An Introduction to Criminology and Criminal Justice

An Introduction to Criminology and Criminal Justice

CHRIS CROWTHER
CONSULTANT EDITOR: JO CAMPLING

First published 2007 by
PALGRAVE MACMILLAN
Houndmills, Basingstoke, Hampshire RG21 6XS and
175 Fifth Avenue, New York, N.Y. 10010
Companies and representatives throughout the world

PALGRAVE MACMILLAN is the global academic imprint of the Palgrave Macmillan division of St. Martin's Press, LLC and of Palgrave Macmillan Ltd. Macmillan® is a registered trademark in the United States, United Kingdom and other countries. Palgrave is a registered trademark in the European Union and other countries.

ISBN-13: 978-1-4039-1215-2   hardback
ISBN-10: 1-4039-1215-7   hardback
ISBN-13: 978-1-4039-1216-9   paperback
ISBN-10: 1-4039-1216-5   paperback

This book is printed on paper suitable for recycling and made from fully managed and sustained forest sources. Logging, pulping and manufacturing processes are expected to conform to the environmental regulations of the country of origin.

A catalogue record for this book is available from the British Library.

A catalog record for this book is available from the Library of Congress.

10 9 8 7 6 5 4 3 2 1
16 15 14 13 12 11 10 09 08 07

Printed and bound in China

For Helen, with love. Thanks for everything.

Contents

Tables

Acknowledgements

The writing of this book has taken a long time, far too long a time, and I am grateful to Palgrave for their tolerance over the last few years. In particular, I would like to thank Emily Salz and Sheree Keep for their patience and extremely supportive guidance at all stages the publication process. Sarah Lodge, Tina Graham and Anna Reeve were at all times excellent in bringing this book into production. I am very appreciative of the hard work of the copy editor Susan Curran, who has dramatically improved the quality of the text in so many areas. All of the aforementioned team also very kindly worked, with great commitment, around my trip to Australia to watch some of Australia's 5-0 drubbing of England in the 2006–07 Ashes series.

An extremely important person who made this project a reality from day one was Jo Campling. Unfortunately Jo passed away in the summer of 2006 and I never had the chance of thanking her personally for her warmth, professionalism and wisdom through-out the years I knew her. However, I feel very privileged to have worked with Jo and hope this book is in the spirit of what she imagined when she backed it. Jo, thank you.

While all omissions and errors in this book are entirely my own, I am indebted to all the academic – and administrative – staff I have worked with, and the many students I have taught. Your mainly indirect influences have shaped this book although quite probably not in ways you would recognize. In particular, I would like to thank Paul Senior, Roger Hopkins Burke, Marisa Silvestri, Anthony Whitehead and Matt Long. In short, thanks to everyone in criminology who is committed to keeping the discipline alive and kicking.

All of the comments of the reviewers of drafts of this text were gratefully received, even the more negative responses. A special thanks to those of you who understood the aims of this book and for your encouraging words.

Because of the pressures of working in higher education in the early twenty-first century, projects like this one are rarely supported by employers, and the completion of this book has depended to a great extent on family and friends. My Mum, Dad and brother Simon have continued to give their love and support even when I have done things that may seem a little crazy. Just to say, the roots and wings are still there.

In 2004 I became a husband, son-in-law, brother-in-law, and nephew-in-law and I would like to thank all of the Dowey family for their warmth and generosity. You have all helped me to get this book done. I am blessed with many good friends although due to work and life commitments we seldom speak to, let alone see, each other. However, Steve, Tanya, Katie and Zoe Lightfoot deserve a heartfelt thank you for their great company and sharing the good times.

Finally, this book would not have been possible without Helen. I can never thank you enough for what you do for me each and every day. Helen, now this project is out of the way I hope you, Daniel, Jack and Rosie share a home with a less grumpy person.

Chris Crowther
January 2007

Introduction

These days crime would appear to be almost everywhere. Crime is simply the breaking of a legal code, or lawbreaking, and it is an issue that is often in our minds, or if not, it is quite likely to be in front of our eyes. It is highly likely that most people have been exposed to crime as a result of watching or simply being in close proximity to a television. Popular television dramas such as *The Bill* and *Bad Girls* are all about the police and prison life respectively. Other popular programmes such as *Footballers Wives* and *Coronation Street*, which are not crime dramas, have had plots involving crime, ranging from antisocial behaviour and drug use to fraud and murder. Movies and films, screened either at the cinema or watched at home on the television, all too often include a reference to crime or the agencies belonging to the criminal justice system, which include the police, the courts and prisons. The same observation applies to novels, the theatre and radio, where crime stories or stories involving an aspect of crime are commonplace. These examples are all fictional, of course, and are primarily there to entertain us, but the television (and radio) also feature factual programmes. For example, documentaries and news programmes regularly feature crimes. In other words, society is awash with both fictional and factual images and words about crime.

The news is an important source of information, and the case study below shows the extent to which crime and crime-related stories are a key element in a newspaper on any single day. There follows a case study looking at the issue of gun crime, illustrating some of the links that are sometimes said to exist between this type of crime and popular music, in this instance hip-hop.

CRIME IS ALWAYS IN THE NEWS

The stories below are all taken from the *Guardian* of 3 November 2006. The full stories are accessible at: guardian.co.uk. The headlines are listed, then there is a brief précis of each story. There is then an attempt to identify the key themes, and to extract from these news stories the issues and debates that are of some criminological significance.

- ■ 'Rapper who killed producer for "disrespect" gets 30 years'
- ■ 'Controversy as Moss wins fashion Oscar'
- ■ 'Man jailed for life for killing daughter'
- ■ 'Italian killings spree blamed on amnesty'
- ■ '"Scandal" as officials try to deport British prisoners'
- ■ 'Brown hints at creation of homeland security department'
- ■ 'Outrage as Greek youths charged with gang rape of Bulgarian classmate'
- ■ 'Google "will be able to keep tabs on us all"'
- ■ 'We are already at the gates of the surveillance society'

After glancing at these headlines some astute readers may be puzzled about one or two of the stories, as they do not appear to have any relationship with crime. The connections will become apparent shortly.

'Rapper who killed producer for "disrespect" gets 30 years'

The 'grime' rap star Carl Dobson, commonly known as Crazy Titch, was given a 30-year prison sentence because he shot dead a music producer, Richard Holmes. Dobson shot Holmes because the record producer had released a track on which a 16-year-old 'garage' star Shaba Shah (known as Shaba Shak) had insulted Dobson's half-brother, Dwayne Mahorn (known in the rap world as Durrty Goodz).

'Controversy as Moss wins fashion Oscar'

Another story involving a celebrity concerned the fashion model Kate Moss, who attained adverse notoriety as a result of her misuse of drugs and relationship with singer and songwriter Pete Doherty. Despite her criminal past Moss was named model of the year at the British Fashion Awards.

'Man jailed for life for killing daughter'

Gavin Hall drugged and suffocated his three-year-old daughter, Millie, because he found out that his wife had been having an affair with a district judge. The story outlined in some detail the 'emotional disturbance' Hall suffered as a result of discovering this affair. Hall committed the murder while taking prescribed anti-depressants. Hall was given a 'life' sentence of a minimum of 15 years. The judge passing sentence said that the murder was 'planned and premeditated' once Hall had discovered the affair. The judge also revealed that Hall had killed the family cats the day before he killed his daughter.

'Italian killings spree blamed on amnesty'

This story concerned a spate of fatal shootings in and around the city of Naples, in southern Italy. It referred to 12 killings in 10 days, claiming that a number of the murders had been carried out in the style of the *Camorra* (the Neapolitan mafia). The article suggested that the murders were connected to a government decision to release prisoners from an overcrowded police system. Up to 24,000 prisoners were released, many of whom were left homeless and jobless.

'"Scandal" as officials try to deport British prisoners'

A number of prisoners who were British nationals and people who had spent more than 30 years in Britain were threatened with deportation. This story referred to the confusion arising between the prison service and immigration service, and problems in differentiating prisoners who were foreign nationals from those who were British nationals. British nationals are allowed to live in Britain on release from prison, but foreign nationals are supposed to be returned to their country of origin.

'Brown hints at creation of homeland security department'

In the aftermath of the terrorist bombings in London on 7 July 2005 there was increased concern about national security in the United Kingdom. Since 11 September 2001 when terrorists bombed the Twin Towers in New York, the home secretary, John Reid, showed that:

■ 387 people had been charged with terrorist offences
■ 214 had been convicted
■ 98 were awaiting trial.

Gordon Brown, chancellor of the Exchequer, called for a more integrated and seamless counter-terrorist service by joining up the work of police and security services. This would involve cross-departmental work between the Home Office, the Ministry of Defence and the intelligence services (such as MI5 and MI6).

'Outrage as Greek youths charged with gang rape of Bulgarian classmate'

This was another story involving immigration, but this time in another country. It described a case in Greece where four Greek schoolboys were charged with the rape of a 16-year-old Bulgarian girl. The girl had migrated to Greece with her mother a few years before the assault. The article drew attention to the racism directed at the victim not only by her attackers but also by many establishment figures in Greek society. It also described how three Greek schoolgirls watched and recorded the rape on their mobile phones. If the boys were found guilty and convicted for the offence they could spend up to 20 years in a juvenile detention centre or prison.

'Google "will be able to keep tabs on us all"'

This story concerned the Internet, and claimed that the search engine Google holds so much digital data that it could let someone know what another person is doing at a particular time. For instance, it would be possible to put electronic chips in people's clothes to track their movements. This data could then be transferred back to the

Internet via video recordings or data banks. This innovation is attributed to the 'surveillance society', and presents crime-fighting institutions, such as the Serious Organised Crime Agency (SOCA) with a chance to tackle a criminal minority and to protect the safety of most of the population.

'We are already at the gates of the surveillance society'

This was not a news item but a comment by the London editor of the magazine *Vanity Fair*, Henry Porter. It described the so-called 'surveillance society' in which all citizens are being watched nearly 24/7 by close circuit television cameras (CCTV) and monitored on the basis of the information that is stored on their credit and ID cards. The article also drew attention to the police and their legal right to take a DNA sample from people they arrest, and the proposed introduction of a National Health Service (NHS) database to hold all kinds of sensitive information about individual health and other personal data. Porter argued that these developments create a tension between one the one hand, freedom and privacy, and on the hand, the state and government potentially restricting and curtailing these freedoms.

THE CRIMINOLOGICAL SIGNIFICANCE OF THE NEWS STORIES – SOME EMERGENT THEMES

Crime

The stories refer to a diversity of crimes, although serious and violent offences such as murder and rape are prominent. While these crimes do occur, and rightly cause alarm, they are relatively rare in comparison with other types of crime. The articles mentioning surveillance discussed the threat of terrorism and other unspecified crimes. Crucially, the articles reviewed were all of some criminological significance, but there is far more to criminological study than the serious crimes these stories cover.

Offenders and suspects

As well as identifying specific crimes, the articles also identified specific offenders or suspects. In the Hall and Dobson cases there were identifiable offenders because these people have been convicted of murder. The individuals responsible for the murders in Naples were not known and had not been called to justice at that time. The rape in Greece was slightly different because the boys who were facing trial had not yet been found guilty and were therefore suspects rather than offenders. They cannot be named as offenders until their guilt is established and they are convicted of an offence.

Victims

The accounts of the murders and the rape all have clear victims. In other stories the discussions about crime was at a more general level, and there was no obvious immediate victim. For example, the story about Kate Moss referred to her misuse of drugs. On the surface this would appear to be an offence that is victimless. In a sense this is an understandable response, but in England and Wales when someone commits a criminal offence the status of victim is assumed by the state, largely because a crime is a violation of a written statutory code. More than that, the state is representing the interests of society as a whole.

Criminal justice agencies

The stories about the murder cases and the rape trial all referred to different players in the criminal justice system, in particular the courts and the police. In the surveillance pieces it was clear that the issues facing the police and courts also had resonance for other areas of public policy, including immigration and health. In other words, there are specified criminal justice institutions but the effects of crime are far-reaching and have an impact on other organizations too.

These examples have served to identify some everyday examples of crimes, and to illustrate some of the complex issues surrounding the issue of crime. A limitation of the illustrations above is that they are merely 'news flashes' and lack any sense of context. In other words, they just cast light on a few of the elements involved in understanding and coming to terms with criminology and criminal justice. The next example provides some more detail about crime in context, and serves as an initial taster to give more of an impression of what is involved in criminological study.

GUN CRIME AND HIP-HOP CULTURE

Many students of criminology find great interest in the problem of gun crime.[1] Violent crime involving the use of firearms is a problem throughout the world, and Britain is no exception. In comparison with the United States, for example, there is limited use of guns by British criminals, but since the late 1990s there has been a perception, certainly in the media, that gun crime in Britain is increasing and that society is becoming increasingly unsafe.

For example, in 2003 in Birmingham there was an incident at a New Year's Eve party where two young Black women, Letishia Shakespeare and Charlene Ellis, were shot dead. In 2004 Danielle Beccan, a 14-year-old Black girl, was shot dead while walking home from the Goose Fair in Nottingham. The media was quick to make links between these events and a south London rap group, the So Solid Crew. Some of the group were convicted for gun-related violence, and the mass media focused on this case and the Birmingham shootings of these young females. The negative influence of the rapper 50 Cent is also frequently mentioned in newspapers. This is perhaps not surprising given the violent imagery of his 2005 album, which was entitled *The Massacre*, and the sound-track he produced for the 2005 film *Get Rich or Die Trying*. The video game he released in 2005 was called *Bulletproof* (see 50 Cent's homepage: www.50cent.com).

The reality of gun crime and the paraphernalia surrounding it cause considerable fear and anxiety in some communities. We can add to this the sensationalized stories about young people carrying high-powered weapons who are prepared to kill other kids for small quantities of money, or because they have been shown signs of 'disrespect' ('dissed'). The case of Crazy Titch outlined above lends some support to such worries, even though crimes of this kind are relatively rare.

There is a tendency for some commentators to make a link between the phenomenon of gun crime and popular culture, in particular hip-hop music. Popular newspapers, police officers and politicians frequently cite stories suggesting that hip-hop somehow causes people to shoot and seriously injure or kill other people (Bullock and Tilley, 2002; Dodd et al., 2004; Nicholas et al, 2005; Metropolitan Police Authority, 2004). There is no evidence to support such accusations, and some writers have instead focused on the poverty and deprivation existing in these cultures (Sanders, 2005).

If we are to make sense of the supposed linkages between gun crime and hip-hop it is necessary to look a little more closely at these two issues separately, before considering any possible interrelationship between them.

Hip-hop culture

You are probably familiar with hip-hop and rap music. It is a musical genre originating in the 1970s in the South Bronx, New York, describing the social tensions found in urban areas where life is hard and opportunities are limited (Rose, 1994). Poverty is endemic in these communities and their inhabitants all too often experience marginalization from mainstream life, with few having well-paid jobs and economic security.

Artists producing hip-hop sing about their own experiences – often in the past tense – and there is a tendency for rappers to celebrate their success and achievement. Many hip-hop tracks talk about how the artist managed to escape from poverty and marginalization, and the singers subsequently embrace the celebrity lifestyle. For some hip-hop artists this celebration is manifest in the form of 'gangsta rap', a variant of rap music in which the possession and possible use of a gun is a status symbol (Sanders, 2005). It should be noted that there are multiple versions of hip-hop, although its most extreme versions tend to attract most publicity. It is also now a multi-billion-dollar industry, which has achieved commercial success in a global media market. The origins of rap may be located in the ghettoes of the United States but it is now a big business, extending beyond the music to the designer clothes, 'bling' (jewellery) and other accessories that go with it.

Although there is no universal connection between hip-hop and violence, lyrics such as those found on G-Unit's 2003 album *Beg for Mercy* would not persuade many critics to argue that there is *no* connection between hip-hop, guns and violent criminality. Verse three of the track 'Eye for an eye' illustrates this link quite clearly. In this track 50 Cent raps about the use of high-powered firearms and how they are used by the rapper to kill his perceived enemies.

The reality of gun crime

Firearms crime is not new to the streets of Britain, and since 1946 – a year after the end of the Second World War – there have been six gun amnesties where the police allowed people to hand in unregistered firearms at police stations with no questions being asked or action taken. The National Criminal Intelligence Service reported in 2003 that

250,000 firearms had been taken out of circulation. On the surface that suggests a problem dealt with, but there is a downside because those criminals who are most likely to hand guns in are those least likely to use them, meaning that the guns not handed in are the ones most likely to be used. In reality from the late 1990s onwards there has been an increase in the use of guns, despite the ban on the legal use of handguns in 1997 following the mass murders in Dunblane in Scotland in 1996. (A lone gunman, Thomas Hamilton, walked into a school and killed several children before turning his gun on himself and committing suicide.)

The word 'firearm' is defined in legislation in section 57(1) of the Firearms Act 1968 as 'a lethal barreled weapon of any description from which any shot, bullet or other missile can be discharged'. The Home Office has expanded this definition, stating that a firearm is considered to have been used if it is fired, deployed as a blunt instrument or even used to threaten someone. Firearms are used for a variety of purposes such as to carry out a robbery, to hurt someone or to threaten an individual. Statistical evidence shows that in England and Wales in the period from June 2004 to June 2005, 11,160 firearm offences were recorded (Nicholas et al., 2005). This amounts to a 5 per cent increase over the previous year, including a 55 per cent increase in cases involving the use of imitation weapons (Dodd et al., 2004). Out of all the offences involving firearms, 60 cases resulted in a fatality. The message that can be taken from this is that while gun crimes are on the increase, most weapons used in a criminal manner are not used to kill people.

Gun-related crime is a problem, but many offences are limited to a relatively small number of inner-city areas. Over half of all firearm offences occurred in three police force areas: the Metropolitan Police District (Greater London), Greater Manchester and the West Midlands (Nicholas et al., 2005).

This data is very interesting, and it tells criminologists something about the use of firearms although it does not say much about why guns are used or the cause of gun-related crime. Knowledge and understanding of gun crime is limited largely because of the nature of this type of offending, although there is some limited information that focuses on the connections between the illegal use of firearms and hip-hop.

Does hip-hop culture cause gun crime?

Hales (2005), for example, published some research that examined gun crime in an area of London. Among the key points made in this study, Hales observed that gun crime 'encompasses diverse symbolic and instrumental motivations'. Interestingly Hales comments that gun crime is not exclusively carried out by particular ethnic groups, and the perpetrators of such crimes are not just young people. Crucially, Hales did not find sufficient evidence to confirm a link with 'gangsta rap' in particular and hip-hop more generally.

The Metropolitan Police Authority (2004) produced limited evidence to show that hip-hop culture had some tangential links with gun-related violence, but no more than any other style of music. Rather the music had an influence on fashion and more general cultural attitudes and beliefs.

Obviously the data here is rather limited, which is perhaps inevitable given the sensitive nature of the topic. On the basis of the information from these studies, it is not possible to say either way whether there is a causal link between hip-hop culture and the use of firearms. The reasons for this are complex, but one is that the examples given so far have not shown an attempt to study crime systematically and logically. That is the job of students of criminology and criminal justice.

INTRODUCING CRIMINOLOGY AND CRIMINAL JUSTICE

Criminology and criminal justice are very popular issues for study. There are many reasons for their popularity, and you, the reader, will bring with you your own ideas and feelings about the topics they address.

- Some readers will have quite clear preconceptions concerning what criminology is all about. This book will either confirm or challenge these assumptions.
- Perhaps you have direct experience of criminological and criminal justice topics, either as a result of working in the sector or because you know of the experiences of partners, family members or friends, as workers in this field, victims of crime or even criminals.
- Perhaps you have plans to work in the criminal justice sector on graduating from university, and see studying criminology as a way of gaining an insight into criminal behaviour and the various methods of addressing it.
- Perhaps you do not have a very clear idea yet of why you should study criminology and criminal justice, but you have chosen to do so – or to read this book because you are considering doing so – because you think it will prove an interesting subject.

You might be reading this book for some other reason, but these are reasons often given by students who are asked why they have enrolled on a course on criminology. They are all good reasons, though having an interest and an open mind is perhaps most essential. You do not need a clear career plan in order to find many of the issues covered in the book interesting. Criminology, or the study of crime, is fascinating in itself. Of course many of those who find crime interesting do not study criminology and criminal justice, and many people who have not done so are quite happy to talk about crime and offer their opinions on the causes of and solutions to crime. However, criminology offers a more balanced view and informed perspective. This book introduces to you to the ways in which it does so.

This book has been written primarily for students who have no, or very little, prior knowledge of criminology and criminal justice. It is particularly suitable as a core course book for first-year undergraduates, to provide an accessible general introduction to some of the issues and debates, but it should also provide a refresher overview to students later in their studies, and it will be of interest too to many who are not studying in a formal way, but wish to learn a little more about the subject.

Before continuing any further we need to outline the key features of criminology and criminal justice.

WHAT IS CRIMINOLOGY AND WHAT IS CRIMINAL JUSTICE?

These are sometimes seen as two separate areas of study, but the aim of this book is to use elements of both to introduce students to the topic of crime.

In general terms criminology is the study of crime. It looks at how crime is:

- defined
- measured
- conceptualized.

For example, a question students frequently start with is, what is crime? This is a *definitional* issue. For the purposes of this book, a crime can initially be defined as the action committed when a person breaks a legal code: in this case, the criminal law. This definition tends to be favoured by those who take the 'black letter law' approach (see Chapter 1). The chapters that follow expand on this definition.

Once crime has been defined, criminologists want to measure it. In short, how much crime is there out there? There are various sources of data that are used to answer this type of question, as well as different methods of obtaining this data.

More than that, criminology pays attention to conceptual issues such as the causes of crime, asking big questions like 'what is the cause of crime?' Criminology focuses on the offender, who is at the heart of the subject. Without offenders there would be little point in studying criminology. Where there is an offender there is also a victim, and increasingly victims too are coming to the forefront of criminological study. Criminology draws on a range of disciplines to assess the causes of offending behaviour, especially sociology and psychology, but also social policy, law and politics. In fact the list of influences is much more extensive than this, and may include history, design and engineering.

Attempts to conceptualize and explain criminal behaviour have resulted in *criminological theory*. This is an useful definition of criminological theory:

> In attempting to explain the facts that we know about crime we use theoretical perspectives. Theories are part of that explanation and, according to Vold et al. 'an explanation is a sensible way of relating some particular phenomenon to the ... information, beliefs and attitudes that make up the intellectual atmosphere of a people at a particular time or place'.
>
> (Harrison et al., 2005: 67)

As well as looking for sensible explanations of the causes of crime, criminologists study attempts to prevent and reduce crime. In other words, what does a society do to stop people committing crime? Criminology demonstrates that it is not possible to stop crime altogether, but there are institutions in place that attempt to tackle criminality. This refers to the criminal justice system, which in basic terms includes the following services:

- the police, who are responsible for the maintenance of social order, and the detection and prevention of crime

■ courts: these are the places where criminal trials occur and where sentences are passed
■ prisons, where convicted offenders given a custodial sentence are sent
■ the probation service, which manages offenders who are given a community based or non-custodial sentence
■ to some extent all public-sector agencies, as well as the private and voluntary sectors, since crime affects everyone, at work, at home and at play.

Criminal justice focuses on many of the issues mentioned above, but it pays most attention to the criminal justice system and the principles and values underpinning its policies. For example, the study of criminal justice involves asking questions about the extent to which policing and sentencing policies are fair. Criminal justice is also preoccupied with legislation and its impact on criminal justice policy and practice. Perhaps the main thing separating criminology from criminal justice studies is that criminology also examines research methods and draws more extensively on theoretical debates produced in other disciplines, such as sociology.

This is to a certain extent an over-simplification, but it captures the essence of these two areas of study. In this book the two areas are brought together in order to study criminology and criminal justice systematically and logically. A proposition of this book is that in order to begin appreciating criminology and criminal justice we need to consider four broad themes:

Definitions and conceptions of crime

■ Legal
■ Common sense
■ Theoretical

Crime data

■ Sources of information
■ Methods of interpretation

The criminal justice system

■ The police and prosecution
■ The courts
■ Prison
■ Probation
■ Other aspects

Theories of crime

■ Sensible explanations of why people commit crime
■ Sensible explanations of the criminal justice system response to crime

These four themes are reflected in the structure of the book. As an introductory text, it aims is to describe the core issues in each area systematically, and by the end of the book students will have a basic introduction to each. Further study in this area will involve making connections between these different themes, and formal students of criminology will go on to do this, especially in their dissertation or final-year project. For the moment, coming to terms with each theme on its own is a sufficiently demanding task.

STRUCTURE OF THE BOOK

Part One of the book comprises two chapters, and introduces various definitions and conceptions of crime. **Chapter 1** attempts to define crime and what is involved in the study of criminology and criminal justice. It shows that crime has captured the public imagination since the origins of human societies, but it is only during the last 20 years that a large number of undergraduate students have studied the subjects of criminology and criminal justice. The chapter describes how crime has been defined in legal, media, and political and academic terms. Special attention is given to the different ways in which crime has been represented and studied in a diversity of social and historical contexts.

Chapter 2 introduces some key issues in criminology and criminal justice. As well as defining crime it is important to be aware of the different ways in which crime impacts on different groups of people. Chiefly, it focuses on offenders and victims and their differential experiences of crime. Students need to be aware of the significance of social divisions, especially the class, race, age and gender dimensions of offending behaviour, and patterns of victimization in relation to different types of crime.

In the second part of the book the emphasis is on understanding crime data. Building on Part One, the chapters in this part introduce and evaluate various sources of crime data available to criminologists, and the many different ways of understanding it. In **Chapter 3** a range of the different sources of crime data are identified, including quantitative and qualitative types. It shows that these can give very different impressions of crime and its impact. It is often argued that quantitative and qualitative data are incompatible, but the overarching aim of the chapter is to show that they may be effectively integrated and used to complement each other.

In **Chapter 4** some of the different methods of interpretation are introduced. It is necessary to introduce not only the various sources of crime data, but also the different methods criminologists use to gather and analyse crime data. To complement Chapter 3 the focus is on some of the research methods commonly used by criminologists, which tend to be used to obtain and interpret quantitative and qualitative data respectively. Since undergraduate students frequently undertake mini-research projects as part of their studies there is a discussion of the relative advantages and disadvantages of using different sources of data and research methods. There is no attempt to explain the technical issues involved in doing research, but rather the aim is to outline key themes and principles.

The third part of the text moves on to assess the criminal justice system in context, beginning with **Chapter 5**, which takes into account the criminal justice system and its processes. In particular, it introduces the criminal justice system in the United Kingdom in relation to the welfare state and society as a whole. Taking the criminal justice system in England and Wales as an example, it charts its emergence and the philosophical and political values which underpin its workings, and looks at how these affect suspects, defendants and the convicted as well as victims of crime in different social groups (differentiated by class, gender, age and race). It discusses what is meant by the concept of justice in relation to crime from legal and sociological perspectives. The central argument is that the criminal justice process cannot be understood in isolation from the many complex causes and consequences of, and responses to, crime.

The police, frequently cast as gatekeepers to the criminal justice process, receive attention in **Chapter 6**. The police organization is the one most commonly identified as the key agency responsible for responding to crime and disorder, although a whole range of other statutory, private and voluntary organizations also work alongside the police. However, the police have special importance because they have the power to refer the people they deal with to the next stage of the criminal justice process, and also influence the experience of victims. The chapter examines the origins of the modern police service, and outlines its core responsibilities and functions. In determining what the police do, the chapter identifies two key sets of interrelated tasks, which are identified here as first, peace keeping and crime fighting, and second, caring and controlling. Drawing on a range of studies the chapter also scrutinizes macro (social structural) and micro (individual) approaches in studies of the workings of police organizations, and their effects on different social classes and ethnic groups, as well as men and women, and people from different age groups.

The prosecution process, the courts and sentencing are the topics covered in **Chapter 7**. Traditionally it is in the courts that the administration of justice takes place. Although the police play a pivotal role in deciding who enters into this stage of the criminal justice process, a specific set of principles and practices are applied in the courts, which are primarily concerned with balancing the rights of offenders against the needs of wider society and individual victims. However, if ethnicity, class, age and gender are considered this balance is not always struck. After describing the legislative and policy context, the chapter focuses on the role of the prosecution and the courts in processing individual cases. The courts also perform a major role in sentencing policy, determining whether offenders are punished in prison or in the community.

In **Chapter 8** the discussion concentrates on the prison. Contemporary discussions of penology or the study of punishment concentrate on the relative significance of custodial and non-custodial sentences, and incarceration versus community-based punishments, for reducing crime and the harmful effects of victimization. This chapter outlines the philosophical and practical considerations underpinning the use of prison as a means of punishment. It traces the emergence of the prison as the preferred option for policy makers in the United Kingdom, and critically considers the arguments for and against this development in policy in the context of wider changes in society and in the criminal justice system. Racialized and gendered forms of discrimination in relation to imprisonment are examined.

Chapter 9 concentrates on the activities of the probation service, and what is known as community-based punishment and community justice. The existence of the probation service demonstrates that imprisonment is not the only form of punishment in modern societies. This organization is responsible for the provision of non-custodial or community-based punishments. The chapter introduces students to the range of punishments available in this context, and their philosophical and professional rationales. Although policy makers and the public tend to express strong support for the use of prison as the main method of punishment, there is a credible case for using alternative measures provided by the probation service and other agencies, such as drug treatment and testing orders (DTTOs) and electronic monitoring.

At the time of writing the activities of the prison and probation services were being brought together to create the National Offender Management Service (NOMS). The rationale for creating NOMS was to establish stronger connections between prison and probation, ranging from sentencing to the resettlement of offenders in the community following their punishment. Because NOMS had not been properly established when this book was written there is a dearth of literature on this topic, and for this reason the prison service and probation service are introduced in separate chapters.

For many years academics, politicians and practitioners in the field of criminal justice have argued that individual agencies cannot effectively reduce crime and disorder if they do not work together. Following this logic, **Chapter 10** assesses multi-agency and 'joined-up' approaches to criminal justice policy. There is also a view that criminal behaviour can only be addressed by looking beyond the criminal justice system towards wider society, including a host of statutory as well as voluntary and private agencies. The causes of and solutions to crime are dependent on recognition of the complex linkages between institutions and processes at macro and micro levels. In England and Wales, for example, there has developed 'joined-up' thinking and policies to reduce crime and disorder and create safer communities. The chapter outlines the structure of these ideas and practices, and assesses their impact and effectiveness.

The fourth part of the book introduces a range of theories of crime, which help us to understand different aspects of crime and crime control, particularly its racialized, gendered, age and class dimensions. Many of the debates addressed in these chapters are foregrounded in earlier chapters, but this part examines them in a more sustained way. Throughout the chapters in Part Four the policy implications of these theories are addressed, and there are examples of different applications of these ideas to explain the workings of the criminal justice system outlined in Part Three. It demonstrates that there are many traditions and perspectives within criminological theory, and although it is not the aim to impose intellectual coherence where it does not exist, there are some emergent themes. Conventionally, key debates included the relative significance of agency or structure, micro or macro levels, the individual or society, and voluntarism/ free will or determinism. These are the criminologies of modernity. More recently these ideas have been challenged by an array of critical and deconstructive perspectives, including feminism, anti-racism, poststructuralism and postmodernism.

The aim of **Chapter 11** is to summarize those theories of crime that devote most attention to the individual human subject. Many theories of crime have centred on the individual, ranging from those emphasizing the human subject as a free agent (such as classicism and rational choice theory) to ones that suggest individuals are driven to commit crime by their innate characteristics (such as biological and psychological positivism). The first part of the chapter considers the nineteenth-century legacy, including positivism and classicism, and the second part the contribution of microsociological perspectives such as labelling theory and symbolic interactionism, as well as social psychology. The chapter uses various examples from the existing literature to reflect on the policy implications of these different theoretical approaches in relation to the various criminal justice agencies.

Chapter 12 evaluates more sociological explanations of criminality. This tradition in criminological theory holds the view that criminal behaviour needs to be understood in its wider macro or structural context. These theories incorporate explanations that argue that social forces are deterministic (sociological positivism) and other more nuanced accounts that take into consideration the relationship between structure and agency (such as subcultural theory and left realism). There are many examples of these ideas being applied to explain particular aspects of offending behaviour and the response of the criminal justice system.

Chapter 13 discusses critical and deconstructive perspectives on crime. It assesses the contribution of the criminologies of modernity discussed in Chapters 11 and 12 in light of critical and deconstructive approaches to the study of crime. Since the late 1970s many scholars have subjected the criminological literature to extensive criticisms, including feminist, anti-racist, poststructuralist and postmodernist perspectives. This rich, diverse and complex literature does not altogether jettison the more traditional concerns of criminological theory, but pushes to the forefront of analysis issues such as risk and surveillance.

The conclusion offers a very brief summary of the main issues and themes addressed in the book, and outlines a vision for the future. It restates the importance of understanding the relationship between what we think and claim to know about criminal behaviour, and the institutions and resources available to policy makers to address this problem at macro and micro levels.

With the exception of this introduction and the conclusion each chapter includes some questions exploring the themes addressed inside the chapter. There is also a glossary at the back of the book containing brief definitions of the key concepts introduced in the main body of the text.

Finally, throughout the book the focus is mainly on the criminal justice system in England and Wales. In a book of this size it is not feasible to cover jurisdictions in other parts of the world, although some of the theoretical examples used are drawn from American and Australian literature. Comparative criminology, which compares criminal justice policy and practice across the world, is a separate and more advanced topic. However many of the ideas (such as justice, race and gender) and theoretical debates are of universal significance and relevant in any part of the world.

PART ONE

Definitions and Conceptions of Crime

1 Defining Crime and Studying Criminology and Criminal Justice

---

OVERVIEW

The aim of this chapter is to provide:

- an explanation of legal definitions of crime, drawing attention to the fact that the law is not static and changes over time
- an outline of some methods of classifying criminal offences, drawing attention to the differences between summary, indictable and triable either way offences
- a discussion of the influences of common-sense thinking, paying attention to personal experience, the mass media and political power, as well as theory
- two historically informed case studies of the police power to stop and search suspects and different approaches to the policing of drugs.

INTRODUCTION

This chapter shows that crime has captured the public imagination since time immemorial, and begins with a description of how crime has been defined in legal terms. This will be referred to as the 'black letter law' approach to criminology and criminal justice. It is an influential perspective in the study of crime, not least because it governs the activities of agencies such as the police service and the courts. However, beyond the criminal law there are other factors influencing the way crime is defined. For example, crime is defined partly through the sensory perceptions of people in their day-to-day experience. Such definitions form part of a common-sense understanding of the world. This knowledge of crime is backed up by information gleaned from the mass media, through exposure to television and newspapers, for example.

The capacity to comprehend crime from lived experience and mediated versions of social reality is important, but powerful and influential groups in society, including politicians and policy makers, also define crime. It is shown that each method of defining crime offers a partial and limited view of the complex processes surrounding the production of definitions of crime. However, taken together they provide a complementary overview.

The chapter is split into four main parts. The first provides a rudimentary answer to the question, what is crime? After providing a legalistic definition of crime, the second section shows how crime is understood in common-sense or everyday terms. It looks at five main ways in which crime is seen: on the basis of personal experience, popular press (mass media), political power, practical and professional perspectives, and theoretical perspectives. In the third part, there is a case study tracing the development of legislation related to the police power of stop and search. It examines the various uses of stop and search in relation to a range of different offences, including vagrancy, street crime and terrorism. The fourth section is another case study, the Lambeth cannabis experiment, which explores the changing nature of drugs crime and the legislative and policy response to it.

WHAT IS CRIME? – A LEGAL DEFINITION

This section:

- considers the processes involved in defining crime according to a legal perspective
- demonstrates that the criminal law changes over time
- provides an overview of the official methods and terminology used to classify criminal offences.

It is only necessary to turn on the television or glance at a newspaper to see that crime is always in the news (Jewkes, 2004). Society is awash with crime, whether it is represented in factual or fictional terms. Crime is an issue that concerns everybody in one way or another, and this is a situation that is unlikely to change. The very fact that you have picked up this book and decided to read it suggests that crime interests you in some way. A possible explanation is that crime is as old as humanity itself, suggesting that it is an enduring and maybe permanent feature of social life. The history books show that ever since human societies came into existence there have been crimes. People stole from and hurt each other in Athens in 10 BC, they do so in 2007, and most likely they will do so on dates in the future like 2020. Furthermore, these actions have always tended to be considered as wrong, immoral or illegal.

Before we continue there is a need to ask a very basic question: *what is crime?* The more thought is given to this simple question, the more complex it becomes. We can ask ourselves or our friends and family this question, and while there will be a diversity of answers it is highly likely that some behaviours will be mentioned by almost everyone. One obvious response is homicide, or the unlawful killing of a human being. There are few, if any, contemporary societies where this act is treated as anything other than a crime. However, while taking the life of another human being may be perceived as immoral or wrong, this in itself is not a sufficient reason for defining this behaviour as a crime. After all, in times of war it is quite legitimate for one human being to take the life of another.

For behaviour to be recognized as a crime there is the need for a statement prohibiting or banning an act. In other words, a crime is a violation of a written code or the law, or to be even more specific, the criminal law. It is necessary to focus on the matter of defining crime in more detail.

It is beyond the scope of this book to ask profound and deep philosophical questions about why particular types of behaviour have been criminalized, but it is necessary to understand the processes leading to the defining of particular actions as criminal. In essence a crime is an act banned by the state. There are some instances when judges rather than Parliament make the law. Most crucially, the conduct defined as criminal by the state has a punishment attached to it. This is a universal definition of crime applying to all societies, and without these characteristics no crime is committed. However, a degree of relativity informs this definition, because the conduct defined as criminal will vary over time and space. While there may be universal themes in the content of the criminal law found in different jurisdictions, there are variations in the conduct defined as criminal in particular countries. An obvious example is the side of the road people drive on in England and in France. In England people drive on the left, but to do the same in France is to commit a criminal offence, as well as most likely to be responsible for a traffic collision.

The criminal law also changes over time, and a particular type of conduct defined as a crime in one period may be decriminalized in another or vice versa. This will depend on the ideology, morality and values of particular governments, and their influence on the types of social issue that are considered to be in need of a legal response. A frequently cited example is the age of consent for homosexual acts.

An example: the age of consent

Any history of sexuality shows that public attitudes and government responses to homosexuals are different from those directed at heterosexuals (Weeks, 1981). For most of the heterosexual population, adult sexuality is an area where legislators have rarely intervened. It is regarded as a private matter that should not be unduly influenced by the state. Those laws that do exist focus on the issue of consent between the individuals involved in a sexual act, to protect children and young people from sexual exploitation by adults.

According to prevailing public morality, often underpinned by religious principles, heterosexuality has tended to be considered the norm and homosexuality as deviant and immoral. The Criminal Law Act (1885) actually criminalized consensual sex between homosexual adults (Weeks and Porter, 1998).

It is felt by some people that consent is exercised differently by homosexuals than by heterosexuals. There is a deeply entrenched and highly prejudicial view in many cultures that homosexuals are less responsible for their conduct, and that they must be treated differently from their heterosexual counterparts. It is also argued that homosexuals have been stigmatized to such an extent that they cannot take rational and fully informed decisions about their sexual behaviour.

The impact of the Criminal Law Act on homosexuals was harsh, and for many years there was a campaign to obtain for them the same basic legal rights as heterosexuals. For heterosexuals the age of consent was 16 years. Over time successive governments indicated that they were considering the possibility of reforming the legislation on homosexuality, but the reform tended to reflect the view that a different age of consent was appropriate for homosexuals. For instance, in 1967 the passing into law of the Sexual Offences Act resulted in the decriminalization of homosexual acts for people aged 21 years and over. Over the course of the next two and half decades or so, pressure groups continued to lobby the government to bring the age of consent for homosexuals into line with the prescribed age for heterosexuals (Weeks, 1981). In the mid-1990s the Criminal Justice and Public Order Act (1994) made some concessions, and the age of consent for consensual sex between adult homosexuals was reduced from 21 to 18 years. There was still differential treatment until 2000, when the age of consent for homosexuals was eventually reduced to 16 in line with heterosexuals. Even then the government met with opposition from the House of Lords.

WHAT IS CRIME? KEY POINTS

■ Criminal behaviour is a form of rule breaking, particularly a violation of criminal law.
■ There is a degree of relativity involved in defining crime.
■ Legislation changes over time and adapts to changes in social attitudes.

Classifying offences

As well as recognizing that law making is part of an ongoing process and that specific pieces of legislation are amended over time, it is necessary to note that criminal offences are defined and classified in different ways.

One method refers to the source of legislation, of which there are three main types. First, there is common or judge-made law. Second, there is statutory law, which is set out in Acts of Parliament, and third, regulatory law, which is set out in delegated legislation.

A more popular classification is based on an assessment of the type of harm caused by a crime. Again, there are three main categories:

■ offences against property
■ offences against the person
■ offences against public order.

There are other ways in which offences are classified, and these are related to the activities of criminal justice agencies, in particular the police and the courts. The police service use a method of classifying offences that is in line with some of the key activities of the organization, namely arresting and detaining any individual person suspected of committing a crime. The issue of arrest is important in categorizing offences. For example:

- There are serious arrestable offences, comprising murder, manslaughter and rape.
- The Criminal Justice Act (1967) highlights arrestable offences where the sentence is fixed by law, or offences where the maximum sentence is at least five years imprisonment. Parliament also has the powers to make any offence an arrestable offence.
- Finally, there are non-arrestable offences.

There is a different methodology used in the courts. Chapter 7 focuses exclusively on the courts, but it is appropriate to mention at this stage that in the criminal justice system in England and Wales there are two main types of court, the Crown court and the magistrates' court. These different institutions are charged with the responsibility of dealing with different types of criminal offence. There are indictable offences, consisting of the more serious offences, including:

- murder
- manslaughter
- rape
- blackmail
- robbery
- malicious wounding with intent to do grievous bodily harm
- arson with intent to endanger life.

Each of these offences is first heard in a magistrates' court, but those charged are then committed to Crown court for trial, where they are tried on indictment.

Second, there are summary offences, which can only be tried in a magistrates' court. Summary crimes comprise:

- assaulting a police officer
- common assault
- exceeding the speed limit
- driving with excess alcohol in the blood
- threatening behaviour
- disorderly conduct
- being found drunk
- not possessing a required vehicle licence
- not possessing a required television licence.

The third type of offences is triable either way, which means an offence can be tried on indictment at the Crown court or summarily by magistrates. The trial court is determined by the mode of trial procedure. Some examples of triable either way offences are:

- theft
- burglary

- assault occasioning actual bodily harm
- obtaining property by deception
- violent disorder
- affray
- possession of an offensive weapon.

COMMON-SENSE DEFINITIONS OF CRIME

This section discusses the significance of:

- personal experience for understanding crime
- the influence of the popular press and mass media on defining crime, drawing attention to the concepts of newsworthiness and moral panics
- the role of politicians and politics in shaping understanding of crime
- the different types of knowledge possessed by people working in the criminal justice system.

Personal experience

The first source of knowledge is our own personal experience of crime, as an offender, a victim or a witness. For reasons of ethics and privacy you are not expected to admit to your first-hand experience, as this is a deeply personal matter. Whether you have committed a crime is between you and your conscience. Beyond your first-hand experience, you may also have some awareness of crime as a result of the experiences of your family, friends or acquaintances. This may be uncomfortable territory, but it is not territory that you should completely avoid in your study of criminology, since your experiences at either first or second hand are likely to affect your thoughts and opinions.

It is important to be aware of your personal attitudes and feelings about offending behaviour and victimization. Your emotions will teach you a lot. This is particularly important if your current or future employment is in the criminal justice sector. You need to appreciate whether your gut reaction to offenders and victims is based on empathy, sympathy, fear, contempt or possibly indifference. The potential reactions you might have to a crime are limitless. However it is important to bear in mind that your initial response to a particular case is unlikely to be based only on detailed information, or even basic facts, about it: it will depend too on the past experience of you and those close to you.

When you have no immediate experience of a crime, your response might instead be based on 'common-sense' understanding and knowledge. This will be defined in a moment, and we shall go on to discuss why it is advisable to refer to other sources of information and knowledge about crime. The aim is to encourage you to deconstruct or challenge your common-sense view of the world of crime, by reconstructing your views on the basis of established criminological knowledge. You will learn that while criminology does not altogether dispense with common-sense explanations, these need to be either supported or refuted through research studies. This research is based on students of criminology asking questions and finding the best methods of obtaining an answer to them. These issues are discussed in more detail in Chapter 4.

'Common sense' refers to the general world-views people hold, which are a reflection of their personal experience and the attitudes and beliefs they have developed. It is based on what people have seen and heard for themselves, and what others have told them. This type of understanding is an inherent feature of our outlook on the world. Even though people do not necessarily express a coherent view on their experience and perceptions of the world, each person draws on essential taken-for-granted understandings.

For example, a group of your friends who have never studied criminology might state with confidence that burglars commit their crimes because they are high on class A drugs. This kind of view is expressed frequently in social settings, and often it meets with general agreement. However accurate this assessment turns out to be, it is interesting to consider where it comes from. If your friends have no direct experience of criminology and criminal justice, as either students or practitioners, what makes them so sure about this?

Common-sense understanding is actually built up from various sources of information, which people draw on with care as they construct an apparently coherent explanation of criminological matters. As we have already noted, one major source is personal everyday experience. Another is the popular media, which are saturated with both sober and sensationalized stories about crime (Jewkes, 2004).

The popular press (mass media)

The use of media sources for understanding crime raises profound philosophical questions about the nature of reality and how it is represented. There are factual and fictional media representations. The former include newspapers and the popular press, television news and Home Office press releases. The latter include television dramas, movies/films, plays and novels. Although each of these sources are important, the focus in this chapter is on factual representations, and in particular the popular press.

It needs to be appreciated that the mass media is an invaluable source of information about crime and deviance, but it is just one source, and one that must be treated with varying degrees of scepticism. For example, it may be tempting to read an article from a newspaper (hard copy or electronic) and treat what it says as 'facts'. The notion of a 'fact' has been debated at length by social scientists. One school argues that there is no such thing as a 'fact' that exists independently of human consciousness and interpretation. Another position is that facts undoubtedly do exist independently of individuals: for example, if nobody witnessed something happening, that does not mean it did not happen. A resolution of this debate is beyond the scope of this book, but you do need to appreciate the complex nature of 'facts', and that they are rarely straightforward to deal with. Take this example:

- A piece of closed-circuit television (CCTV) footage shows two males, A and B, standing in a crowded street talking to each other.
- A and B are surrounded by shoppers and commuters who are all walking by the two men.

- A little later on, A pulls out a gun and shoots B in the head.
- B falls down dead.
- Shortly after this a police officer walks up to A, who gives him the gun.
- The police officer then handcuffs A.
- Both wait for three minutes for the arrival of a police van to take A away.

In this case the fact that B has died is hardly in dispute, and is likely to be confirmed in due course by police officers and a coroner. But what are the 'facts' about the role of A in causing this death? They too will be considered by the police, forensic experts and professionals throughout the prosecution process. At this stage it is highly likely that the media will also enter the equation. There is likely to be a lot of missing information about the causes and circumstances surrounding the events, and this will leave considerable scope for speculation and interpretation. It will not take long before the basic facts outlined above are lost in a spectacular tale that draws on the accounts of a host of eyewitnesses, observers, criminal justice professionals and other experts. Most likely some of them will disagree with others about what actually happened. The crude existential facts can be mediated through many different perspectives.

A useful concept in considering the role of the media in relation to crime and disorder is 'newsworthiness' (Chibnall, 1977). This focuses on how or why some items of news are regarded as relevant and given coverage, when many other occurrences are not.

Criminology looks too at the various effects and consequences arising from media representations of crime. In other words, it considers what the media do to shape public understanding of crime and give a direction to societal responses to it. In some instances newspapers provide essentially neutral and balanced accounts of events, where the priority is the dissemination of information, but in other instances they are overtly (or more covertly) subjective in what they report. People with direct experience of, or expertise in, the issues addressed might be asked to comment, with the suggestion that the aim is to 'tell it as it is', while in fact what are being expressed are subjective opinions.

At the far end of the spectrum, mass media reportage may generate 'moral panics' about crime (Cohen, 1973, 1980). This is a complex idea, but in brief a 'moral panic' occurs when coverage of an event or an issue is blown out of proportion. This raises anxiety levels among sections of the audience or population, so they become out of line with the actual pervasiveness or seriousness of the problem (Hall et al., 1978).

This part of the chapter concludes with a general appraisal of the undoubted benefits of media coverage of crime and disorder, but also draws attention to some of the limitations and resultant problems.

'Newsworthiness'

A cursory glance at a handful of daily newspapers shows that almost any topic can be considered newsworthy, although the actual decision on what to cover depends on the type of newspaper (for instance, racy issues in a tabloid and more serious coverage in a broadsheet) and its editorial and 'political' stance. Journalists also play an important part, as what is covered can depend on the 'professional ideology of reporters, their intuitive sense of newsworthiness, what makes a "good story"' (Reiner, 2000: 143).

In spite of the differences between publications, some important principles apply to all newspapers and the methods they use to represent crime. Chibnall (1977) identified five 'rules of relevancy' which, he argued, together determine whether a story gets coverage:

1. The news needs to refer to *the exceptional*.
2. The item must have *social connotation*.
3. It must lend itself to a *graphic representation*.
4. Notions of *individual pathology* (that is, an individual's motives and actions) are important.
5. It must be capable of leading to *demands for a firm deterrent and retributive response*.

We can illustrate and expand on these rules by looking at the Jamie Bulger case, which occurred in 1993. Jamie Bulger was a toddler who was abducted in a shopping centre in Bootle, Merseyside, by two young boys. Later they murdered him alongside some railway tracks. The crime itself was particularly brutal and horrific, but it was made even more disturbing because there was CCTV footage of Jamie, which showed him with his hand being held by one of his abductors as he was walked away from the crowded shopping mall.

1. The news needs to refer to the *exceptional*. This means that the crime reported needs to be out of the ordinary and not a run of the mill offence. It is unlikely that anyone would be interested in a story about a suburban burglary, or the theft of a Ford Escort. The more unusual or atypical an offence is, the more likely it is to attract and maintain the interest of an audience. The Bulger case was exceptional inasmuch as the boys who killed Jamie were very young. Children of this age rarely commit such serious offences. The image of Jamie being escorted from a crowded shopping centre was also unusual, as the boys were surrounded by shoppers in a busy public area. The question asked was, how could this all happen in broad daylight?
2. The item must have *social connotation*. In this case the events tapped into public anxieties about youth crime. The claim that young people are out of control and something needs to be done has been repeated periodically throughout history (Brown, 1998; Pearson, 1983), but it still carries great resonance.
3. The *graphic representation* is provided by the image of Jamie with his hand held by his abductor. Arguably this image had such a powerful effect because at first sight it appears so innocent. It just shows a small boy holding hands with another, who might be taken for his brother. But those looking at it know that something much more tragic and sinister lurks beneath the surface, and this meant that the fuzzy picture became lodged in the consciousness of the public.
4. This case provided a good basis for exploring *individual pathology*. There was lengthy debate in the media about the actions of the boy killers. Some suggested that their backgrounds helped to explain why these children had deviated so far from the norm. Others claimed that they were simply 'evil'. Were they redeemable, through punishment and treatment, or were they 'beyond the pale'?
5. This case certainly sparked demands for *a firm deterrent and retributive response*. The media could do little else but respond to a shocking crime with calls for the police and

courts, as well as the wider society, to tackle its perceived causes. Later on in 1993, for instance, at the annual conference of the Conservative Party, the home secretary made a speech calling for more criminals to be locked up. There were also calls for the age of criminal responsibility to be lowered so the killers of Jamie could be treated in the same way as adults.

Chibnall (1977) is very helpful in explaining why some crime makes the news. His concept of 'newsworthiness' also leads to broader questions about what the media is attempting to represent. The popular media undeniably make an important contribution to public understanding of phenomena like crime. People learn from the papers what is going on at a particular time. This source of information is also crucial as it provides a documented history of both what happened in the past, and how it was seen and discussed at the time. However, there is more to the role of the media than straightforward reporting of what has happened.

There is not a clear divide between journalists and fiction writers: rather, there is a continuum of ways in which writers including journalists deal with the world around them. Some claim to be intent on describing things 'as they happen' and 'as they are', while others treat 'real' events as something they can manipulate for the sake of a good story, or the argument they want to draw out of them. Even though journalists may not make up a story in its entirety, as many novelists do, they can be economical with the truth. This raises an important question about media representations of crime. Can they ever be value-free accounts of real events, or are they always selective and partial accounts? In other words, are media representations objective or are they subjective?

We can approach this question from a slightly different angle by considering how media accounts interact with the wider social structure. Is what people read in the newspapers a simple reflection of cultural attitudes to crime and disorder, or alternatively do media accounts of criminality shape and create norms and values? These questions lead towards a discussion of the effects and consequences of media representations of law breaking and deviant behaviour.

The media may produce a distorted picture of 'true crime', which is at odds with the reality of crime. In research examining media coverage of police work, Reiner (2002, 2003) shows that there is a tendency for the media to over-report serious and violent crimes, such as murder or rape, in comparison with their coverage of lesser crimes. These crimes are relatively rare, and the bulk of offending behaviour actually consists of more minor property-related offences. So the media provide a distorted reflection of both the quality and quantity of criminality 'out there'. The media also focus most on crimes that have been solved (generally again, those of a more serious nature). This reflects 'organisational pressures' (Reiner, 2000: 142). Many crime stories are obtained from coverage of court cases: this is convenient and effective for journalists, and provides an 'event-led' structure and often good headlines.

Other coverage is derived from contact with the police, who control information about crimes under investigation, and often form a 'symbiotic relationship' with the media. It should be noted, however, that many crimes do not come to the attention of the police, and even when they do, a successful conviction is not always the outcome.

An effect of this distortion is that unusual and somewhat atypical offences actually become stereotypical images of crime, criminals and the workings of the criminal justice system. This in itself is not necessarily a problem, but research shows that the reaction and response of the popular press to crime may lead to an escalation of anxiety and fear (Jewkes, 2004).

Factual media representations of crime have a number of other effects. In particular they help to define and maintain *moral boundaries:* to identify behaviours that are normal and consistent with the prevailing status quo. Media agents and organizations also play a part in shaping what is thought and said about crime control policy, and in some instance their actions result in 'moral panics' (Cohen, 1973).

Moral panics

The notion of 'moral panic' has been influential in criminology, especially in association with the idea of 'deviancy amplification'. Croall (1998: 63) characterizes the process as a spiral. If intolerance is shown to deviant behaviour in the first instance, any recurrence of the deviance is likely to attract a stepped-up response. In other words, the response is amplified.

To give a concrete example, young people have been involved in anti-social behaviour for decades. For example, they may hang around in groups outside shops. They are not necessarily breaking the law, but they can be a cause of concern to shop managers who think others will find them intimidating and be put off from shopping. The managers might then call the police, who ask the kids to move on. Over a period of time if the deviance continues, the police may adopt more forceful tactics. Eventually the police may be given more powers (they can force the kids to move on, instead of asking them to), and this ends with the stigmatization and criminalization of behaviour that once was just irritating. Basically, there is less tolerance of behaviours that were once tolerated as formal action increases, and the process ends up creating a group of stigmatized deviants. The stigmatized people are then likely to react to the police action with resistance and worse behaviour. The outcome is a spiral of deviancy amplification (Croall, 1998: 63).

This idea was developed by Cohen (1973) in his study of 'moral panics', which focused on violent clashes between gangs of 'mods' and 'rockers' in Clacton, Essex in 1964. The media gave a great deal of coverage to these incidents, exaggerating the extent and prevalence of the violence. Eventually these rival gangs were scapegoated by society, who made them into 'folk devils'. Hall et al. (1978) looked at much the same issues in the response to street crime in the 1970s, and showed how the police worked closely with the government to criminalize young black men. The popular press honed in on several atypical examples of mugging, including one where the victim died, and their sensational coverage tended to stir up fear in the community. The stories were about muggers who either were, or were implied to be, African-Caribbean, and it did not take long for the view to spread that this was a crime mostly committed by young black men. Hall et al. (1978) did not deny the involvement of some black men in street crimes, but they argued that it was grossly distorted and exaggerated by the media. Arguably this criminalization of ethnic minority communities gave the state an opportunity to divert criticism from an economic and social crisis.

Political power

Common-sense views, as opposed to an understanding based on criminological research, may also be expressed by people with a direct involvement or interest in various aspects of crime. Politicians frequently express opinions about crime. Sometimes they actively seek out 'evidence-based' research, but at other times they put forward politically motivated arguments, possibly to win votes in a parliamentary debate or an election. What they actually say may lack any supporting evidence, but their power and authority as politicians gives weight to their common-sense understanding. This may go on to influence criminal justice policy (Walters, 2003).

Professional and practitioner perspectives

Similarly, professionals working in the criminal justice field, such as police officers, have a well-developed bank of common-sense knowledge. Because they deal with crime on a day-to-day basis, it is perhaps not unreasonable to expect this understanding to be based on their real-world experiences. This is not necessarily the case, though: the police are as liable as the rest of us to develop stereotypes and prejudices that are not borne out by evidence.

When prejudicial preconceptions are held by police officers, their sense of reality may become distorted, and this can lead to discriminatory policing. There is significant research to show that the police service has routinely perceived that certain minority ethnic groups are disproportionately involved in criminal activity. This opinion is not always justified, and the police focus on these groups can then be described as *institutionally racist* (Macpherson, 1999; Rowe, 2004). These examples show that common-sense explanations of crime exist in most social domains, even amongst people with a personal investment and involvement in the crime industry.

As student of criminology, you need to develop an understanding of criminality and social control, and therefore you must beware of common-sense explanations, which can be of limited utility. Common sense is necessarily dependent on knowledge that is at best partial and incomplete. It is based on broad-brush generalizations and assumptions about the world. The danger in having only a snapshot or limited view of an issue is that inevitably there are inaccuracies. In the last analysis you will need to adopt certain methods for conducting any criminological inquiry, and you will be taught that relying on your own perceptions, attitudes and beliefs is not necessarily the best method. However, it is arguably a good starting point, so long as you look carefully at *why* you hold your opinions and perceptions.

In this context, you should also be aware of the strengths and weaknesses of the *ethnographic* tradition in criminological research. In this type of research, academic researchers engage first-hand with crime or the criminal justice system, and write about what they do and see (Hobbs, 1998; Winlow; 2001; Holdaway, 1983). It is important to appreciate that the writers of these works observe strict methodological rules. They are not simply describing things as they see them, but rather are attempting to represent the reality of the world as seen by the people who are being researched. In doing so they are attempting to make a contribution to criminological knowledge, so they work within a framework of concepts derived from previous research. These points are expanded in Part Two.

Theoretical perspectives

What is criminological theory? Answering this question is far from straightforward. Indeed it is probably more difficult than describing a more specific theoretical approach, such as 'labelling theory'. We try to answer it in some detail in Part Four of the book.

One way of looking at criminological theory is to see it as a toolkit used by criminologists, to offer explanations of the reasons that crime occurs. It is worth revisiting the definition given by Harrison et al. (2005) in the introduction before reading on.

The question 'what are the causes of crime?' is a theoretical one. In Part Four we sketch out many different theories that are drawn on in criminology, including classicism, positivism, subcultural theory and strain theory. Some of these theories are attributed to schools of thought such as Marxism, the Chicago School and feminism, and it would be doing a disservice to criminological theory and the writers who have produced it to present the theory as a single package. For this reason Part Four is divided into three chapters. An attempt has been made to outline and facilitate the understanding of criminological theory on the basis of three distinctive approaches. This attempt also draws on the history of criminological theory. At this stage, you just need to be aware that criminology developed out of a number of other disciplines, especially the human and social sciences. Many of the debates in criminological theory reflect wider debates in sociology, and to some extent psychology.

Criminological theory is very much a product of the principles of the Enlightenment, which commenced in the early eighteenth century, and the period of modernity that began towards the end of the eighteenth century. These developments refer to the displacement of religious attitudes and beliefs by the development of scientific ideas and the principle of rationality. Perhaps the *leitmotif* of the Enlightenment was the belief that human beings could exert control, or at the very least influence, over the social environment. Human subjects are able to emancipate themselves from the state of nature (Bauman, 2000). Added to this was a conviction that the outcomes of modernization were social progress and a more civilized society (Elias, 1978, 1982). The Enlightenment was very much the product of the European imagination, but it was exported to other parts of the world through colonialism and imperial expansionism. Throughout the twentieth century scientific reason and rationalism had uneven impacts across the globe, and this led to uneven social development, degrees of civilization and modernization (Lea, 2002; Bauman, 1991).

Amongst the issues that have concerned individuals attempting to write a science of society are many that are as relevant now as they were when they first came to prominence. Discussions tend to focus on a key question. In one way or another criminology focuses on an entity called 'society', or to be more specific, the nature of the relationship between the individual and society. There are two fundamental orientations, and to reduce the distinction between them to its bare bones, one approach suggests that society shapes the individual person, whereas the opposite argument is that it is individuals who make up society. This is an over-simplistic representation, of course: the theoretical explanations are multidimensional, and many different words are used to describe this complexity.

Theorists who work from the perspective that society influences the individual are often described as *structuralists*. This refers to the fact that in this view, society is seen as an objective structure, external to the individuals within it, which in turn influences or limits what they do. This is also described as a *macro-level approach,* a term that acknowledges the two levels of analysis: individuals (the micro entities) and society, characterized as an impersonal phenomenon external to and independent of them (the macro entity). According to the macro structural perspective, human behaviour is caused or influenced to some degree by factors in the social environment (such as social class or economic circumstances). An analogy is the rocks making up a mountainous landscape. An individual can chip away at the rock face – that is, his or her personality can shape his/her path in life – but the difference he or she makes to the originally predicted outcome is likely to be minimal. Although the structuralist approach tends to downplay the role of the individual, the actions of people are not always determined, and they can adapt to the structural environment in creative ways. This is demonstrated in Chapter 12.

In contrast to this way of looking at the social world, there are theories that focus on the individual, which view society only as the sum of individuals, who are both atomized and alone, and involved in interaction with each other. Some advocates of the micro perspective hold the view that individuals have considerable freedom to choose and act as they wish, although not without some influence from external factors such as the social environment. This leads to attempts to explain crime which focus on the degree to which individuals consciously and actively choose what they do. Other researchers, whose focus is still on the individual, concentrate on the degree to which human behaviour is determined by people's psychological or biological make-up, rather than by their free choice.

These perspectives can be represented as a set of dualisms:

- individual versus society
- micro versus macro
- free will versus determinism
- subjective versus objective.

The words on the left-hand side are generically defined as the 'agency' perspective, and those on the right-hand side as the 'structure' perspective. The structure may be social, psychological (concerned with the workings of the mind) or biological (concerned with the body). Various scholars have questioned the usefulness of these dualisms. Some have argued that it is not a case of either the structure or the agency perspective being right, and the other being wrong: the two are interrelated and work together. However, in the last analysis researchers do tend to attach slightly more weight to one than to the other.

Other theories move beyond looking for explanations that rest on distinctively sociological and psychological assumptions about the causes of crime. Among these perspectives, covered in Chapter 13, are the feminist, anti-racist and postmodern or poststructural perspectives. Criminologists focusing on race and gender show that traditionally criminology has treated offenders and victims as if they are white, male and working class. The sex and gender, as well as the race and ethnicity, of offenders and victims have not been made explicit. Subsequently feminist and anti-racist writers have shown how all aspects of crime and criminal justice are both gendered and racialized. Scholars representing these schools of thought have over the years brought about a rethinking and reorientation of criminological theorizing.

Other approaches have challenged in more fundamental ways our understanding of society, the individual and the relationship between the two. These approaches, referred to as poststructural or postmodern, have drawn on disciplines other than the social sciences, including philosophy and cultural studies. It will be shown in Chapter 13 that variants of this so-called radical and deconstructive framework have challenged criminologists to rethink what they mean by everyday concepts we take for granted: crime, the offender, the victim, the criminal justice system; and the idea of justice. They even question conceptual categories such as the individual and society. It is shown that in many of these commentaries society is the product of neither structure or individual agency, but an effect of discourse or language. Indeed in some extreme cases it is claimed that there is no such thing as society, and everything is reducible to text (including words and images). This is a thought-provoking assertion, and one that it is sometimes difficult to understand.

So far the discussion has taken place at a general level. The next part examines how criminal behaviour has been defined, and the legislative response to criminality.

Crime is defined and understood in terms of:

■ legislation, in particular the criminal law
■ personal experience, as well as the experiences of family, partners and friends
■ media-led accounts
■ political debate
■ theoretical perspectives.

STOP AND SEARCH: A CASE STUDY

The example of stop and search shows how legislation is developed to tackle different types of offending behaviour. In this case the law relating to stop and search has changed substantially in response to sociohistoric changes, changes in the nature of offending behaviour and varying statutory responses to a range of crimes.

In this case study:

■ stop and search is examined from an historical perspective
■ the links are traced between nineteenth-century legislation on vagrancy, and policing in England and Wales in the 1970s and 1980s
■ the notions of reasonable suspicion and discretion are discussed
■ key legislation is introduced, including the Police and Criminal Evidence Act (1984), the Public Order Act (1994) and the Terrorism Act (2000).

The power to stop and search people has existed since the Metropolitan Police was first established in London in 1829. Stop and search is at the heart of police work, and an understanding of its utility for police officers as part of their day-to-day contact with the public cannot be overstated. Stop and search is a power exercised by police officers in public places if they are suspicious about the behaviour, actions or appearance of an individual. The purpose of the stop is to assess whether the suspicion a police officer holds about a person is accurate, through asking the stopped person questions relating to that suspicion. If the questions are answered in such a way that the suspicions held by the officer are allayed, then the interaction is over; if not, the individual may be searched. Because this power has been in existence for a considerable time, it is useful to trace its development from an historical perspective.

Many studies of stop and search refer back to the Vagrancy Act (1824), but before we focus on this legislation we need to put the problem of vagrancy into context. The reason for this is to show how legislation is adapted to respond to different crime problems at different times.

Vagrancy

'Vagrants' is a rather vague and loose term. It's dictionary definition is a person with no settled home. It is used to apply to a disparate group of individuals, ranging from those genuinely seeking work to beggars and tramps who are not looking for work. The law on vagrancy has a particularly lengthy history, and although it is not necessary to dwell too long on this, it is essential to be aware of its past because there have been a number of shifts of emphasis, which show the extent to which legislation is adapted to different social conditions and to reinforce social control.

Chambliss (1969) suggests that early legislation in the fourteenth century was prompted by the decimation of the population by the Black Death. As a result of the plague there was a shortage of labourers, and it was necessary to ensure that those who had survived did work regularly, to sustain the weak economy. One way to do this was to restrict – or even prevent – the mobility associated with vagrancy. It was also considered socially desirable to deter idleness and begging.

During the fifteenth century socioeconomic conditions generally became more stable, coinciding with the declining importance of feudalism and its suppression by commerce and industry. So the economic need to make people work still existed, but in a different context. Vagrants were in a position to undermine the social changes through their behaviour, and it was considered desirable to control them for this reason. Also by the sixteenth century there was a growing concern with the criminality of vagrants, hence the appearance of words like 'ruffian' and 'vagabond'. In a statute of 1530 it was written:

> Whoever man or woman, being not lame, impotent, or so aged or diseased that he or she cannot work, not having whereon to live, shall be lurking in any house or loitering or idle wandering by the highway side, or in streets, cities, towns, or villages, not applying themselves to some honest labour and so continuing for three days; or running away from their work; every such person shall be taken for a vagabond.
>
> (Chambliss, 1969: 58)

The vagrancy laws continued to be subjected to amendments and revisions in response to changing perceptions of social problems, and arguably they functioned as a buffer against social revolt. The seriousness of the threat posed by vagrancy worsened as Napoleonic war veterans returned to England, only to meet unemployment and high bread prices. Many resorted to begging and stealing in order to survive. For instance, during the period from 1806 to 1826 crime increased by almost three times, despite the fact that the population only increased by a half (Rose, 1988). It was Sir Robert Peel who responded to this with reforms of the police in the years 1823–7 and the transformation of the archaic criminal code to ensure that it was enforceable. Indeed, concerns with criminality had become extremely important, the most notable example being the problem of juvenile delinquency. This was regarded as a crisis, and as the 1815 Select Committee put it, two-thirds of London beggars were in fact children who were 'on course to becoming the very worst criminals' (Rose, 1988: 5).

Demuth (1978) comments that the 1824 Vagrancy Act demonstrated a clear commitment to rectifying these deficiencies, and therefore gave more power and responsibility to magistrates. The law became increasingly codified. The Act defined three categories of vagrant. First were the idle and disorderly, or those individuals who neglected their families and begged within the parish of settlement. Those found guilty of this offence were punished with a maximum of one month in prison. Second were rogues and vagabonds, consisting of those who deserted their families and fell back on parish relief, travellers, reputed thieves and suspected persons loitering and appearing 'to be up to no good'. The latter offence required no concrete proof apart from suspicion. The consequences of committing such a misdemeanour were three months in jail. Third were 'incorrigible rogues', encompassing those previously convicted of being a rogue or vagabond. The punishment for such an offence could include a whipping and imprisonment for one year.

This legislation was directed at tackling the problem of people wandering around aimlessly with no sense of purpose, or to be more specific, without a commitment to productive work. In sum, the Act prohibited the telling of fortunes, sleeping rough, exposing wounds as a means of begging, collecting alms under false pretences, indecent exposure, carrying offensive weapons, being found on enclosed premises for unlawful purposes, and suspected persons. In section 4 it is stated that:

> Every suspected person or reputed thief, frequenting any river, canal, or navigable stream, dock, basin, or any quay, wharf or warehouse near or adjoining thereto, or any street, highway, or avenue leading thereto, or any street (or any highway place adjacent to a street or highway) with intent to commit an arrestable offence.
>
> (Demuth, 1978: 11)

Section 4 was directed not just at vagrants but towards a whole class of 'shady people', and guilt under the section had to be denied and innocence proven by the defendant, rather than it being necessary for the person making the accusation to prove it.

The relevance of criminality is consolidated by the clause detailing the consequences of escaping from a place of legal confinement. This offence was responded to by labelling a person as an 'incorrigible rogue', also resulting in the individual being committed to a Crown court and sentenced to up to one year in prison. Indeed as Archard (1979) argues, the Vagrancy Act (1824) was essentially a 'criminalising instrument'. There are also links with psychiatry and the medicalization of vagrancy: thus common lodging houses, hostels and reception centres perform the function of an 'open asylum' (Archard, 1979: 21).

It was not only 'unmeritable wanderers' who were problematic: fears were expressed about the possibility of individuals predisposed towards participating in such activities forming communities, hence the notorious 'dens of thieves and infamy'. The Act permitted the search of houses, ostensibly because of a concern with living conditions, but in actual fact because of the perceived threat to 'respectable society' (Pearson, 1983). It was suggested the existence of lodging houses, 'clustered in the labyrinthine rookeries, linked by secret passages and the roof top escape routes', corrupted youngsters, leading them into vice and crime. The rookeries of central London were considered to be the 'hot beds' not only of disease (primarily cholera) and political activism (in the form of Chartism) but also crime and the 'dangerous classes' (Stedman-Jones, 1971: 167). Unscrupulous proprietors, some acting as 'fences', often controlled these areas, aiding and abetting criminal clients, as well as being the victims of theft from clients.

To summarize, in an earlier period the legislation to tackle vagrancy was prompted by the perceived problem of idleness and the avoidance of work, which was seen as detrimental to economic growth. Then came a clear shift of emphasis towards criminality, and the perceived threat vagrants posed to wider society. The statutes outlined punitive measures intended to deter people from the pursuit of this 'lifestyle choice'. Critics argue that this showed a failure to recognize the extent to which socioeconomic conditions dictated the actions of certain sections of the population. For some people, such as destitute former soldiers, vagrancy was one of the more viable ways for them to subsist and survive. Beresford sums up the issue of vagrancy with the pertinent observation that it served as 'an umbrella for activities offensive to the state' (Beresford, 1979: 144).

The history books tell us that the police power to stop and search can be traced back to the Vagrancy Act (1824). This was known as the old 'sus' law, and was in place to prevent 'any person or thief' from hanging around or loitering in a public place with the intent to commit an arrestable offence. In 1839, section 66 of the Metropolitan Police Act (1839) gave the police further authority to stop and search a person if an officer had reasonable suspicion that he or she was in possession of something that was either stolen or unlawfully obtained. The principle of 'reasonable suspicion' is of exceptional importance, as will be shown later in this chapter. The police therefore clearly have considerable powers to stop and search individuals they suspect of criminal intent.

This power was used extensively throughout the nineteenth and twentieth centuries, but it did not appear to a noticeable extent on the criminological agenda until the 1970s. During that decade the 'sus' laws, or section 4 of the Vagrancy Act, were used – arguably to excess – against minority ethnic groups, especially young black men in inner city areas (Hall et al., 1978). At that time the power to stop and search was also given to the police by other pieces of legislation, in particular section 6 of the Drugs Act (1971), which stated that police constables may search people if they have reasonable grounds to suspect they are in possession of controlled drugs (such as cannabis and heroin).

Several research studies expressed concern about the use of stop and search, especially the finding that officers did not always observe the 'reasonable suspicion' requirement found in the legislation. Most crucially, these studies found that the powers of stop and search were being used disproportionately against black people (Sanders and Young, 2003; Bowling and Foster, 2002). Research also shows that since the late 1960s researchers have uncovered evidence of racism among police officers, in the form of stereotypes and prejudicial attitudes and beliefs (Rowe, 2004). There is ongoing debate whether police racism is a problem confined to a minority of racist individuals, or is institutionalized. If it is to be understood as the latter, it is an inherent characteristic of the organizational outlook and activities of the police service (Waddington, 1999). This dispute is revisited throughout this book. The point to be made here is that the 'sus' laws gave the police officers considerable discretion in whom they stopped, and they arguably used this discretion in a racist way (Reiner, 2000; Gelsthorpe and Padfield, 2003).

One of the first lessons students of the police and policing are taught is that even though the police are there to enforce the law, it is impossible to interpret literally and enforce absolutely all laws, at all times and in all places. This would be unworkable mainly because there are simply not enough police officers with sufficient resources to fully apply the law. In addition, operational policing is influenced by other factors such as the discriminatory stereotypes mentioned above, and non-legal or extra-legal policy frameworks. Perhaps the most significant issue, though, is police discretion (Choongh, 1997; Reiner, 2000), which amounts to a degree of subjectivity and selectivity in the maintenance of the rule of law. Historically the 'sus' laws were used in a discriminatory fashion, often in ways that were perceived to be illegitimate and unjust. Moreover, the police lacked the consent of sections of the community they were policing, in particular locales or geographical areas (Scarman, 1981).

Given these contextual factors, it is perhaps not surprising that there was a high degree of conflict and tension between the police and sections of black communities, especially young males. The situation finally came to a head in 1981 in Brixton, an area of the south-east London borough of Lambeth (Bowling and Phillips, 2002). The police decided to use section 66 of the Metropolitan Police Act (1839) to implement 'Operation Swamp '81'. This operation involved a massive police presence, used for extensive surveillance to detect and arrest burglars, stopping, searching and arresting supposedly suspicious people on the streets, and then taking them to the police station for interrogation. This and the more general insensitive use of the 'sus' laws antagonized some of the community to such an extent that 'Swamp '81' was a trigger or 'flashpoint' precipitating major riots.

Arguably the community of Brixton had been placed under such 'endless pressure' (Pryce, 1979) for so many years that these riots could have been predicted. In the aftermath of the Brixton riots the government appointed Lord Scarman to conduct an inquiry into these events. The Scarman (1981) inquiry covered a lot of ground, as it investigated the circumstances surrounding and factors causing the riots. Among the principal causes of the unrest was the 'sus' laws, and this resulted in the repeal of the Vagrancy Act. The story does not end here, though.

Another of the many recommendations made by Scarman was a fundamental change in policing, including the use of stop and search. There was no call to entirely jettison this approach, and it was recognized as an important investigative power to detect or prevent offending by particular individuals in a particular time and place. However, the suggestion was that stop and search should be used with more caution and sensitivity. This can be seen in the creation of a new piece of legislation, the Police and Criminal Evidence Act (1984).

The Police and Criminal Evidence Act (1984)

PACE, as this Act is commonly known, led to major reform of police powers, procedures and properties (Sanders and Young, 2003). It is Section 1 of this Act that is important for the purposes of this chapter. The rationale for introducing PACE was to add much-needed clarity to the circumstances when it would be appropriate for a stop and search to be conducted. It also included safeguards to protect the rights of the individuals concerned.

The PACE Code of Practice A states that the main purpose of the power is to 'enable officers to allay or confirm suspicions about individuals without exercising their power of arrest'. As a result of PACE, police officers have a general power to stop and search any person or vehicle in a public place if they have a reasonable reason to suspect that they will find stolen or prohibited articles. To check out this suspicion an officer can carry out a full search of individuals, any baggage they may be carrying with them, or any vehicle they may be in. The kinds of possessions the police look for include drugs, offensive weapons and stolen property. The reasonable grounds for stopping and searching someone must be at the same level as the grounds used to justify the arrest of a suspect. In section 23, which relates to section 1, it is written that the reasonable grounds to which a police officer refers depend on the particular circumstances. For example, the suspicion must be based on 'facts, information, and/or intelligence'. To put it more concretely the Act states that:

> Reasonable suspicion can never be supported on the basis of personal factors alone without reliable or supporting intelligence or information or some specific behaviour by the person concerned. For example, a person's race, age, appearance or the fact that the person is known to have a previous conviction, cannot be used alone or in combination with each other as the reason for searching that person. Reasonable suspicion cannot be based on generalizations or stereotypical images of certain groups or categories of people as more likely to be involved in criminal activity.

An important factor to note is that the decision to stop and search is an individual decision, and the police officer deciding to stop and search a person is individually accountable. This is partly achieved under Section 1, where it is stated that the police officer is required to produce a record of the stop, including details about the officer's identity, where he or she is stationed, and the grounds for the search (that is, what he/she is looking for).

There are various other pieces of legislation relating to stop and search, and here we need to consider two of them: section 60 of the Criminal Justice and Public Order Act (1994) and section 44 of the Terrorism Act (2000).

Section 60 of the Public Order Act (1994)

This was introduced to help the police respond to intelligence that there is liable to be an outbreak of major disorder. It enables the police to identify a geographical location where individuals may be searched on the basis of information about potential trouble-makers. The use of this Act is different from PACE in that it can only be applied by a constable who has received authorization by a senior police officer. For authorization to be given it is necessary for there to be 'a reasonable belief that incidents involving serious violence may take place or that people are carrying dangerous instruments or offensive weapons within any locality'. Once the senior officer has issued authorization, constables are in a position to legitimately carry out a search. There are some safeguards to protect suspects, because officers are required to provide a justification of the grounds for making a stop and to keep a record.

Section 44 of the Terrorism Act (2000)

Police officers have the power to stop and search individuals if they have reasonable suspicion that a person is either a terrorist or is suspected of having an object in his/her possession, which would count as evidence of involvement in terrorist activity. The focus of this Act is extremely clear, as is demonstrated by section 2.22 of Code A:

> The powers must not be used to stop and search for reasons unconnected with terrorism. Officers must take particular care not to discriminate against members of ethic minorities in the exercise of these powers.

Perhaps the main difference between these different Acts is that stop and search under PACE must be based on 'reasonable suspicion', which amounts to an 'objective basis'. By contrast the Criminal Justice and Public Order Act (1994) is used if the police 'believe serious violence will take place'.

Clearly this chapter is concerned with legal approaches to understanding criminal justice, but it should be borne in mind that there are also non-legal influences on this area of study. In 1993 a young black man, Stephen Lawrence, was brutally murdered in an unprovoked and racially motivated attack in London. The men responsible for killing him were never successfully convicted, and in response to this the government of the day set up an inquiry to examine the circumstances surrounding his death and the police investigation of the case. The outcome was the Macpherson report, published in 1999. Although stop and search was not directly relevant to the Lawrence case, it was discussed as part of the Macpherson inquiry, mainly because there was a view that in the post-Scarman era (1981 onwards), it had continued to be used in a discriminatory way, especially against African-Caribbean communities (Bowling and Phillips, 2002). In total Macpherson made 70 recommendations, including Recommendation 61, which said:

> That the Home Secretary, in consultation with the Police Services, should ensure that a record is made by police officers of all 'stops' and 'stops and searches' made under any legislative provision (not just the Police and Criminal Evidence Act). Non-statutory

or so called 'voluntary' stops must also be recorded. The record to include the reason for the stop, the outcome, and the self-defined ethnic identity of the person stopped. A copy of the record shall be given to the person stopped.

(Macpherson, 1999)

This case study has shown that:

■ legislation changes dramatically in response to changing social conditions and historical events.
■ law enforcement involves discretion, and the law is enforced selectively.

STOP AND SEARCH AND THE POLICING OF DRUGS

This case study:

■ focuses on the Lambeth cannabis pilot scheme and the reclassification of cannabis
■ is an historical example, but illustrates how legislation is related to policing and government policies
■ considers the contextual factors surrounding the Lambeth experiment
■ examines the implementation of the scheme
■ reviews the impact of the scheme
■ discusses some of the responses to the experiment, especially those of the police, politicians and media.

This next part of the chapter focuses on these difficulties, and discusses the ways in which policing drugs has changed in Britain, drawing on Brixton as a case study. As noted above, following the 1981 Brixton riots there was a reappraisal of police policy and practice, and this area has continued to attract innovative approaches to policing, such as the Brixton drugs experiment. This was followed by the reclassification of cannabis from a class B to a class C substance by the Home Secretary in early 2004.

The Lambeth cannabis pilot scheme

What is the background to the Brixton or Lambeth cannabis pilot scheme? There is a relatively long and troubled history of policing in this deprived and socially excluded community, because of police raids of the streets and 'shabeens' (social clubs) aiming to disrupt a sometimes busy drugs marketplace. While there is evidence to show the trading of soft drugs such as 'ganja' (cannabis) was commonplace, and the presence of hard drugs was an undeniable reality, the police response to crime, including drug-related criminality, was at best characterized as hard and aggressive.

Following Scarman the style of policing in Brixton changed to reflect a view that police work is best done when the police converse and communicate with the people they police. The logic of this approach is that the police need the consent of the community if they are to effectively address crime problems such as selling and misusing drugs. In the post-Scarman era officers were actively discouraged from making arrests for the possession of cannabis for personal use, especially on or near to the 'Front Line' (Keith, 1993). If any arrests had to be made, officers were told that it should be done away from this tension-ridden area, to avoid increasing the potential for any conflict and full-scale riots like Brixton 1981. The unthinking and uncritical enforcement of the drug laws was likely to be counter-productive and create more social harm than public good. The legalization or decriminalization of cannabis was not on the public policy agenda, but there was a different understanding of how drug misuse should be resolved.

Thus in the early to mid-1980s the police began using new methods of controlling drugs, but these were not altogether unproblematic. One unintended but anticipated outcome was that the prioritization of peace keeping, and the residualization or decreased use of crime-fighting tactics, allowed the drugs trade to expand, especially the market for hard drugs. At times the police were not able to distinguish the antisocial behaviour associated with the use of cannabis and alcohol from the more serious threats posed by organized gangs selling hard drugs (Keith, 1993). These drugs caused ill health through addiction and interpersonal violence. When the police did use coercive methods the outcome was the displacement of drugs crime to other parts of the Metropolitan Police District (MPD). Additionally the idea of allocating officers to an area to ensure a visible police presence still left communities feeling exposed to unnecessary surveillance and over-policed. Moreover, the Scotland Yard Drug Squad eventually proved the alleged involvement of officers from the CID (the Criminal Investigation Department) in the recycling of drugs following a raid of Brixton police station (McLagan, 2003).

The late twentieth-century legacy

So far it has been established that the policing of drugs in Lambeth, and many other areas like it, has been fraught with difficulties. At this stage, three interrelated points need to be made clear. All drugs classified under the Misuse of Drugs Act (1971) are illegal, and the police are required to apply the letter of the law, albeit under the influence of discretion and policy directives. The use of drugs may pose an immediate threat to the physical and psychological health of individual users. More than that, drug users may harm the communities in which they live, because of their antisocial behaviour and involvement in various crimes to fund their habits. Suppliers may also cause social harm, as rival gangs become embroiled in turf wars to maximize their control and influence over global and local, or glocalized, drug markets (Lee and South, 2003; TDPF, 2004). Such a situation requires the police to respond to the supply and use of illicit substances in social settings where interpersonal and communal violence are never far away.

Lambeth Cannabis Warning Scheme: contextual factors

The story recounted above perhaps explains an event that occurred at the end of 2000. In December that year a police officer in Brixton was arrested and charged because of a failure to deal with cannabis properly. The police officer in question had exercised his discretion in not making an arrest, as many officers had done previously, but on this particular occasion a criminal charge was made. It is not surprising that the colleagues of this criminalized officer reacted in the way they did: to ensure they did not end up being arrested and charged, they stated that they would arrest every individual they found in possession of cannabis. As was argued above, it is highly improbable that they could have done this, nor would it have been particularly desirable.

Shortly after this incident Commander Brian Paddick was appointed to lead and manage policing in Lambeth. Paddick was concerned by this event, and investigated possible ways of responding to cannabis without exposing his officers to any danger of facing an arrest for not doing their job properly and according to the letter of the law. As well as this legal conundrum, Paddick identified a range of political and economic problems with arresting people for cannabis use. Some of his arguments were also found in a report published before his arrival, entitled *Clearing the Decks* (Metropolitan Police Service, 2000). He argued that arresting people for cannabis placed a considerable burden on the police because of the limited availability of time and money. More than that, the outcomes in the prosecution process did not justify the investment of resources. For example, the results of arrests were frequently cautions, small fines (around £50) or conditional discharges at court (PSS Consultancy Group, 2002).

The problem of finite resources experienced in Lambeth was part of a more general problem faced by the police service throughout the other 42 forces in England and Wales, specifically the influence of the 'New Public Management' (NPM) or 'managerialism' (Long, 2003; Neyroud, 2003). These ideas gained ascendancy throughout the public sector during the 1980s, and while they refer to a set of complex political rationalities, it is possible to identify some broad tendencies for the purposes of this discussion. In essence, providers of public services must satisfy the government and the wider public that their activities are 'cost-effective', provide 'value for money' and are evaluated according to their effectiveness, efficiency and economy (Fionda, 2000). The police are now required to adopt more businesslike styles of service provision, in order to deliver more economic, effective and efficient services. The significance of the 'three Es' can be seen in the emphasis now placed on value for money, performance targets and auditing, quality of service and a consumer orientation. The introduction of market and private-sector values also constrains professionals through the introduction of national standards and objectives, systems to measure financial accountability and increased external scrutiny and monitoring (Senior, Crowther-Dowey and Long, 2007). The theme of managerialism is revisited in Chapter 5.

To address this problem Paddick explored various possibilities, including an idea called the 'seize and warn scheme'. This concept was based on the commander appreciating the riot-torn history of Lambeth,[1] and an acceptance of Scarman's view that arresting everyone the police stopped and searched who possessed cannabis would put already fragile police–community relations under considerable strain, possibly culminating in yet another major outbreak of public disorder.

There were further continuities with the 1980s, inasmuch as Lambeth was affected by the problems of ill health and violence caused by hard drugs. According to community leaders – not just the police – crack cocaine and heroin, along with gun-related violence and street robberies, blighted the quality of life of residents in this locality. There was a view in the community that these harder drugs should become police priorities rather than cannabis. In addition, community representatives argued that a shift of emphasis along these lines might curb any continuation of the often poorly conceived usage of stop and search by police officers against African-Caribbean youth.

The controversial changes suggested by Commander Paddick clearly presented problems. An obvious criticism is that the police might have been seen as giving the impression to the wider public, particularly those who do not use drugs, that they were abnegating their responsibility to enforce the law and protect people from the harm caused by an unregulated drugs market. Moreover, Paddick did not have the authority to implement a pilot without the approval of the ACPO team, consisting of Sir John Stevens, now former Commissioner of the Metropolitan Police Service, and his team of senior officers, headed by deputy Commissioner Mike Fuller. In short, it was necessary to broach the subject with the community and the higher echelons of the police organization.

Paddick announced in the *Evening Standard* (on 29 March 2001) that the police in Lambeth were considering taking a softer line and not arresting people for cannabis. Following this the police met on three occasions with the Lambeth Police Community Consultative Group. Throughout these discussions the group made it absolutely clear that they were opposed to all kinds of illegal drugs, but that they supported the philosophy underpinning the plan outlined by Paddick (Dapp, 2002). Senior officers overseeing Paddick adopted a similar position, and despite some scepticism, it was seen that the court results did not fully justify the cost of prosecuting people. Indeed the way drugs are currently policed is placing the criminal justice and penal systems in a state of permanent crisis (TDPF, 2004: 8).

Implementing the Lambeth Cannabis Warning Scheme

By 4 July 2001 the Lambeth Cannabis Warning Scheme had been implemented, initially for six months (*Evening Standard*, 4 July 2001), but it actually ran for just over a year, until 31 July 2002. On 1 August 2002 the discretion to arrest individuals in possession of cannabis was returned to police officers, raising questions about the need for an exit strategy (Metropolitan Police Authority, 2002: 3). The rationale of the initiative was to reduce the time the police dedicated to dealing with individuals caught in possession of cannabis, thus freeing up time for the police to respond more effectively to serious offences, including class A drug offences, burglary, gun crime and robbery (PSS Consultancy Group, 2002). What actually happened?

Immediately prior to the initiation of the scheme it was necessary for an officer to devote considerable time to filling in forms after making an arrest, which acted as a disincentive and frequently led to officers 'turning a blind eye', thus avoiding taking any further action. Any adult who was found to be in possession of small quantities of cannabis for personal use had the substance confiscated. There were two outcomes: individuals admitting this offence were given a 'formal warning', while those who did not admit to it were issued with an 'informal warning' instead. In both instances, the course of action taken avoided making an arrest (Metropolitan Police Authority, 2002).

As part of the pilot police officers were told that if young people were found to be in possession of the drug that it must be taken off them. Young people were not just left to walk away following the confiscation of the drug, but were automatically referred to the Youth Offender Team (YOT). These teams were set up by the 1998 Crime and Disorder Act (Home Office, 1998) to provide 'joined-up' inter-agency solutions to problems with complex causes. In the case of cannabis possession the individuals referred to YOTs would be offered counselling, support and advice. More than that, their parents were also invited along to receive similar support.

The impact of the Lambeth scheme

The response of senior Metropolitan Police officers was positive, and the then deputy commissioner of the Metropolitan Police, Ian Blair, declared the scheme 'undoubtedly a success – in statistical terms'. Mike Fuller, the deputy commissioner in charge of drugs strategy, was also positive, referring to the project as 'a godsend' (*Guardian*, 2 July 2002). To put these perceptions into context it is necessary to scrutinize the impact of the scheme.

The PSS Consultancy Group (2002) evaluation focused on the impact of policing activity on drugs in Lambeth and adjoining boroughs. It examined data about particular offences and disposals, as well as gleaning some of the perceptions of police officers through a questionnaire survey and focus groups.

A key priority of the pilot was to reduce the pressures the policing of cannabis placed on scarce resources. The police achieved this goal, and more time was made available for the police to focus on more serious offences. For example:

> During the 6 months of the evaluation, Lambeth officers issued 450 warnings. This released at least 1350 hours of officer time (by avoiding custody procedures and interviewing time), equivalent to 1.8 full time officers. A further 1150 hours of CJU staff time was released by avoiding case file preparation.
>
> (PSS Consultancy Group, 2002: 1)

The warning scheme was still bureaucratic, because officers had to fill in a crime report, a stop and search form and possibly a criminal intelligence sheet. They also had to produce a written record of what happened to the seized drugs. Despite the considerable work involved there was an 110 per cent increase in the number of interventions concerning cannabis, and 1,390 warnings were issued, in contrast to 661 arrests in the previous year (MPA, 2002: 6) The MPA suggested that the PSS calculations above might be an underestimate of the total resource saved, but the time saved worked out as the equivalent of 1.8 officers per annum, or up to 2.75 more officers if the increased enforcement activity was also integrated into the costing methodology (MPA, 2002). The availability of more resource may account for the finding that 'Lambeth also increased its activity against Class A drugs relative to adjoining Boroughs' (PSS Consultancy Group, 2002: 1).

It would appear from these points that the pilot had some success, inasmuch as the costs of controlling cannabis supply had been reduced, and some police time had been liberated to direct more resources towards harder drugs, especially in relation to class A drug trafficking enforcement. For example:

There was an increase in police activity in relation to class A drug trafficking enforcement in Lambeth, which increased 19% (89 in 2000, 106 in 2001), when compared with a 3% increase in adjoining boroughs. The increased performance against class A trafficking continues to be sustained, particularly against crack cocaine. The total number of drug offences, which denotes arrests, increased from 1367 to 1733 (26%) during the period from April–March 2001–2, when compared with the same period the previous year. Arrests for drug trafficking have also increased from 288 to 344 (16%) during this period. This would indicate that one objective of the pilot scheme has been achieved, which was to release officers' time to carry out more class A drug enforcement.

(MPA, 2002: 10)

It should be pointed out that even though police in Lambeth make a contribution to intervening in such drug markets there is also the work of national bodies such as the National Criminal Intelligence Service (NCIS)[2] and Customs and Excise.

Despite the 'statistical' success story, the MP for Vauxhall (the area covered by the scheme), Kate Hoey, vehemently opposed the scheme, and argued that it had caused far more harm than good by giving the message to children that 'cannabis is no worse for you than sweets' (*Guardian*, 2 July 2002). There are in fact real risks from cannabis-taking to the physical and psychological health of young people. This view was backed up by anecdotal evidence from other residents living in the areas.

The evaluation also focused on the perceptions of police officers. Among the main findings was that some officers still felt the public did not understand the aims and objectives of the policy. Some of the officers surveyed also voiced concern that the policy was resulting in the restriction of their powers to address drug offences, and that a valuable source of intelligence was being lost. Indeed most officers felt that the policy would lead to an increase in general drug use in Lambeth, and for this reason the policy should not be rolled out to the rest of the MPD (PSS Consultancy Group, 2002: 2).

The community also had its own views about the scheme, some of which were gathered by a survey instigated by the Police Foundation and delivered by MORI. This report highlighted that there was a notably high degree of apprehension that young people were increasingly more likely to come into contact with and misuse drugs. Lambeth police were naturally worried about these concerns, and conducted a survey of local schools. It found that neither the experiment nor the home secretary in his discussions about reclassifying cannabis had led to any increases in dealing or the confiscation of cannabis in schools. Some critics also argued that the borough had become a site for drug tourists making the best of the lax enforcement strategy, but this claim was not borne out by the evidence. There was also a belief that the experiment signalled the legalization or decriminalization of cannabis, demonstrated by a comment made by Deputy Assistant Commission Mike Fuller: 'The public were very unclear about what was happening and thought drugs were being legalized and this wasn't the case' (BBC News, 21 March 2002). This suggests that communication about the strategy could have been improved. The MORI poll has found that there was more support among white rather than black and Asian residents (BBC News, 21 March

2002). Finally, there was no evidence of formal complaints being made by members of the public against the warning scheme pilot.

As was indicated above on 1 August 2002 the police reverted to the original policy of making arrests for the possession of cannabis. However, during the trial period public debate had been preoccupied with the reclassification of cannabis, and it was appreciated that simply returning to the ways things had been done before could create tensions between the police and community.

The reclassification of cannabis

10 July 2002 was a significant date in the history of the policing of drugs in British society, because the home secretary announced that the reclassification of cannabis from a class B to class C drug was high on the political agenda (Home Office press release, 10 July 2002). Research had indicated that this reclassification would result in some financial savings, and give police officers more time to patrol and respond to calls for public assistance. There might be slightly fewer serious crimes detected, but the savings in police time elsewhere would compensate for this. There would also be non-economic benefits, specifically fewer adversarial contacts between the police and young people (May, Warburton, Turnbull and Hough, 2002).

After taking advice from the Advisory Council on the Misuse of Drugs (ACMD) the home secretary was made aware that cannabis could not be decriminalized and had to remain illegal because it is a harmful drug. It was acknowledged that cannabis carries health risks of an acute and chronic nature, and can also lead to dependency. However, it was agreed that cannabis was not as harmful as either class A drugs (such as heroin and crack cocaine) or class B drugs (such as amphetamines), and for that reason cannabis, including resin, should be reclassified as C. The government has therefore adopted a clear position: cannabis is illegal and poses risks to the health of users. In practical terms, though, it is not feasible to criminalize adults possessing cannabis, mainly because resources are finite and class A drugs should be prioritized.

Cannabis was reclassified from a class B to a class C drug on 29 January 2004. As a controlled drug, the production, supply and possession remains illegal but the penalties imposed have been altered. The maximum penalty for producing and dealing in all class C substances is now 14 years. The maximum penalty for possession has been reduced from five years to two years imprisonment, but for adults the aim is to avoid making an arrest. This is typical for class C drugs. The preferred penalty for possession is confiscation of the drug (in the case of adults) and a warning unless there are aggravating factors. An aggravating factor could be public disorder associated with the use of cannabis; if a person smokes cannabis openly in a public place; if a young person aged 17 years or under is found in possession of cannabis; people who are in possession of the drug in close proximity to places such as schools, youth clubs or areas where children play. Young people (under 18) offending for the first time will be arrested and given a formal warning or reprimand. If perpetrators reoffend they will be given a final warning or be charged.

Obviously the Lambeth pilot scheme was only tried out in one area of London and therefore too much should not be read into this.

The Lambeth experiment – key observations

Despite the limitations of this example the following points are important.

- Changes in legislation and criminal justice policy and practice are situated in a wider historical and social context.
- Changes in legislation involve the government, criminal justice agencies (such as the police), the media and the general public.
- Changes in legislation and policy are contentious and controversial, producing complex debates.

CONCLUSIONS

This chapter has shown that crime is defined in various ways, in particular through the criminal law. However, an initial understanding is based on common sense, which consists of personal perceptions which are influenced by contact with friends, families and significant others. The media is also an influential shaper of our assumptions about crime and disorder, which in turn are influenced by political ideas and the views held by policy makers and practitioners. This information is important as a starting point for understanding crime and criminal justice, but it provides a partial view of the problem. The case studies, concentrating on stop and search and the control of drugs, illustrate the complex linkages between changes in legislation, the policy response and the perspectives of policy makers, practitioners and media representations of what goes on.

FURTHER READING

For a more detailed introduction to the issue of defining crime read Chapter 1 in J. Muncie and E. McLaughlin (eds), *The Problem of Crime* (London: Sage, 2001). This advanced text will expand some of the basic points made in this chapter. There are many introductory texts on the shelves of libraries and learning centres which cover similar ground. The discussion on pp. 5–7 of Roger Hopkins Burke, *An Introduction to Criminological Theory* (Cullompton: Willan, 2001) is particularly helpful. If you are using a different edition of this text, look up 'defining crime' in the subject index. Also see Chapter 1 of S. Hester and P. Eglin, *A Sociology of Crime* (London: Routledge, 1992).

For excellent, although quite advanced, guides to some of the issues related studying criminology see Chapters 1 and 2 of D. Downes and P. Rock, *Understanding Deviance: A guide to the sociology of crime and rule breaking* (3rd edn, Oxford: Oxford University Press, 1998) and Chapter 1 of F. Heidensohn, *Crime and Society* (Basingstoke: Macmillan, 1989).

Students interested in reading more about the media influences on common sense and political debates about crime should consult Y. Jewkes, *Media and Crime* (London: Sage, 2004), S. Cohen, *Folk Devils and Moral Panics* (London: Paladin, 1973) and D. Glover, *The Sociology of the Mass Media* (Ormskirk: Causeway, 1985).

STUDY QUESTIONS

After reading Chapter 1 in this book and Chapter 1 in Muncie and McLaughlin (2001) (see above), answer the following questions:

Defining crime

1. What is meant by the word crime?
2. Consider (a) legal (b) common-sense and (c) social definitions of crime and identify their relative strengths and weaknesses.
3. Why should students of criminology be concerned with these definitional problems of crime?
4. Definitions of crime change over time. Explain why this happens with reference to material in this chapter that focuses on stop and search and the Lambeth cannabis pilot scheme.

Media influences on defining crime

Pick a day to read two national newspapers of your choice. You can access newspapers on the Internet, but on this occasion you will gain more from the study task by looking at a hard copy of a newspaper. Answer the following questions:

1. How much space is devoted to crime and disorder in each newspaper?
2. Are there any particular types of crime (see the section in this chapter on classifying offences) that are mentioned more frequently than others?
3. Are there any significant differences in the style and approach of the two papers in they way they report crime?
4. Is there any evidence of a 'moral panic'?

Repeat this exercise by selecting a local newspaper, and compare and contrast your answers to see whether there are any significant differences.

2 Key Issues in Criminology and Criminal Justice

OVERVIEW

The aim of this chapter is to:

- provide a description of offending behaviour and the main features of the offender
- outline what it means to be a victim of crime
- provide an understanding of the relationship between the offender and victim
- provide an introduction to the key social divisions, in particular social class, age, race and ethnicity, and sex and gender
- give evidence of the significance of these social divisions for interpreting offending behaviour and victimization
- highlight the potential importance of these social divisions for understanding the workings of the criminal justice system, discussed in Part Three of this book.

INTRODUCTION

As well as defining crime it is important to be aware of the different ways in which crime impacts on different groups of people. Accordingly this chapter focuses on offenders and victims, and their different experiences of crime. It is also necessary to be aware of the significance of social divisions, especially the class, race, age and gender dimensions of offending behaviour, and the patterns of victims of different types of crime.

Criminology and criminal justice focus on a wide range of practical and conceptual issues and debates, and no attempt will be made to provide a definitive account of the field. Nonetheless it is fair to say that criminology would not exist without two key actors, the offender and the victim. It is imperative to explain what is meant by both of these terms, which may seem to have obvious meanings.

Before reading the next section, give some thought to the following simple question: what and who is an offender? Make notes of your answer, and when you have read the rest of this chapter compare your response with what you have read.

THE OFFENDER

Before we consider what an 'offender' is, it is helpful to consider what is meant by the term 'criminal offence', because for reasons that will soon be made clear, the offence precedes the offender.

In a narrow sense, a criminal offence is an action that violates the criminal law. In many instances there is a victim of the crime who first brings it to awareness. There may be one or more witnesses, or the crime might be uncovered through the activities of law enforcement professionals like the police. It is important not to forget that sometimes an offence is not noticed by any of these actors. Some crimes are in a sense victimless: for instance, drug misuse can be a crime, but it may hurt only the criminal him or herself. Other crimes are neither seen nor heard, and that they have taken place at all might not be realized for some time, if ever.

For an offence to be committed, there must be one or more people who commit it, and these are the offenders. In this context the word 'perpetrator' is also often used. A perpetrator is someone who carries out an act, which is usually (but not inevitably) in this context a criminal act. So in a technical sense, this is a more correct term when the act that has been committed has not been proven to be a criminal offence.

In most instances it comes to light that an offence has occurred before the person(s) responsible for it are identified, and it is in this sense that the offence precedes the offender, at least as far as the criminal justice system is concerned. In the case of a burglary, for instance, there is likely to be a broken window or lock; perhaps a smashed-down door in the house of a neighbour; or the disturbing discovery that someone has entered your own home and rummaged through your personal belongings or taken an item of your property (Mawby, 2001). To take another example, it might become apparent that graffiti artists have been active in a neighbourhood because there are murals and 'tagging' on the walls of buildings. The likelihood of someone being seen producing the graffiti is relatively remote, but the fact that the graffiti are there suggests there has been both a crime and an offender.

Being called or known as an offender is both a status and a form of identity. It is so in at least two different senses. One relates to the criminal justice system: an offender is someone who has been convicted of committing a crime. In the second sense, the offender might not have been identified, but nevertheless he or she exists, as an unknown person who committed a crime. We might say that there is a 'virtual' offender in this case: the police know that there is an offender, but do not know the person's identity. (And in converse, of course the offender is a real person, even though he or she is not yet known to the criminal justice system.)

When a crime is reported, the police have several options available to them. However we do not need to consider them all at this point, because the only ones that are relevant to us here are those that are taken when the police either know, or believe they know, who the perpetrator is; or they do not know the identity, but believe there is an opportunity to find the perpetrator, however slim the chances of success may be. When they do not judge that there is a chance of identifying the perpetrator, obviously there will be no action proceeding through the criminal justice system.

The police investigate different crimes in different ways, but there are several tasks they regularly carry out to assist them in identifying offenders. They may appeal for witnesses, for example, or they may have access to video footage from a closed-circuit television (CCTV) system (Coleman, 2004; McCahill, 2002). Later in the investigation, when a suspect has been identified, witnesses may be called to attend an 'identity parade'. Here the police line up the suspect alongside individuals who had no possible connection with the crime, in front of a one-way screen. Witnesses are brought to view the line-up covertly, from the other side of the screen, to see whether they can identify the person they saw at the crime scene. However this staple of television cop shows does not take place all that often in real life.

When the offenders were not seen by witnesses or victims (or were seen, but not clearly enough to be confidently identified), the police may concentrate on other forms of evidence: personal belongings or items of clothing left at the crime scene, or known to have been at the scene and later found in the suspect's possession; the tools used to commit the crime; and personal identifiers such as fingerprints, bodily fluids and other substances that may contain DNA (deoxyribonucleic acid). The generic name for this material is *forensic evidence* ('forensic' simply means with reference to the legal system). The police may then be able to match some of this material with their records of known suspects and past offenders.

This brings us to a point where the police either identify an individual or individuals who are suspected of the crime, or they fail to do, and run out of lines of inquiry they can actively pursue. Again, this latter case is not our concern at this point.

If the police do have a suspect, they will make a first judgement whether they have sufficient evidence for a charge to be laid. If they do not, they continue their enquiries until they do (or put the case on hold, should they not succeed). If and when sufficient evidence exists to justify doing so, the case will be referred to the next stages of the criminal justice process, which are discussed in detail in Part Three of this book.

It is not until individuals have been identified as suspects, charged with a crime, been tried, found guilty and sentenced that they are officially 'offenders' in the view of the state (and, in a sense, of the wider public). It is quite wrong to describe people as offenders in the legal sense before this process has been completed. To call someone a criminal or an offender has profound consequences. The fundamental rule of the criminal justice system is that a suspect must be treated as innocent until proved guilty. The burden of proof is on the prosecution, and guilt has to be proven beyond reasonable doubt (Ashworth, 2003).

So now at last we have an offender: someone who has first been identified as a suspect, then accused and tried for a crime, and proven beyond reasonable doubt to have perpetrated it. The person will have been sentenced: given either a fine, a period 'inside' (a prison sentence), or a non-custodial or community-based punishment (see Chapters 8 and 9). For the duration of the sentence and a period beyond that, the individual is a known offender with a criminal record.

In the technical sense, the person's status and identity as an offender lasts as long as the conditions attached to the sentence are in place. Under the Rehabilitation of Offenders Act (1974), a system was introduced to ensure that many criminals would not be permanently classed as offenders. After the sentence has been performed, and a period of rehabilitation and resettlement has passed, then if the individual has not reoffended, a criminal conviction is classed as 'spent'. The aim is that it should not continue to stigmatize the person beyond a reasonable time period. However, this applies only to relatively minor crimes: prison sentences of two and a half years or more are never treated as 'spent', so those who have committed these crimes continue to be treated as past offenders. The more serious the offence, the longer the official label or 'tag' remains in place. For some individuals who have been to prison, such as murderers and paedophiles, the 'past offender' label is indelible. This is not only for reasons of retribution, but also (arguably, primarily) for reasons of public safety and security. For example, sex offenders convicted after the Sex Offenders Act (1997) need to remain on a sex offender register to ensure that criminal justice agencies can monitor their movements after they have completed their sentences (Kemshall et al., 2005; Lieb, 2003; Maguire and Kemshall, 2004).

The consequences of becoming an offender vary, but they are rarely if ever positive. At best, they may involve a minor inconvenience such as the payment of a fine. At worst, they will be calamitous for the individual. For some people, their status as a criminal offender is their core identity. Offenders are often distinguished from 'normal' and 'law-abiding' folk, and felons are sometimes represented as a criminal 'other' element in society. The criminal 'other' is frequently excluded from normal society by the state, communities and individuals, including friends, family and acquaintances, as well as total strangers (Young, 1999).

Offenders are seen as having – and arguably do have – psychological, environmental, cultural or social characteristics that separate them from those who do not offend. Offenders are routinely stigmatized because of their offending behaviour, whatever their crime and irrespective of its seriousness. Sex offenders tend to be vilified more than thieves, but all known criminals are likely to be treated with suspicion and hostility by many people. For example, convicted thieves may find it difficult to find employment when they are seeking resettlement in the community following their punishment (Home Office, 2001a).

Some individuals are less negatively judgmental, and may empathize with offenders. In a more positive manner, too, offenders are often seen to be in need of some additional support and care. Invariably, though, the status of offender is associated with problems, and offenders are treated differently from the non-offending population.

THE OFFENDER: KEY POINTS

In sum, then, an offender is a person who has been found guilty of breaking the law and committing a criminal offence, and subsequently sentenced for this crime. There is normally a penalty imposed as a sanction against the offender, and to this is added a criminal record. Minor criminal records are treated as spent in due course, and these individuals may eventually escape the status of criminal, but for some unfortunates it becomes the defining characteristic of their identity and may never truly disappear.

VICTIMS OF CRIME

The victim has always been a central component of the crime equation for one simple reason: in most instances, whenever a crime is committed, there are one or more victims. However, victims of crime did not consistently attract the attention of policy makers and many academic criminologists until the late 1980s and early 1990s (Goodey, 2004; Spalek, 2006). This may come as a surprise to many students, especially because everyone is potentially a victim of crime. In response to the relative absence of the victim from criminology, a number of writers have contributed to the development of a subdiscipline of victimology, or the study of victims (Zedner, 2002; Mawby and Walklate, 1994).

The reasons for mainstream criminologists neglecting the victim are complicated, but it is true that since the emergence of the criminal justice system the most important player, as far as the administration of criminal justice goes, has been the suspect and offender. The victim is at best peripheral to the system. As was mentioned above, victims do of course play a vital role in drawing the attention of the police to the fact that a crime has taken place, and they are often witnesses in criminal trials. Victims should receive a courteous response from the police when they report crimes, and nowadays they can expect to be kept informed of any progress made with the investigation into the crime (Home Office, 2005d). Apart from that, the role of the victim is marginal to what goes on. For the most part, if a suspect is identified the victim will not be in control of what happens to that person: it is the state, not the victim, that acts as prosecutor in a criminal case.

In traditional societies before the state came into being, communities typically addressed offending behaviour by bringing together the offender and victim and solving any dispute between the parties involved (Christie, 1977). The creation of complex criminal justice systems led to a fundamental change of orientation, as the state now takes a lead in determining the treatment of a suspect. The police and subsequently the Crown Prosecution Service (CPS) determine whether a case is prosecuted at all (see Part Three), judges and juries determine whether those charged are found innocent or guilty, and judges usually determine the sentence for those found guilty, within a framework of legal guidance. The original victim of the crime does not perform any of these functions. Basically the system is based on the argument that state is the victim of the offence, and accordingly the state assumes responsibility for the correction or amendment of the harm caused.

Before we consider these issues in further detail, spend a few moments thinking about the knowledge you already have about the victims of crime and their experiences of criminal justice. Note down a summary of your knowledge about crime victims. Next ask yourself, do you consider yourself to be a potential victim of crime? If your answer is yes, why? If you answered no, why?

So far we have talked about victims in the abstract, and that is reasonable, because 'the victim' is an important concept in criminology. But victims are also individuals, and we need to consider them from this perspective too.

It is helpful to think about individual victims in two ways: looking at their individual characteristics, and the types of crime they have experienced. Both these aspects ensure that different victims have very different experiences. It is also true that people have different likelihoods of becoming victims of crime. The risk is related to a person's age, sex/gender, race/ethnicity and class (Spalek, 2006). Certain individuals are also more vulnerable than others because of where they live, their occupation and/or their lifestyle. Some people become victims of crime on more than one occasion, or experience 'repeat victimization' (Farrell and Pease, 1993, 2001).

One important distinction is between victims of crimes against property (such as burglary and vandalism) and victims of crimes against the person (such as assault or homicide). Some victims suffer from crime in public places – for example, mugging in the street – and others from crimes that take place behind closed doors (like domestic violence and child abuse).

Who is the victim?

We have already seen that 'the offender' is a complex concept, and the same is true, of course, of 'the victim'. There is both a colloquial and common-sense definition of 'the victim', and a more formal criminological definition. Initially 'the victim' is the person who is harmed or damaged by an offence, but as we explained, it does not take long in most instances for the state to take on board the status of victim. 'The state' is a rather abstract concept: it is perhaps easier to see it as an embodiment of all the members of a society. Although the crime might have been directed at one individual, all the members of society can in a real sense see themselves as 'the injured party', since we all suffer from living in a society where crime takes place. In this sense, both the individual concerned and the state may be described as the *direct victims* of crime.

There are *indirect victims* too of many crimes. For example, the immediate family and friends of a victim will be affected to a greater or lesser extent by the experiences of the victim they know and care about. In extreme cases, such as murder, the family and friends of the victim are likely to experience acute distress and possible psychological disturbance. In these tragic cases the victim is clearly not present to experience long-term pain and suffering, but those left behind are likely to do so. They may be required to identify the body, and they will probably have to endure a long-drawn-out and possibly well-publicized trial. There are arguably sound reasons to view these unfortunate people as victims of the crime.

Sometimes indirect victimization is less clear-cut. People who are extremely fearful of crime, however real their risk of becoming a victim actually is, could be seen as victims of living in a society blighted by crime (Hough and Mayhew, 1983). It can be argued that corporate negligence leading to pollution and environmental damage affects us all to some degree (Braithwaite, 1984; Tombs and Whyte, 2005). Another group who may adopt the status of indirect victimization are consumers, who have to pay higher prices to compensate for wrongdoings by providers of goods and services.

It is also necessary to be aware of the relationship between the victim and the perpetrator. With some offences (like burglary and the theft of a motor vehicle) it is unlikely that the victim will meet the offender face to face. Sometimes the offender and the victim are acquainted, but only casually; sometimes they meet but the victim is not consciously aware of the crime taking place (as with drug-assisted rape). In crimes of interpersonal violence (physical assault, rape, domestic violence), the victim will come into close contact with the individual carrying out the attack, but might not know him or her from other contexts. Some victims and offenders are, in contrast, close friends or married couples (Mirrlees-Black, 1999; Myhill and Allen, 2002a, 2002b).

It should be apparent by now that there are many different types of victim, and that everyone is, at least in principle, a potential victim. And you should appreciate that it can be argued that we are *all* victims of crime to some degree (although you might not consider that a helpful position to take).

Support for victims

Once a victim of crime has been recognized or acknowledged, what does society do in response? Offenders are likely to be drawn into the criminal justice system, and one aspect of this is the existence of various rights to safeguard them from abuses of power by statutory agencies like the police and the courts. But victims have few comparable rights, and the kind of response they receive is something of a lottery (Ashworth, 2003). Unfortunately from time to time victims of crime may be victimized again by the criminal justice system. The police might disbelieve a victim, or victim's character might be assassinated in the courtroom. This is known as *secondary victimization* (Zedner, 2002). There have been various criticisms of this tendency, resulting in fundamental reforms and gradually the enhanced status of crime victims.

Family and friends often support victims of crime, and in close-knit communities they may receive informal support from neighbours more generally. Charitable organizations like Victim Support offer help and assistance for some victims, often following referral by the police. The Criminal Injuries Compensation Scheme was set up in 1964 to provide financial compensation to some victims of violent crime.

Successive British governments introduced 'Victims' Charters' in 1990 and 1996 (Home Office, 2001a), and these were followed by the Victims' Code of Practice, which came into effect in 2004 with the passing into law of the Domestic Violence, Crime and Victims Act (2004). First the charters and then the code have raised the profile of crime victims. They have not given victims rights comparable to those possessed by offenders, but at least victims can now expect a better quality of service and some additional support throughout the criminal justice sector. The police are also required to provide more information and support. In the courts victims can expect to be kept informed of the cases in which they have an interest, and special arrangements may be made for vulnerable witnesses and victims who are testifying in court. Child victims may be allowed to give their evidence by video live-link. Even the probation service, traditionally an offender-oriented agency, now undertakes victim contact work, particularly focusing on the victims of violent crime (Home Office, 2005d). As a result of these initiatives, victims may not be centre stage but they are now entitled to basic support in the form of information, and in some instances this is backed up with services.

These changes have been welcomed by many organizations campaigning on behalf of victims, as well as by victims themselves. However, it is quite clear that the delivery of services and support to victims is uneven and lacking in equity. This is partly because of the lack of formal rights, which means victims have limited scope to question the treatment they receive, but it is arguably also because of the distinction that is frequently drawn between two types of victim, the 'deserving' and the 'undeserving' (Mawby and Walklate, 1994).

This distinction is based on the personal characteristics of victims, and the argument that some people contribute to their own victim status. Early victimologists (Von Hentig, 1948) adopted the concept of 'victim precipitation' to explain how some victims brought about their own suffering. In cases where this was claimed to have happened, the victim could be judged to be 'undeserving' of sympathy and support. An example is the treatment received by victims of rape. A sex worker with a drug misuse problem is much more likely to be cast as an 'undeserving' victim than an educated professional woman, who is well spoken and appears to come from an affluent background. Those judged as 'respectable' are often seen as 'deserving' victims (Zedner, 2002).

The notion of the victim and *victimhood* has also been treated as problematic by some 'victims' because it is patronizing, and treats people as passive agents to whom something awful happens. These critics argue for an emphasis on the capacity of the individual to become a survivor by transcending the experience of crime. This approach is about individuals taking control over their own lives and not allowing external interference to take away that control (Walklate, 2004).

THE VICTIM: KEY POINTS

The victim has always been a key element of crime, a fact that has tended to be recognized only implicitly. The criminological gaze has to all intents and purposes rested on offenders and the agencies dealing with them. The growing subfield of victimology has made victims more visible and their role more explicit, and over the course of several decades students of crime, as well as policy makers and practitioners, have come to take victims seriously. It is now not possible nowadays to talk about an offence without simultaneously acknowledging the existence of a victim. Victims still lack the formal rights that protect offenders, but they are currently given more credibility and attention, placing them in a stronger position in the administration of criminal justice.

SOCIAL DIVISIONS

Among the other concepts that are important in criminology is that of social divisions. Governments, policy makers and practitioners categorize individuals on the basis of particular physical or social characteristics and features. These classifications tend to be

used to describe and explain various intellectual and practical problems studied by criminologists. At a very basic level the main social divisions may be used to describe the pattern
and distribution of offending behaviour and victimization, as well as the experiences of
professionals working in the criminal justice system. This is demonstrated in Part Three,
which introduces the work undertaken by criminal justice professionals. Part Four shows
that these methods of differentiating human beings are also a trait of some approaches in
criminological theory, which have looked at the impact of factors such as social class,
gender, race and ethnicity, and age (Bowling and Phillips, 2002; Walklate, 2004).

We shall consider here the practical and conceptual relevance of the prime markers
of social difference, but before we do so it is necessary to acknowledge other forms of
social division. In particular people can be categorized by their sexual orientation, their
abilities or disabilities, and their religion. These topics are all important, but criminological research into them is still at an early stage, and they are not discussed in detail here.
However, you will doubtless be aware that religion is a subject of much debate over criminal activity at present, particularly in the context of terrorist attacks like those that
occurred on 9/11 (11 September 2001) and 7/7 (7 July 2005). These have been blamed on
Islamic militants, and have given rise to 'Islamophobia', or the irrational fear and
malign misrepresentation of Islam (Spalek, 2002).

Social class

For many centuries categorizations of people by social class have been used for various
purposes. Theorists such as Karl Marx have based historical analyses on class divisions;
marketers have used highly technical methodologies to look at how people in different
classes behave in different ways. Some cultures are seen as having a relatively highly
structured social hierarchy (Devine et al., 2004). However although the concept of social
class is a central concern for many social scientists, it has been contested by politicians
and academics. In the 1990s there was widespread debate about the 'death of social class'
(Pakulski and Waters, 1996) and the emergence of the 'classless society'.

Categorizations are not necessarily based on hierarchies (with some classes being
'higher' or 'better' than others), but the concept of social class is sometimes interpreted
as social stratification. (The word 'strata' (the plural of stratum) is important in this
context.) Although there is disagreement between analysts about how best to divide
people up into categories, most social classifications are based on people's occupations.
There is a close relationship between jobs, income and wealth, so these latter factors are
sometimes also brought into play. This kind of thinking underpins the Office for
National Statistics (2001) *National Statistics Socio-economic Classification Analytic Classes*,
which classifies people according to their occupations. There are eight main classes, one
of which is subdivided:

1 Higher managerial and professional occupations
   1.1   Large employers and higher managerial occupations
   1.2   Higher professional occupations
2 Lower managerial and professional occupations
3 Intermediate occupations

4 Small employers and own account workers
5 Lower supervisory and technical occupations
6 Semi-routine occupations
7 Routine occupations
8 Never worked and long-term unemployed.

Evidence suggests that most (certainly not all, but many) crimes of acquisition (that is, burglary, theft of and from motor vehicles, and robbery) are committed by individuals in the lower social classes. This is especially true of class 8, which is sometimes referred to as an *underclass*. However there is more to the concept of social class than this, and we need to look at a brief history of the concept before we consider how it applies to an understanding of criminal justice in the contemporary world.

For the purposes of this book, perhaps the most influential ideas about class are those associated with Karl Marx (1848) and Max Weber (1968). Marx's contribution to twentieth-century social science was immeasurable, and although he had nothing much to say directly about crime, his ideas have provided a framework within which many criminologists have worked. (Students who have studied sociology and are familiar with Marx's ideas may wish to skip this section and go to page 58, 'Age'.)

Marx, and his co-author and friend Frederic Engels, provided a historically informed explanation of the social changes that occurred in some parts of the world during the eighteenth and nineteenth centuries (Marx and Engels, 1848). Marx used the socioeconomic transformations in the United Kingdom as an example. Prior to the eighteenth century this country was a simple rural society, but it was transformed into a complex urban industrial society. For Marx, the core change lay in the workings of the economic system, and specifically the development of capitalism (that is, a system where the overriding objective is the production of profit). Marx was highly critical of the organization of capitalist societies, because their profit is made by a relatively small group of powerful people who employ the remainder of the population. The dominant group have a negative impact on the quality of life of most of the population, and indulge in exploitation and oppression.

The core Marxist conception is of a capitalist society split into two classes that are in direct conflict with each other. The ruling class, which Marx called the bourgeoisie, own the means of production (that is, the factories), and the working class (Marx's proletariat) own nothing beyond their ability to sell their labour. The proletariat are dependent on the bourgeoisie for work, to ensure they have sufficient money to satisfy their basic human needs. The bourgeoisie therefore have considerable power, which they exploit by paying their workers as little as possible. The difference between the value added by labourers and their pay becomes the profit of the bourgeoisie.

Marx argued that the tensions this caused would eventually result in revolution, with the proletariat overthrowing and disposing of the bourgeoisie. He believed this was historically inevitable, and that the end product would be a communist society: one that was classless, where everyone was equal. Some societies did indeed develop a political system known as communism (most notably the Soviet Union and the Republic of China), although it is questionable whether they fulfilled Marx's predictions and would have met with his approval. After the Second World War there was a 'cold war' between the capitalist bloc (led by the United States of America) and the communist bloc (led by the Soviet Union). In 1989 the Soviet Union's government collapsed, and capitalism transformed the economies of the former communist-bloc countries. Marx's critics claim this to be evidence of the failure of his ideas. Communism is still influential in China, but capitalism is starting to exert an influence, as is apparent from a number of economic reforms.

Marx's ideas about social class are relevant to criminologists for two reasons. First, they deal with issues of power and control, both of which are concentrated in the hands of the bourgeoisie. The most powerful group in society controls not only its economy and infrastructure, but its superstructure, which consists of all social institutions, including the government, schools, the health service, the media and (most importantly, for the purposes of this text) the criminal justice system. Indeed economic interests more or less determine the nature of all social relationships. All these social organizations are used to regulate the behaviour of the proletariat, not only at work but also during their leisure time, to ensure the capitalist system can continue to make profits. So the capitalist system provides a structure within which crime is defined and dealt with.

Second, class has a strong link with income. In crude terms, the working classes have less wealth than the ruling class, and the underclass have less wealth even than the working class. As we noted above, most (though not by any means all) offenders and victims are found in the underclass, and it can be argued that this is because of the income differentials in society. However, before we consider the underclass in more detail we need to introduce the thinking of Max Weber (1968).

Many criticisms have been levelled at Marx over the years, and arguably his critics were right, given the collapse of communism in the Soviet Union. However long before this took place, Marx's critics objected to his economic determinism, or his tendency to argue that the economy influenced everything that went on in all areas of society. Weber (1968) was among those who thought this was too simple. He introduced two other factors to explain the class structure and the workings of society: status and party. Party is not considered here, but we do need to review Weber's ideas on class and status.

'Class' refers to economic factors such as property and markets, whereas 'status' relates to those differences between people that are based on cultural rather than economic factors. Both share a relationship with power. People of 'high' class have power because of their economic control, but people of 'high' status have power for wider reasons: their social standing in the community, and the role they play within it. In a nutshell, there are powerful and influential groups in society who do not simply represent economic interests, but are powerful because of the status attached to their role or function. Criminal justice agencies like the police and the courts are examples.

The underclass

The idea of an underclass has been around in one form or another for centuries (Crowther, 2000a; Devine et al., 2004). In the nineteenth century commentators spoke of the dangerous classes, or the 'residuum', particularly in major cities like London and Manchester. During the twentieth century and into the twenty-first, the term 'underclass' became less popular, but we have seen a replacement in the term and concept of the *socially excluded*. So definitions vary, depending on fashions and preoccupations, but the group being described tends to be more or less the same. It is characterized by, for example, low educational attainment; a lack of adequate skills, which make it difficult for people to find paid work; a tendency to live in specific areas; a dependency on welfare; unemployment and underemployment, or an unstable relationship with the labour market; pathological (that is, abnormal) family structures, and the inter-generational transmission of poverty; involvement in the unreported economy; and crucially, a predisposition to criminal and disorderly behaviour (Townsend, 1990; Walker, 1991; Westergaard, 1992). Thus the underclass is made up of the poorest sections of society, and its members' poverty is usually related to their being out of work.

Interestingly Britain has been very slow to produce an official definition of poverty. Many indicators of relative deprivation are available, but governments were reluctant to base a definition of poverty on them. The closest thing to an officially recognized indicator is the reference to those living on less than half the average household income (Cook, 2006). There were 5 million people below this line in 1979, but by 1991 there were 13.5 million (almost a quarter of the population), including 3.9 million children (Department of Social Security, 1993). More recent evidence indicates that social policies have started to improve the material conditions of some poor people, but low income and multiple deprivation remain persistent and intransigent problems (Hills and Stewart, 2005; Department of Social Security, 2001; Rahman et al., 2000, 2001). Crucially, the poorest and most socially excluded members of society are most susceptible to becoming victims of crime, and the bulk of offenders are drawn from this social stratum.

SOCIAL CLASS: KEY POINTS

The idea of social class can be traced back to the beginnings of social science, and Marx and Weber both defined class with varying degrees of reference to a person's job. Over the course of the twentieth and twenty-first centuries the concept of class has been called into question, although the concept of the underclass has proven to be popular and influential. This stratum or layer of the population is said to be the one most affected by crime (as we shall see in Part Three, where the focus is on the workings of criminal justice agencies). It has also proven to be important in the field of theoretical criminology (see Part Four).

AGE

Categorizations of people by age are also important for understanding patterns of offending behaviour and victimhood. The popular belief that young people commit most crimes, and when they get older people tend to stop offending, is for once borne out by the evidence. It is uncommon to find senior citizens or elderly people on the list of usual suspects, at the police station, in the courtroom or in prisons (Wahidin and

Cain, 2005). Old age does not stop everyone offending, but crimes by the old are relative rarities in comparison with those committed by the young.

The age structure of victims of crime is rather different. People of all ages can be victims. To take extreme examples, newborn babies are sometimes physically abused (Thomas, 2005), and individuals nearing the end of their lives can suffer from elder abuse (or 'granny bashing') (Brogden and Nijhar, 2000; Penhale, 2005).

Understanding youth crime

Young people are frequently associated with troublesome behaviour and perceived to be a problem (Smith, 2003; Omaji, 2003). Many negative images surrounding youth are connected with delinquent and antisocial behaviour, and the involvement of young people in crime is often taken as a fact (Muncie, 1999). Throughout the twentieth century the dominant representation of young people was as a social problem. There is also a tendency for people to look back to a 'golden age' when young people were calmer and did not upset the public peace. However, those who complained about the teddy boys in the 1950s and mods and rockers in the 1960s tended not to see it that way (Pearson, 1983; Cohen, 1973).

In the early twenty-first century there has been a lot of talk about young people's binge drinking, particularly their consumption of 'alcopops' (Dingwall, 2005), as well as their antisocial behaviour (Squires and Stephen, 2005). These behaviours do exist and are rightly viewed as social problems, but the negative images are often stereotypes and are not representative of many young people. Arguably the notion of rebellious teenagers is even rather out of date now: there is plenty of evidence that many young people have generally positive relationships with their parents, and tend to accept parental values in preference to the attitudes and beliefs of their peers (Davies, 1990: 10). However, there is an overwhelming sense that 'something ought to be done about young people', who are basically either 'out of order' or 'out of control'.

Pitts puts the youth problem into perspective and links it to our discussion on social class. He asks, 'Are young people an unruly "underclass" whose behaviour and attitudes must be modified in order to bring them back into line, or are they socially excluded citizens who have been denied both the right and duties of citizenship?' (Pitts, 1998: 95). There is no clear-cut answer to this question, but it is beyond doubt that there remains plenty of concern about young people and crime.

Perhaps the question that ought to be asked is why young people are so involved in crime. There are several possible reasons. Since the 1970s there has been a tendency for poor families to be concentrated in areas that are characterized by a high degree of social exclusion. The young people living in these areas are approximately five times more likely to have a criminal record by the time they reach their early 30s than people growing up in more stable and cohesive communities (Pitts, 1998, 2003). This is not altogether surprising if the fact that vulnerable communities experience disproportionate amounts of crime, victimization and tension is acknowledged. To illustrate this starkly, the Association of Chief Police Officers (ACPO) (2004) reported that 1 per cent of the population suffers 59 per cent of all violent crime, and 41 per cent of property crime is experienced by 2 per cent of the population.

In deprived areas the level of fear of crime is higher, as well as the risk of becoming a victim. For instance, people in these poor geographical areas are four times more likely to be burgled than the general population. The risk is even greater for individuals from a minority ethnic background (ACPO, 2004). Social exclusion also accounts for relatively high degrees of victimhood.

AGE: KEY POINTS

People of all ages offend, and people of all ages can be victims of crime. A consistent trend over time is for young people to be prone to offend, and although most grow out of it, there is still considerable anxiety about youth offending. However, a closer look at some research evidence suggests that many young offenders and victims belong to an underclass living in poor, socially excluded communities.

RACE AND ETHNICITY

It is neither possible nor desirable to place ways of classifying people in any hierarchical order, as they are all important for understanding variations in the pattern of offending and victimhood. However, some markers of difference between human beings have attracted more attention than others, from sociologists in general and criminologists in particular. Race and ethnicity, for example, have proven to be important and contentious issues in relation to criminal justice. They are topical because of the existence of a form of discrimination called racism: the tendency to treat people differently on account of their race. (See Chapter 13 for a discussion of different attempts to theorize racism.) In this section there is a brief history of the concept of race, which considers how individuals are categorized into racial and ethnic groups for the purposes of understanding what goes on in the criminal justice system.

A brief history of the concept of race

Over recent years there has been a burgeoning interest in empirical, theoretical and methodological issues regarding race and ethnicity (Mason, 2000; Solomos, 2003). I cannot offer a full summary of the voluminous literature here, so I focus on some topics of particular relevance for understanding debates in criminology. Conceptualizations of race and ethnicity are not natural and a given, but are contextually specific. Race and ethnicity are socially constructed categories which are shaped by complex and interactive dynamic processes involving economic, ideological, political and social factors which change across time and space.

Since human societies first came into existence, people have focused on physical, biological and genetic differences in order to classify each other. This is perhaps inevitable to some degree, although the consequences of separating individuals into discrete categories on this basis can be extremely problematic. The concept of race is relatively modern: it was first developed during the Enlightenment. The Enlightenment resulted in the replacement of religion as the main way of thinking about the universe by a new way of seeing the world, based on the values of scientific reason, which was seen as the highest achievement possible in civilized societies. Using scientific principles, human beings could control their environment rather than be at the mercy of divine forces.

The Enlightenment was seen as progressive, inasmuch as it could liberate society from the forces of nature, but it defined the principle of reason in a way that was essentially western and European. Because western Europe back then was mainly populated by people with white skin, philosophers such as Hume, Kant and Hegel tended to view non-western European and non-white people as not only different, but also inferior. In addition to skin colour, facial features, head shape, hair type and other physical attributes were linked to racial difference. In sum, what occurred was the creation of a hierarchy of races. How did this develop?

Carl Linne used the term *homo sapiens* to identify white people as superior, and the German physiologist Blumenbach (1776, cited in Mason, 2000) created a racial typology consisting of five racial groups: Caucasian, Mongolian, Ethiopian, Malay and American. Another thinker, Gobineau (1853, cited in Solomos, 2003), explicitly referred to the 'inequality of the human races' and identified social qualities with physical characteristics. According to Gobineau there were three main races: 'negro', 'yellow' and 'Aryan'. The 'negro' was described as being animal-like and aggressive, in contrast to the 'yellow' race which was labelled weak, apathetic and mediocre. These negative qualities stood in stark contrast to the Aryan, who was represented as strong and beautiful. Charles Darwin (1968) wrote an important book, entitled *On the Origin of the Species*, in which he discussed 'natural selection' and the 'survival of the fittest'. Darwinian thought upheld a view that over time inferior races would disappear and the white race would prove to be the strongest, with the best fit with the environment.

What these early ideas did was to effectively categorize certain racial groups, based on skin colour, and arrange them in a hierarchical order. White Europeans were at the apex of this hierarchy and non-whites at the bottom. This method of classification was more than just a system of thought: it influenced social action, particularly colonialism and the slave trade. Some British imperialists sensed that it was their duty to civilize the world, and as they colonized countries on the African continent they regarded the indigenous black population as inferior. Black people were compared to children or animals, and seen as in need of care and nurturing, as well as improvement (Gilroy, 1987).

A consequence of dividing people into races is that some racial groups are excluded from doing things that are enjoyed by other racial groups. For example, in some societies such as South Africa, black people have lived separately from white people in a system known as apartheid. In other societies black people have been excluded from activities or prevented from receiving resources enjoyed routinely by white people. In the United Kingdom the Eugenics movement, pioneered by Sir Francis Galton (1907), raised concerns about 'racial hygiene' and the need to maintain and improve the quality of 'human stock'. This system of thought referred to the poor in terms of their biological and hereditary defects, or as the 'biological dregs of the population' (Wootton, 1959: 55). The movement formulated:

> A programme for the gradual 'improvement of the race' by deliberate modification of the relative fertility of the various groups in society. The eugenic programme, which was most readily justified if evolution was a predictable process, amenable to gradual redirection by the cumulative effects of continuing small scale interventions, was one manifestation of the reformist, interventionists' strands of thinking associated with the rising professional middle class.
>
> (Barnes, 1977: 60)

The Eugenicists focused on reproduction and maintaining racial purity, including a recommendation to sterilize certain groups who were considered to make unsuitable parents. The logic of this type of thinking was applied brutally in Germany by the Nazis throughout the 1930s and 1940s, leading to the genocide of over 6 million Jewish people.

By the twentieth century there was a clear method of allocating individuals to racial groups. This was achieved by appealing to scientific values about physical differences, especially skin colour. It has been shown that ideas of race have been used to justify treating people differently. The most interesting point is that the concept of race has been used to measure the relative social status of people with reference to their phenotypic or physical characteristics. This necessarily brings us to an important concept in criminology, namely racism, which is examined in more depth in Chapter 13.

Over time the concept of race has been questioned, and it has been argued that there is no scientific evidence that skin colour is a valid method of classifying people. For that reason the concept of ethnicity was introduced, but as will be made clear shortly, ethnicity and race are used interchangeably by the government and criminal justice agencies.

Ethnicity and minority ethnic group

Rather like race, ethnicity is a quality that every individual has. Although there is a tendency to apply it to visibly different minority groups, that is not central to the concept. Unlike race, the concept of ethnicity does not appeal to notions of inferiority and superiority. Nor does it not normally refer exclusively to skin colour and other physical markers of difference: it includes cultural factors. Although there is no single definition of ethnic groups, according to most definitions an ethnic group is distinguished by:

- a shared geographic origin
- common ancestry and shared historical origins
- migratory status
- language
- religious beliefs
- shared traditions, values and symbols
- artistic and culinary taste.

Phenotypical or physical features may still be relevant, but this is not the only factor to highlight difference, and it is not regarded as the most important variable. Above all, ethnicity is all about a distinct culture, way of seeing, thinking, feeling and interacting with others. More generally, ethnic groups have a sense of identity which makes them distinct from others. An ethnic group has both internal and external distinctive features, so its members are recognized both by other members of the group and by those who are not members (Mason, 2000).

All complex societies include many different forms of ethnicity, and the groups within them can be categorized in a number of different ways. But in most societies there is a core ethnicity: that is, the ethnic identity of the majority of people. Other groups are labelled as ethnic minority or minority ethnic groups. The word 'minority' is not used in a negative sense: it is just an indication that the group contains less than half of the population.

For example, the UK 2001 Census (Home Office, 2005c: ix) gives these figures for the percentage of ethnic groups in the general population (aged 10 and over):

White 91.3%
Black 2.8%
Asian 4.7%
Other 1.2%

This shows that the majority ethnic group is white. There are two reasonably sizeable minority ethnic groups, and a number of smaller ones which have been lumped together in this summary. At first glance these figures may appear to be unproblematic, but it is necessary to scrutinize them more closely.

Clearly there are some dangers attached to the concepts of race and ethnicity, but they are both used to classify people for administrative purposes. Without this kind of classification, it would be impossible to tell whether one group was being discriminated against. Since 1991, statistics on race and the criminal justice system have been produced annually. These are collected in response to Section 95 of the Criminal Justice Act (1991) which states that:

(1) The Secretary of State shall in each year publish such information, as he considers expedient for the purpose of:
(a) enabling persons engaged in the administration of justice to become aware of the financial implications of their decisions; or
(b) facilitating the performance of such persons of their duty to avoid discriminating against any persons on the ground of race or sex or any other improper ground.

(2) Publication under subsection (1) above shall be effected in such a manner, as the Secretary of State considers appropriate for the purpose of bringing the information to the attention to the persons concerned.

This is an example of *ethnic monitoring* of the activities of the criminal justice system. It was introduced in response to a growing concern about race relations, and recognition of the need to collect accurate information about the experiences of different ethnic groups in the criminal justice system. Since the turn of the century, increased attention has been given to ethnic monitoring as a result of the Race Relations (Amendment) Act (2000), which followed the publication of the Stephen Lawrence inquiry (Macpherson, 1999).

(As noted earlier this was a government-commissioned inquiry into the circumstances surrounding the racially motivated killing of a young black man, Stephen Lawrence. The murderers were never convicted, and the case raised important issues about policing and society in relation to ethnic minority groups.)

We return to this subject in Part Three, where we look at the different criminal justice agencies and their contact with ethnic minority offenders (and to some extent victims). Here, we need to look at how the Home Office suggests people be put into ethnic categories. In 2005 there were four main methods of classification, which belong to two broader subgroups: 'visual identification' and 'self-classification' (Home Office, 2005c: 111). We outline each method, and consider how they relate to the ideas of race and ethnicity.

With four methods in use, the picture can become confusing. This is a confusion practitioners and policy makers have to work with, so you need to come to terms with it as a student of criminology.

Visual identification

This approach is used by police officers when they have to visually categorize a person. For instance, they may be required to do this if they stop a person in the street or when they make an arrest. The 'Census 4 Point classification ('4+1')' consists of the following categories:

- White
- Black
- Asian (Indian sub-continent)
- Other
  (Home Office, 2005c: 111)

The +1 refers to the cases that do not seem to fit any of these four categories. These people are described as 'unknown'.

Another method of visual identification used by the police is the 'Phoenix classification', which comprises six identity codes or ICs:

- White European (IC1)
- Dark European (IC2)
- Afro-Caribbean (IC3)
- Asian (IC4)
- Oriental (IC5)
- Arab (IC6)
- Unknown (IC0)
  (Home Office, 2005c: 111)

Although these categories have been recognized as meaningful to criminal justice agencies, they are unusual since they refer to racial characteristics such as skin colour (such as white) as well as physical differences associated with geographical factors such as place of origin (Asian, Oriental) or culture (Arab).

These methods of identification are intended to be used by people who know a minimum about the person being categorized. They are based on visible markers of difference, including some cultural signifiers as well as physical characteristics. The classifiers presumably realized that it might not always be easy to categorize people correctly: while it *might* (my emphasis) be possible in most cases to decide whether someone is an African-Caribbean from his or her skin colour and hair, identifying an Arab is much trickier.

Self-classification

Again there are two systems. Firstly there is the Census (Standard Home Office) 5-Point Classification:

- White (1)
- Mixed (2)
- Black or Black British (4)
- Asian or Asian British (3)
- Chinese or Other minority ethnic group (5)
- Not stated.
  (Home Office, 2005c: 111)

Like the 'visual identification' system above, this leads on to a more detailed methodology, a '16 Point Classification ('16+1'), with a number of further subdivisions. White is made up of British (W1), Irish (W2) and any other white background (W9). Here a physical marker of difference is supplemented by information about the ethnic or national identity of a person, although the W9 could include many different ethnic groups from various parts of the world who have white skin. The ethnicity of these peoples (perhaps Jewish or Bosnian) is not taken into consideration.

Mixed (M) includes White and Black Caribbean (M1). This corresponds with Black on the '4+1' mentioned above, as does White and Black African (M2). There is also White and Asian (M3), which is comparable to Asian on the '4+1'. A final category for those of any other mixed background (M9) maps on to 'Other' on the '4+1'. The Black or Black British (B) category refers to ethnic factors including Caribbean (B1) and African (B2). The additional B9 and A9 subcategories cover those with other Black or Asian backgrounds. Similarly the next category, Asian or British Asian (A) joins together racial and ethnic differences, with the subcategories Indian (A1), Pakistani (A2) and Bangladeshi (A3). Finally, there is O, the label for Chinese and other minority groups, which includes O1 (Chinese) and other (O9).   Again, there is some confusion here between physical or race characteristics like skin colour, and cultural or ethnic factors. The main point is that these divisions are meaningful for criminologists, practitioners and policy makers.

The significance of race and ethnicity in the criminal justice system and for criminological theory is examined again from time to time in Parts Three and Four, but we need to note here that research evidence shows consistently that there are profound ethnic differences in patterns of offending and victimization (Home Office, 2005c). A disproportionately high number (relative to their proportion of the total population) of African-Caribbean and black people register in recorded crime statistics and in the prison population (see Chapter 8). In the past there was a relatively low proportion of Asians, but since 9/11 there has been an increase in the proportion of convicted and sentenced criminals from this ethnic group. The evidence on victims of crime is mixed, but in cases of racially motivated violence the perpetrators are mainly white and the victims Asian (Bowling and Phillips, 2002).

RACE AND ETHNICITY: KEY POINTS

Race tends to refer to visible physical differences, and although it is not regarded as a scientifically valid concept, racial categories such as White, Black and Asian are used to classify people. Because of the scepticism about race, the notion of ethnicity has been introduced. Here the emphasis is placed on culture. In practice ethnic and racial categories are used interchangeably. Evidence suggests that the experiences people have of criminal justice are related to their ethnicity. The reasons for this are explored at various stages later in the book.

Sex and gender

A person's sex and gender probably make the most difference to their type of relationship with the criminal justice system. The proportions of people of each gender who are suspects, offenders, victims and employed by the sector very greatly.

'Sex' is the word for the biological differences between males and females. In most instances (there are a few exceptions, of hermaphrodites and transsexuals), a person's sex is beyond dispute. In the social sciences the word 'gender' is used more widely than 'sex', as it recognizes that there is more to being male or female than biology. This term encompasses the strong social influences on what it means to be a woman or man. This issue is investigated further in Chapter 13. For the purposes of this section, we use the word 'gender' for purely descriptive purposes.

Key questions that need to be asked regarding sex and gender are:

- How often do men and women offend?
- Do men and women typically commit the same types of crime as men?
- Are women looking more and more like men in terms of their offending behaviour?
- Are the causes of female crime different from the factors that cause men to commit crime?
- Do men and women have common experiences as victims of crime?

To help us answer these questions it is best to start with the basics. We look at first, male and female patterns of offending behaviour, then the different experiences of males and females as victims of crime. From time to time a link between gender and age is highlighted.

Gender and offending behaviour

There is broad agreement amongst criminologists that most crimes are committed mainly by men. Criminologists tend to accept as an unmistakable truth that women are far less likely to be involved in criminal behaviour than men (Heidensohn, 2002). However, even though there is no profound disagreement about this fact, criminologists still find plenty of gender-based issues to research and argue about.

In more recent times there has been mounting concern about the involvement of females in crime, and in particular the 'girl gang' phenomenon (Laidler and Hunt, 2001; Burman, Batchelor and Brown, 2001). There is also tentative evidence that the proportion of women becoming involved in crime has risen, from 7:1 (that is, seven male criminals to every one woman) in the 1950s to 6:1 in 1999 (Home Office, 2004b). However, there are differences between offence types. The Home Office-funded research of Tarling (1993, cited in Walklate, 2004) shows that the male/female ratio for sex offences is 105:1, while it is only 3:1 for theft and handling. Meanwhile, 'Murder is predominantly a male activity' (Walklate, 2004: 6).

In 2001, 42 per cent of female victims of homicide were killed by their partner, compared with 4 per cent of male victims who were killed by a female partner. Taking an extreme example, even though there are female serial killers (Hickey, 1991), there are far fewer of them than men, and their motivations are very different. Women killers in general seem to be driven by different factors from those compelling male killers: most of them kill violent partners with whom they have had abusive relationships.

It is not yet clear whether there are more crime-prone females in society today than before, and if so, why. Any change could be a result of demographic factors, or there might be other social and cultural factors accounting for it. In general there appear to have been some changes over time, reflected by Gelsthorpe (2002). Although they observed that in comparison with men women commit fewer offences, they also noted that in the early 2000s women were committing more crime than ever before, and that this was most evident for drug-related offences.

The different victim experiences of men and women

Evidence shows that men and women experience being victims of crime differently. For example, men are more likely than women to become victims of violent crime in general, but women are at a greater risk from violent crimes in the private sphere, such as sexual and domestic violence, and from stalking (Home Office, 2004b; Walklate, 2004).

CONCLUSION

This chapter has just scratched the surface of criminological study by looking at two of its central characters, the offender and the victim. The offender is a figure who is often taken for granted, but there are complex processes leading to the application of this status. The status of offender is very much a product of the activities of state agencies such as the police, who in turn are dependent on the wider public. Before being labelled an offender a person is known as a suspect, and in that role he or she has fundamental rights, especially the right to be treated as innocent until proven guilty beyond reasonable doubt.

All convicted offenders are punished by the state for their behaviour. The nature of the punishment meted out to them varies, as does the impact it has on their future lives. For some people offender status is more permanent than it is for others.

This chapter has also shown that for every offender there is a victim. Before the 1990s the victim was relatively marginal to the proceedings of the criminal justice system, and the state assumed the status of victim on behalf of the offended person. In the final stages of the twentieth century the victim was increasingly brought into the criminal justice system. Now victims can expect improved services, but they still lack formal rights.

The offender and victim are both at the heart of criminology, but social divisions are important too, especially class, gender, race/ethnicity and age. This chapter has done little more than outline their main features of these classifications, but they are revisited later, mostly in Parts Three and Four.

FURTHER READING

The main focus of criminology is on the offender, although this is often taken for granted. In a sense there is no single text dedicated to the offender, but this entity is a feature of all books. There is a body of work examining victims of crime, who were neglected until the emergence of the subdiscipline of victimology. For comprehensive introductions to this area see J. Goodey, *Victims and Victimology: Research, policy and practice* (London: Longman, 2004) and B. Spalek, *Crime Victims: Theory, policy and practice* (Basingstoke: Palgrave, 2006).

This chapter has examined a number of social divisions including race/ethnicity, gender and age. General texts which elaborate on the data included here are S. Walklate, *Gender and Crime* (Cullompton: Willan, 2004), B. Bowling and C. Phillips, *Racism, Crime and Justice* (Harlow: Longman, 2002) and S. Brown, *Understanding Youth and Crime* (Buckingham: Open University Press, 1998).

STUDY QUESTIONS

1. Earlier on you were asked what and who is an offender. Try this exercise again now you have read this chapter. How does your response now compare with your earlier answer?
2. Earlier on you were asked to write a list demonstrating your knowledge about crime victims. Now describe the main characteristics of victims of crime.
3. Describe the significance of sex and gender for explaining offending behaviour and victimization. Base your answer on this chapter and Walklate's book (see above).
4. Repeat exercise 3 for race and ethnicity. Base your answer on this chapter and Bowling and Phillips' book (see above).
5. How important is age for explaining crime and offending?
6. Discuss the relevance of social class to our understanding of offenders.

PART TWO

Understanding Crime Data

3 Understanding Crime Data I: Sources of Information

OVERVIEW

The aim of this chapter is to:

- explain the importance of having sound information about crime
- discuss different types of crime data, paying attention to the differences between quantitative and qualitative sources of information
- provide an understanding of the relative strengths and weaknesses of qualitative and quantitative data
- give a basic introductory overview of official sources of crime data, including recorded crime statistics and the British Crime Survey
- consider the relevance of social divisions for understanding crime data
- provide a case study focusing on the quantifiable costs of anti-social behaviour and the relative merits and demerits of this type of information.

INTRODUCTION

This chapter introduces students to the two main types of crime data, quantitative and qualitative. It shows that these can give very different impressions of crime and its impact. It is often argued that the two are incompatible, but the overarching aim of the chapter is to show that they may be integrated effectively and used to complement each other.

Perhaps the first point to make is that this chapter is concerned with the data itself and not the research methods criminologists use to get hold of data. The ways in which information is collected are examined in Chapter 4. The purpose of this chapter is therefore restricted to briefly introducing different types of data to show how they contribute to our understanding of crime, disorder and victimization. After a brief outline of what is meant by quantitative and qualitative data, two of the main sources of crime data are identified, recorded crime statistics and the British Crime Survey (BCS). These two data sources may be categorized as official information, and it is shown that they tend to prefer quantitative data. The strengths and weaknesses of this type of data are rehearsed. Following that some examples of qualitative data are considered, and its merits and demerits relative to quantitative data are evaluated. The final part of the chapter draws on some basic research carried out by this author, which focused on the costs of antisocial behaviour, to illustrate the different insights quantitative and qualitative data offer to criminologists. It is concluded that while there is a tendency for social scientists to prefer one or the other, it is possible to accept that both have something to offer and that they may, if used carefully, be mutually complementary.

INTRODUCING QUANTITATIVE AND QUALITATIVE DATA

In this section:

- the main features of quantitative and qualitative data are discussed
- two perspectives on crime data are contrasted: the state administrator perspective and the questioning academic perspective
- some of the issues relating to these different times of data are illustrated with reference to examples.

Students of sociology will know that since the emergence of the social sciences there has been an ongoing debate between two often diametrically opposed schools of thought. On one side there are the positivists, and on the other the interpretivists. This classification is arguably over-simplistic, but it is a useful starting point for coming to terms with quantitative and qualitative data.

QUANTITATIVE DATA

Positivist social scientists hold that criminology can produce the type of data that is obtained by natural scientists such as physicists and chemists. The work undertaken by scholars working in these fields is complex, but a central organizing principle of what they do is an assumption that the natural world can be measured through the use of mathematical formulae, especially statistics. The emphasis is on quantifying phenomena. Quantification is, inescapably, about counting the number of cases. There is a belief that the number of cases provides a reliable measure of a particular aspect of the social world. For example, if a student is asked to consider media accounts of crime (for a discussion of reports in the popular press, see Chapter 1), a commonly cited source of information is crime statistics released by the Home Office. There is a view that statistics (what is sometimes called *hard data*) cannot be reasonably questioned. They are facts about an objective reality.

Why statistics?

The dependence of criminological researchers on statistics can be traced back to the Enlightenment period of modernity, and in particular the emergence of the so-called 'age of reason' associated with the transition of societies from a domination by divine values to a secular social order. This is linked with the expansion of positivism and the belief that human society can be examined in the same way that scientists study natural phenomena. For instance, crime can be measured in the same way that reactions between particles can be observed by physicists. The growing influence of scientific values occurred in many areas of social life, including urbanization and industrialization. However, it was the rationalization of society resulting from the expansion of huge impersonal bureaucracies that brought about a major change to the way society was organized. There was an increased emphasis on quantifying social phenomena and measuring various aspects of day-to-day life. The use of statistics by state administrators and social scientists was a consequence of this transformation.

Official statistics are therefore an important source of information if a student or researcher wishes to gain some understanding of the volume of crimes committed. A modicum of caution needs to be exercised because there is sometimes a tendency to give criminal statistics too much power. It is not unusual to hear politicians debating law and order present statistics as if they capture the 'true' facts about offending behaviour. Because these figures are treated as facts they are seen as being beyond dispute and debate. Statistical facts are claimed to be more relevant than opinions, which are perceived as subjective and less reliable.

To gain a fuller understanding of the different uses of statistics it may be helpful to consider how they are used in relation to two main perspectives, the state administrator perspective and the questioning academic viewpoint.

The state administrator perspective

This is underpinned by a 'consensus' approach advanced by functionalist sociologists such as the nineteenth-century writer Emile Durkheim. In his famous work *Suicide* (1970), Durkheim showed how official statistics about this phenomenon could readily demonstrate something about its reality. The statistics produced by various government agencies were treated as incontrovertible social facts, with the implication that it could be taken for granted that they provided a firm basis for an account of the way things were.

What Durkheim did was take at face value the judgements taken by state officials on what counted as a suicide. He did not make a particular attempt to consider the criteria officials used to arrive at this judgement. In other words, the methods used to decide whether a person had committed suicide were never called into question. In reality, there are complex and multifaceted meanings attached to the act of suicide, but Durkheim did not take stock of this. There are also a number of factors that influence how and why officials designate an unnatural death as a suicide. It could be argued that they are actually involved in the creation of social facts. However, in Durkheim's research there was no attempt to address wider societal attitudes to suicide and how these could have a bearing on how deaths are recorded.

The questioning academic perspective

Other social scientists take exception to the view that statistics provide an adequate representation of the social world. It is here that interpretivist sociologists, such as symbolic interactionists, enter the fray. Adherents to this approach are not satisfied with the idea that statistics are social facts, but focus instead on how social reality is created by the meanings human beings attach to their own behaviour and the actions of other people. In other words, they reject the possibility of social facts existing independently of human perception and social action. Consequently, the interpretivist sociologist would question the claim made by Durkheim that there are social facts about suicide, arguing instead that official statistics are social constructs.

For example, Douglas (1967) looked at how categorizations of deaths as suicides were arrived at. Coroners (the officials who investigate causes of death) used certain 'cues' to help them make sense of an often mucky and messy reality. The coroners actively looked for evidence that would help them piece together the circumstances accounting for the dead body. A suicide note or a history of mental illness, for instance, might be treated as evidence of suicidal intent. To put this in different terms, 'suicide' is less a fact with an independent and tangible existence than a category. Deaths are assigned to this category (or another, such as accidental death or murder) as part of the mundane work undertaken by coroners. Suicide is not a crime today (although it was treated as one until recently), but clearly the same applies to other categorizations of deaths. We can see how subjectivity becomes an important factor in the recording of crime statistics (Elgin, 1987).

Atkinson (1968) has written a well-known critique of the type of arguments forwarded by Durkheim, especially in work focusing on police practice. The main findings highlighted by Atkinson are supported by various writers who have shown how contextual factors influence the decisions the police take over what they record on paper and present to the public (Bittner, 1967a, 1967b, 1974; Cicourel, 1976; Manning, 1977). What is recorded as a crime in one week might not be classified as one a week later.

Let us start grounding these debates by looking at some concrete examples.

Example 1: burglary in Westshire Constabulary

(This is a fictitious example.) The chief constable of Westshire Constabulary decided to take a 'snapshot' of the number of burglaries committed in the force's area on one day. He ordered every police station to inform him of the number of confirmed burglaries that had taken place in the chosen 24-hour period.

'Burglary' has a legal definition, so arguably there should be no scope for disagreement on what counts as a burglary and what does not. A burglary tends to be a self-contained incident, so it should also be easy to identify each one, and counting up the number that takes place is an elementary procedure. So the suggestion here is that the number of burglaries reported will be a fact that cannot be disputed. It could then be used, for example, to inform members of the public about levels of crime in the area. It could be presented to the government as part of a request for more resources, or compared with data gathered on an earlier occasion to show that the force has a higher (or lower) workload as a result of the amount of crime that requires investigation. It could also be combined with data on convictions for burglars in the area's courts, to suggest that Westshire Constabulary has got better (or worse) at catching burglars. It might be necessary for someone to check the arithmetic, or the reports on which it was based, but arguably the basic assumptions cannot be challenged effectively.

Imagine you work in the Westshire Police media relations department. Write a report (a short paragraph will do) identifying the strengths and weaknesses of this exercise.

Example 2: the prison population

This is a real-life example, but it serves similar purposes to example 1. On 9 April 2006 the *Observer* newspaper reported on the number of prisoners in Britain. This short piece provides an excellent example of how statistical data are used. On the date of the survey, there were 77,141 prisoners. The method used to calculate this figure is not discussed here (but see Chapter 8), but you can it take for granted that it was used consistently and there are no grounds for doubting its accuracy. This is a statistic, a hard fact, and there is no sound reason to disagree with it.

The article then made a prediction: that if current trends in criminal behaviour and sentencing continue, the prison population will rise to 84,260 in 2007 and 90,800 in 2011. The article also 'forecast' in statistical terms the consequences of this for the prison service, reporting that 'Britain's 136 prisons will be able to hold only 80,700 prisoners at most in 2007, resulting in a potential shortfall of 3,500 prison places' (*Observer*, 9 April 2006). These are predictions and therefore the methods used to derive the figures can be challenged, but if the methods used are agreed, the results do not lie open to question. In a sense the numbers speak for themselves.

In sum, it has been shown that:

■ quantitative data are numeric and concerned with that which is countable
■ there are different views on the utility of quantitative data
■ while quantitative data is not without its limitations it is an indispensable source of information, and some counting of crime and related phenomena is absolutely essential.

QUALITATIVE DATA

What is meant by qualitative data? In this section:

■ the main features of qualitative data are outlined
■ it is explained that qualitative data is non-numerical and tends to consist of words or text
■ it is shown that this type of data can be used on its own or can be used to complement quantitative data.

Qualitative data is in some senses much more difficult to define than quantitative data. In essence, criminologists whose preference is for qualitative data express scepticism about the assumptions held by positivists, and question whether counting objects in the world tells us anything significant or interesting about social life.

Interpretivists can argue that the methods used by positivists are faulty (see Chapter 4), but more fundamentally they object that quantitative data does not capture the complexity of human experience. It is not possible to use it to deal with human emotions and subjectivity. Statistics are not facts that exist independently of human interpretation: they can only be made meaningful as part of an interpretive process.

Qualitative data does not attempt to quantify human experience. Instead, it is based on the recognition that the universe is not subject to being counted. Human experience cannot be contained in this way and is much more open-ended. To illustrate this, let us look again at the first of the examples above.

Westshire revisited: a qualitative perspective

The recording of crime is not, in fact, as straightforward as people might expect, and human intervention sometimes gets in the way of the production of objective numbers. True, there is a legal definition of burglary, but you will remember from Chapter 1 that the police use discretion in how they apply the law. They can also make mistakes, and be uneven and inconsistent in their decisions. And the facts are not always clear: it is not difficult to think of cases that might or might not be classified as burglaries. It is quite feasible that some burglaries might not be counted, or they could be over-counted if there was an incentive to do so. Burglaries *reported* on the day in question, for example, could be judged as having *occurred* that day (if the message was that a high number reported would be well received), or having occurred the previous day (if the officer received a hint to keep the number down), if it was not clear which was the case.

All this would affect the number of burglaries reported. As a former British prime minister once remarked, 'there are lies, damned lies and statistics'. The lesson to be learnt is that the statistics produced are not simple facts. On the contrary, they are artefacts made by creative social actors who are consciously interpreting and shaping the world around them.

Another criticism levelled at quantitative data is that simply counting the number of burglaries does not tell us what each burglary means for the different players involved, who include the offender (we might want to know why he or she did it, and how), the police (who, as noted above, have plenty of discretion in how they respond), witnesses and the victim(s).

As we discussed in the last chapter, victims of crime can have very different experiences, and this is true even within a single category of crime such as burglary. A victim who was asleep in her bed until she was disturbed by the burglar would have a qualitatively different experience from someone who returned home from work to find that her home has been burgled. One burglar might have stolen a DVD player, another one thousands of pounds worth of jewellery. Yet another offender might have taken nothing, but have gone through the personal possessions of the victim and destroyed items with a high sentimental value. In the chief constable's count all these incidents would rate the same, but that would not reflect the variable experiences of the victims.

Is a snapshot of the number of burglaries taking place in Westshire in one day useful? Would a more, or differently, useful report be possible if it looked at qualitative data too?

You might like to think about the second example in a similar vein. Now let us go on to introduce the main sources of information about crime and disorder.

OFFICIAL SOURCES OF CRIME DATA

The purpose of this section is to:

- introduce the main sources of data used by criminologists, in particular recorded crime statistics collected by the police and published by the Home Office and the Home Office's British Crime Survey (BCS)
- discuss how the data is gathered for each of these methods
- provide some examples of what can be learnt from these sources of crime data.

Recorded crime statistics

The Home Office publishes recorded crime statistics, which include all notifiable offences that the police record (Home Office, 1992–; www.homeoffice.gov.uk). From what you learnt in Chapter 1, you should appreciate that this does not mean all criminal offences are counted. In practice most more minor summary offences are not included, even if the police record these crimes for the purpose of their own investigations. The word 'notifiable' is significant here, because all the offences that are listed have been notified to the Home Office. They are called *recorded crime* (Coleman and Moynihan, 1996).

To understand this more fully it is necessary to look at the different processes involved in a crime being recorded. There are three main stages. First, either a person contacts the police (in person or by telephone) to report that a crime has been committed, or the police themselves see or discover that a crime has been committed. If either of these happens, the police register a crime-related incident, then the police officer allocated to the incident decides whether it should be recorded as a crime. There is a considerable degree of subjectivity in this decision, and in addition, each of the 43 police forces in England and Wales used to have slightly different recording practices, so this too affected the overall count.

Historically the Home Office has produced 'counting rules' to guide the police and to ensure that there is a degree of consistency across the board. One issue, for instance, is what counts as one crime, and what as more than one crime. A rule that applies is known as 'collective protection'. Imagine a car park with five cars parked in it, all of which are broken into one night. However, the car park has a barrier surrounding it, and that means it counts as a single location. Only one offence is recorded. Another counting rule is the 'continuous series'. An individual is walking home after an evening out drinking, and on one street attempts to steal eight cars, but is only successful on the eighth attempt. In this case only the eighth attempt is recorded as part of a 'continuous series'.

Overall, the police do record reported notifiable offences unless there is evidence to suggest that no offence has been committed. The fact that there was some variation was a cause of some concern, though, and this resulted in a relatively recent change: the introduction of the National Recording Standard in April 2002 by the Association of Chief Police Officers (ACPO). The reason for introducing this standard was to ensure compliance to a uniform decision-making model, and greater consistency and clarity of recording practices throughout England and Wales. It was also intended to make crime statistics more victim-focused.

The second stage is the recording of crime. Once the police have taken the decision to record a reported crime, they need to determine the number of crimes recorded and the category of offences to which a crime belongs. The Home Office provides the police with some guidance in the form of the 'Counting Rules for Recorded Crime' to assist them in the classification of crime. There are nine categories:

- violence against the person
- sexual offences
- robbery
- burglary
- theft and handling stolen goods
- fraud and forgery
- criminal damage
- drug offences
- other offences.

These rules tend to be quite clear because most crimes are counted as one crime per victim, and the offence committed is self-evident (for instance, a burglary). There are some more complicated cases where more than one offence has been committed, or an offence may have been committed more than once over a period of time, or the crime involves more than one victim or offender.

The third stage is detecting a crime. If a crime is recorded it will also be investigated. This part of the process includes the gathering of evidence, where an attempt is made to link the crime to a particular suspect. The Home Office has issued 'Detections Guidance', which sets out the criteria used to detect crimes so they have a fit with the counting rules. It covers cases where a person is charged or cautioned, or the court takes another offence into consideration (TIC) (see below), as well as those where no further action is taken by police. The Detections Guidance is very strict about which approach is appropriate, and considerable emphasis is placed on the quality of the evidence. A charge is only laid if the evidence is thought sufficient that when it is presented in court it is likely to result in a conviction.

Throughout the 1990s and into the 2000s the performance of the police service was exposed to more and more scrutiny by the government. League tables and 'hit teams' were introduced to measure police effectiveness, and there was the very real prospect of police managers being put on short-term contracts to improve their productivity. The league tables measured various aspects of police work, and not just criminal detection, but the reduction of crime was an important aspect. The reputations and future funding of different police forces were both increasingly determined by these league tables, and because of the pressure this created, there was an inbuilt incentive for police forces to misrepresent or 'fiddle the figures'. For example, Her Majesty's Inspectorate of Constabulary (2001: 13) carried out an inspection of a Basic Command Unit in Colchester, Essex, and found evidence that crimes were being under-recorded. Only 61 per cent of incidents were judged to have been classified properly.

This was not the first time the police had manipulated crime statistics to show them in a more favourable light. For many years the police were able to clear up crimes by gaining admissions from individuals who in fact had not committed the offence to which they were pleading guilty. It was not uncommon for police officers to negotiate with suspects by offering them the prospect of less severe punishment if they asked to have x number of offences TIC. This 'trade-off' clearly distorted the statistics for solving crimes, and as a result of this practice the police were made to appear more efficient than they actually were. TICs were abolished in 1999 to counter any distorting effect they were having on crime figures. Another method of massaging crime statistics is known as 'cuffing'. In this, offences are downgraded, giving the impression that the police are not struggling to deal with more serious offences. For instance, 'attempted burglary' could be recorded as 'criminal damage', and failure to detect the perpetrator then does not look as bad as far as police performance is concerned (Bottomley and Coleman, 1981; Coleman, 1981; Bottomley and Pease, 1993).

All this means that there appear to be some problems with the statistics produced by the police. Perhaps the most significant omission from the police statistics is the so-called 'dark figure' of crime, which includes those offences that are not reported to them as well as those they do not record (Coleman and Moynihan, 1996). To counter these problems, alternative sources of information have been developed, including the British Crime Survey.

The British Crime Survey (BCS)

The first BCS was produced in 1982 (Hough and Mayhew, 1983), followed by sweeps in 1984, 1988, 1992, 1994, 1996, 1998, 2000 and 2001 (see for example: Mayhew et al., 1989, 1992; Mirrlees-Black, 1998). Since 2001 the survey has been published on an annual basis. It covers England and Wales, which is in line with the administrative structure of the criminal justice system.[1] It is intended to provide as true a measure of the extent of crime as possible, and to complement the criminal statistics produced by the police.

Policy makers and practitioners working in criminal justice regard this source of crime data as invaluable. It is also essential reading for teachers and students of criminology. It is so popular and useful because it provides a wealth of evidence about the level of crime, public attitudes to crime and the criminal justice system (including the police and the courts). The main purpose of the BCS is to measure the number of crimes committed in England and Wales in a particular year. It does this by asking adults (people aged 16 and above) in private households about their experiences of crime over a period of 12 months. Clearly it is not possible to interview every adult in England and

Wales, so the survey takes a sample of addresses throughout the country. At each address one person is randomly selected for interview. In 2000, 20,000 people were interviewed, and by 2002 it was 40,000. Some years include a booster sample to cover the experiences of ethnic minorities (4,000 in 2000).

The interview itself is conducted by a computer-assisted personal interviewer (CAPI). Towards the end of the questionnaire there are two self-completion sections, which focus on sensitive issues such as sexual assault and domestic violence. At this stage respondents are handed the CAPI's laptop so they can tap in any information they wish to give privately and anonymously (Koffman, 1996).

The BCS is considered so important because as was noted above, the police do not record all the crimes reported to them. It also asks people about those crimes that they decide to not report to the police. There are many reasons for victims to not report crime to the police. It is possible that the victim feels the police would be uninterested, insensitive or unable to do anything. Some people fear reprisals from the offender. There may also be a lack of willingness to report some property offences because it would cause the individual to lose the no-claims bonuses on an insurance policy. These are all valid reasons in their own way, but they do mean that the police's picture of crime is incomplete. The BCS can go some way to fill this gap in the knowledge base, and it does this by producing a lot of very useful information about unreported crimes. In addition to counting crimes, the BCS also focuses on fear of crime, which from the 1990s onwards has been taken as seriously as actual crime because of the negative impact it has on people's daily experience.

Over the years the BCSs have focused on a range of topics, including victims' experiences of personal and property crime; the security of homes and motor vehicles; employee experiences of violence at work; sexual victimization; drug use; volunteering and community work. There is a long list, and it is well worth paying a visit to the Home Office website to explore the different data sets and data analyses, which are readily downloadable (www.homeoffice.gov.uk).

The BCS is far more than a simple data-gathering exercise, and it has many practical uses. The survey helps policy makers to identify the people or places that are at most risk of different types of crime. For example, the survey might show that individuals who lived in rented, multi-occupancy accommodation in inner-city areas are more likely to have their home burgled than a retired affluent couple living in a rural area. To take another example, it might show that while young men are more likely to be the victims of violence in a town centre on a Saturday night, they are less afraid of this happening than young women are. Thus the BCS provides agencies with the information they need to plan appropriate crime prevention programmes.

By measuring public perceptions of and attitudes towards crime, including fear of crime, the BCS can provide data that feeds into public information campaigns. It possible to inform people about various actions they take to avoid the crimes they are worried about.

Let us look briefly at some examples of BCS data, with particular reference to some of the factors examined in Chapter 2, including patterns of offending and victimization related to age and gender.

Victims of crime

What can be learnt from attempts to quantify or count the number of victims who are out there in society? This will have a link with the number of crimes committed, although it is quite possible for there to be more victims than recorded offences. This is demonstrated well by the BCS, which estimates that there are between three and four times more crimes committed, and hence victims, than are suggested by the recorded crime statistics produced by the police (Koffman, 1996). Following the first BCS (Hough and Mayhew, 1983), researchers identified a 'statistically average victim', showing that for many people becoming a victim of crime is a relatively unusual experience. However, some criminologists have questioned the notion of this statistical average because it conceals differential tendencies to become victims. A number of local crime surveys have supported this assertion, showing that some groups, particularly the poorer sections of a community and women at home, are even more likely to become a victim than the BCS suggested. Examples are the Islington (Jones, Maclean and Young, 1986) and Merseyside (Kinsey, 1984) crime surveys.

Gender and offending behaviour

Another example of criminological data is the pattern of criminal behaviour by sex. A cursory glance at official statistics and a range of secondary sources shows quite clearly, in statistical terms, that there are more male than female offenders.

In 2002 there were 316,000 known offenders in the general population. Of this figure, 19 per cent were female (Home Office, 2004b: 4). If the statistics are examined a little more closely to take into account the age of the offender, the gap is smaller for younger age groups. Put another way, there is a relatively high proportion of female offenders among the younger subgroups of the population. The peak age for offending behaviour varies by gender: it is 19 for males, and 15 for females. Overall, girls desist from crime much earlier than boys, and this pattern is confirmed in adulthood (ibid.).

Another indicator of the relative commitment males and females have to crime is that women (74 per cent) are more likely to be convicted only once than men (50 per cent) (ibid). Similarly there are fewer male offenders (55 per cent) with a criminal career lasting less than a year than female offenders (80 per cent). Indeed only 7 per cent of females who offend do so for ten or more years, whereas the proportion for male criminals is 24 per cent. In other words, males have a greater disposition to being involved in crime for longer periods, as well as a higher rate of recidivism (that is, repeat offending) (Home Office, 2004b: 5).

Of course this offers just a glimpse or a snapshot of the pattern of offending behaviour, but a similar pattern has been highlighted in research conducted over an extended period of time. Some researchers followed the development of a cohort of individuals born in 1953, and found that the males offended more often than the females (Farrington and West, 1990 cited in Farrington, 1994). By the age of 46, 9 per cent of females had offended compared with 33 per cent of males. This shows that there is a persistent pattern across time in the UK, but what about different societies in other parts of the world?

Internationally relevant research commissioned by the United Nations (Harvey et al., 1992, cited in Walklate, 2004) considered this issue. It was found that across the world criminal justice agencies were more likely to suspect men than women of committing an offence, and that they were more likely to be apprehended, prosecuted, convicted and imprisoned than women.

The Home Office (2004b: 3) shows that self-report data does not contradict what we can learn from official data sources. This is illustrated by the finding that men are more likely to have committed an offence in the previous 12 months (26 per cent) than women have done (11 per cent). The peak age for female offences (age 14) is younger than for males, and like other data sources, it appears from this research that females are far more likely to grow out of crime and desist by their mid to late teens.

So far attention has been directed at a high level of generality about offending in general. Are the conclusions likely to be any different if specific offences are scrutinized?

Heidensohn (1996) has shown that first and foremost it is necessary to spell out that women do appear as offenders in all categories of crime, and therefore criminality is not the exclusive property of males. Despite this it appears that men are more likely to commit some types of offence than women. The available evidence suggests that women are more likely to commit relatively minor offences than are male offenders. The proportion of all female offenders committing the most serious type of offence, indictable offences (in 1999, 30 per cent; and in 2002, 28 per cent) is lower than it is for males (in 1999, 33 per cent, and in 2002, 30 per cent). This percentage tells only part of the story, however, because in absolute numbers the figures are in the region of half a million males and 100,000 females (Home Office, 2004b). Female offenders tend to commit more trivial offences. In 2002, for example, 57 per cent of known female offences were theft and handling, followed by 11 per cent for both drugs offences and violence against the person.

Gender and victimization

When we look at the extent to which men and women have markedly different experiences of being victims of crime, again among the potential sources of information are official statistics (Koffman, 1996). These focus on conventional crimes, and show that overall men are more likely to become victims of crime, and especially of violent offences. This finding is reinforced by BCS data for 1999–2000, which demonstrated that young men aged 18–24 years were the group most at risk of becoming victims of a violent crime (18.8 per cent) (Home Office, 2004b). A more current BCS (2002/3) showed a gender difference when looking at the victims of violent crime over a 12-month period: 2.9 per cent of adult females had been victims, compared with 5.3 per cent of adult males. This perhaps explains why the risk of becoming a victim is greater for men aged below 25 (15.1 per cent), than for women in this age range (6.9 per cent).

Robbery is another example. The BCS (2001/02) data shows that 39 per cent of victims are female, while 25 per cent of victims are young males aged from 14 to 17. The general pattern is that the victimization rate for females is lower, and there is a more even spread across the different age groups, with the notable exception of elderly women: 15 per cent of female victims of robbery are aged 70 and above. Statistics also show that female victims are more likely to be robbed by a stranger instead of a person with who they are acquainted in some way (Home Office, 2004b).

These findings are not applicable for all crimes, and if attention is switched to less 'visible' and more 'unconventional' types of crime, the impression gained is very different. A good example is indecent assault. Female victims of this crime tend to be older than male victims: nearly half the female victims are aged 16 and under, but for males the figure is 70 per cent (Home Office, 2004b: 44). Females are also more likely to be victimized by a stranger: 37 per cent of females compared with 27 per cent of males. The difference is starker when sexual violence against women is taken on board.

According to recorded crime statistics the victims of rape are overwhelmingly female, and in 2002/3 there were 11,441 offences of female rape and 852 male cases. This figure is likely to underestimate the extent and prevalence of this crime, and the BCS showed in its 1998 and 2000 'sweeps' that of females over 16, 9.7 per cent – almost one in ten – had experienced some form of sexual victimization, including rape. More specifically in relation to rape, 4.9 per cent – about one in 20 – of females had experienced this crime in their adult lives (since turning 16). Contrary to what many people believe, most rapes are carried out by the partner of the victim, or an individual with whom the victim is acquainted (however casually). Thus it is perhaps not surprising that 'strangers' are responsible for 8 per cent of offences in this category (Home Office, 2004b: 45).

Another criminal offence where women are at greater risk of becoming a victim is 'stalking' (White-Sansom, 2004). The 1998 BCS showed that three-quarters of victims are female and that 16.1 per cent of women are likely to be stalked at some stage in their lives. Only 6.8 per cent of men are likely to experience similar victimization (Home Office, 2004b).

Age and offending behaviour

In 2002/03 there is statistical evidence showing that 268,500 juveniles (aged 10–17 years) were arrested for notifiable offences out of a total population of nearly 5.5 million (Audit Commission, 2004: 8). This is a sizeable problem and perhaps accounts for public anxiety about juvenile crime. For example, only 21 per cent of the public have any confidence in the capacity of the criminal justice system to deal with the criminality of young people (ibid.). The 2003/04 BCS found a similar view, noting that over a quarter of the population think vandalism, graffiti, litter and rowdy teenagers hanging around on the street to be a problem in their local area (Dodd et al., 2004). Interestingly not all of the behaviours mentioned above are considered to be crime: many are examples of incivility and low-level disorder. However, disorderly conduct is significant because there is research evidence to show that disorder is a reliable predictor of crime, and that by tackling nuisance behaviour there will be substantial payoffs in terms of attempts to reduce crime.

OFFICIAL SOURCES OF CRIME DATA: THE KEY POINTS

■ The recorded crime statistics are a reflection of the methods the police use to record crime.
■ Statistical data produced by the police do not present a complete picture of all the crimes that are committed.

- ■ The BCS has been introduced to supplement and complement recorded crime statistics.
- ■ The BCS shows quite clearly that there are more crimes committed than the police either record or are aware of.
- ■ The BCS provides invaluable information about various aspects of offending, such as the experiences of victims and the different experience men and women have of crime.

THE QUANTITATIVE AND QUALITATIVE DIMENSIONS OF ANTISOCIAL BEHAVIOUR (ASB)

This case study:

- ■ focuses on the issue of antisocial behaviour (ASB), drawing on research by the author
- ■ defines the nature of ASB and discusses the problems it presents to the government and policy makers
- ■ considers qualitative and quantitative data on ASB
- ■ suggests that quantitative data provides useful information about the costs of ASB but there is a need for more qualitative data to explore the underlying issues.

This section draws on a piece of research by the author and a colleague (Crowther and Formby, 2004). It is a rather limited piece, and the purpose of this section is to highlight some of the problems with certain sources of information. The study focused on the costs of ASB in a small town called Westport, set in the county of Westshire.[2] It is a small and rather simple study in contrast to the BCS, and many of the other research studies students are likely to be exposed to as part of their course. Nonetheless it is a good illustrative example of the different ways quantitative and qualitative data may be used to present a multidimensional overview of the financial and other costs of ASB. Also, in contrast to many criminological studies which are methodologically sophisticated, this piece of research can be understood without any prior knowledge of research methods. It is based on simple statistical (quantifiable) data made available by a range of agencies in Westport that are affected by ASB, plus qualitative data which was derived from telephone interviews (effectively short conversations) with representatives of agencies and key policy documents. There are six main sections to this case study.

1. The background to and rationale of the study.
2. Counting the costs of ASB.
3. Defining ASB.
4. Government approaches to ASB.
5. Research on ASB.
6. The limits of counting ASB – other issues.

Background to and rationale of the study

The study was a snapshot evaluation of the direct (economic) and indirect (social) costs of responding to and preventing ASB in Westport. The direct costs were measured on the basis of quantitative data (i.e. pounds and pence). The financial costs told only part of the story, though, and it was necessary to also consider the indirect costs of the ASB, which is where the qualitative data proved necessary.

Before discussing how to measure the costs of ASB, it is necessary to briefly set the scene and describe the nature of the problem. According to Section 1 of the Crime and Disorder Act (1998), ASB includes those actions 'that caused, or was likely to cause harassment, alarm or distress to one or more persons not of the same household as the perpetrator'. The available remedy is an anti-social behaviour order (ASBO) (Home Office, 1998a). The ASBO is a civil response, which may be used against any person aged 10 years or over who behaves antisocially. As Hopkins Burke and Morrill (2004) show, ASBOs concern civil matters where 'behaviour need only be proved on the balance of probabilities' rather 'than beyond reasonable doubt' as it is in criminal cases. Crucially an ASBO can be imposed against people who have not done anything criminal, but it is a criminal offence to breach an ASBO, possibly leading to a five-year prison sentence.

This simple definition of ASB immediately demonstrates the difficulties involved in measuring it, because there is significant scope for subjectivity (for example, for value judgements, and the use of evidence from 'professional witnesses'). The Home Office's 1999 guidelines were not particularly helpful in clarifying matters, but nuisance neighbours were identified as a priority. At a later date, the Police Reform Act (2002) gave registered social landlords and British Transport Police the power to apply for ASBOs. Early research shows that a housing management perspective was dominant (for example, there have been injunctions under the Housing Act (1996)). However, research published by Burney (2002) points out that young people and their rowdy and unruly behaviour were treated as a priority by key agencies on the ground, largely in response to calls from members of the general public. For example the UK government published a white paper, *Building Communities, Beating Crime* (Home Office, 2004a), which called for crime reduction partnerships to respond more effectively to antisocial behaviour (Squires and Stephen, 2005). In addition the National Policing Plan 2003–06 directed chief officers and local authorities to include in their local plans a strategy to address youth nuisance and antisocial behaviour (Home Office, 2005a: 9).

In 2003 the New Labour government launched a new major initiative to tackle ASB as part of its 'Respect' agenda (Home Office, 2003c). In this the frame used to define the problem was changed to include agencies involved in addressing more general crime and disorder problems, especially among socially excluded groups, or the underclass (see Chapter 2). For example, one of the key aims of government plans was to deal with problems that were identified as obstructing the regeneration of disadvantaged areas and leading to crime. There are several strands to the action plan, which are intended to have an impact on the prevention and clearing-up of ASB. For example, the government wishes to improve the response of different agencies to ASB through:

- improved training for police officers
- issuing new guidelines for magistrates
- establishing a new national team of specialist prosecutors
- providing more money for crime and disorder partnerships.

There was a range of specialist initiatives and pilot programmes for:

- nuisance neighbours
- beggars
- abandoned cars
- graffiti.

Responses were intended to be cross-departmental. For instance, the Home Office (2003c) specifically called for the wider use of fixed penalty notices for matters such as truancy and graffiti; more police powers to disperse groups in some circumstances; and increased powers for social landlords to take action against antisocial tenants (faster evictions and removing the right to buy).

ASB was therefore the number one priority for central and local government agencies. ASB also affected the voluntary and private sectors. Why did ASB preoccupy the government so much? The main reason was that the problem impacted on almost everyone: people suffered from it at home, at work and out and about in their spare time. Most people know from personal experience that ASB can affect their quality of life, and it creates a sense of insecurity and fear for many people, although the government and media can overstate such fears (Cook, 2006). ASB refers to many issues, including:

- criminal and subcriminal behaviour
- disorder and incivilities
- community safety/public protection
- fear of crime
- quality of life issues.

More specifically it may refer to:

- drinking
- vandalism
- noise (i.e. nuisance neighbours and 'neighbours/families from hell')
- threatening behaviour
- joy-riding
- violence
- racial harassment
- dropping litter
- verbal abuse.

In 2000 the Home Office-funded BCS identified drug dealing/misuse, litter, teenagers hanging around (with rude or abusive behaviour) and disputes between neighbours (especially on low-income housing estates) as key ASB issues. Even these behaviours refer to many different activities. For example, ASB related to drinking may occur in subways and public parks in the daytime, but outside pubs and clubs in the context of the night-time economy. In short ASB refers to a diversity of behaviours, which suggests that identifying and measuring it is far from straightforward.

Counting the costs of ASB

The Crowther and Formby (2004) study was influenced by an approach used in research undertaken by Elizabeth Stanko (2001). Similarly to the ASB audit produced by the ASB Unit that followed her work, Stanko set out to audit the cost to society of domestic violence, and in discussing her method of gathering data, highlighted the problem of agreed definitions of the problem when asking agencies to compile data. There was also no set definition of ASB agreed by the participants in the Crowther and Formby (2004) study. For instance, many of the statistics appear to focus on vandalism, but other figures also included burglary and other known crimes. In her work, Stanko decided that agreed definitions did not need to be in place, however.

Crowther and Formby (2004) differed from Stanko's methodology in that they did not seek to carry out a systematic audit on one day; rather, organizations were asked to estimate the cost over a period of one year. Many provided responses based on known costs for the last year, although some information was based on calculations from previous years.

There were two phases to the study, introduced by a letter asking for quantitative information from a variety of agencies/organization operating in Westport, and a follow-up telephone interview asking for more qualitative information on, and a discussion around, the issue of ASB and its relationship to respondents' work.

Defining ASB

In the past, the term ASB was used to focus on behaviour in relation to housing, but this definition was broadened to encompass a variety of civil disobediences and criminal activity. ASBOs have been used, for example, as a measure to tackle prostitution, racial abuse, verbal abuse, criminal damage and vandalism, graffiti, noise nuisance, threatening behaviour in groups, begging, kerb crawling, throwing missiles, assault and vehicle crime (www.renewal.net). This obviously impacts upon the recording and measurement of ASB incidents, and hence the type of the data produced.

We mentioned above the Home Office definition of ASB, contained in section 1 of the Crime and Disorder Act (1998): 'Acting in a manner that caused or was likely to cause harassment, alarm or distress to one or more persons not of the same household as [the defendant]' (Home Office, 1998). However, the Home Office did not indicate that this was to be used as a guideline in any monitoring or measurement of data.

Whitehead, Stockdale and Razzu, in attempting to produce a universal definition of ASB, said that:

> ASB is defined in relation to the harm caused to others .... ASB is also defined by categories of behaviours or activities, some of which directly harm people, others of which damage property and some of which are simply a nuisance.
>
> (Whitehead et al., 2003: v)

They also highlighted the diversity of definitions in use: 'Most definitions of ASB involve some overlap with definitions of crime. Some indeed include all crimes' (ibid.). They therefore conclude that 'Given the difficulties of definition ... it is hardly surprising that measurement of the extent of ASB presents considerable difficulties' (ibid.). They drew attention to the resultant variance in the quality of measurements recorded in different localities, and by different agencies.

Government approaches to ASB

ASB was a key area of recent government concern and policy development in the early twenty-first century, highlighted by the establishment of an ASB Unit within the Home Office in January 2003. It is also evidenced by the passing into law of the Anti-Social Behaviour Act (ASB Act) in January 2004, introduced to help agencies respond to ASB problems such as nuisance neighbours and teenage gangs. This legislation allowed the dispersal of teenage groups from the streets, and permitted local newspapers to 'name and shame' teenagers given ASBOs, although ASBOs themselves had first been brought in under the Crime and Disorder Act (1998).

The Home Office has not yet produced a more formal common definition of ASB, but its website indicates the variety of behaviours that can be grouped under this term: in 2004 the site introduction commented, 'ASB includes a range of problems – noisy neighbours, abandoned cars, vandalism, graffiti, litter and youth nuisance' (Home Office, 2004c). However, the website then immediately moved on to concentrate on reactions to, and ways of dealing with, ASB, rather than any in-depth discussion of the variety of definitions used. Whitehead et al. (2003) also commented on the recent, and increasing, increase in the formal steps being taken to address ASB.

Policy developments in this area included the 'Together' campaign, part of a government 'Action Plan' on ASB, published in October 2003. This includes a new 'ASB Academy' (the Together Academy), launched on 3 March 2004. The objective was for the academy to train police, local authority and courts staff in how to deal with ASB. Ten events were held throughout England and Wales in areas where pilot schemes were operating, aimed at particular ASB problems. A national telephone advice line (Action Line) also accompanied these events, helping to explain the new powers brought in under the ASB Act. A Together campaign website was also launched in 2004.

The Together campaign aimed to disseminate ideas about good practice in ASB strategies. The new legislation is applied in many different ways, but as far as young people are concerned there is an emphasis on dispersing youths who throw fireworks or stones, and responding to under-age drinking and joy-riding. Between October 2003 and September 2004 over 400 dispersal orders were issued. During the same period there were also 824 parenting orders and 5,383 antisocial behaviour contracts issued (Home Office, 2005b: 39). This shows quite clearly that the government was pressuring crime and disorder reduction partnerships into an enforcement role with regard to the antisocial behaviour of young people.

Previous research on ASB

Previous research has estimated the cost of ASB to be high. For example, at the turn of the twenty-first century the cost of obtaining a single ASBO was estimated at an average of £5,000 and a maximum of nearly £200,000 (Burney, 2002), although there is evidence to suggest that the cost falls as local authorities grow more experienced in their use (www.renewal.net). The research also highlighted how the cost is affected by how local authorities choose to tackle ASB. Mediation services, for example, are more popular than ASBOs in some areas (Burney, 2002). The complex variety of powers open to local authorities and the police in tackling ASB should not be underestimated. Acceptable behaviour contracts (ABCs), for instance, developed in 2001, bypass the legal process and therefore may well prove cheaper than ASBOs (Burney, 2002). The underlying importance of partnership work in all these new measures leads to the need to consult with a wide variety of agencies and stakeholders when looking at this issue. Whitehead and colleagues also emphasized the wide range of costs to society. As well as the costs of prevention and alleviation, there are also long-term costs to victims: both a direct financial impact (higher insurance premiums, lower property values and so on), and the general toll that ASB has on people's health and well-being (Whitehead et al., 2003).

In 2003 the ASB Unit undertook its own research into the extent – and cost – of ASB in England and Wales. A day-long audit of incidents recorded by a variety of statutory and voluntary agencies was carried out from midnight on Tuesday 9 September 2003, to midnight on Wednesday 10 September 2003. This was the first national count of its kind to be undertaken concerning ASB, with more than 1,500 organizations taking part. In total (based on updated figures), over 72,000 reports of ASB were recorded in this period, equating to more than one report every 2 seconds (which suggests approximately 16.5 million incidents every year). It should be highlighted that this study only records the number of ASB incidents that were reported to agencies taking part in the research, not the actual number of incidents that took place on that day. Whitehead et al. (2003: vii) noted, 'It is clear that there are far more gaps than there is evidence, although both the qualitative and quantitative material available gives useful indications of what is required.'

The ASB Unit estimated from this information that ASB in England and Wales costs agencies a minimum of £14 million a day (about £3.5 billion a year). A breakdown of the results is given in Table 3.1.

We now turn our attention towards ASB in a local area.

The costs of ASB in Westport

Table 3.2 shows how much the council, the voluntary sector, local and national businesses claimed to spend as a result of, or in attempts to anticipate, ASB in Westport.

In summary, the information provided by the participants shows that approximately £3.3 million a year on average is spent in Westport because of ASB. This could rise towards £4 million if the costs known to be excluded in this initial estimate (for example, police

Table 3.1   ASB Unit day count results, 10 September 2003 (in order of highest cost)*

Category of ASB incident	No. of reports	Estimated costs to agencies per day (£000)	Estimated costs to agencies per year (£ million)
Criminal damage/ vandalism	7,855	£2,667	£667
Intimidation/harassment	5,415	£1,983	£496
Litter/rubbish	10,686	£1,866	£466
Nuisance behaviour	7,660	£1,420	£355
Vehicle-related nuisance	7,782	£1,361	£340
Rowdy behaviour	5,339	£995	£249
Noise	5,374	£994	£249
Drugs/substance misuse and drug dealing	2,920	£527	£132
Street drinking and begging	3,239	£504	£126
Animal-related problems	2,546	£458	£114
Abandoned vehicles	4,994	£360	£90
Hoax calls	1,286	£198	£49
Prostitution, kerb-crawling, sexual acts	1,011	£167	£42
Total	66,107*	£13,500*	£3,375*

*pre-updated figures

staff costs) are added in. These figures are very similar to the estimate from the Leeds local authority of £3–5 million a year spent on ASB (Social Exclusion Unit, 2000).

It is possible to draw a conclusion similar to Stanko's. Criticisms were made of her methodology, but she responded, 'Whatever might have been said, it was clear that the audit made one point very clearly. Domestic violence is very visible in the UK' (Stanko, 2001: 224). In this case, the effects of ASB are very visible to agencies and organizations in Westport. It should also be noted, however, that this research also suffered from the same weakness as the ASB Unit's day audit: it does not take full account of the financial and psychological costs to victims of ASB.

The limits of counting ASB: other issues

The costs of ASB only tell part of the story, though: ASB raises a range of other issues. In other words the quantitative and qualitative information outlined in this case study is incomplete because it glosses over four key considerations:

First, definitions of ASB are ambiguous, and many discussions of this phenomenon concern the acceptability of behaviour rather than behaviour that is criminal.

■ Defining acceptable behaviour is a subjective exercise, and actions that are thought acceptable by one person may not be acceptable to another. For example, there are certain types of behaviour that young people consider acceptable (such as 'hanging around') but that are not acceptable to older people.

Table 3.2   *Spending by the council, the voluntary sector, local and national businesses as a result of or in attempts to anticipate ASB in Westport*

Organization	Annual cost	Range of activities that costs cover	Extra comments
National Postal Service	£12,200	Vandalism Arson	Does not include: compensation for fire-damaged letters the cost of time off for staff as a result of pricks from hypodermic needles the cost of counselling for staff as a result of assaults
Westport Primary Care Trust	£13,464.80	Vandalism Graffiti Loss of staff time due to injury	A fall in costs from figures published last year
Westport Passenger Transport Authority	£450,589.07	Vandalism to bus shelters Interchange graffiti CCTV at Westport Interchange	
Westshire Police Authority	£240,000 728 hours over-time at time + 1/3 343 person weeks	False 999 calls Cost of staffing football matches Vandalism Days lost because of violence towards staff Staffing of weekend activities/events	13,091 ASB incidents recorded in the period 1 August 2002– 31 July 2003
Clear and Safe Streets	£2,111,524	Graffiti Litter collection CCTV costs Woodlands vandalism Fly tipping Cost of Neighbourhood Warden Service Dealing with car dumping Dog warden service Chewing gum removal Cost of Antisocial Behaviour Unit Cost of Mediation Service Housing costs due to neighbour nuisance resulting in termination of contract and properties left void	Does not include:· legal costs, ranging from £500–£10,000 per case depending on whether the case goes to trial (e.g. possession hearings, ASBOs) costs to tenants when insurance premiums rise

Table 3.2   *Continued*

Organization	Annual cost	Range of activities that costs cover	Extra comments
National Telecommunications Ltd	£167,003.00	Vandalism to phone boxes	
Westshire Fire and Rescue Service	£186,264	Cost of malicious false alarms Cost of malicious fires	
Westport Education Department	£140,746	Theft from colleges and schools Vandalism	
Westport Culture and Leisure Department	£21,630	Vandalism Theft Arson damage	
Westport Chamber of Commerce		Graffiti Vandalism Cost of CCTV	77% of businesses surveyed said they spend up to £1000 a year as a result of ASB 23% said over £1000 a year as a result of ASB 43% said up to £1000 a year on prevention of ASB 25% said £1000–5000 annual cost on prevention 8% reported £5000+ on prevention
Total	£3,343,420.87*		

* Plus police staff costs, compensation for fire-damaged letters, the cost of time off for postal staff as a result of pricks from hypodermic needles, the cost of counselling for postal staff as a result of assaults, legal costs, rise in insurance premiums, cost to private businesses, cost of Westport Community Safety Unit, costs to support Crime and Disorder Partnership

- Acceptability concerns not only behaviour, but factors such as dress codes. The clothes young people wear (currently, hooded tops) may symbolize ASB.
- ASB also includes criminal behaviour and behaviour that any civilized person would find unacceptable.

Second, the government's emphasis on ASB is full of contradictions.

- When ASB legislation was passed into law the New Labour government at that time was concerned with addressing poverty and neglect amongst young people.
- At the same time, ASBOs were being used to target young people. Rather than having their problems addressed, young people were at greater risk of being labelled as criminals.

Third, the ASB agenda tends to concentrate mainly on the individual offender, and as a result it ignores wider social and economic factors (Cook, 2006).

■ The thinking behind ASBOs is an example of being tough on crime. ASBOs can be used to coerce people to conform to wider expectations about behaviour.
■ A consequence of paying too much attention to controlling the people who act antisocially is that the wider socioeconomic causes of this behaviour are not addressed.

Finally, the civil standard of proof effectively opens a back door to criminal conviction (Hopkins Burke and Morrill, 2004: 236).

■ The ASBO is a civil order, which means that antisocial persons are not necessarily arrested and read their rights before an ASBO is served on them. They are also not required to attend the court for a hearing.
■ If an 'offender' does not comply with this order there is a law enforcement sanction.
■ As a result, civil law can be used as a crime reduction tool.

CONCLUSION

This chapter has introduced some of the different sources of crime data, drawing attention to both quantitative and qualitative forms. Since the election of the first New Labour government in 1997 there has been a commitment to open government, and the student of criminology is nowadays inundated with crime data. Before moving on to the next chapter, you must visit the Home Office website to familiarize yourself with the type of statistical data that is readily available.

FURTHER READING

An essential starting point for information about crime is the Home Office website: www.homeoffice.gov.uk. Visit this link and locate the relevant sections on crime statistics and the British Crime Survey. It is possible to access and download many documents, which can either be printed off or saved on your PC.

An excellent introduction to crime data is C. Coleman and J. Moynihan, *Understanding Crime Data: Haunted by the dark figure* (Milton Keynes: Open University Press, 1996). There is a discussion about sources of crime data, including the BCS, in L. Koffman, *Crime Surveys and Victims* (Cardiff: University of Wales Press, 1996). For a more advanced account of crime surveys read P. Mayhew, 'Researching the state of crime: local, national, and international victim surveys', in R. King and E. Wincup (eds), *Doing Research on Crime and Justice* (Oxford: Oxford University Press, 2000).

STUDY QUESTIONS

1. Describe the main features of:
   a) quantitative crime data
   b) qualitative crime data.
   Write a case supporting the use of both of these sources of data.
2. What are the main statistical sources of information about crime? Using the index of Coleman and Moynihan (1996) to help you, answer these questions below:
   a) Describe the main differences between the sources of information.
   b) Identify the strengths and weaknesses of the sources of information.
3. What is meant by the 'dark figure' of crime?
4. How useful is the British Crime Survey for understanding the relationship between crime and social divisions?
5. This task is more tricky and it may be necessary to seek advice from your tutor. Visit the Home Office website (www.homeoffice.gov.uk) and search for statistical information about a type of crime of your choice (such as homicide or burglary). Write a summary of what this statistical information tells you. Also discuss what it does not tell you.

4 Understanding Crime Data II: Methods of Data Collection

OVERVIEW

The aim of this chapter is to provide:

- an outline of the different methods used by criminologists to collect crime data
- an introduction to the basic principles used to set research questions and formulate hypotheses
- a description of the main qualitative research methods, including interviews and the ethnographic approach
- a discussion of the uses of quantitative research methods, including the use of questionnaires and surveys and a brief acknowledgement of SPSS
- an explanation of the significance of sampling for criminological research.

INTRODUCTION

It is necessary to introduce not only the various sources of crime data, but also the different methods criminologists use to collect crime data. To complement Chapter 3, the emphasis in this chapter is on some of the methods that tend to be used to obtain and interpret quantitative and qualitative data. Bearing in mind that undergraduate students frequently undertake mini-research projects as part of their studies, there is a discussion of the relative pros and cons of using different sources of data and research methods. There is no attempt to explain the technical issues involved in analysing research data: the aim instead is to outline some of the key themes and principles related to organizing the collection of empirical data.

This chapter asks what is meant by criminological research. This may appear self-evident, but the rationale underpinning the activity needs to be made explicit, and this is done by focusing on the issue of research design, and in particular the setting of the research question and the hypothesis or hypotheses. After fixing this initial starting point, researchers need to decide on the type of data they wish to gather, for example either qualitative or quantitative. This will have an immediate bearing on the research methods selected.

Chapter 3 showed that qualitative researchers are interested in looking for non-numerical data, and the methods they use will reflect this. According to this view of the social world there is little point in looking for causal links between social phenomena, because society only exists as an outcome of meaningful interaction between social actors. Subsequently it is the social actor who is most suitably positioned to define society. Research to validate society involves working towards creating mutually respectful dialogues between the researcher and the researched, in the form of qualitative data. Conversely, quantitative criminologists draw on methods that enable them to produce statistical information. Society is seen to be a system made up of social phenomena that are linked together as part of a causal chain. An external observer who has expertise in understanding causality in social environments best defines the nature of society. Testing hypotheses in light of quantitative data collected according to rigorous methods validates any claims made about society. In contrast to qualitative researchers, then, quantitative investigators are looking for an objectivist rather than subjectivist viewpoint. The construction of meaning is secondary to the search for data that gives reliability and comparability, and for data that can be aggregated. Above all, the aim is to formulate concepts that are measurable on the basis of indicators and variables.

The chapter has four strands.

- The process of setting research questions is outlined.
- Those methods preferred by qualitative researchers are considered, in particular the use of interviews and ethnographic approaches.
- Social surveys and questionnaires are introduced. These are tools favoured by researchers who are inspired by the quantitative tradition.
- There is a discussion of an important concept in social scientific research, sampling. In doing social research it is not possible to look at everything that is relevant to a topic. Most researchers look at a microcosm or a small part of a particular social phenomenon, but many hope that their findings will be representative of wider trends.

SETTING RESEARCH QUESTIONS AND FORMULATING HYPOTHESES

This section:

- describes what is meant by the terms 'research question' and 'hypothesis'
- considers research as a process.

The first point to note is that research design and data collection are not the same thing. It is not possible for researchers to collect any data without at least some idea, however vague, of what they are looking for. There must be some initial thought and groundwork. There are two main approaches, deductive and inductive. *Deductive* research refers to pre-existing ideas and theories, which are used to develop research questions, on the basis of which empirical work is undertaken. In contrast to this, *inductive* research starts with more of a blank canvas, where data is gathered and this in turn produces theory. The data collection thus follows the setting of a research question, followed by the research design.

Data refers to the observations collected by a fieldworker, such as the answers to a questionnaire, or responses given in an interview. In quantitative research the data is generally in the form of numbers, while qualitative data tends to appear in a textual form.

The research process

There are five key stages in this process, and all criminological researchers follow a similar course.

- The first stage begins with a research question or a hypothesis.
- Second, there is the selection of appropriate data collection methods.
- Third, the researcher will go out into the field to collect the data.
- Following this stage, it is necessary to analyse and test the data in light of the original hypothesis.
- The research process ends with drawing some conclusions, and an evaluation or appraisal of what has been achieved and areas where further work needs to be done.

Setting a research question

At the outset of the process all criminologists ask themselves a fundamental question: what am I going to research? Although this may seem like a straightforward task, a researcher needs to spend considerable time getting this absolutely right, or the research might never take off, and even if it does it will in all likelihood never be finished satisfactorily. There are two types of research question: those that are researchable or doable, and those that are not.

First-year undergraduates are on the whole not required to carry out any research, but it is necessary to be aware of how criminologists set a research question which is sufficiently clear to enable them to arrive at some answers, however provisional and inconclusive.

To illustrate this part of the process a little more concretely, let us look at a sample research question: 'What is the cause of crime?' This is an interesting question, and the contents of this book go some way towards addressing it. However it is not necessarily a good research question, principally because it is too big and lacking in focus. As a result it would prove difficult to answer it without infinite time and resources. In the earlier chapters I explained that crime is a complex conceptual category, and there would be all kinds of problems in lumping together sometimes tenuously linked forms of behaviour. Offences committed against property (such as theft) are different from violent crimes committed against the person (like assault). Also an assault involving two young men fighting in a pub is very different from a sexual assault, such as a rape. This difficulty becomes much more apparent when the researcher looks for the cause of the crime. The causes of rape are likely to be different from causes of theft.

To cut to the chase, this sample question is too broad. Most criminological and common-sense thought would recognize that there is no single cause of crime. A better, or more doable, research question would be narrower, and it is usually very specific. Rather than asking 'What is the cause of crime?' the question could be revised to 'Why do men commit rape'? or 'Why do people commit the act of theft?' However, these questions are still quite broad, and might still cause problems. For this reason it may be appropriate to have some related subquestions. For instance, it would not be surprising if there was found to be more than one factor accounting for the involvement of men in rape. Subquestions could consider the age of the men committing this crime, or the relationship between men committing rape and their consuming drugs or alcohol. There are many possibilities, but researching a question about rape is much more manageable and ultimately doable than the big question about the causes of crime in general.

Beyond setting a research question, it is also obligatory to formulate a hypothesis.

The hypothesis

A hypothesis may be defined as a *statement of expected outcome*. It is a rudimentary proposition concerning the relationship between variables. Prior to describing a hypothesis, a researcher must be clear about what is meant by the term *variable*. In simple terms, a variable is 'a particular characteristic upon which a group varies'. A variable is also a way of measuring a concept. If a criminologist were to distribute a survey to her colleagues to find out about their experiences of crime (the concept), she would try to measure this using a variable, such as 'Yes (I have been a victim of crime)' or 'No (I have not been a victim of crime)'. There are two main types of variable, *independent* and *dependent*. Briefly, an independent variable is one that causes something to happen, while a dependent variable is something that is caused to happen (as a result of the independent variable). So the answer to yes/no question (have you been a victim of crime?) might form the independent variable, and it could lead on to a question that produces a dependent variable, such as the answer to 'On a scale of 1 to 5, how worried are you about being a victim of crime?'

Now let us return to the hypothesis. Researchers interested in obtaining quantitative data express a hypothesis through a formula such as $X \Rightarrow Y$. In plain English this means the researcher is expecting to find that X causes Y. The research will consist of obtaining data, then analysing it to see whether there is any statistical association between these variables. There are several possible relationships between the variables. As noted above, X (the independent variable) may be the cause of Y (the dependent variable) (which is stated as $X \Rightarrow Y$). Alternatively it could be the other way around, and Y turns out to be the independent variable which is the cause of X (the dependent variable) (i.e. $Y \Rightarrow X$). To complicate the situation slightly the research might uncover another variable – an *intervening variable* – which can be called A. The formula would then become: $X \Rightarrow A \Rightarrow Y$. Alternatively the data analysis might show that both X and Y are related to A. Forgetting A for a minute, it may turn out that there is a spurious or false relationship between X and Y, so neither one causes the other.

A hypothesis is different from a research question in three main ways.

■ A hypothesis is more specific than a research question because it identifies variables.

■ A single research question is likely to generate more than one hypothesis.

■ A hypothesis refers to a population (see page 118) and situation to which the results of a study could be extended.

In sum, the planning of a research project, whatever its scale and size involves the following stages. A research question and one or more hypotheses are first identified. This is followed by the identification of concepts, variables and appropriate measuring instruments. Data is needed to provide information about the variables.

Finally, there are two other key concepts that influence the research process, reliability and validity. *Reliability* refers to the degree of consistency in the measurement of a concept. Put another way, it is a matter of stability: when researchers use a concept, they need to use it in the same way to ensure that they are measuring the same thing. *Validity* determines, in a nutshell, whether a concept measures what it claims to measure. One aspect of validity is *measurement validity:* this assesses whether the way in which a concept is measured actually reflects the concept. (These are brief definitions, obviously, and you can expect to learn much more on this topic when you study research methods in depth.)

You may also come across the terms *internal* and *external validity*. Internal validity refers to the extent to which a research finding shows that there is a causal relationship between two variables. External validity concerns whether or not the findings of a particular piece of research can be extended beyond the immediate context in which the research was conducted. These are technical questions that have a bearing on all criminological research, although they have only been touched upon here.

RESEARCH QUESTIONS AND HYPOTHESES: KEY POINTS

■ There are certain rules that researchers need to observe.

■ Questions and hypotheses need to be focused to ensure that they are researchable.

■ Research considers the relationship between dependent and independent variables.

■ Researchers expect certain things to occur during their research, but the world is an unpredictable and uncertain place, so questions and hypotheses may be refined and revised.

Now we need to look at qualitative and quantitative methods of collecting data.

QUALITATIVE RESEARCH METHODS

The purpose of this section is to:

■ review some of the qualitative methods most widely used by criminological researchers

■ introduce the interview method, including structured, semi-structured and unstructured interviews
■ introduce ethnographic research techniques
■ introduce the main methods of quantitative research, including the use of SPSS, different types of variables and questionnaires
■ discuss the issue of sampling in criminological research.

Interviewing: an overview

Many criminological researchers have used interviewing as a method of gathering evidence. Like all research methods there are variations on a theme, and there are four main types of interview: structured, semi-structured, unstructured and focus group. It is helpful to look at the three main types of interview as points along a continuum:

structured ⇒ semi-structured ⇒ unstructured

Interviews tend to involve two individuals, an interviewer and an interviewee, whereas focus groups involve more: possibly two people in an interviewer-type role, and a group of respondents.

The structured interview

The name of this type of interview gives a clear clue about what is involved. The interview schedule, or the list of questions asked of an interviewee, will be all agreed prior to the interview being arranged. The person conducting the interview (the interviewer) is required to ask each person interviewed (the interviewees) the same questions, as far as possible in the same manner. The interviewer needs to adopt a standardized approach to ensure that all respondents are asked exactly the same questions, and the interviews must be handled as far as possible in the same way. For example, the layout of the room and the type of interaction between the researcher and the interviewee should be similar. The purpose of structured interviews is to obtain simple and descriptive information, which sometimes errs on the side of being quantitative rather than qualitative.

Structured interviews are commonly used as part of the survey method. For instance, the British Crime Survey (see Chapter 3) uses this type of interview to find out the number of times an individual has been the victim of a crime in the previous 12 months. The data produced by structured interviews tends to be easily interpreted. Using the crime survey as an example, it is possible to find out the number of times an individual has been the victim of a violent crime, or the number of occasions he or she has reported crimes of which he/she was the victim to the police. The data produced may be numerical and quantitative, or it might involve simple verbal responses, such as answering in the positive or negative.

Responses of this type often tell the researcher little about the subjective experience of victimization. Being a victim of violent crime is experienced in diverse ways. Some of the differences in experience might become apparent if variables such as age and gender are considered, although even these factors do not show the meanings attached to the lived experience. Do young men feel the same about becoming victims of violent crime as elderly women? The data churned out from structured interviews cannot always provide adequate answers, so there is arguably a need for less structured interviewing.

Some criticisms of structured interviews

Various philosophical arguments for relying less on structured interviews have been advanced by advocates of the interpretivist qualitative approach. According to this perspective, structured interviews actually lead to the distortion of the lived experience of the respondents, because the meaning they attach to a given social phenomenon is channelled into the over-rigid and too narrow categories created by researchers. As a corollary of this, the meanings a social actor attaches to specific phenomena are not reflected in the data collected. Facts and figures tend to provide a partial and fractured view of human existence. Interpretivists also do not agree that hard statistical data is value-neutral, in the sense that the facts speak for themselves.

Semi-structured and unstructured interviewing

These types of interview are principally concerned with producing data that is more qualitative than that produced by structured interviews. It is an approach that enables the researcher to build up a more in-depth impression of the views people hold about a social issue. Unlike structured interviews, semi-structured interviews allow more flexibility for the researcher, and he/she may carry out additional interviews to follow up a topic. This is not possible with a structured interview approach, because it means leaving behind the standardization that is core to the structured approach.

The main difference is that respondents or interviewees are given more autonomy and space to express their own attitudes and feelings more freely. These approaches do not jettison altogether the strategies used in structured interviews, as it is possible to combine closed with more open questions. For example, it is not uncommon for a semi-structured interview to include closed questions to obtain background information such as sex/gender and age, and snippets of factual information.

For example, a researcher might be investigating the influence of sexist discrimination and its effects on the career progression of police officers (Silvestri, 2003). It would be quite reasonable to expect different people to hold diverse views on this, and closed questions alone would not, in all likelihood, result in a revealing set of answers. However, it makes sense to include closed questions to obtain information about respondents' sex and age, and their length of career in this case. These would then need to be supplemented with open-ended questions that allow the research subjects to say more about their lived experience. These questions offer room for more in-depth and descriptive replies. Respondents are able to use their own words and tell the researcher how they see things. It creates space for them to articulate their attitudes, feelings and experiences.

Now let us look more closely at unstructured and semi-structured interviews.

Unstructured interviews

The unstructured interview is, for many qualitative researchers, an 'ideal' research method, as in a sense it gives them a licence to ask a person anything they wish, and there are no necessary constraints or restrictions on what can be said. This style of interviewing is often described as naturalistic. Unlike other methods, especially quantitative ones, researchers make no attempt to control the research environment. They ensure as far as is practicable and ethical that interviewees are in their own world, and that what they have to say is not unduly influenced by the researcher. In ideal circumstances an unstructured interview can be viewed as autobiographical, in as much as respondents can tell their own story at a particular moment, producing a narrative or storyline that is as detailed as the interviewee desires it to be.

In enabling the interviewee to 'tell it as it is', the researcher is relatively passive. The openness and spontaneity of an interview mean that the criminologist cannot impose artificial coherence on the data, and that any preconceptions the researcher has may be unfounded.

However, this 'ideal' methodology is not without its own problems. At a practical level it can produce a rather unwieldy data set, making the task of interpreting the data difficult. Because of this problem researchers may use an unstructured interview as precursor to a more structured method of data collection, hence the semi-structured interview. This is arguably the better method of interviewing for many qualitative researchers.

Semi-structured interviews

These are less formal than the structured interview method, but more formalized than the unstructured style. Researchers normally have quite clear ideas about what they are looking for, and a specific agenda. Interviewers have preselected several themes they wish to examine, and these feature in an interview guide. The guide may be seen as a framework, with a list of key questions designed to explore common themes, although there is also an opportunity for interviews to follow up ideas.

For example, say a researcher is interested in asking a group of criminal justice professionals, such as chief constables, about the influence of political values on police policy making (Reiner, 1991). Questions could be asked at a fairly general and abstract level, making it possible for the chief constables to express their own views without feeling pressured to pursue a particular line.

The semi-structured interview does let respondents answer in a way that they choose. Despite this freedom some initial parameters are set by the interview guide, limiting the scope of the research at least to some degree. The results are a set of responses that are easier to interpret than the outputs of an unstructured interview, and while interviewees are not given absolute freedom, they are free to express their own perceptions within some predefined boundaries.

You might think that an interview is basically a conversation, and anyone can do it. But conducting a decent interview is not a straightforward task, and successful interviewing is dependent on the interviewer having well-developed skills. Unlike a conversation, interviews have aims and objectives, a rationale and a purpose. A researcher has consciously gone into the field to find out something. Conversations may be used to the same end, but on the whole we converse with family and friends for many reasons, and the instrumental and utilitarian requirements of the social scientist do not explicitly influence everyday social interaction. Also, with the exception of some unstructured interviews, interviews do have more of a structure than a conversation. Conversations can meander and flow in many interconnected directions, with no clear beginning, middle or end. Even the most unstructured interview is not without an end, and there are certain assumptions governing it, if only the amount of time a respondent is prepared to give up to speak to an interviewer.

Although there are clear differences between an interview and a conversation, in some ways a conversation can provide an important template. Both interviews and conversations are dependent on trust. In criminological research this is very important, because an offender, victim or professional is likely to be talking about private and personal matters. Rather like talk between friends, it is understood that the contents of any conversation are not the business of anyone other than those immediately involved. Indeed, for ethical reasons many researchers ensure interview data is anonymized, so the consumers of research are not able to attribute views and opinions to particular named persons. Interviewers need to be aware of this need for trust, not only for ethical reasons but also to make sure interviewees feel sufficiently comfortable to open up and be honest about what they are thinking. When people engage in conversation with friends, most people are sensitive to the needs of the person with whom they are communicating. If, for example, you are talking to a friend and something you say appears to upset him or her, you would treat this as a cue to change the course of the chat. Similarly, an interviewer needs to be sensitive to any reactions from respondents that indicate they are inappropriately perturbed by a question.

I referred above to friendship, and this is another crucial consideration when carrying out an interview. It is not unusual for researchers to feel warmth towards the people they interview, and it is not impossible for a researcher to start to chat, as if to a real friend. This raises issues about the degree of involvement a researcher has with those being researched, and the extent to which detachment and an objective distance should be kept. Again, the subject matter of criminology makes it particularly necessary to maintain a distance, but in wider contexts too it is not good social science to turn an interview carried out for academic reasons into an informal discussion. Even those qualitative researchers who embrace subjectivity are required to remain objective and to keep their personality separate from the research project and the researched subject.

The twin themes of subjectivity and objectivity are also relevant in relation to exploitation. It can be argued that some interviewers take advantage of their respondents, exploiting their knowledge and experience without giving them anything in return. Even worse, the interview situation can be used to degrade and dehumanize an interviewee. If objectivity is not treated as important, researchers can impose their own world-view on the interview and the outcome. In other words, the methods can be used in such a way that they bring about a change in the research subject.

This is still more vital an issue when power is brought into the equation. Power is a complex concept, but for the purpose of this discussion we can think of a researcher as having power in several senses. First, the researcher is the one asking the questions that he or she (or a research centre or government department) has set. Second, respondents may be obliged or even compelled to respond to questions an interviewer asks because of their professional status. If an interviewee is speaking to vulnerable groups, such as prisoners, they will have to give their consent to be interviewed, but even so in most cases the interviewer is in a more powerful position than the respondent.

Interviewers tend to be disproportionately white, middle class and university educated, whereas especially if the research is looking at offenders, the respondents are likely to be lower class, possibly from a minority ethnic group, and lacking basic key skills such as literacy and numeracy. This clearly places the interviewee at a relative disadvantage, and again this can create room for exploitation. Some qualitative researchers are sensitive to this, and those using unstructured interviews do indeed give some space for the researched to assert their authority or influence over the situation. However, it is still the case that the researcher decides the questions that are asked, and at a later stage when reproducing the interview transcript, he or she has an opportunity to edit and interpret the data that has been gathered.

An important skill required of any researcher using interviews is *self-reflexivity*. In plainer English this means researchers must analyse their own position and general world-view in relation to the research they are involved in and their method of doing it. In particular they need to be aware of the power relations existing between the researcher and researched, and the factors that make them different. If for instance the researcher is a white middle-class male, the impact of this on the respondent needs to be considered. The social status of researchers can influence both how they apply the interview method and their interpretation of the data.

Focus groups

Like interviews these are used as a source of qualitative data, and they are often used together with other research methods. Their origins can be found in market research. Focus groups are normally formed of individuals with specific common characteristics. For example, a crime reduction partnership (see Chapter 10) may wish to explore the fear of crime among pensioners living in local authority housing, so these are the focus group members they would bring together. Rather than being spoken to on a one-to-one basis, the focus group members are interviewed collectively. Focus groups are coordinated and managed by a facilitator and moderator. Usually the facilitator asks the questions and the moderator makes sure the responses are tape recorded, or takes notes.

What do focus groups achieve? They generate information that is based on collective rather than individual views. As there are many views being expressed, there are likely to be many uncertainties and ambiguities. The moderator will often explore those uncertainties by asking further questions to assess the degree of disagreement between those involved. On many occasions it proves to be more a difference of emphasis than a difference of opinion, and by the end of the focus group there tend to be normative understandings, or if there is a diversity of views, each view is shared by several members of the focus group. This is not because the researchers have manipulated what has been said: rather they have assessed the ambiguities that reflect both substantial and superficial differences.

INTERVIEWING: KEY POINTS

■ Interviews are a popular method of gathering data.

■ There are several different types of interview. Structured interviews produce data that may be quantifiable, such as yes/no responses, whereas unstructured and semi-structured interviews produce data that is more qualitative.

■ Interviews are sometimes compared to conversations, but the interviewer must observe strict methodological rules.

■ While interviews are widely used, one problem with them is that it is possible for the interviewer to affect the respondent's feelings and thoughts, and subsequently the quality of the data produced.

ETHNOGRAPHIC RESEARCH

This section:

■ outlines the ethnographic approach
■ considers the issues of reliability and validity
■ examines the benefits and some of the practical issues involved in doing this type of research.

Starting with the basics, what is ethnography? To answer this, it is helpful to look at some related terms. It is first and foremost a qualitative method that is interpretive. Ethnographic research is synonymous with certain variants of the case study approach, and with fieldwork based on participant observation. All of these terms are used in different ways over time by different researchers from different social science disciplines, including criminology (Hobbs and May, 1993).

There are several enduring questions that characterize ethnographic research:

■ Who are these people?
■ What is the situation?
■ What was the researcher doing there?
■ How did the researcher get access?
■ How did the researcher build up rapport?

Before looking at the potential uses of ethnography in criminological inquiry, it is necessary to introduce some of its philosophical and methodological assumptions. Ethnography is sometimes described as 'writing culture'. Among its main advantages in criminological research is the fact that it attempts to reflect the world-view of participants, who might for example be offenders (Hobbs, 1988, 1995), rank and file police officers (Holdaway, 1983) or nightclub bouncers (Winlow, 2001). The ethnographer has several strategies to employ in the field, such as observing, listening and 'knowing' the data. Crucially, the approach, its methods and the final product are *all* part of ethnography.

To understand more fully the fit between ethnography and qualitative research, we need to consider some key points. Like all qualitative research, ethnography aspires to reflect the views of participants through providing a description of the context or the social world the participants inhabit. Considerable attention is given to understanding the processes involved in the construction and shaping of the social world. There is recognition of the flexible nature of social reality, whereby the creativity of individual actors is recognized. Finally, data is of central importance to ethnographic researchers. Theory and concepts are embedded or grounded in data.

Ethnography, reliability and validity

Qualitative researchers approach validity and reliability in a way that is markedly different from quantitative researchers. In relation to ethnography, for instance, ethnographic research can be seen as having external reliability because it can be replicated, and internal reliability because of inter-observer consistency. Interval validity is achieved because there is a high degree of congruence between concepts and observations. However, the degree of external validity is rather low because of the lack of generalizability.

General principles of ethnography

The ethnographer is interested in describing and analysing everyday contexts. Data are acquired mostly by observing social activity and listening to conversations. Ethnography is perhaps the least structured, or most unstructured, approach to criminological investigation. Ethnography is normally based on a small number of cases or an in-depth study, and interpretation of the meanings social actors attach to reality. The material consists primarily of verbal descriptions, explanations and understandings.

Ethnography is more often than not an inductive rather than a deductive approach to research. It generally sets out to gather new and original data, and derive understanding and theoretical insight from the data amassed. However, ethnographic approaches such as participant observation can also be deductive and about theory testing.

Now that some of the ideas surrounding ethnography have been outlined, let us consider the practical issues involved in doing ethnographic research. The first consideration is, why ethnography? Is it the most appropriate research method to answer the research question set? A big question often asked by the ethnographer relates to whether the research should be covert or overt (that is, whether or not the participants realize they are being researched). There are questions of a more subtle nature too, such as what kind of data is needed to reflect the meanings of the participants.

The practicalities include the choice of site or sites where the research takes place. The availability of a site and the way of gaining access to it may be issues. Researchers' success in setting up the situation will have an impact on how they present themselves to the intended participants, and on the rapport they can build (Bryman, 2001: 114). The researched need to accept the researcher, and let him or her into their world, so the researcher can see how they live, talk to them about their lives, and maybe manage to be treated as a member of the group.

Perhaps the most significant issue is deciding whether the research is to be covert or overt (Bell, 1969). Most, but by no means all, research is undertaken overtly, so the researched are aware that a researcher is physically present.

Overt research

This has a number of advantages, but it also presents some problems. Among the strengths is the ability for the researcher to ask questions outright by interviewing participants, and taking notes if appropriate. The research process runs smoothly because researchers are honest about their status and do not have to maintain any pretence. From an ethical perspective, it is useful and desirable for the researched to give their informed consent to the researcher. This does not overcome, but minimizes, the potential for the researcher to exploit the researched.

However, unfortunately overt research faces the problem of reactivity. Because people know they are being studied, they may adapt their behaviour, perhaps to the extent that they behave in a way that is totally different from their normal behaviour. It is also quite likely that the researcher will not have access to all situations. This is especially apparent for criminal justice researchers looking at ethically sensitive and politically contentious issues.

Covert research

This also has its pros and cons. A major advantage is that if the researcher behaves as 'one of us', he or she might also come to be treated as a member of the group being studied. The fact that the fieldworker is fully participating in the routines of social life makes it more likely that the researched will behave naturally. Covert research is also often the best – or indeed the only – way to find out some things, especially in areas that are inaccessible for many researchers. An example of this is an empirical study by Holdaway (1983). The author explored the existence of an occupational culture among rank and file police officers (see Chapter 6), and did so by actually becoming a serving police officer. For most of the study, the officers Holdaway worked alongside were unaware of his dual status as a police officer *and* an academic researcher. He was able to observe the activities of his colleagues in a way that would have been impossible for a researcher who was not a member of the police service. However eventually the people with whom Holdaway was working realized that he was different in some way from them, and he then had to terminate his fieldwork.

All research methods have drawbacks, and ethnography is no exception. Participant researchers have to live out a role within a setting, which may involve their being put in a difficult and compromising position. For example a criminological researcher who becomes a member of a criminal gang might witness, or be pressured to commit, illegal activity. Research carried out by Winlow (2001) illustrates this. He used his insider status as a bouncer to gain access to the working environment of this group. Not surprisingly it is a violent world, and Winlow was put in a position where he faced and had to use violence, with all the risks attached to it. The end of his involvement in this research came when he expressed concern about the near-fatal beating of a man he witnessed. This was not an acceptable thing to do in that particular world, and his cover was almost blown.

Another potential problem is that the researcher might be put in actual danger should his or her covert identity be uncovered. (This would compromise the research too, as Winlow (2001) discovered.) As well as these practical issues, there is an ethical dimension to this kind of research. Because the researcher is acting covertly, those being researched are not in a position to give their informed consent. They might justifiably regard this as a form of exploitation or breach of confidentiality.

Access

Access to a research environment can be a problem, in both closed and open settings. Job situations tend to be relatively closed. It is difficult for students of criminal justice and criminology to undertake ethnographic work in the police service or the courts. Of course it is possible for some students to work in these environments, perhaps on voluntary work experience or a temporary basis, but this might not give them the access that is hoped for, and to take advantage of this kind of position to do covert research is generally regarded as ethically questionable.

'Open' situations include, for example, observing a street corner gang (Whyte, 1983) or firm of football hooligans (Armstrong, 1993, 1998), but there are risks attached if the researcher's identity is not kept secret. More than that, most universities will not allow students to do any empirical research with offenders for ethical reasons, and also because of health and safety considerations.

The negotiation of access is a highly complicated activity, and is fraught with all kinds of moral and practical difficulties. It is not simply a case of identifying a site; the problem is also to speak to the right people. Contacting a sympathetic person is crucial for facilitating access. The key people who can provide access are known as *gatekeepers*: it is essential to identify and cultivate them, in order to open up opportunities as a researcher (Whyte, 1983).

Level of involvement

We touched on the level of the researcher's involvement in outlining the Holdaway (1983) and Winlow (2001) examples, but a few additional points need to be made. Ethnographic research is based on different degrees of involvement, which may be best understood as a continuum. At one end there is the active participant and at the other the passive observer. The active participant becomes completely immersed in the field, and at the level of surface appearances there is nothing to separate the researcher from her/his subjects. Other criminologists become 'observational participants' who hold on to their role as a researcher more firmly, by acting as observers. They may also participate in the activities observed, but not fully: they retain some detachment. 'Participatory observers' are more interested in participating in the social world they inhabit, but again they keep their distance in their capacity as an observer. At the other end of the continuum there is the 'complete observer'. This is often not considered to be a form of participant observation at all, because there is no interaction with others in the setting (Bryman, 2001).

These are ideal types, and real situations tend to be more complex than they might suggest. As Gans (1968) has observed, it is possible for the status of the researcher to vary as a research study continues, so at times he or she might act as a 'total participant', 'researcher participant' and 'total researcher'.

Taking notes

The tools used in ethnographic research include a notepad, tape recorder and computer. The ultimate aim of any research method is to gather data, and ethnography is no different. The method most commonly used is note taking, of which there are three main types. Fieldworkers may make *mental notes,* storing in their memory details of what they have witnessed and writing this up at a later date. This approach is likely to be adopted by a covert researcher who is not in a position to let his or her status be known. Mental notes are not likely to be particularly reliable and valid, because there is no scope for verification or replication. However, sometimes the end of gathering obscure and difficult knowledge may justify the means.

Second, a practical solution to the problem of over-relying on memory is *scratch-notes*. Here researchers temporarily absent themselves from a research setting to make (often rather rudimentary) notes. For example, a researcher studying gang members might try to write up notes when he goes to the toilet, the most private place where he is least likely to be followed. This approach is more likely to produce reliable data, but there are other problems. However discreet the researcher is, the activity might cause suspicion: why is this guy using a cubicle rather than a urinal, for instance?

Finally, *full field notes* tend to be compiled by an overt observer of a social setting. Here the researcher has much more time to produce a record of what is going on, and because the researcher's presence is seen as legitimate and accepted by the group being studied, there is no need to be secretive and there is less pressure on the researcher.

Some criticisms of the ethnographic approach

Perhaps one of the most serious criticisms levelled at ethnographic research, and one of the issues ethnographic researchers need to bear in mind at all times, is the danger of 'going native'. The phrase refers to the tendency for researchers to act like (or perhaps even come to think like) the people they are studying. To some extent this is unavoidable for researchers in an occupational environment, such as a serving police officer studying other serving police officers (Holdaway, 1983), but in other cases too it is possible for researchers to do things that they normally would not do. Researchers need to understand the people they study, and it is only a small step from understanding to empathy, and from empathy to identification. The researcher might take on, assume and assimilate the concepts and theories of his or her research subjects.

All researchers are to some extent susceptible to 'doing things' and 'thinking like' the people they are studying, and this is not necessarily a major problem, but it does become so when this is all that a researcher thinks and does. This is what 'going native' means. At all times ethnographers must 'come back' to academic concepts and theories in order to present their work to their peers.

Ethnographic research is not just about the expansion of academic research, and some ethnographers have acted as 'brokers' between different cultures or groups. It is quite conceivable for researchers to think and express themselves in a meaningful way to their academic colleagues as well as participants in the research.

ETHNOGRAPHIC RESEARCH: KEY POINTS

- This approach belongs to the interpretivist tradition of social scientific research, and the aim is to ensure that the data produced by research is consistent with the views of the researched population.
- Ethnographic research may be done covertly or overtly, which means that the researched population may either be unaware or aware that they are being researched.
- Ethnographic researchers need to be aware of their status as researchers, which sometimes may become compromised. Some researchers 'go native' and start to think and act like the group they are researching.

QUANTITATIVE RESEARCH

Now that the main qualitative methods have been outlined, we move the focus to quantitative methods, beginning with a quick overview of statistics and the main methods used to gather this type of data, and looking too at questionnaires and surveys. This section:

- talks about statistical methods
- introduces SPSS
- discusses variable values, including categorical and continuous variables
- outlines different types of questionnaire and survey.

Quantitative research is a topic many students find difficult, mainly because it involves mathematics and statistics. Indeed quantitative criminological research *is* complicated, but at this introductory level only the basics are sketched. It was demonstrated in Chapter 3 that statistical data is a source of information frequently used by many criminological researchers to produce explanations of crime. For that reason, students are expected to have some understanding of research based on statistical evidence and explanation, if not at this stage of the actual statistical techniques used. Later in your studies you will need to explore the methods used to perform and evaluate quantitative research.

Quantitative research is carried out to gather a structured data set, which is then subjected to statistical tests. There is no need to be too daunted by the word 'statistics': it simply refers to a mathematical toolkit applied by criminologists, which enables them to arrange numerical data in a way that can answer questions and test theories (Bryman, 2001).

Beyond this general definition, statistical analysis has five main aims.

■ Statistical data is used in order to make comparisons between groups of people who share the same characteristics. For instance, a criminologist may be interested in examining the number of crimes reported to the police by people in specific geographical areas. The statistical data might show that a particular housing estate or cluster of streets has a higher than average number of crimes recorded.
■ Statistical analysis is used to identify trends. To take the previous example, the researcher might go on to see whether there are any changes in the number of crimes reported to the police over a period of time, such as one or five years.
■ Statistical analysis is widely used as a method of identifying causal links between two or more variables. In this example, it might be possible to show that two variables, housing tenure and social class, account for the differential reporting of crime.
■ A major aim of statistical analysis is to make generalized statements about groups of people and their behaviour. For example, the data could show that there is a relationship between social class and housing tenure, and the reporting of crime to the police.
■ The underlying rationale is for criminologists to make a causal inference from statistical data, to enable then to make predictions about future behaviour.

SPSS

If you are studying for a degree in the social sciences, you are highly likely to be required to do some statistical analysis using a personal computer. Among the most widely used tools is the 'Statistical Package for the Social Sciences' known as SPSS. This package is periodically revised to make it more sophisticated and user-friendly, but the organizing statistical principles remain unaltered. At the most fundamental level SPSS enables students to operationalize concepts and theories. The package lets researchers manipulate variables and produce data matrices, even if they are not expert mathematicians.

In essence a data matrix is a table of results. It is used:

■ to categorize answers
■ to find relationships between different variables
■ as a basis for the statistical manipulation of data.

A data matrix is sometimes described as a variable by case table. This means that it comprises variables, variable attributes and cases (units of analysis). Each case (in this context, each person studied) is a unit of analysis, and each *type* of information about that case is a variable. Each *piece* of information about the person forms an *attribute* attached to the variable. So the variable might, for instance, be age, and the attribute for an individual case might be '16–18 years'.

Research using statistics is all about facts and figures which are generated from a questionnaire or other type of survey. This provides data that is suitable for inputting into a data matrix. SPSS also churns out statistical data into various formats, including frequency tables and graphs.

Variable values

In a survey or questionnaire a respondent will be presented with a range of questions requiring an answer. Each answer to these different questions (that is, each attribute of a variable) is given a value. This value may be of mathematical significance, like a person's age. Alternatively it is possible to allocate numbers to answers as a form of 'code', where there is no mathematical significance attached. For instance, 'lives in a town' might be designated '1', and 'lives in the country' might be designated '2'. There is no mathematical relationship here between the 1 and 2, as there is between the ages 16 and 18; they are just symbols used. It is important that non-numerical data are coded in this way so that statistical interpretation is possible. We shall come back to coding once we have discussed the differences between types of variable.

In this context we can classify variables in two ways, *categorical* and *continuous*.

Categorical variables

Categorical variables, as implied by the terminology, are those that fit into social scientific categories such as class and sex. These categories were discussed in Chapter 2. While a category such as social class does not provide a perfect method of classifying people, it is generally quite useful. Of course, there are fewer potential values for the 'sex' variable: any individual will either be male or female.

Continuous variables

Continuous variables are those that can take any value within a range, and not just discrete values such as '1' or '3'. Age and income might be thought of as fitting into this category. A person's age can be measured in years, but also in months, days, or even minutes, creating a virtually continuous spectrum of possibilities. However, continuous spans are not easy to work with statistically, and often the continuous spectrum of potential values is grouped into ranges. Allocation to one of these ranges then creates a set of categorical data (for instance, 0–10 years, 11–20 years; £0–10,000, £11–20,000).

To complicate things further, there is another distinction you need to bear in mind, between *ordinal* and *nominal* data. Nominal data are data given in numeric form, but with no inherent ranked value. For instance, a researcher might wish to explore the factors motivating a person to steal, and ask this question accordingly:

Which of the following points best describes why you stole?

1. To buy food.
2. To buy clothing.
3. To pay household bills (gas, electricity, council tax etc.).
4. To pay off debts.
5. To buy drugs.
6. To deposit in a bank account.
7. Other (please specify).

There is no attempt to rank these categories, so that number 7 is in some way 'bigger' than number 1; they are just codes, as we discussed above. In contrast, ordinal data is presented in a way that implies there *is* some ranking. However, the differences between the categories are not necessarily directly quantifiable. Take the following example:

When you were a burglar, how often did you offend?

1. Every day.
2. 4–6 days a week.
3. 2–3 days a week.
4. Once a week.
5. 2–3 times a month.
6. Once a month.
7. Less than once a month.

Clearly these are listed in a specific sequence, but the sequence is not a straight numeric sequence, so point 4 is not exactly half-way between point 1 and point 7.

SPSS presents nominal and ordinal data in bar charts and pie charts.

Continuous variables can also be placed on what is known as a *ratio or interval scale*. In this instance they *must be* real numerical values, and the same interval *must* exist between the cases. This means, of course, that it is possible to carry out a wider range of statistical operations on the data.

QUESTIONNAIRES AND SURVEYS

This section:

■ introduces questionnaires, focusing in particular on self-completion questionnaires
■ considers the design of questionnaires
■ identifies the features of both 'good' and 'bad' questionnaires
■ considers how questionnaire data are measured
■ acknowledges some of the limitations of questionnaires.

A research method utilized by many quantitative criminologists is the questionnaire. This section considers why they are so popular, and reviews the advantages and disadvantages of their use. It is shown that a common difficulty experienced by researchers is a poor response rate, although there are some precautions researchers can take to make sure this does not become an enduring problem.

Questionnaires often fall under the more general heading of *surveys*. Chapter 3 discussed the British Crime Survey (BCS), and this is one of the main types of criminological survey, but other surveys are used by many researchers for a variety of purposes. A significant number of criminology undergraduates employ surveys in their final-year dissertations or projects.

Generally speaking there are two types of questionnaire: those that are administered by a researcher (including the use of IT), and those that are self-administered or self-completed. The situations where surveys are used vary significantly. On one level they may appear to be remarkably similar to structured interviews, but as I shall explain they are actually rather different.

Self-completion questionnaires

By far the most widely used type of social survey is the self-completion questionnaire. This normally consists of a list of questions, each with a set of possible answers. The respondent is asked to choose an answer and tick the appropriate box. Usually the survey asks the respondent first to give basic information like his or her age and gender. This is followed by questions which might, for instance, ask respondents whether they agree or disagree with a statement, or ask them which of two alternatives they prefer. This method of data collection is popular for practical and methodological reasons. On a practical level the production of a survey is relatively cheap, amounting to the costs of printing it off and distributing it to the respondents. It is also a quick way of data collection. For experts who are skilled at survey design it does not take long at all to produce and distribute a questionnaire. Surveys are also relatively convenient for both researchers and respondents.

Two strong methodological justifications are used to argue that surveys are more reliable and valid than structured interviews. Because the questionnaire arrives in the hands of the respondent via snail mail (for a postal questionnaire) or electronic mail (e-mail, for an electronic survey) the respondent never meets the researcher. However well designed an interview schedule may be, there is always the chance that the interviewer will, however unintentionally, influence the responses of an interviewee, but there is no such risk for a self-completion questionnaire Also, when interviews are administered by a team of interviewers there is the possibility that their influence on the outcomes of research may be variable. Because the self-completion questionnaire is distributed in the same way to all respondents, there will be less researcher variability.

Questionnaires are not without their limitations, though. There are at least seven.

■ There is no one to prompt a potential respondent to fill in the survey. At least with an interviewer present there is human contact, and it tends to be more difficult for people to say no to participating in research if they have a person in front of them, than if they are facing a pamphlet with a basic covering letter.

■ The types of question are restricted, and the focus is necessarily on quantifiable data.

■ It is difficult to make sure the order of questions is right. The questions need to grab the interest of the respondent, and their relevance needs to be clear from the outset.

■ Because self-completion questionnaires are filled in without a researcher being present, nothing is known about the identity of the respondent.

■ At best the only data that will be gathered is that requested by the survey: no additional data will be amassed. It may be that informative and crucial data remains untapped.

■ Because there is no interviewer present, completion of all the questionnaire is dependent on the goodwill of the respondent. It is clear that many questionnaires are returned with data missing, and this affects the quality, and indeed reliability and validity, of the data analysis.

■ Perhaps most important is the damaging problem of the notoriously poor response rate to self-completion questionnaires. Basically it is possible to send out a perfectly well-designed questionnaire to several hundred addresses but get only a handful back. Even fewer are likely to be completed fully and properly. A low response rate can lead to a flawed piece of research, and as this is so important, most researchers anticipate the problem by taking a number of precautionary steps.

Improving poor response rates

How can response rates by improved? Many researchers devote considerable time and attention to drafting covering letters to 'sell' their research to potential respondents. A good letter will be pithy, to the point and polite, explaining the research objectives, and the importance of the respondent and his or her personal views. Researchers will try any trick, as long as it is ethical, to persuade respondents to participate. It is all but essential for the researcher to include a stamped addressed envelope to encourage a response. This is necessary because there is no reason for a respondent to pay for the privilege of completing an unsolicited survey to further the career of a criminologist. Including a stamped addressed envelope may subconsciously influence some people to respond because they do not want to waste the stamp. Similarly, some might feel guilt about not giving up their time to answer some questions in the interest of science.

Other simple but fundamental actions can be taken. The length of the questionnaire can be crucial: the larger and longer it is, the greater the likelihood of non-completion. It takes exceptional skill to produce a questionnaire that will obtain all the information needed over as few pages as possible. The instructions and layout need to be clear and comprehensible to the intended recipients. The wording of a survey targeting a professional group such as barristers would be different from one targeting the general population: barristers can be expected to understand complex language and instructions, while some members of the general public might find them difficult, and will need a simpler approach. It is also helpful to include some interesting questions. Even if the research is not on the most interesting of subjects, the questions could possibly be phrased in an interesting or attention-grabbing format and style. It is also not unknown for researchers to offer bribes or incentives, such as cash, novelty gifts, and a ticket for a prize draw to entice as many people to respond as possible.

Designing self-completion questionnaires

As noted above, a good design is essential. The questionnaire must have clear instructions, so readers are left in no doubt what the survey is about and what they are being asked to do. The main body of the questionnaire should be laid out clearly, so respondents know what boxes to tick. Both these considerations will affect the response rate and the quality of the information that is gathered.

Question type

The types of question appearing on a survey fall into various categories. There will be factual questions of a personal nature, such as the sex, age and ethnic group of the respondent. Respondents may be asked questions about other people. Other questions may refer to facts about which the informant is aware, possibly relating to the roles and responsibilities of a criminal justice professional. Questionnaires are not exclusively interested in facts, though, and there will be questions about attitudes and beliefs, and normative standards. For example, a survey may wish to explore public attitudes to the restoration of capital punishment. As well as asking people whether they would like to 'bring back hanging', the researchers might ask questions which ascertain their more general attitudes towards punishment, sometimes regarding specific types of offence (say, comparing burglary with paedophilia). Finally, a survey may be used to assess the knowledge a population has of a particular issue.

Some basic rules of questionnaire design

It must be made clear that designing a survey questionnaire is not necessarily straightforward, and that a researcher must observe some important rules. The questions on the survey must refer to the research issue, and should focus precisely on the relevant issues. It is, in short, necessary for researchers to decide exactly what they want to know.

It is important that each question is also very focused and that it concentrates on a single issue. The research topic as a whole might be phrased as a single question, but in the questionnaire it will be broken up to form what might be thought of as sub-questions. It is essential that the sub-questions are made distinctive, so there is no confusion between the questions. The data produced by the survey needs to be clear, and give answers that specifically address the issue they are supposed to address. If a question is especially complex, it may be necessary to break it up into different components or subquestions: the data will not be useful if respondents are confused or misled. In writing each question, the researcher must try to avoid using 'leading' wording. In other words, there must be no attempt, consciously or subconsciously, to influence the respondent into replying in a particular way.

It is also good practice to avoid the use of technical terms, especially in surveys addressing a lay (non-specialist) audience. For example, if a criminologist were exploring the experiences of repeat victimization among a population (see Chapter 2) it would not be good practice to ask a question like, 'Have you experienced repeat victimization in the last 12 months?' Most members of the public would not necessarily know what is meant by 'repeat victimization'. Alternatively they might pretend to understand it to avoid the embarrassment of appearing clueless or ignorant, but guess wrongly. Instead it is appropriate to ask a more straightforward and direct question. This one might be along the lines of, 'How many times have you been a victim of [a specific crime] in the last 12 months?'

Designing questionnaires takes a lot of practice over the course of many years, and it is worth giving some quick examples of good and bad practice in phrasing questions.

The main requirement is to be precise in the expressions and language used. A researcher asking about the frequency of cases of victimization would show bad and good practice in using these phrases:

Bad practice	**Good practice**
Very often	More than once a week
Quite often	Once a week
Not very often	Two or three times a month
Not at all	Once a month
	Once a year
	Less than once a year

The phrases on the left-hand side are too vague and imprecise: one person might interpret 'very often' as meaning 'more than once a week', while to another person it means 'at least once a year'. The phrases in the left-hand column are not perfect, but it is easier for respondents to tell what answer is needed.

A popular method of measuring responses is the Likert scale. On the surface it might look rather like the bad practice list above, but the difference is that it is used in cases when the answer is not easily quantified: for example, when respondents are asked to judge to what extent they agree with a statement. It provides a clearly numbered scale with a hierarchy of preferences:

Strongly agree = 5
Agree = 4
Undecided = 3
Disagree = 2
Strongly disagree = 1

QUESTIONNAIRES AND SURVEYS: KEY POINTS

■ This quantitative method is widely used by researchers to gather numerical data.
■ Many questionnaires are self-administered or completed by the respondent.
■ They are relatively cheap and straightforward to administer.
■ They are useful for discovering facts of a quantifiable nature.
■ Questionnaires are not without their limitations. For example:
  – the response rate can be low
  – they are not particularly good at capturing the subjective experience of respondents
  – quantitative data may be of limited use.

SAMPLING

In this section:

■ the principles underlying sampling procedures are introduced
■ the difference between probability and non-probability sampling is outlined.

Sampling: the issues

Sampling is a key concept in research methodology, and it is necessary to explain why this is so. An important consideration in any form of research, whether it is in the natural or social sciences, is the notion of *generalization*. This is also known as external validity, which refers to the extent to which the findings of a particular piece of research are relevant beyond the immediate context where the research was done. This has implications for the credibility of the conclusions arrived at. (We shall revisit this idea shortly.)

Sampling is concerned with four broad questions. First and most important, who or what is to be researched? Second, how is it to be researched? The third question concerns the number of people or things that are to be researched. Finally, how are they to be selected? These are big questions, and before they can be answered it is necessary to come to terms with some other key terms.

Essentially a sample is part of a whole, or what is called the *population*. The term 'population' in a lay sense is used for the number of people in a particular geographical area, but social scientists use it in a wider sense, to mean the people or items of interest to the research. So these could be the people in a particular town or city, or they could be, for example, all male prisoners in the UK, or women over 70 who have been victims of crime in the last year. The population need not consist of people: it could equally comprise all thefts from vehicles in a certain period.

Often the population of interest contains more individuals (or things) than can be researched individually. As a result, the researcher needs to choose a segment of the population to investigate. This is the *sample*. The selection of a sample must be done with care, to ensure that the results obtained from the sample are likely to apply to the population as a whole. Researchers use a *sampling frame*. This lists all the units that are available in a particular population, from which the sample is to be taken. They must then decide how to select some of these units for research. There are two main types of sampling, known as *probability* and *non-probability* sampling.

Probability sampling

There are several approaches under this subheading, but they all fall under the general category known as *random sampling*, where each unit in a population has a known chance of being chosen.

Simple random sampling refers to those instances when each unit is selected by chance, but every unit within a population has an equal chance of becoming part of the sample. The starting point is the population and the sampling frame. Once these have been determined, the researcher must decide on the size of the sample. For example, say the researcher is interested in the extent of self-harm among 8,000 offenders detained in prison. She decides that a sample of 400 prisoners will give her sufficient information. In other words, the probability of any prisoner being included in the population is 400/8,000, or one in 20. This may be expressed in the form of an equation:

Sampling fraction = n/N (n = sample, N = population)

To generate the sample, the researcher assigns a number to each of the cases appearing in the sampling frame. A table of random numbers is then used to select the 400.

A variant of this is *systematic sampling*, where rather than randomly selecting numbers from a sampling frame, cases are taken at fixed intervals. For instance, the researcher begins by selecting a number less than (in this case) 20 at random. Say the number identified is 07. The researcher then uses the seventh unit in the sampling frame, and every 20th number after this one, to make up the sample.

Another slightly different approach is *stratified random sampling*, which is used when a population has characteristics that make simple random sampling an inappropriate option (for example, minority groups that must be adequately represented in the sample). Here the population is divided into various categories or strata. Either simple random sampling or systematic sampling is used to identify a preset number of units from each category. To further complicate the situation there is *multi-cluster sampling*, which is again based on the principle of dividing up the population into segments, and sampling a proportion from each segment. Sticking with the example of prisoners and self-harming, it would be possible to select a sample of prisons, and then a sample of prisoners from each prison in the sample. Alternatively, prisons could be grouped by regions and a random sample could be taken from, say, two regions.

Non-probability sampling

This is the opposite of probability sampling in that the method of selecting units for analysis is not random, and therefore it is more likely that some units will be selected from a population than others. There are various types of non-probability sample, but here we consider two of them, the convenience sample and the snowball sample, which share much in common. Adherents to these approaches are less likely to be quantitative researchers, and they are not as likely to be committed to positivist values. These kinds of sampling are likely to be justified by appealing to interpretivist principles. However, both quantitative and qualitative researchers use non-probability sampling.

A *convenience sample* is a sample chosen by a researcher on the basis of what is readily available. For example, a serving police officer who is an area commander in charge of several police stations in a basic command unit may be interested in the attitudes of rank and file officers to the capabilities of their managers. She might decide to administer a questionnaire to all the police constables and sergeants in the police station where she is based. In this situation she is likely to be able to ensure that many of the questionnaires are returned, and hence there will be a decent response. The findings may be of interest, but it would not be possible to generalize them, because they reflect only the views of officers working in that station and not others, either in the same force area or in other forces across the country.

Convenience sampling therefore lacks scientific rigour. Regardless of this criticism, it can be used to test out a questionnaire before it is administered as part of a proper research project. Also, it may be difficult to access some groups because it is difficult to identify a population (for instance, of people committing street crimes in Nottingham) or the population may prove hard to access (such as homeless persons who have been the victim of a physical assault). In these instances, a researcher may come across a chance to obtain data from a sample, which is too good an opportunity to miss. The findings will not necessarily be fully representative but they will arguably be better than nothing.

Snowball sampling is very similar to convenience sampling. In this methodology, researchers make contact with just one person, or a handful of people, then use those connections to make further contacts. The initial contact might say, 'Have you met x and y?' The image to bear in mind is a small snowball being pushed from the top of a hill, and growing in size as it rolls downwards. Again, rather like convenience sampling the data is not likely to be representative, and for the most part this method of sampling is preferred by qualitative researchers.

SAMPLING: KEY POINTS

■ When studying a criminological problem it is not always possible to consider every case.
■ For each problem there is researchable population, and usually the researcher will only be able to look at a part of it, a sample.
■ In an ideal world, the researcher needs to select a part of a sample that is representative of the characteristics of the whole sample.
■ Some researchers are more purposive than others in their selection of a sample. The outcome is less representative of the population as a whole.

CONCLUSION

This chapter has looked at some of the different methods used by criminologists when they carry out research. Many criminologists rely on qualitative methods, and in particular interviews, to gain an insight into research problems. The interview is an important research method, and can be used to explore issues with offenders, victims and people working in the criminal justice system. In the third year of undergraduate study students sometimes do some interviewing as part of their dissertation, although for reasons of ethics or health and safety it may not be possible for them to speak to criminals or victims. (They can still interview friends or fellow students about their perceptions of crime.)

Ethnographic approaches are also popular, but again there are ethical constraints.

Other researchers use quantitative methods. One of the advantages of this is that are many readily available data sets which can be used for analysis. This chapter briefly outlined some considerations in statistical analysis, but much greater depth is given in dedicated research methods modules. Above all, this chapter highlighted some of the issues that students will need to consider before embarking on criminological research later on in their studies.

FURTHER READING

Students are spoiled for choice when it comes to texts focusing on methods of data collection. An accessible introduction to social research methods in general is T. May, *Social Research: Issues, method and process* (London: Sage, 1997). An extremely comprehensive albeit slightly more demanding read is A. Bryman, *Social Research Methods* (Oxford: Oxford University Press, 2001). Other books by Bryman are also useful for those trying to come to terms with research methods, perhaps for a course module that deals more generally with social science research rather than with criminology research.

As your confidence grows it is recommended that you dip into a range of methods texts. Good starting points are M. Bulmer, *Social Research Methods* (London: Macmillan, 1984) and R. Sapsford and V. Jupp (eds), *Data Collection and Analysis* (London: Sage, 1996).

Key methods texts that focus on research methods with a direct reference to criminology include two edited collections: V. Jupp, P. Davies and P.Francis (eds), *Doing Criminological Research* (London: Sage, 2000) and R. King and E. Wincup (eds), *Doing Research on Crime and Justice* (Oxford: Oxford University Press, 2000).

STUDY QUESTIONS

1. Referring to the section on 'setting research questions and formulating hypotheses', describe:
   a) a research question
   b) a hypothesis.
2. Formulate a potential research question and hypothesis. Put this to one side because we shall return to it in a while.
3. Interviews are widely used in criminological research. Why do researchers use interviews? Also identify the problems with different styles of interview.
4. Describe the main features of ethnographic research, and list the advantages and disadvantages of adopting this type of methodology.
5. Questionnaires and surveys are also popular in criminological research,
   a) Describe the different types of questionnaire and how they are constructed.
   b) Identify the main problems with using questionnaires.
6. What is sampling, and why is it used in criminological research?

Study task

Revisit your response to study question 2, and select a particular methodological approach to answer your research question. This is intended to be a desk-based exercise, and you must not actually do any research without speaking to a tutor or lecturer. It is necessary to consider:

■ the type of data required (is it qualitative or quantitative?)
■ the research method or methods to be used
■ any actual or potential problems with the research proposal.

PART THREE

The Criminal Justice System in Context

5 The Criminal Justice System and its Processes

OVERVIEW

This chapter aims to provide:

- an initial introduction to the criminal justice system, highlighting the role of the state and central government
- a description of the welfare state and social policy, drawing attention to the relationship between different areas of public policy and criminal justice
- a brief introduction to debates about welfare and crime
- a discussion of the centrality of the idea of justice to crime policy, with reference to the control of offenders
- an understanding of the major influence of managerialism on crime and public policy.

INTRODUCTION

This chapter introduces the criminal justice system in the United Kingdom, and its policy-making processes in relation to the welfare state and society as a whole. Taking the criminal justice system in England and Wales as an example, it charts its emergence and the philosophical and political values that underpin its workings, and how these affect suspects, defendants and the convicted, as well as victims of crime in different social groups (categorized by class, gender, age and race). It discusses what is meant by the concept of justice in relation to crime, from legal and sociological perspectives. The central argument is that the criminal justice process cannot be understood in isolation from the many complex causes and consequences of, and responses to, crime.

The chapter consists of four main parts. First, the structure of the criminal justice system is outlined, referring to the Home Office, the police service, the magistrates' and Crown courts, and the prison and probation services. The chapters that follow are each dedicated to examining the work of one of these agencies, and a final chapter looks at attempts to join up the activities of these different players.

The core aim of this section is to put it across that there is a system, and within this system there a range of processes.

Although the main focus of this book is on criminal justice policy, the understanding of this needs to be related to the wider issues of social policy. Accordingly, the second part of this chapter situates the criminal justice system in the context of the welfare state, as understood from what is called a social policy perspective. As well as describing the welfare state, it indicates that issues such as health are related to criminal justice matters. This is only a preliminary outline, and the links between the welfare state and the criminal justice system are made more explicit in Chapter 10 where the topic is joined-up approaches to social control. Another reason for exploring the relationship between welfare and crime is that the issue of justice is key for both.

The third section moves on to consider the relevance of the concept of justice in public policy, albeit with an emphasis on crime policy. The Police and Criminal Evidence Act (1984) and the principles of crime control and due process are used to illustrate some tensions in criminal justice. In the fourth section, it is argued that while the word 'justice' is still a key element of crime reduction policy, this is just one priority. Since the late 1980s the values of managerialism and new public management (NPM, see Chapter 1) have also had an influence on the workings of the criminal justice system.

THE CRIMINAL JUSTICE SYSTEM

In this section the macro-level organization of the criminal justice system is described, including the Home Office, the Department of Constitutional Affairs and the Office of the Attorney General. The relationship between crime and society is not only complex, it is also ambivalent. While few would argue seriously against the view that crime is generally harmful and undesirable, it has been argued, most notoriously by Emile Durkheim (1984) and later by Michel Foucault (1977), that crime is in certain ways functional. For Durkheim, crime can bring about social solidarity. In societies increasingly characterized by anomie or normlessness, where individuals lead increasingly atomized lives, the universal condemnation of crime can bring people together. In short, it is an expression of shared norms and values.

Foucault's observation about the social benefits of crime is slightly different, but Durkheimian in tone, when he talks about the many organizations in society that deal with various aspects of crime. If it were not for crime and disorder, there would be no need for the police, the courts, and the prison and probation services. There would also be no need for the burgeoning private security sector, or the increasing levels of participation by volunteers. In the words of the eminent radical criminologist Nils Christie (1993), there is actually a 'crime control industry', which like any other enterprise seeks to expand and grow. It might sound cynical, but crime creates jobs. For example, the criminal justice system (CJS) is a major public-sector employer, and there are in the region of 400,000 staff working in the sector. The CJS is a complex and dense body of agencies and networks. The police, court, probation and prison services attract most attention, and the important behind-the-scenes influence of three powerful departments tends to be overlooked or ignored.

There are three main departments that are key drivers of criminal justice and public policy:

■ the Home Office
■ the Department for Constitutional Affairs
■ the Office of the Attorney General.

These players are situated at the macro level of the criminal justice system. The police, court, probation and prison services exist at a meso level, and the work done in each of these agencies occurs at a micro level.

THE HOME OFFICE

This government department is mainly based in London, and has overall responsibility for three key CJS agencies: the police service, the prison service and the probation service. The latter two are in the process of being joined together, to create the National Offender Management Service (NOMS).

Perhaps the most crucial point is that the Home Office is ultimately responsible for the effectiveness of each of these players, and for this reason there are inspectorates responsible for inspecting the operational efficiency and effectiveness of each of these players, including Her Majesty's Inspectorate of Constabulary, Her Majesty's Inspectorate of Prisons and Her Majesty's Inspectorate of Probation. The Home Office is also responsible for the:

■ **Youth Justice Board**: this was set up to oversee the youth justice system, including youth offending teams (YOTs), which are multi-agency teams set up by the Crime and Disorder Act (1998) to deal with youth justice matters
■ **Criminal Injuries Compensation Authority**: this administers a state-funded scheme which compensates some victims of violent offences
■ **Criminal Cases Review Commission**: which exists to examine suspected miscarriages of justice.

DEPARTMENT FOR CONSTITUTIONAL AFFAIRS

This department emerged in 2003 and is responsible for the day-to-day running of the court service, in particular the magistrates' courts, the Crown court and the Appeals Court. It appoints magistrates and judges. It also oversees the Legal Services Commission.

THE OFFICE OF THE ATTORNEY GENERAL

This looks after the Crown Prosecution Service (CPS), the Serious Fraud Office and HM Revenue and Customs prosecutors.

These three separate arms of the CJS are joined up and integrated by the Office for Criminal Justice Reform (OCJR), which reports to ministers in the three departments. The OCJR is the main mechanism used by ministers and civil servants belonging to the National Criminal Justice Board as they implement initiatives and reforms. At a local level there are 42 local criminal justice boards, which were set up in 2003 and charged with the responsibility for running criminal justice policy in their area.

As indicated above, the voluntary sector also makes a significant contribution to the CJS. For example:

- **Victim Support** is a charitable organization first introduced in 1974 to provide support and services to victims of crime
- the **National Association for the Care and Rehabilitation of Offenders (NACRO)** is a pressure group that disseminates information about, and contributes to debates on, criminal justice matters.

THE WELFARE STATE, SOCIAL POLICY AND CRIME

In this section:

- a social policy perspective is introduced
- there is a description of the structure of the state and government
- the origins and main functions of the welfare state are outlined
- there is a rehearsal of some issues and debates about welfare
- the relationship between health and crime is used as a short case study.

Social policy can be very broadly defined as actions taken by organizations in society to promote social well-being or welfare (Dean, 2006). 'Welfare' has both an individual and a social focus, in the sense that it is concerned with the needs of individuals but also with the needs of society as a whole. Indeed a good deal of debate is generated by the difficulty of reconciling these two dimensions. The most important organization that acts to promote well-being is the state, although it is not the only one. Voluntary organizations, private-sector organizations and informal organizations like the family also play an important role. However, since the start of the twentieth century there has been an enormous growth in the range of activities and areas of social and economic life in which the state has a direct influence, and social policy has become the largest area of public expenditure. This has in turn caused considerable political debate, since it has increased both the amount of taxation and the amount of compulsion to which individuals are subject.

Social policy is at the forefront of the battle between the major political parties in Britain. For most of the twentieth century this involved the Conservative Party on the political right and the Labour Party (renamed New Labour in the mid-1990s) representing the political left.

A major turning point came in the period after the Second World War, when a series of Acts of Parliament created what has become known as the *Welfare state* (Fraser, 1984). Before this time, social provision was piecemeal and often restricted to the lower paid, whereas the welfare state sought to promote the well-being of all citizens as well as to assist underprivileged groups and individuals. A key document was the Beveridge Report (1942), which called for the abolition of the 'five giants': want, disease, squalor, ignorance and idleness. Drawing on Alcock, Erskine and May (2003), the broad aims might be summarized as:

- to provide a minimum standard of living for all citizens (including a basic income but also health care, education and housing)
- to compensate for inequalities in income and property so that all have equal opportunity to develop to their full potential
- to provide a safe and healthy environment for all.

Legislation laid out the responsibilities of public authorities in relation to these aims. Some examples of key post-war legislation are the 1946 National Health Service Act, which guaranteed all citizens free medical treatment at the point of need, and the 1944 Education Act, which provided for compulsory state-funded education for all, with provision tailored to reflect the aptitude and ability of different types of pupil.

To a great extent this legislation defined the area of study for social policy, which includes health, education, housing, personal social services and social security. Until relatively recently, policy on crime was excluded largely because it was seen as a punitive, offender-based system, and the social causes and consequences of crime received little attention (Crowther, 2000a). This has now changed, and the connections between policies on crime and other social policy areas are an important field of study. An example of the enduring relationship between crime and health is given a little later on with reference to prostitution (Walkowitz, 1980) and victimization (Dixon et al., 2006).

THE STRUCTURE OF THE WELFARE STATE

Since a great deal of welfare is provided through public authorities via legislation, it is important to understand something of the structures through which the welfare state operates.

Central government

This refers to the prime minister and the Cabinet (the senior ministers responsible for particular departments, such as the Home Office). The government derives its authority from having been chosen by the electorate. The party with most seats in the House of Commons forms the government.

Parliament

This includes both the elected House of Commons and the non-elected House of Lords. All legislation is debated and scrutinized by Parliament and must have parliamentary approval before it becomes law. The House of Commons is the most powerful body, and can override a decision by the House of Lords.

The state

'The state' is not the government. It is the more or less permanent legal and organizational framework through which society is managed and controlled, and which defines the competencies and powers of its agents (such as judges and civil servants). The state is the totality of institutional structures that legitimately make the collective decisions for society. It is not a single organization but a series of bureaucratic organizations with different powers and functions (such as the police, the judiciary, local government and the armed forces). Its actions are taken in accordance with agreed procedures, in particular laws passed by Parliament. More simply, in terms of social policy, it is the apparatus through which welfare legislation is implemented and enforced.

THE STATE AND WELFARE

Two of the most important state organizations for social policy are the Civil Service and local government. They are the bodies charged with the major responsibility for providing the services required by legislation.

The Civil Service

Each of the major areas of government has a department headed by a minister who is responsible for government policy in that sector. Each department is staffed by a body of professional civil servants responsible for advising the minister on policy and making sure that it is implemented.

The minister is assisted by a number of politically appointed junior ministers (who are normally elected Members of Parliament – MPs) and by special advisers, who are politically appointed, but not elected, individuals. Junior ministers may take on responsibility for a particular area of policy within the department. The minister is also assisted by permanent (non-political) civil servants in the department, who are headed by a permanent secretary, and civil servants in the agencies that fall within the remit of the department.

Agencies

These are the branches of the Civil Service that are most directly concerned with the day-to-day running of services and policy implementation. In 1988 every government department had to conduct ongoing analyses of its activities. If an activity or service could be run without day-to-day ministerial control and was large enough to justify organizational change, then it was transformed into an executive agency. The executive agencies are headed by a chief executive recruited by open competition and employed on a renewable fixed-term contact, with salary linked to performance. The principle was to decentralize managerial and service delivery functions while keeping control over policy in the hands of the minister and department.

Local government

The network of local authorities is a major provider of welfare services, which the state provides under legislation passed by Parliament. At a sub-regional level there are county, district and borough councils. In 1997 limited powers were devolved by Westminster to the regions, resulting in a Scottish Parliament, National Assemblies for Wales and Northern Ireland, and a Greater London Assembly (Cochrane, 2003). London boroughs, metropolitan boroughs and unitary authorities are single-tier councils that provide all local authority services in the geographical area they serve. In many non-metropolitan areas of England there is a two-tier system, with the counties providing the bulk of services such as education and social services, and districts providing other services such as housing.

For example, in education local authorities are responsible for building and maintaining state schools, and employ teachers and other staff. Each local authority has an elected council which controls the apparatus of the local state: the council departments and their officers. The elected council is responsible for ensuring that both local and national policies are implemented in its area. However, there are crucial differences between local and central government:

- Except for some minor areas (where by-laws can be passed), local authorities are not law-making bodies.
- Local authorities can only spend money in policy areas in which central government commands them to do so (mandatory legislation) or grants them the power to do so (permissive legislation).
- Local authorities are dependent on central government grants for most of their funding, and must account for their spending.
- Should a local authority fail in an area of its duties required by law, that function may be taken over by central government.
- The structure and functions of local government are in the hands of central government, and may be altered according to the policies, ideologies and priorities that central government has at any time.

GOVERNMENT AT A DISTANCE

One of the significant features of British government is the relatively large proportion of what might be termed the public sector that falls outside both the Civil Service departments and agencies, and the local government sector. Many people who work in the public sector are neither civil servants nor local government officers. They work for what are known as quangos, or non-elected quasi-autonomous governmental organizations. Such organizations share many of the key features of government bodies. In practical terms, they are publicly funded, they are entrusted with duties prescribed by law, and their chief officers are appointed by a minister or her/his department. However, in their day-to-day operations they work with a degree of independence from the minister and the Civil Service, and are less subject to scrutiny by Parliament.

THE PRIVATE SECTOR AND THE VOLUNTARY SECTOR

It is necessary to be aware that many of the services that come under the heading of social policy are provided outside the public sector. Private, profit-making organizations are clearly important in sectors like pensions, housing, education and health. Voluntary non-profit-making organizations have always played a key role in the development and provision of welfare services. Many services that are now provided by statutory public authorities have their origins in the voluntary sector. Before 1870 education was provided largely by voluntary bodies, even though some of these received government grants. The probation service has its origins in the Police Court Missionary Society, which pioneered work with offenders, and so on. This is not simply a matter of historical interest, since voluntary organizations continue to play a key role as pioneers of new services, as identifiers of new social needs, and in supplementing and supporting services provided by the state.

The distinction between the public sector and the private and voluntary sector is becoming less easy to draw, as public authorities enter into more and more partnerships with bodies outside the realm of the state. A good example is to be found in local government, where the 1980 Planning and Land Act and the 1988 Local Government Act required local authorities to put certain services out to competitive tender. The Local Government Act (1999) replaced this system with 'best value' as the mechanism by which local authorities ensure the economy, effectiveness and responsiveness of service delivery. Since the passing into law of the Local Government Act, local authorities have been required to develop more robust and effective mechanisms to consult members of the public, to inform the planning and delivery of services.

The 'best value' ethos requires organizations to base their service provision on a review of the so-called 'four Cs': challenge, comparison, consultation and competition (Newburn, 2002). Let us consider challenge first. It is no longer acceptable to simply provide a service: it is necessary also to know why and how it is being provided. 'Comparison' in this context refers to the indicators that need to be developed so the performance of different agencies can be compared. The views of service users and suppliers are important. Performance targets are based on consultation with taxpayers and the users of services. Finally, competition is the mechanism used to deliver effective and efficient services (Newburn, 2002). However local authorities may still look beyond their own organization to the private and voluntary sectors to provide services.

THE WELFARE STATE: DEBATES AND ISSUES

The extent to which the welfare state has achieved its objectives has been an issue of intense debate. Indeed the debate encompasses disagreement about what those objectives are or should be. To illustrate this, think about the following question: should the welfare state be concerned with providing an efficient and effective safety net for the poorest, or should it aim to produce a more equal distribution of income, wealth, goods and services?

This relates to a wider question about *social justice*. A major debate on this subject took place from the mid-1970s into the early 1990s. The dispute was based on the arguments of the Conservatives, influenced by the New Right (Murray, 1997, 2000), and the socialist stance of the Labour party (Walker, 1991).

On the one hand there are those who argue that the welfare state is an outmoded and cumbersome institution, which makes worse the very problems which it is trying to solve. The benefits system is too generous, and encourages a dependency culture in which there are considerable disincentives to obtain work and financial independence. The poor are actively discouraged from the kinds of behaviour that could lift them out of poverty. Many of the services provided by the welfare state are inefficient and unresponsive to consumer demand, and could be better provided by the private sector or the voluntary sector. Further, a great deal of money is wasted in providing services to people who do not need them, either because they could afford to provide for themselves, or because they are encouraged by the system to exaggerate the extent of their needs. The result is a system which demands ever greater increases in taxation, and this in turn discourages enterprise and risk taking. If public expenditure could be reduced, there would be lower taxes, which would encourage greater investment and economic growth, and create more jobs. Those who take this stance do not see inequality as a problem in itself; indeed inequalities in reward are seen as a necessary stimulus to economic growth. As the rich become richer, the fruits of their endeavours will 'trickle down' to the poorest in society.

On the other hand there are those who argue that a major objective of the welfare state should be to reduce the inequalities in society, and that from the outset the welfare state has failed to do this (Lister, 2004; Hills and Stewart, 2005). Indeed it could be argued that the welfare state has reinforced existing inequalities. Statistical investigations from the 1960s onwards show that there has been little economic redistribution from the better off to the worse off (JRF, 2004). People who rely solely on state benefits for their income have fallen well below the average standard of living, as have those on low or irregular earnings. Poverty and unemployment are still major causes of inequality, and tend to be located in the same geographical areas and among the same social groups as suffered before the welfare state. These inequalities are not simply a matter of income (Levitas, 1998). The poor suffer multiple deprivations, and they:

- live in worse housing
- have less access to health and education services
- have lower life expectancy
- have fewer chances to escape deprivation by obtaining qualifications and paid work.

Although the welfare state has succeeded to some extent in solving absolute poverty – lack of the basic resources to sustain life – it has failed to reduce relative poverty – the gap between the 'normal' or 'average' standard of living and that of the poor. A series of reports published throughout the 1990s seemed to reinforce the view that social divisions are becoming wider (Rahman, Palmer and Kenway, 2001). The number of people living on low incomes relative to the average is far higher than it was towards the end of the 1970s.

The method of measuring poverty that is used by the government is 60 per cent of median income. According to Cook (2006: 24–5), in 2003 this meant in real terms that a couple without kids had to live on £200 per week before housing costs. For a single person the figure was £118. The equivalent figure for a family comprising two parents and two children was £283, and a single parent with two children had £207. In 2003–4 12.4 million people – 21 per cent of the population – had incomes below the 60 per cent of median income threshold.

These figures are an improvement on the widening gap between the rich and poor that materialized in the 1980s and 1990s (Rahman et al., 2000). Poverty in general and child poverty in particular remains a serious problem. As Harker (2006: 11) puts it:

> Child poverty has fallen substantially in recent years – some 700,000 children have been lifted out of poverty since 1998/99. Given that child poverty rates tripled during the 1980s and then remained persistently high during the 1990s, this sharp fall in child poverty has been a remarkable achievement. The child poverty rate is now at a 15-year low and the UK no longer has the highest child poverty rate in the European Union.

The last point is especially important, because it is children and young people who are the most vulnerable when it comes to crime and disorder, especially those concentrated in the poorest families (Farrington et al., 2006).

Although measures of both poverty and inequality are to some extent controversial, both official figures and those produced by independent bodies point to the same conclusion: that a significant proportion of the population now lives 'outside' the mainstream of society (Hutton and Giddens, 2000). The explanations of how and why this has happened and what the implications are for social policy, have tended to divide between those, like the New Right, who see the responsibility lying with the perverse incentives of the benefit system and the characteristics of the poor themselves, and those who seek an explanation in structural changes – the interplay of social and economic forces – which have marginalized large groups of people who are more or less permanently outside the labour force.

This latter approach can be summarized in the term 'social exclusion', and a number of possible factors may be identified as contributing to this phenomenon (Lister, 2004; Levitas, 1998). Among them are:

■ structural changes in the labour market, such as the decline in staple industries and the failure of successive governments to maintain full employment

- insecurity in employment and low wages
- the failure of the education and training systems to ensure equality of access for the development of the appropriate skills
- the failure of benefit levels to keep pace with the rise in average living standards
- changes in the taxation system which have disproportionately benefited the better-off
- demographic changes such as the increase in the number of elderly people
- cultural and social changes such as the increase in divorce and lone parenthood, and the failure of social policy to adapt to change
- lack of investment in public services
- failure of investment in public services to address the problems of inequality.

These points all require the priorities of social policy to be rethought, and bring into question the efficacy of the traditional approach of the post-war welfare state. This might be summarized as an approach based on universal benefits and services to guarantee equal citizenship rights. The challenge is to find a solution which will maintain this fundamental value while redressing inequality. The problem can be illustrated by some examples.

- Child benefit is a universal benefit paid to all children at the same rate regardless of parental income or circumstances. Simply to raise the level of child benefit would be expensive, and would not necessarily close the gap between children in poor families and those in better-off families.
- The National Health Service (NHS) is a universal service, access to which does not depend on either income or national insurance contributions. However, evidence suggests that the better-off in society make more use of the NHS than the worse-off, that they live in areas where the services are of higher quality, and as a result, that existing inequalities in health are compounded by the NHS.

This is necessarily an over-simplification of the issues, but it will serve to raise the question of the extent to which those most in need should be targeted by social policy and welfare spending. The issue of targeting or selective social policies is highly controversial, and involves a number of important questions:

- Is it possible to find an exact measure of need, or should a range of criteria be used?
- Should individuals, groups or geographical areas be targeted, or some combination of all these?
- Is it possible to target services and benefits without stigmatizing recipients?
- Does targeting raise questions of equity?

What is the relevance of this to crime and criminal justice? This section has been rather sketchy, and Chapter 10 revisits the linkages between the welfare state and criminal justice policy, with a focus on joined-up approaches to crime reduction, but we shall explore here some of the connections between crime and health.

A SHORT CASE STUDY: THE LINKS BETWEEN HEALTH AND CRIMINAL JUSTICE

The relationship between health and crime can be demonstrated with a historical and a more contemporary example.

A historical illustration: prostitution

Prostitution is often described as one of the 'oldest professions', and strictly speaking there is no such thing as a criminal offence of prostitution. Rather there are the criminal offences of soliciting, loitering, living off the earnings of prostitution and 'brothel keeping'. Most attention is directed towards prostitutes – or sex workers – who 'work the streets', mainly because they are visible and are linked with other social problems like drug misuse, violence, fear of crime, threatening behaviour and being a general nuisance. In the past, though, legislators and policy makers were far more preoccupied with the danger prostitution posed to public health.

In the nineteenth century prostitution was a major problem in Victorian London. The policy response to prostitution at that time was underpinned by a concern with contagion or the spread of disease – both moral and spiritual, and physical – amongst the population. A key reference is the Contagious Diseases Acts of 1864, 1866 and 1869, which were passed into law in order to require women involved in prostitution to register for a medical examination. Women who worked the streets were seen to be 'disease carriers' (Scrambler and Scrambler, 1997) in need of surveillance and regulation. If a prostitute was believed to be suffering from a venereal disease (the term used then for what is now known as a sexually transmitted disease), she could be detained in hospital for up to three months (Walkowitz, 1980). This legislation was used alongside the anti-vagrancy legislation (see Chapter 1), which was also used to prosecute women.

This raft of legislation reflected the ambivalent attitudes to prostitution in Victorian society, demonstrated by on the one hand the widespread use of prostitutes, and on the other, the fear and contempt with which they were held. Not only were women seen as the 'carriers' of disease, the men who used them were cast as 'blameless victims' (Scrambler and Scrambler, 1997). This can be understood in relation to more general views about women in nineteenth-century English society (O'Neill, 1997).

The imposition of contagious diseases legislation did meet with some resistance from women's rights campaigners such as Josephine Butler, who, inspired by her Christian faith, set up the Ladies National Association. This eventually led to the repeal of the contagious diseases legislation in 1886 (Self, 2003: 2). Self (2003) adds that support for this change was also gained as a result of newspaper articles recounting stories of men using young girls as prostitutes. This resulted in pressure from concerned and anxious parents who called for the protection of children. Thus an issue that is today to some extent regarded as a criminal justice issue has also been regarded as a health issue, as well as an issue of child protection or welfare.

Now let us consider a more up-to-date illustration of the linkages between health and crime.

A CONTEMPORARY EXAMPLE: VICTIMIZATION AND HEALTH

According to a recent report published by the Institute of Public Policy Research (IPPR), there is growing evidence that there is a link between inequality in general and the tendency to become a victim of crime (Dixon et al., 2006). For example, victimization and ill-health are interrelated in the context of social exclusion in general, and various forms of discrimination. It would appear that living in social housing and being unemployed also have a bearing on ill-health and victimization. It is also known that a person who is experiencing poor health is more likely to achieve victim status. The poor health is demonstrated in a variety of ways, for example by sleeplessness and depression, and an increased reliance on cigarettes and alcohol (ibid).

There are also strong links between ill-health and specific crimes such as domestic violence (Refuge, 2004). Domestic violence is officially defined by the Home Office (2001b) as 'Any violence between current and former partners in an intimate relationship wherever and wherever the violence occurs. The violence may include physical, sexual, emotional and financial abuse.' Grace's (1995) definition is similar: 'any form of physical, sexual or emotional abuse which takes place within the context of a close relationship'.

Domestic violence is sometimes categorized under family violence. The reasons for this are made clear in a quotation from Gelles and Cornell: 'people are more likely to be killed, physically assaulted, hit, beaten up [and] slapped ... in their own homes by other family members than anywhere else, or by anyone else in our society' (1985: 12).

In short, domestic violence refers to both physical and psychological violence shown by a man or woman to his or her partner (in a context that includes marriage, cohabitation, heterosexual and homosexual partnerships, and separated couples). The definitions are important because they make it clear that violence is not exclusively a physical act consisting of slaps, punches and kicks: it also includes more insidious forms of mental abuse, such as verbal abuse and mind games, where the cuts, bruises and scars may not be as visible. All these kinds of domestic violence affect both physical and mental health. The effect of domestic violence on mental health is shown in increases in sleeplessness and anxiety, depression, and alcohol and drug dependency (Refuge, 2004). There are also links between domestic violence and physical health, especially relating to maternal health and obstetric outcomes (Mezey et al., cited in Stanko, O'Bierne and Zaffuto, 2002).

There are correlations between domestic violence and:

- drug misuse and smoking
- general social problems and social needs
- depression and gynaecological problems
- more previous pregnancies and becoming pregnant at a younger age.

Women who have been assaulted in a domestic setting in the last 12 months:

- begin antenatal care later than the average
- experience more false labour than the average

- suffer from hyperemesis (excessive vomiting)
- suffer from significant levels of backache and headaches.

If domestic violence is experienced during pregnancy, women are more likely to be admitted to an antenatal ward with unresolved physical complaints. Refuge (2005) shows that young children who witness domestic violence are more likely to be abused and also to engage in offending behaviour, including cruelty to animals.

THE WELFARE STATE, POLICY AND CRIME: KEY POINTS

- The state and government play an important role in the distribution and allocation of resources, as is demonstrated by the existence of the welfare state.
- The state is not the only provider of welfare services: there are also the private and voluntary sectors.
- Social policy is a highly contested area of activity, and heated debate is not uncommon.
- Traditionally social policy has not encompassed criminological issues, but the relationship between crime and welfare issues (such as health) is now widely acknowledged.

JUSTICE AND CRIME POLICY

In this section:

- a simple definition of justice is used to explore the extent which offenders are treated in a way that is fair and right.
- the Police and Criminal Evidence Act (1984) (PACE) is given as an example of how legislation is intended to ensure fairness and justice.

The concept of justice has been debated by philosophers and politicians for centuries. The related concept of *social justice* is 'concerned with who gets what in society and whether it is "right" or "fair"' (Dean, 2006: 58). There are plenty of controversies surrounding this idea, but we shall not explore them here: the purpose is simply to introduce what justice means in the context of the study of crime. Conveniently Dean's terminology is useful, and we can take it as a helpful starting point alongside the following definition taken from the Home Office website (http://www.homeoffice.gov.uk/justice/):

> Along with two other government departments we are responsible for ensuring that justice is done in the UK. Justice means ensuring people who break the law are punished fairly and rehabilitated if possible, victims of crime are supported, and our communities and families are safer and happier as a result.
>
> We're reforming the justice system to make sure we achieve these goals, moving the focus away from the offender, and towards the needs of victims and witnesses.

> The justice system – meaning the process that starts with a crime being reported and ends with an offender being punished – is a complicated process.

This has a fit with the overarching aims and objectives of the Home Office.

> The Home Office is the government department responsible for internal affairs in England and Wales. We work to build a safe, just and tolerant society, to enhance opportunities for all, and to ensure the protection and security of the public is maintained.
>
> (http://www.homeoffice.gov.uk)

It is clear from the first quotation that there is a lot to this idea, and it is necessary to unpack it to consider the detail. The notion of social justice has already been discussed, and while the focus in this section is on criminal justice, the two are interrelated. As Cook (2006) shows, for example, some social groups such as minority ethnic groups and women experience various injustices in their day-to-day lives which are replicated in the criminal justice system. Although the concepts of social justice and criminal justice are linked, the fact that criminal justice is being discussed suggests it has a specific meaning.

The Home Office definition uses the word 'fairness', and this is central to the concept. Basically, the question is whether offenders and victims are treated fairly when they have contact with the criminal justice system. The answer to this question is far from straightforward. We shall consider it with regard to first offenders, then victims.

Criminal justice and the offender

> Justice means ensuring people who break the law are punished fairly and rehabilitated if possible.

The first point to note is that in breaking the law the offender has caused a social harm, which attracts censure, or disapproval and criticism, from the state. The offender may have harmed a person (as in rape), property (as in theft) or a principle (as in the possession of drugs). Chapter 1 examined how behaviour may be labelled as criminal, but what is crucial here is the role of the criminal justice system in responding to law breaking.

'Justice' in this context refers to the activities of various agencies in attempting to detect, prosecute, convict, punish and possibly rehabilitate offenders. Crucially all of these activities – with the exception of rehabilitation – are bound by the rule of law. Indeed the rule of law is key to understanding how justice is put into practice to ensure that all persons are treated the same, or in a way that is fair. Perhaps surprisingly, even people who break the law are in principle, if not always in practice, protected by the law and have certain rights.

In modern society the state is the main player responsible for delivering criminal justice. Individual citizens are not allowed to take the law into their own hands. A person who confronts a burglar in his or her own home is only able to ask the intruder to leave, and is not legally permitted to use physical force unless it is in self-defence. A good example of this is Tony Martin, a farmer from Norfolk, who fired shots at two men – injuring one and killing the other – who had broken into his home. Martin was convicted of manslaughter although he claimed he was acting in self-defence. The jury concluded that Martin had used more than reasonable force, and that self-defence was not an adequate defence to the charge.

If an offence is committed the victim or a witness is expected to report this to the police, who will then investigate the crime. The police need to perform their duties in such a way that they ensure justice is realized. As Chapter 6 shows, the police have many powers, in particular the power of arrest and the legitimate authority to coerce (which can including stopping, searching or even shooting) a person when carrying out their law enforcement duties. The police are answerable to the law inasmuch as the way they deal with an offender must be seen as fair and just, or put another way, lawful. The rule of law is therefore important for regulating the actions of criminal justice agencies. An example of this is the Police and Criminal Evidence Act (1984) (PACE).

PACE covers many issues relating to police work, but for the purpose of this section the focus is on the use of the law to make sure suspects are treated fairly, with the principle of justice in mind, on the streets and at the police station.

To begin, why was PACE introduced? The main reason was a concern about police officers, and the use and sometimes misuse and abuse of their discretion (see Chapter 1) in their dealings with suspects, both on the streets and when they took them back to the police station. There were rules to govern the police's behaviour, known as the Judges' Rules, but these were considered by many to be inadequate. The Judges' Rules were created in 1912, and according to Reiner (2000: 65), were 'non-statutory administrative directions laying down procedures for questioning and taking statements'. The rules stated that a police officer could not question suspects without cautioning them first. If an officer arrested a person and questioned him or her about an offence, the Rules should have prevented the officer from threatening or offering any inducements to the suspect. Arrestees were also to be told that they had a right to consult a solicitor in private at any time.

In reality the Judges' Rules did not prevent a range of abuses. For example confessions were sometimes obtained prior to a suspect being cautioned, and officers often failed to inform suspects of their right to seek legal advice. A number of notorious cases made it clear that the rules did not stop the police from extracting false confessions from innocent suspects. The rules were ambiguous, which meant the police could manipulate them, and officers were also helped by magistrates and judges, who tended to interpret the rules flexibly and often in favour of the police (Choongh, 1997).

The Phillips Commission on Criminal Procedure discussed these abuses of power, and illustrated how criminal justice was being compromised. Phillips influenced the creation of PACE, which established a framework for police investigation, setting out the rights of both the police and arrested persons.

To illustrate the importance of PACE for criminal justice, we can consider the example of arrest. Section 24 of PACE revised section 2 of the Criminal Law Act (1967) to define an arrestable offence, and make it clear when an officer can and cannot make an arrest. (The police cannot automatically arrest and detain those suspected of many minor breaches of the law, although they can initiate criminal proceedings against them.) According to section 24 an 'arrestable offence' is a crime for which the sentence for an adult aged 21 or over is a prison sentence of five years or more. Some offences that attract a sentence of less than five years also come into this category, including going equipped to steal (Theft Act 1968, s.25), taking vehicles without consent (Theft Act 1968, s. 12) and indecent assault on a female (Sexual Offences Act 1956, s. 14).

Any person, and not just a police officer, is allowed to arrest somebody without a warrant if the person 'is, or is reasonably believed to be, in the act of committing an arrestable offence' or 'where an arrestable offence has been committed, anyone who has, or is reasonably believed to have been guilty, of the offence'. Police officers do have other powers, though, which other citizens lack. An officer can arrest a person if he or she has *reasonable grounds* to suspect that the person has committed an offence. He or she can also arrest a person who is, or is reasonably believed to be, *about to* commit an arrestable offence. In contrast to an ordinary member of the public, a police officer can enter any place where a suspect may be in order to make an arrest, and can use force if necessary to carry out the arrest. In other words, the powers of the police are greater than the powers of other individuals in this context.

Section 25 of PACE outlines police powers of arrest in connection with non-arrestable offences, which might sound rather contradictory and paradoxical. This section states that an arrest may be made in response to any criminal conduct, even if the goal is limited to identifying the suspect. The purpose of this section is to simplify the law, otherwise an officer would have to remember more than 100 statutory powers. The arrestee does not need to be taken to a police station if he or she cooperates with the police and provides any information requested. Arrests may also be made preventively if an officer has reason to believe that an offence has been, or is actually in the process of being, committed. It is legitimate to arrest someone to prevent physical harm, either self-harm or harm of another. An arrest may also be made if it is necessary to prevent the loss of or damage to property. The powers to arrest are widened to include offences concerning public decency and the obstruction of a public highway.

Section 27 states that if a person is convicted of a recordable offence (those offences recorded in police statistics), he or she may be called in for fingerprinting. Anyone who fails to attend the police station for this purpose may be arrested.

These examples show how the police are answerable to the law, and how the law is in place to make sure arrestees are treated fairly. Section 37 of PACE also states what counts as a lawful arrest. A lawful arrest must be reasonable and involve notification. It is important that there are reasonable grounds, because the liberty of a person is potentially at stake. It is necessary that the grounds for making an arrest are made clear, with particular reference to the circumstances of the case. At the outset the officer will be suspicious, but he or she needs to gather sufficient evidence to ensure that a charge can be made. The evidence used by an officer may be provided by another person, such as a store detective, but only if that other person is known to be a reliable witness or observer. For instance, an anonymous tip-off which cannot be used in evidence would not count as grounds for making an arrest.

The requirement for notification means that the suspect must be given a valid reason for the arrest. In other words, suspects need to be told why they have had their liberty taken away, and this needs to be expressed in clear-cut terms so there is no room for any misunderstanding. The law also takes account of the fact that on some occasions a suspect may escape, or try to escape. In these circumstances it is not always feasible to notify the person before making an arrest, so it is not a requirement in these cases.

Following an arrest the next stage in the criminal justice process is for the suspect to be taken to a police station, where he or she is detained. In an attempt to treat all suspects fairly, following a valid arrest the police must maintain a complete custody record, which nowadays is computerized, timed and dated. The detention of a suspect is not taken lightly, as it involves a fundamental deprivation of the person's civil liberties. For instance, no one can be forced to go to a police station unless there is a proper reason (such as following a lawful arrest). A valid reason also needs to be given for the detention itself. It is also not allowable for the police to force people to give evidence against themselves. However, although a detainee is under no obligation to 'help the police with their inquiries', if he or she fails to cooperate the police are entitled to draw adverse conclusions from this.

Under PACE there are two main types of requirement regarding detention, administrative requirements and detainees' rights.

Administrative supervision

The police are nowadays required to produce a lot of paperwork, and they have to keep a written record of what they do. This is important as far as justice goes, because the police can then be called to account. A *custody officer* supervises a suspect's case. This officer is a police officer, but is expected to act in a way that offers some impartiality, and ensures the detainee is correctly dealt with. A paper record is essential so officers can justify their actions if they are subsequently questioned.

Detainees' rights

Section 56 of PACE states that detainees have the right to inform someone (for instance, a family member) of their arrest and of their whereabouts. The suspect needs to be made aware of this right promptly, and a delay is only acceptable if a serious arrestable offence has been committed, such as serious harm against the state, or if the case involves financial loss. A senior officer (such as a superintendent) may decide to stop a suspect making a call if he or she suspects the call will be used to contact an accomplice, for example to advise him or her to dispose of stolen property. It is not possible to delay the right to notification for more than 36 hours, whatever the circumstances.

Section 58 concerns access to legal advice. The same rules apply as in section 56: detainees have the right to obtain legal advice, subject only to safeguards to ensure they do not use this right to subvert the course of justice. If an arrestee wishes to decline the opportunity to contact a lawyer, he or she must sign a waiver. Of course, not all individuals have equal access to legal advice. A well-off suspect may have an existing relationship with a solicitor, and the ability to call on help immediately, whereas others might not know whom they should call on, or have the funds to pay for advice. To address this problem there is a publicly financed duty solicitor scheme, which effectively gives all suspects the ability to access legal advice at a police station. From time to time the police may deny a suspect legal advice, for example if an officer has reasonable grounds to believe it would obstruct the gathering of evidence. It is also possible for the police to commence an interview with a suspect who has not yet obtained legal advice, if he or she has requested a solicitor who is not available or contactable, and has declined the offer of the services of the duty solicitor.

A SUMMARY OF THE PACE CASE STUDY

■ This section has attempted to demonstrate that the criminal justice system, in this instance the police, is controlled by the law in an attempt to ensure that justice is done.

■ Even though a suspect may turn out to be guilty of a particular offence, a police officer cannot assume this without gathering evidence. The suspect is treated as innocent until proven guilty beyond reasonable doubt.

■ There are essential safeguards in place for suspects, such as those provided by PACE.

There is a long-standing debate in criminal justice studies about the relationship between crime control and due process (Packer, 1968). This is a complex debate, and in part concerns the extent to which the police should either follow the letter of the law (observing due process), or take short-cuts so they can arrest and charge a suspect (putting the emphasis on crime control). These opposing principles also apply in the courts and to all professionals involved in the administration of justice.

Crime control

This approach prioritizes efficiency above justice. The aim is to deal with a suspect as speedily as possible and to ensure there is finality about a case. The guilt of the suspect is presumed to be clear-cut, so it is argued that the quickest route to proving guilt and convicting the defendant is the best. Adherents to this view have faith in the law and the procedures in place in the criminal justice system. For example, they take it that PACE will ensure everything is done properly. This approach has been likened to 'assembly line justice' (Packer, 1968).

Due process

In contrast to the crime control model, those who prioritize due process have less faith in the competencies and morals of criminal justice professionals. There is a view that experts, such as police officers, are prone to error, and that it is essential to observe the proper procedures to safeguard against mistakes being made. There is a firm belief in the principles that the suspect is innocent until proven guilty, and that there needs to be robust fact-based evidence to prove that a person is guilty beyond reasonable doubt. All suspects must be treated equally, and they all share in common the fact they are treated equally. Those who take this approach insist that officials observe very closely the formal rules set out in legislation and procedures. Because of this, the due process model is sometimes compared to an obstacle course (Packer, 1968).

MANAGERIALISM

We now need to consider the impact of the ideology of managerialism. This has had a profound influence on social policy and the administration of criminal justice. In short, this set of principles does not directly challenge the concept of justice, but it does place some constraints on the realization of a fair and just society.

Managerialism, or the new public management (NPM) as it is also known, started to have an influence on public policy in the 1980s. Effectively its impact has been to subordinate social policy – and sometimes justice – to the requirements of economic policy. More specifically, it has resulted in:

■ devolved responsibility (especially budgetary or financial)
■ more economic, effective and efficient delivery of services
■ increased targeting of resources.

There are many accounts of these processes, but here we follow the model offered by McLaughlin et al. (2001: 302), who identified nine features of NPM. These were summarized by Senior, Crowther-Dowey and Long (2007).

1. More emphasis is placed on the achievement of results than on the administration of processes

During the period in social history known as the 'welfare society' (broadly from 1945 to 1979), public-sector organizations such as the NHS attached considerable importance to gaining as many 'inputs', or resources, as possible. In the case of health policy for example, the government, welfare professionals and the wider public agreed that the state had a moral obligation to procure the resources needed to provide health care that was free to all at the point of need. When the New Right arrived on the scene (with the election of Margaret Thatcher's government in 1979), the weight given to *inputs* was questioned, and public-sector organizations were instead required to show the *outputs* they were delivering. This shift of emphasis also signalled a trend towards public-sector institutions such as the police playing an enhanced role in service delivery, and a reduced role for the state and government.

2. There was a requirement to set targets and to formulate explicit and tangible performance indicators (PIs). These PIs were introduced to facilitate the auditing of effectiveness and efficiency.

This tendency is clearly related to the growing influence of a performance culture. Rose and Miller (1992) talked about 'centres of calculation', which existed to set targets that public-sector agencies were expected to achieve. An example is the Audit Commission, which has helped the government to set targets for institutions such as the police. The Home Office embraced the performance culture, evidenced by Home Office Circular 114, which aimed to improve the 'effectiveness, efficiency and economy' of the police service. It proposed that this could be achieved in various ways, for example by creating more civilian posts (*civilianization*) to carry out tasks that did not need to be done by a police officer.

3. League tables were published to show comparative performance

As well as target setting and the development of appropriate indicators to measure and quantify performance, *benchmarking* was also significant. According to the principle of benchmarking, public-sector organizations were required to demonstrate to taxpayers how well they delivered services in comparison with other organizations. This resulted in a requirement to produce performance data that was comparable. From the 1990s onwards 'league tables' have been published so comparative performance against specific criteria can be ranked, with the aim of identifying the best-performing police forces, hospitals or schools.

4. Core competencies were identified

Advocates of the New Right political ideology made a concerted effort to claim that public-sector institutions lacked a focus. They did this by casting into doubt what these organizations were attempting to do. The public sector was contrasted with the private sector, with the argument that private-sector organizations had a clear objective: they served the interests of shareholders by maximizing profits. A profit margin is much easier to quantify than good health or a reduction in the fear of crime. The private sector was also seen as more adept at identifying its core business, which is usually measured in terms of the number of items made or sold, and the profits resulting from those activities. In the public sector this is trickier, and core and non-core tasks are less easily distinguishable. The New Right encouraged public-sector organizations to identify and focus more on core activities and competencies.

5. All activities were market tested and costed to make sure the services provided gave value for money

The managerial stance argued that once public-sector institutions knew their core business, it would become easier to evaluate the added value of their activities. For example, the practice of 'activity costing' was introduced, with the aim of learning in more detail how much money was spent on different activities. It would then be easier to judge whether the money spent on each activity represented good value. This can also be seen as a move towards institutions monitoring their own activities.

6. Responsibilities deemed to be non-core were hived off to external bodies

After public-sector organizations had determined their core functions, they externalized, or contracted out, responsibilities that were judged to be non-core. (For example, it could be argued that while catching criminals is a core function of the police, keeping the police station clean and providing meals for officers are not core functions.)

The argument was that if these non-core tasks were not discarded, organizations would stay unfocused and fail to satisfy the 3Es – effectiveness, efficiency and economy. 'Compulsory competitive tendering' is also a term used in this context: the activities that were outsourced were required to be put out to tender, with normally the lowest tenderer obtaining the contract.

Many public-sector institutions were not comfortable with identifying what was core and what was non-core or ancillary. Taking the police as an example, there was no attempt to radically reform police practice. However, a number of specific functions were externalized, such as catering services and managing wide loads on motorways.

7. A purchaser–provider split was introduced

This relates to what is known as the *marketization* of public services. New Right thinkers argued that the market place, where *laissez faire*[1] economic principles applied, was infinitely preferable to the interventionism associated with the welfare state, so the aim was to inject the disciplines of the market place into public-sector institutions. However, what was introduced was not a full market, but rather a form of quasi market, or internal market. The argument was that this too would guarantee more economy, effectiveness and efficiency. The internal markets introduced in the state sector were based on a split between a purchaser and a provider. This purchaser–provider split is perhaps most apparent in the reforms that took place in the National Health Service throughout the 1990s. The purchasing organizations were health authorities, which commissioned services for people at a local level, and the providers were the hospitals and other bodies that actually carried out the services.

8. Inter-agency cooperation was actively encouraged

This aspect of NMP was developed later than those described above, and is more clearly associated with the New Labour government of Tony Blair. Rather than focusing exclusively on the organizational outputs of individual institutions, it introduced a requirement for agencies to work together. The Morgan Report (1991) recommended inter-agency cooperation in the criminal justice sphere, and this was eventually enshrined in legislation by the Crime and Disorder Act (1998). (This is discussed further in Chapter 10.)

9. Clients were redesignated as 'customers'

In the context of the welfare state citizens were perceived as recipients of welfare (Clarke and Newman, 1997). There was a tendency to see citizens as being passive, and to take the approach that the state had a moral obligation to provide welfare services to those who were unable to provide for themselves and their families. As part of the NPM, these passive recipients came to be seen instead as customers of public services. The argument was that customers would question the quality and standard of services, and as they were paying for them, would demand more and better products: a demand that the providing bodies were expected to respond to by becoming still more effective and efficient. This shift to the redesignation of clients as customers implies a far more active and participatory relationship between the public and state (Clarke and Newman, 1997).

The implications of NPM for welfare and justice

It is undeniable that many public-sector organizations, including welfare and criminal justice institutions, were in need of reform and that they needed to become more effective, efficient and economic. However, the principles of the NPM are not necessarily compatible with justice, for the following reasons:

■ An emphasis on performance targets, results and league tables can skew and distort the priorities of agencies. Understandably, the aspects that are measured receive more attention than those that are not.

■ In the 1990s the police were required to prioritize volume crimes such as burglary. Because police forces had finite resources, this meant that other crimes were sometimes under-investigated or not investigated at all. In the 1990s, for example child protection was not a priority. The emphasis on burglary certainly produced quantifiable measures of police effectiveness, but was this just and fair as far as child victims of sexual abuse were concerned?

■ Many criminal justice professionals felt it was not possible or practicable, or arguably even desirable, to redesignate offenders as customers. If people are arrested and detained, it is a part of the process that they lose rights such as the right to freedom. It is essential that they are treated legally and in accordance with principles of due process, but it is questionable whether consumer choice is a concept that has any validity in this context. Arguably people should not be allowed to complain if they are rightfully arrested. Likewise, it might be felt perverse to regard a prisoner as a customer. Is it appropriate for prison authorities to be required to consider complaints that prisoners make about the quality or standard of their prison experience?

There are other examples, but these serve to illustrate some of the tensions and contradictions that surface if the values underpinning justice and the NPM are compared and contrasted.

CONCLUSIONS

In this chapter the aim has been to introduce the criminal justice system as a framework. It has drawn attention to the role of the Home Office, but most crucially it has situated criminal justice in the context of the welfare state. An example was given of the relationship between health and crime.

The concept of criminal justice has also been introduced, illustrating how justice ought to look. In reality justice often assumes another shape as a result of organizational pressures and human frailty. Finally, although justice is still an important, and indispensable, principle, since the 1980s other value frameworks have become increasingly important, and in particular managerialism has had an increasing influence.

FURTHER READING

This chapter has introduced social policy, and attempted to explore some of the linkages between the welfare state and the criminal justice system. To the best of my knowledge, no basic introductory text covers all of these issues in a single volume. However there are succinct but comprehensive introductions to social policy in H. Dean, *Social Policy* (Cambridge: Polity, 2006) and P. Alcock, A. Erskine and M. May (eds), *The Student's Companion to Social Policy* (2nd edn) (Oxford: Blackwell, 2003). Use the index to find specific references to crime and disorder.

The concept of justice has been discussed only at a very basic level in this chapter. It is discussed in more depth in Chapter 1 of M. Davies, H. Croall and J. Tyrer, *Criminal Justice: An introduction to the criminal justice system in England and Wales* (3rd edn) (Harlow: Pearson, 2005).

For an excellent discussion of the relationship between social policy and criminal justice policy see D. Cook, *Criminal and Social Justice* (London: Sage, 2006) (especially Chapters 1, 2 and 7).

STUDY QUESTIONS

1. What is the significance of the welfare state for understanding criminal justice policy?
2. What is meant by criminal justice?
3. Is the Police and Criminal Evidence Act (1984) adequate to ensure suspects are treated fairly?
4. Describe the main principles of managerialism (NPM) and consider their relevance for understanding criminal justice.

6 The Police: Gatekeepers to the Criminal Justice Process

OVERVIEW

The aim of this chapter is to provide:

■ a discussion about the ideas of policing and police
■ a brief historical sketch of the emergence of the police service in the nineteenth century and its evolution until the early stages of the twenty-first century
■ a description of the police organizational structure and the relationship between each of the key players
■ an examination of what the police do
■ an appreciation of the significance of police culture, for explaining the gap between what the police are supposed to do in principle and what they actually do in practice
■ an indication of the relevance of social divisions for understanding the complexity of police work.

INTRODUCTION

The police service is widely regarded as the key agency responsible for responding to crime and disorder, although a whole range of other statutory, private and voluntary organizations also work alongside the police. However, the police have special importance because they are legitimately able to use force against another person. They also have the power to refer the people they deal with to the next stage of the criminal justice process, and to influence the experience of victims of crime. The chapter examines the origins of the modern police service and outlines its core responsibilities and functions. In determining what the police do, the chapter identifies two key sets of interrelated tasks: first, peace keeping and crime fighting, and second, caring and controlling.

The chapter is divided into five main parts. First, the twin concepts of policing and the police are examined from a historical perspective. This shows that policing refers to a set of processes relating to social control, and that the police are just one agency involved in the wider activity of *policing*. Policing has been around for centuries, although the specialist police force, or service, was not created until the nineteenth century. After this brief history the second part focuses on the organizational structure of the police service in England and Wales, paying particular reference to the tripartite structure of accountability set up by the Police Act (1964). The rank structure of the police and some of the agencies belonging to the wider 'policing family' are also outlined. In the third part some of the main jobs done by the police are considered. You might think of this as straightforward, but the police actually do many different things. The fourth part introduces an important topic in police studies, the notion of police culture, to show how police work on the ground is often rather different from the formal roles and functions of the police. In this part, it is demonstrated that the police culture results in the differential policing of a range of minority groups, including ethnic minority groups and the underclass. The fifth and final part explores in more depth the theme of social divisions, by considering some police responses to violence against women. This example and the discussion of the police culture show quite clearly that the police do not always do what is required of them by the law, policy makers and senior police officers.

POLICING AND THE POLICE: A BRIEF HISTORY

Although there is considerable overlap between the ideas of 'policing' and 'police' they have separate meanings. This discussion is related to the history of the emergence of the modern police service in the early nineteenth century, which can only be understood with reference to the system of policing prior to that time. It is argued that policing before the police were established was community based, although the deficiencies of this system were exposed as a result of the social and economic changes from the eighteenth century onwards, including industrialization and urbanization. History is sometimes seen as irrelevant to contemporary developments in society, but Sir John Woodcock, a former Chief Inspector of Her Majesty's Inspectorate of Constabulary, made a comment which gave due respect to the significance of the past for understanding what the police do in the present:

> What is happening to the police is that a nineteenth century institution is being dragged into the 21st century. Despite all the later mythology of Dixon, the police never really were the police of the whole people but a mechanism set up to protect the affluent from what the Victorians described as the dangerous classes.
>
> (Woodcock, 1992: 1932 cited in Crowther, 2000a)

Jones and Newburn argue that policing consists of:

> those organized forms of order maintenance, peacekeeping, rule of law enforcement, crime investigation and prevention...which may involve a conscious exercise of coercive power – undertaken by individuals or organizations, where such

activities are viewed by them and/ or others as a central or key defining part of their purpose.

(Jones and Newburn 1998: 18–19)

Other commentators have suggested that:

> 'Police' refers to a particular kind of social institution, while 'policing' implies a set of processes with specific social functions. 'Police' are not found in every society, and police organizations and personnel can have a variety of shifting forms. 'Policing', however is arguably a necessity in any social order, which may be carried out by a number of different processes and institutional arrangements. A state-organized specialist 'police' organization of the modern kind is only one example of policing.
>
> (Bowling and Foster, 2002: 980)

The idea of policing is therefore not restricted to what the police do, and is concerned with a set of processes and practices rather than an institution. In other words, the police perform a policing function, but policing can be undertaken by non-police agencies as well. Indeed the police are, in historical terms, a relatively new phenomenon with a more specific role: 'the police are nothing else than a mechanism for the distribution of situationally justifiable force in society' (Bittner, 1974: 39).

As the quotations above show, a range of individuals and organizations from both the public and private sectors are involved in policing. However they do not make it particularly clear what policing *is*. In essence, policing is a form of social control and security, related to the surveillance of particular geographical areas, but above all of specific populations or groups of people. Examples of surveillance include the CCTV cameras installed more or less everywhere, private security staff at shopping centres, and nightclub bouncers. The list is endless, and it soon becomes clear that the police are just one provider of control, security and surveillance. The underlying aim of these activities is to make sure that society is disciplined and orderly, and that any unruliness and disorder is kept to a minimum.

A history of the police force or service

This section:

- traces the evolution of the modern police service, beginning in the thirteenth century
- demonstrates that policing was carried out by communities
- shows how the police assumed responsibility for policing in 1829
- explains why the police emerged when they did.

Before the creation of the New Police in the nineteenth century, it was the job of notable figures of authority in predominantly small, self-contained rural areas to appoint parish constables and watches to ensure that day-to-day life in communities ran smoothly. Their role included crime prevention, and in particular the control of the vagrancy laws, which required them to observe anyone suspicious, especially outsiders passing through their communities (see Chapter 1). However, most of their time was spent regulating the everyday conduct and behaviour of households within the community, dealing with issues such as personal dress and appearance, and ensuring the community was secure, clean and safe.

In essence, policing can be characterized as a style of communal intervention involving, at least in principle, all members of the community. For example, the Statute of Winchester (1285) established a system called the watch, effectively a community-based method of social control. Under this system householders in communities were required to look out for each other, to ensure that no outsiders intruded into their day-to-day lives, and to make sure that everyone in the community conformed to expected behavioural conventions (Rawlings, 2001). We can see the continuation of communal policing in neighbourhood watch, a scheme set up in England and Wales in the 1980s, which involves neighbours in small areas – such as a few streets on a housing estate – looking out for each other (McConville and Shepherd, 1992).

The watch system evolved over time, and policing became the responsibility of various figures including watchmen, poor law officers, justices of the peace and constables. Rawlings (2001: 43) argues that this form of '[c]ommunal policing was the progeny of feudalism and, like it, depended on the existence of relatively stable communities'. The focus was mainly on order maintenance rather than crime detection. Social order at that time was achieved largely as a result of informal methods of social control rather than by relying on the formal codes of law. Offenders were not prosecuted as a matter of course. If an individual broke the rules, the rest of the community would demonstrate their objections to that person. Invariably a restorative approach was used, whereby offenders were required to apologize and make amends for the harm they caused to their neighbours. For example, a thief might be required to repay the victim from whom he or she had stolen. Occasionally the community reacted in an over-coercive and unlawful way towards a wrong-doer. In contemporary societies the equivalent type of action is known as *vigilantism* (Johnston, 2000).

By the late thirteenth century the feudal system was in decay, and in 1348 the plague devastated many communities. This resulted in a shortage of labour, increased wages and the need for employees to be more geographically mobile. According to Rawlings:

> These problems led many in the political elite to swallow their reservations about encouraging the acquisition of power by the Crown and instead, to support a national strategy that was co-ordinated by justices of the peace appointed by the Crown.
>
> (Rawlings 2001: 43)

Subsequently the arrangements for policing changed, and there was a shift from communal policing towards a different style of policing which was led by 'officials', involving an enhanced role for the Crown. These changes were gradual and incremental, but they accelerated in the eighteenth century, and as Rawlings (2001: 58) puts it, 'By the eighteenth century, active intervention in criminal justice policy had started to become a routine part of the state's functions'. An illustration of this is the role the

Fielding brothers (the novelist Henry and his brother John) played in reforming methods of policing. They were critical of the Westminster watch, arguing that it was far too small and inefficient to meet policing demands, largely because this system had developed in rural communities. Urbanization and the growth of towns and cities exposed the watches as too localized and unsystematic.

As Gattrell (1990) argues, the nineteenth century was a period of dramatic social and economic change which increasingly exposed the inadequacy of this method of maintaining social order. Among the most significant changes was industrialization, which led to the replacement of an agrarian economy mainly reliant on agriculture and farming by an economic system based on manufacturing and factory production. This resulted in the development and rapid expansion of cities such as London, Manchester, Liverpool, Bristol and Birmingham, so vividly brought to life in the novels of Charles Dickens and Elizabeth Gaskell, and in the journalistic writings of Henry Mayhew. The entire socioeconomic and cultural landscape changed so suddenly that it put pressure on what was quickly becoming a fragile social order. The new industrial manufacturing sector, based in a maturing capitalist economic system, required a readily available pool of workers to produce the goods customers were demanding, and many people moved from the countryside to find work. This soon led to overcrowding in areas inhabited by these recently arrived workers. Wages were low, living conditions poor, and long-term and secure employment rare (Emsley, 2002).

In response to these developments the Bow Street Runners were established, and made responsible for policing in the Bow area of east London. This early form of public policing was supplemented by the employment of private watchmen by the affluent who had the means to protect their property and possessions from the masses.

By the nineteenth century there were more street patrols, which started to resemble the type of policing found in contemporary society. Professional watchmen had effectively replaced householders. Partly because a parish-based system of policing was seen to be partial and unfair, favouring the wealthy, the state now had to intervene. Sir Robert Peel (who was home secretary, and later prime minister) saw it as an appropriate time for action, and his initiatives led to the establishment of the Metropolitan Police in 1829. The main purpose of this organization was to prevent crime (crime fighting) and maintain social order (peace keeping) in the London area. Ever since that day the police have been required to undertake these two roles, and at particular moments the police have prioritized one above the other (Crowther, 2000a and b).

By the mid-nineteenth century the rest of England and Wales had introduced similar bodies as a result of the County and Borough Police Act (1856). Although the visible presence of uniformed police officers carrying out these specialized tasks was a new development, many policing functions they performed were long-established.

Explaining police history

Various police historians have attempted to explain the history of the police, although the Reiner (2000) model is the one most commonly referred to. He characterized previous accounts as either 'orthodox' or 'revisionist'. The orthodox explanation is based on a functionalist view of the police, and an assumption that society is organized on a consensual basis. Conversely, the revisionist account is based on the view that society is in a state of conflict. Each of these explanations is now considered in some more detail.

The orthodox and revisionist interpretations both argue that the Metropolitan Police was a consequence of the broad social changes identified earlier by Gattrell (1990). However, they offer contrasting accounts of the relationship between these social changes and the police. Orthodox theorists argue that the creation of the police forces was an inevitable result of social progress, and that the organization exists to control society in a professional and bureaucratic fashion. Modern industrial society is much more complex than earlier societies, and the police symbolize authority, law and order, and are there to protect all people. Revisionists, on the other hand, argue that the ruling classes set up the police to maintain their economic interests. Thus the origins of the police must be seen in the context of class conflict, and the antagonism between the bourgeoisie and the proletariat. Added to this, urbanization resulted in over-crowding, especially amongst the poor. The poorer sections of society posed a threat to the capitalist classes because of their crime and perceived political radicalism. The police were an instrument used by the bourgeoisie to coerce the crime and disorder of the dangerous working classes (Reiner, 2000).

POLICE HISTORY: KEY POINTS

- The activity of policing is a feature of all societies, and concerns surveillance and social control of the population.
- Informal policing methods were the defining features of pre-industrial society.
- The modern police service came into existence as a response to social changes, including urbanization and industrialization.
- The Metropolitan Police Service model, first established in 1829, was a template for forces throughout the remainder of England and Wales.
- By the end of the nineteenth century the police were an important feature of the social landscape.

The relevance of police history for today

Following the introduction of the police in 1829 there was widespread opposition from most elements of society. Affluent groups felt the police were a burden on the taxpayer, and that they were not part of the established English way of life (Emsley, 2002). The working classes were opposed to the police too, but their opposition was related to the perception that the police were in place to enforce ruling class interests. However, over the course of the next 130 years or so the police came to be accepted by most of the population, although the underclass has posed problems (Crowther, 2000a and b). We shall return to this issue after outlining the structure of the police service that emerged out of the 1964 Police Act.

THE ORGANIZATIONAL STRUCTURE OF THE POLICE SERVICE IN ENGLAND AND WALES

This section:

- sketches the organizational structure of the police service
- introduces the tripartite structure of police accountability
- considers the formal roles and responsibilities of the police service.

Before it is possible to start coming to terms with what the police actually do, it is necessary to provide some more background information. At the time of writing there are 43 separate police force areas in England and Wales, all resulting from the Police Act (1964). This piece of legislation followed the Royal Commission of 1962, the first of its kind to review the structure and organization of the police. It effectively formalized the system of police governance in England and Wales. Among its many recommendations was that the number of force areas should be reduced. Before the Second World War there were 180 forces, which were amalgamated into 131 in 1947. In other words, there was a tendency towards centralization before the 1960s, but it was accelerated significantly by the 1964 Act, when the target was set at 43 forces. More crucially, the Act outlined a new set of arrangements to bring together the different players so that there was more power sharing. The aim was to ensure that the police were not just an arm of the state, and that they were also accountable or answerable to the communities they served. The mechanism set up to achieve this was a tripartite structure of accountability, consisting of three players: the home secretary, chief constables and police authorities. The role of each of these players is briefly described below:

The home secretary

The home secretary is the most important player in the tripartite system, and he/she has ultimate influence and control over the direction of policing. The home secretary:

- is accountable to the prime minister
- sets the National Policing Plan
- establishes key performance indicators
- oversees the running of the Home Office
- influences policy through Acts of Parliament and circulars
- receives annual reports from chief constables
- oversees central government expenditure on policing
- approves chief officer appointments
- ensures the resignation of inefficient and incompetent chief officers
- makes decisions regarding future amalgamations of forces.

Chief constables

Although the home secretary possesses most power, chief constables have constabulary independence. This means that the police are accountable to the law and should not be subject to any political interference. As Lord Denning put it, a chief constable 'is not the servant of anyone, save of the law itself …. The responsibility for law enforcement lies on him. He is answerable to law and to the law alone.' Halsbury spells out the significance of this:

> notwithstanding that present day police forces are the creation of statute and that the police have numerous statutory powers and duties, in essence a police force is neither more or less than a number of individual constables whose status derives from the common law, organized together in the interests of efficiency.
>
> (2005, 4th edn, vol. 36, para. 201)

There is a chief constable in each constabulary in England and Wales, and they are in overall charge of a particular geographical area, such as Nottinghamshire, South Yorkshire or Devon and Cornwall. Their main roles and responsibilities are to:

- be accountable to the home secretary
- submit an annual report to the Home Office and police authority
- manage the force budget
- show leadership in terms of operational decision making
- oversee discipline and grievance concerns in the force.

Police authorities

The 1964 Act established an authority in each of the 43 police force areas, so there was alignment between their activities. Police authorities are required to:

- make sure the force is 'adequate and efficient'
- appoint chief officers
- work with chief officers on the annual report
- publish the annual policing plan
- make sure the people they represent have a 'voice' in policing
- ensure that the constabularies they are responsible for are accountable to the public.

A commentary on the tripartite structure

The 1964 Act was a watershed in British policing because for the first time in police history the roles of the home secretary, chief constables and police authorities were explicitly defined. The Act clarified the role of chief officers, who were charged with directing and controlling policing in their respective areas. It affirmed the principle of constabulary independence which was acknowledged above.

The local police authorities, which effectively replaced watch committees and joint standing committees, were made up of two-thirds elected councillors and one-third magistrates. In London, the home secretary acted as the police authority until 1999, when the Metropolitan Police were made accountable to the Greater London Authority. The police authorities were also given more powers and responsibilities than they had previously enjoyed, including responsibility for securing an adequate and efficient force in a given area, and a role in appointing chief officers. However, although on the surface it appeared that the police authorities were being given more power and influence, the powers of the home secretary and chief constables were increased, suggesting that there was actually greater centralization. For example, the home secretary was given the authority to make chief officers resign or retire. Although police authorities had some say in the appointment of new chief officers, the appointments required the backing and approval of the home secretary. The home secretary could also demand annual reports from chief officers, but above all the Home Office provided 51 per cent of police expenditure.

The tripartite structure remained unchanged until the 1990s, with the passing into law of the Police and Magistrates' Courts Act (1994) (PMCA). This brought about changes to police authorities, and they became independent from the local government structure. They had the same duties of overseeing the effectiveness and efficiency of the force, but there were changes to their structure and make-up. The size of each police authority was restricted to 17 members:

- nine councillors
- three magistrates
- five 'independent' members, who were locally appointed.

The thinking behind the PMCA was to increase the influence the police authorities had over policing at a local level. In practice the influence of the centre remained strong, inasmuch as local policing priorities must reflect national objectives. The powers of the home secretary were bolstered in other ways too. Chief constables were subject to fixed-term appointments, and the home secretary could exert more control over the activities of chief officers by setting performance targets. If a force is seen to be failing (that is, not meeting performance targets), the home secretary can intervene and remove the chief constable. The home secretary also has greater power to amalgamate forces, and this debate was reopened in 2005, with the government calling for a further reduction of the number of constabularies. Finally, the home secretary sets an annual cash-limited grant to forces, but the PMCA empowered police authorities and chief officers to decide exactly how that money is spent. However, because the home secretary is able to set performance targets, the influence of managerialism (see Chapter 5) remains strong.

Now we have outlined the formal structure of the police policy-making machinery, we need to sketch the organizational hierarchy of the police service.

The rank structure

The role of chief constables has already been acknowledged. These officers, along with deputy and assistant chief constables, belong to a collective organization known as the Association of Chief Police Officers (ACPO). This agency is the main policy maker in the police service, although its activities are influenced by the state, principally the Home Office. Below the ACPO officers at the top of the force hierarchy are the super-intendent ranks, followed by inspectors. These three ranks are commonly referred to as senior police officers, and they all have managerial responsibility and act as police leaders. The final two ranks are sergeants and police constables, who carry out the bulk of operational police work.

As well as the police service, recognized by its distinctive blue uniform, a range of other bodies perform policing functions. This is sometimes referred to as 'plural policing' (Crawford et al., 2005). As Crawford (2003) shows, there are various specialist policing bodies, including:

- state security services
- HM Revenue and Customs
- the British Transport Police
- state departments (such as the DSS)
- regulatory authorities like the Health and Safety Executive (HSE).

Municipal policing is also important: this includes environmental health officers, public auxiliaries (such as city guards, neighbourhood wardens and local patrols), traffic wardens, community safety partnerships and antisocial behaviour teams. There is also civilian policing undertaken by:

- the Special Constabulary
- citizens' patrols
- neighbourhood watch organizations
- vigilantism.

Last but not least there is commercial security, an expanding sector that provides policing for areas of 'mass private property' (Shearing and Stenning, 1981), such as shopping centres, sports stadia and gated communities. Private security firms that employ 'bouncers' also effectively police the night-time economy – the pubs and clubs in town and city centres (Hobbs et al., 2003).

Observing the police

Most academic research has focused on sergeants and constables, also known as the *rank and file*, and little work has been done on senior police officers (Reiner, 1978, 1991). Indeed most of the knowledge and understanding students have of the police is based on the activities of the lower ranks. Most people's main exposure to the police is via the media, especially fictional representations such as television dramas or movies. In these dramatizations the rank and file, and especially detectives, feature most prominently. Senior officers, especially at the highest level of the hierarchy, are likely to appear in the background and in a rather negative light, as people who are remote and removed from the reality of policing. When people have direct contact with the police, as victims of crime, witnesses or offenders, they are likely to encounter an officer from the rank and file. Also, bear in mind that for many people their contact with the police has nothing directly to do with crime. For instance, people might ask a police officer for directions if they are lost in a strange city centre late at night.

Task

Spend five minutes writing down all the different jobs the police do on a daily basis.

It is highly likely that the list you produce will refer more or less exclusively to the jobs undertaken by the rank and file. The list below is based on a 'thought shower' by a group of undergraduates, and demonstrates this quite well.

- Responding to a report from a student who has had a bag stolen on the bus.
- Catching a thief breaking into a motor vehicle in a car park.
- Monitoring a witness looking at suspects on an identity parade.
- Making door-to-door enquiries in response to a reported crime.
- Stopping motor vehicles at a roadblock.
- Patrolling visibly in a village or the high street in a town or city.
- Emergency response to a 999 call.
- Patrolling in a helicopter to monitor the movements of a suspected group of soccer hooligans at a railway station.
- Evicting a drunk from public transport.
- Arriving at the scene of a road traffic collision.

The police will be involved in all of the above and in 101 other tasks. However the tasks on this list (and on your own) can be put into two broad categories, crime fighting and peace keeping.

Crime fighting

The police are crime fighters when they enforce the law through stop and search, making arrests, detaining, interviewing and interrogating suspects, and observing and monitoring a range of suspects and offenders. Crime fighting is all about the police using their legitimate right to coerce or use force against law- and rule- breakers.

Peace keeping

The police are also peace keepers, meaning that they take an interest in the maintenance of social and public order, where law enforcement is not always necessary. Asking anti-social youths to move on, and preventing people from drinking in public places, are examples. To use discretion by not arresting a person for possessing a small quantity of cannabis for personal use (see Chapter 1) might be seen as a form of peace keeping, if making an arrest is likely to cause alienation and resentment among a particular group of people. Peace keeping also refers to problem solving, and the capacity of the police to act in a social-service type role, caring for victims and some more vulnerable offenders such as drug addicts and the mentally disordered.

So far we have traced the origins of the police, identified some of the things the police do, and showed that the police are just one player responsible for policing. The next section focuses on the characteristics of the police service that are peculiar to the organization, and that for some commentators provide its defining feature.

THE POLICE CULTURE

In this section:

■ the concept of police culture is defined
■ the relevance of the police culture is examined in relation to the ways in which the police treat lower-class and minority ethnic group subjects
■ a case study considers the police service and its treatment of the victims of sexual violence, in particular rape victims.

The police culture is sometimes known as the 'occupational subculture'. It is most apparent among junior or rank and file officers, typically police constables. The police culture is generally characterized as a negative feature of the police service, and is frequently identified as such not just by critics, but also by senior police officers. Among the most serious problems posed by the police culture are its racism and sexism. This section briefly reviews the main traits of the police culture, then considers its impact in relation to social divisions (particularly social class, race and ethnicity, and to some extent gender).

Defining police culture

So how do police officers see the world through the 'cop culture'? Much of the research looks at the links between attitudes displayed by police officers and their behaviour. There is a gap between what is said in the canteen and what is done on the streets (Waddington, 1999). Reiner (2000) identifies two issues:

■ 'cop culture' in terms of what is said, hinted at and actually done when police officers are at work
■ the 'canteen culture', or those values and beliefs police officers express when socializing.

The latter is often about reducing tension through the use of jokes, often in the form of 'gallows humour' (Waddington, 1999). It would be wrong to focus too much on what is said to, or observed by, researchers in trying to assess the police culture. There is a problematic relationship between the words spoken by the police and their working practices. There is far more to the police culture than just attitudes.

What is 'culture'? It refers to a way of life, beliefs, attitudes and institutions. Social values, attitudes and rules are developed as people react to the many situations they face. Culture is also based on prior experiences. Cultures are shaped by the people belonging to them, and a culture is about people making situations meaningful for themselves and for others to act in. Although people make their own cultures, this is not done under conditions of their own choosing, as there are structural or environmental constraints (Reiner, 2000). There is not one cop culture but variants within a broader, ideal-typical version. For example, each officer has a different biography and history, and there are differences between forces. So there are general tendencies based on common experiences, but considerable diversity and internal variation too.

Among the major contributions of research into the police subculture is its investigation of the relationship between decisions and plans made at the top by chief constables, and the translation of these principles into practice by police managers, but especially by the rank and file (constables and sergeants). In this sense, it holds precisely to the distinction between policy as it is written and policy in action, and it also indicates that officers at this level act autonomously and independently. To this must be added the principle of constabulary independence, which is shared by all police officers irrespective of their rank. Holdaway (1983) argues that it is imperative to take into account the existence of the occupational culture among police constables if we are to gain a more rounded view of police policy making. Unless we are aware of the often clandestine activities of the police, it is not practicable to either monitor or limit the power they apply.

In the early 1990s the police staff associations in England and Wales conveyed a similar message in a co-authored report (Joint Consultative Committee, 1990). It was found in one force that the rank and file either rejected or were unaware of the priorities set by their chief constable. Senior officers, on the other hand, assumed that constables had knowledge of force goals and objectives. There can be minimal contact between officers at senior and intermediate levels of the organizational hierarchy and the rank and file, and this obstructs effective communication in the police policy-making process. For example, there is a perception that senior officers do not have enough direct contact with officers under their leadership to make them fully aware of policy changes initiated at the top. There is more to this issue, though.

While each and every police officer enjoys the principle of constabulary independence, the rank and file in particular exercise a considerable degree of discretion because of the low visibility of most of their activities (Sanders and Young, 2003). Many officers hold the view that policing should be done not by the book but by the 'Ways and Means Act'. In the 1960s and 1970s there was concern about the police use of the 'crime control' model instead of the 'due process' model (see Chapter 5). McBarnett's structural critique (1981, cited in Choongh, 1997) argued that the over-reliance on crime control was not the fault of the police, but occurred because of the way the law is written (for instance, that it is flexible and elastic). Blame should be apportioned to political elites and the judiciary, who encourage crime control rather than due process.

However, the law is not the only factor determining what work the police actually do. Much of police work is about shaping practice in relation to particular situations. Thus legal rules are neither irrelevant nor do they determine police practice. It is said that there are three types of rule:

- 'working rules': internalized principles guiding action
- inhibiting rules, which have a different effect: they are concerned with how visible behaviour is controlled
- 'presentation rules', which suggest how people can put a gloss on actions that are actually undertaken for reasons other than those that are apparent (Reiner, 2000).

There is a complex relationship between these rules and the law. Legal rules may be used for 'presentational' purposes rather than as operational 'working rules' or 'inhibitors'.

Thus the legalistic response to police malpractice (to write a new law) is not always the solution. However, 'black letter law' may become an 'inhibitor' or a 'working' rule (as was seen with the complex impact of PACE (1984)) (Sanders and Young, 2003).

Thus the culture of the police is not monolithic, universal or unchanging (Foster, 2003). There are differences between individuals and forces. Despite these variations there are some commonalities because all police officers face similar problems. There are familiar tensions and pressures recurring over time and space, and officers are socialized into this culture (albeit not passively). Stories and jokes are told about good and bad practice. The culture only survives because it has a psychological fit with the many complex demands of the job (Waddington, 1999).

There are a number of core characteristics of the cop culture, including an emphasis on danger and authority, which are both mediated by an attempt to be efficient. Other professionals face dangers, but the police arguably face more of them. It is not clear what is around the corner. Police officers have authority (an ability to legitimately use force), which is intended to minimize the danger to them. It is hoped that the visible presence of a police officer will be enough to keep order, but this is not always so. In addition there is the pressure to get results and to be efficient, which has been magnified by managerialism and the NPM. This can encourage officers to cut corners as they attempt to 'maintain order' and 'fight crime' (Reiner, 2000).

Another integral feature of the police culture is its machismo. Being a police officer is seen as an essentially male activity, and traditionally male officers have suggested that women are not fully capable of carrying out all the duties a police officer must perform (Foster, 2003).

Other elements include a sense of mission and a search for action, underpinned by cynicism and pessimism. Police officers also have an almost religious sense of mission. It is more than 'just a job', it is 'a way of life'. The job is about protecting the weak and vulnerable (that is, victims or potential victims of crime). The job is challenging, exciting and fun. The sense of being on a mission is evidenced by phrases such as 'the thin blue line', the 'noble cause', and the *Dirty Harry* 'make my day' ethic (Reiner, 2000).

The police present themselves as if they are being overrun, and civilization being overturned in the process. Cynicism is most manifest amongst the so-called 'uniform carriers', who are resigned to not being promoted and may be waiting for retirement. For others, the mission is more exciting. Thus a sense of mission, an orientation towards action, and 'pessimistic cynicism' characterize the police culture (Reiner, 2000). These elements are interwoven, and lead to a pressure for results, which can test the principles of due process (Sanders and Young, 2003). Thus the pressures for efficiency are not just externally induced (by factors such as managerialism and the 'three Es') but an inherent part of the job (Long, 2003).

Police culture and social divisions

It is perhaps not altogether surprising that the police culture or occupational subculture has generally been identified as a problem. Much of the literature refers to the occupational prejudices and stereotypes held by rank and file officers. Much of the empirical material used to identify the existence of police culture is based on ethnographic work (see Chapter 4) examining what has been described as 'front line' policing. Perhaps one of the most significant pieces of research was that undertaken by Holdaway, and described in his *Inside the British Police* (1983). Holdaway was a serving police officer when he commenced the empirical research on which the book is based, and it is therefore based on first-hand experience of 'the job'. Much of the work describes the police officer confronting 'The world as a place that is always on the verge of chaos held back from devastation by a police presence. People are naïve and potentially disorderly in all situations; control, ideally absolute control, is the fundamental police task' (Holdaway, 1989: 65).

By watching police officers grapple with the unpredictable nature of their working environment, some observers of the police culture have imputed certain ideas to practitioners. The key issue is how different aspects of policing come to be associated with negative representations of minority ethnic groups, women, and the underclass or 'rougher' sections of the working class.

The work of Banton (1964, 1967), which has been important to police training, focuses (among many topics) on police discretion, or partial law enforcement. Rather than questioning the legitimacy of discretion, Banton mulled over the practical uses of this power in everyday police work, and the impact this had on police relations with the wider community. In their interactions with the public, officers make judgements based on their perceptions of the personal, behavioural and cultural traits of the people they police. Interpersonal relations are also influenced by the kind of language used in particular situations, and officers communicate with different members of the public 'in their own language' (Cain, 1973: 82). Although it contravenes official regulations, the compliance of 'lower-class subjects' in general and 'low-status offenders' in particular is obtained by using coarse language, instead of imposing legal sanctions (Banton, 1964: 183). Because this depends on detainees accepting the classification an officer assigns to them, it may result in a hardening of collective attitudes into an 'us and them mentality' with 'possibly serious consequence{s}' such as an altercation or insurrection (Southgate and Ekblom, 1986: 12).

There is also a spatial dimension to the prejudices belonging to the police culture, and the law is enforced more forcibly in 'rougher neighbourhoods' (Banton, 1964: 131). The rough/respectable dichotomy is peculiar to urban policing, and other kinds of stereotypes obtain in rural areas (Cain, 1973: 82). In terms of the occupational culture, urban policing is made meaningful through the use of a 'fundamental map of the population' (Holdaway, 1983: 81). This enables officers to link the characteristics of an environment with a specific style of police action. One police constable observed by Baldwin and Kinsey described the inhabitants of a housing estate as comprising two kinds of people. On the one hand, there was a 'civilized' majority with whom officers had minimal contact, and on the other hand, the 'priggies' or the 'garbage at the bottom of the bucket' (Baldwin and Kinsey, 1982: 47).

Drawing on American research, Banton assessed social differences in terms of myriad customs and values which differ from one community to another, frequently on the basis of social class (Banton, 1964: 138). The different norms and values held by residents in some areas explain why the police are very selective in their treatment of particular groups. Such action can be influenced by police officers' past experiences with suspects who have had previous contact with the law. Constables may be acquainted with individuals, or alternatively know people as a members of a group or class of person, as inhabitants of particular neighbourhoods, and either as 'villains or as law abiding citizens'. Southgate and Ekblom expand on this point: 'It was certainly clear that, in general, certain classes of person were regarded by officers as "deserving" or "non-deserving" according to the previous experiences of the officer – or his colleagues – with that person or someone seen as similar' (1986: 12). In principle police officers should be unbiased and classless, but in reality there is ample latitude for discriminatory attitudes and practices.

There are many methods of distinguishing members of the public. The idea of 'police property', for example, includes references to the sexual orientation of suspects, their use of illegal substances, and their affiliation with radical political organizations and deviant subcultures. Categorizations of 'rough' and 'respectable' are not based solely on class in socioeconomic terms, but on whether or not a population is a 'nice class of people' (Cain, 1973: 82). The 'rough' is a broad category, including 'the people living "down at the bottom end" plus a number of others' such as 'criminals and coloured people'. It is generally a negative label, but the term is ambivalent and built up of contradictory imagery (ibid: 114–15, 228). Despite this the poorest members of society persistently attract most police attention.

These and other themes are also evident in research published by the Policy Studies Institute (Smith and Gray, 1983), which concentrated on police policy and practice in London in terms of relations between the police and different members of the public, particularly minority ethnic groups. The PSI researchers documented the attitudes of both individuals and groups of officers, and their views about the public. We do not need to consider the findings of the report as such here: the main point of interest is the way the population is classified and differentiated into specific categories. The 'underclass' is one idea:

> A special conception of social class, mixed with an ideal of conventional or proper behaviour [which] is just as important to the police officers as racial or ethnic groups. In this scale, the 'respectable' working class and the suburban middle class stand highest while the 'underclass' of the poor and rootless, together with groups regarded as deviant, such as homosexuals or hippies stand the lowest.
>
> (Smith and Gray, 1983: 111)

Officers labelled the groups situated in the 'underclass' – as well as prostitutes and pimps – as 'slag' and 'rubbish'. Although these make up only a relatively small proportion of the overall population, the police encounter these groups far more than 'ordinary' people, who are property owners and ratepayers. There is also an implicit assumption that the 'slag' and 'dross' have fewer rights than 'respectable' people and should be treated accordingly (Smith and Gray, 1983: 163–5; Choongh, 1997: 43).

American and British research shows that the tendency to divide the population into different subgroups on the basis of the 'rough/respectable' typology is not just apparent when the issue of social class is addressed. Other significant factors include occupation, education, accent and ethnic group. To expand this point, it is assumed there is a connection between minority ethnic groups and the 'roughs', and there is little attempt to consider the impact of discrimination on the poverty and exclusion experienced by these groups. The view that black people are different, disorganized, unpredictable, unintelligible and violent has been consciously and deliberately perpetuated by some police officers, and hence the prevalence of police racism, which has been identified by academic researchers, and even by state-sanctioned commentators such as Macpherson (1999).

POLICE CULTURE: KEY POINTS

■ Numerous academic commentators have highlighted the existence of a so-called police culture.
■ The police culture has been identified most clearly among the rank and file.
■ While the police culture is arguably necessary for the operational activities of the police, it is not without problems, and it may result in the discriminatory treatment of some social groups.

Final thoughts on the police culture

Over the years, then, the view that the police service has a distinctive subculture has attracted substantial scholarly attention. The police culture is generally seen to comprise a negative set of traits, sustaining racist and sexist stereotypes. The sexism sustained by the police culture can be seen in the next section (Brown and Heidensohn, 2000).

THE POLICE AND SEX OFFENDERS: THE CASE OF RAPE

The section that follows:

■ discusses the nature of sex offending and rape
■ describes the scale of the problem the police service face
■ considers the police response to rape and the problems associated with this response
■ provides an account of attempts the police have taken to improve their response to rape.

Background

Now we shall look at the work the police do in response to sex offences, in particular sexual assault and interpersonal violence (Kelly, 2001). Sexual crime and the fear of sexual crime have a profound and damaging effect on individuals and communities. For that reason the government is determined to back the police, to help them do everything possible to reduce this kind of crime. Sex offenders, and especially predatory paedophiles, are a group of offenders who cause widespread public anxiety and fear. In the early twenty-first century high-profile cases included the murder of Sarah Payne in 2000 by the convicted paedophile Roy Whiting, and the Soham murders case in 2002, where Ian Huntley was convicted of the murder of two schoolchildren, Holly Wells and Jessica Chapman. It was found after the event that Huntley was known to the police for offences involving children, but an adjoining police force had mishandled intelligence about him. Tragically the vetting processes in place failed to identify him as a potential danger, resulting in Huntley being employed as a caretaker at the local school where Jessica and Holly were both pupils. To make matters worse, one of the family liaison officers supporting the families of the victims was accused of internet paedophilia offences (Bichard, 2004).

Fortunately cases such as these are relatively rare. However, if we look more closely at the reality of sex offending, most of it is not carried out by monstrous and predatory strangers like Roy Whiting or Ian Huntley, but by people known to the victims. Unfortunately sex offending is relatively commonplace, and is a routine feature of the lives of many people. The crimes of rape (being forced to have sexual intercourse)[1] and sexual assault (which is not rape, but the use of force to commit an offence of a sexual nature) are particularly common. These crimes make the headlines too, although it would appear that they do not arouse such an emotional response as cases involving the sexual abuse and sexually motivated murder of children. More than that, the police treatment of rape victims has been found to be deficient.

This part of the chapter focuses most on rape in attempt to understand the reasons that the police response is sometimes flawed. The crime of rape is very difficult to police, usually because it occurs in private behind closed doors, either in the home of the victim (55 per cent) or the residence of the offender (20 per cent) (Myhill and Allen, 2002a, 2002b). In most instances it is highly unlikely that there will be witnesses, unless it is a 'gang rape', and then the witnesses are not likely to come forward as they are already implicated in the crime. Policing this crime is made doubly difficult because of issues relating to evidence gathering. The investigation and attempted prosecution of rape normally involves taking the word of one person rather than the word of another, and some research shows that police officers and court officials have, at least in the past, regarded the suspect as more believable than the complainant or victim. This relates particularly to the complex issue of consent. In far too many cases the courts have assumed that the victim gave her (or his) consent to the sexual activity, when in actual fact the situation is likely to have been more complicated and less clear-cut. Given the nature of the offence and the time lapse that often occurs between the crime being committed and reported, there is often a lack of adequate forensic evidence, making the situation even more problematic for the police.

Key facts for the police

Chapter 3 provided some statistical data illustrating the proportion of violent crimes of a sexual nature that are reported to the police. Towards the middle of the 2000s there was an increase in the number of sexual offences recorded by the police. It is not clear whether this rise can be attributed to more offending behaviour of this type, or more victims coming forward. This chapter does not intend to revisit the controversies of crime statistics, but a number of research findings do have consequences for police work. The majority – some 80 per cent – of cases of rape and sexual assault are committed by someone known to the victim (St Mary's Historic Database, cited in Yates, 2005). This is significant because the likelihood of a sexual assault being reported to the police is greater if the assailant is a stranger. Reporting is much less likely if the perpetrator is an acquaintance, partner or family member (Temkin, 1999; HMCPSI and HMIC, 2002a). British Crime Survey data shows that most rapes (45 per cent) are carried out by current partners, and a further 11 per cent are carried out by ex-partners or other intimates. Strangers account for 8 per cent of rapes (Myhill and Allen, 2002a, 2002b). Earlier research revealed that there used to be a higher proportion of stranger rapists, ranging between 12 per cent and 30 per cent (Grace, Lloyd and Smith, 1992). This does not mean that there has been a decline in the number of stranger rapes, but rather that more rapes committed by partners and acquaintances are reported to the police.

Looking at the issue of reporting more closely, Myhill and Allen (2002a) found that 18 per cent of rapes come to the attention of the police. An incident is more likely to be reported if the offence was carried out by a stranger (36 per cent) and least likely if it happened during a date (8 per cent). In 1999, 7707 cases were reported to the police, compared with some 61,000 that were identified by the BCS (Myhill and Allen, 2002a). How successful are the police in dealing with rape cases?

According to Yates (2005), in 2001 there were 9450 reported offences and 2650 prosecutions, with a conviction rate of 6 per cent. In 2003 there were 12,760 reported offences and 2790 prosecutions, and a conviction rate of 5.27 per cent. Overall, more rapes are being reported to the police but three out of four of those accused get off towards the latter stages of the criminal justice process. The situation has not always been as bad, though, because in 1985 24 per cent of recorded rapes led to a conviction. However even then the figure had started to decline, and by 1997 it stood at 9 per cent (Harris and Grace, 1999).

Although the police do not have a particularly distinguished track record, it may come as a surprise to find that the BCS shows a third of victims were 'very satisfied' with the way the police handled their case, and only a fifth were 'very dissatisfied' (Myhill and Allen, 2002a, 2002b).

As has been noted elsewhere in this book, statistics are useful as a starting point, but criminologists need to complement them with other sources of data to assess the effectiveness of what the police are doing.

The police response to rape

There is considerable variation across the forces of England and Wales so it is difficult to make any broad-brush generalizations (Harris and Grace, 1999; Lees and Gregory, 1993). On the basis of what has been outlined so far, there are several issues we need to explore, including some of the reasons that rape victims choose not to report their experience to the police in the first place. We then look at the relative success and failure of police work related to rape cases, including the performance in the areas of investigation and detection.

Rape victims: reasons for non-reporting

It may be tempting to criticize the police for the relatively poor rate of reporting, but to offer a more balanced view, it is worth noting that the circumstances surrounding a rape make reporting difficult for many victims (Temkin, 1999). If the offence was carried out by a current partner the victim might fear reprisals if she reports her experience to the police. She (or in a minority of cases, he) might have ambivalent feelings towards the abusive partner, and even if she was hurt by the assault, she might decide that to pursue criminal proceedings is not the right option. Some victims might not define their experience as rape, even though legally that is what has happened to them. This is not altogether surprising given that there was no such offence as rape within marriage until the 1990s: before then a husband had the right to have sex with his wife with or without her active consent (Painter and Farrington, 1998). Deep-seated cultural attitudes like this, however objectionable they might seem to you, still remain an enduring influence. Other victims or survivors may fear retribution from family and friends, and this makes contact with the police even less likely.

The victim might feel that those around her, including the police, will disbelieve her. This fear is not completely irrational, as was made clear by a notorious fly-on-the wall television documentary made by Roger Graef in 1982 entitled *Police*. It showed Thames Valley Police officers interviewing a rape victim, and displaying unsympathetic and insensitive attitudes (Women's National Commission, 1985). This police culture appeared to have macho attitudes that made the officers unable to grasp the complex gender-specific issues surrounding the crime of rape. It was made obvious that they did not believe the complaint by the victim (Stanko, 1990). There was a public outcry, and the general expectation was that changes would result from the showing of this documentary, but a programme screened over 25 years later on Channel 4 exposed similar attitudes in Leicestershire Constabulary (*Dispatches: Undercover Copper*, 27 April 2006).

The police may not be aware of some of the reasons for non-reporting. Victims of rape not only suffer physical harm during the act, there are also psychological repercussions such as rape trauma syndrome (RTS), leading to feelings of shame, helplessness, self-disgust, self-blame, anxiety and shock (Stanko, 1985). RTS can also cause memory loss and confusion. Other victims of rape can become withdrawn. They feel unable or reluctant to talk about their experience, and may not want others to find out. These factors are significant for the police because the timing of the report is crucial to getting a conviction. If a rape is reported within 24 hours the chances of a conviction are much higher than if reporting is left for more than a day (Walby and Allen, 2004).

Rape victims might also fear the trial process, where again they may feel they are being blamed, or fear that their sexual habits will come under scrutiny, causing them considerable embarrassment. These issues too make victims likely to feel confused and frightened (Kelly, 2001).

In the aftermath of the Graef documentary the police were shamed, and efforts were made to improve the quality of their response to victims of rape. Most of the changes related to training. Some advances were made, but the impact of this training was uneven, particularly because of deficient supervision and management. There is still considerable under-reporting, as the BCS makes clear, and there have been estimates that only between one in five and one in ten cases of rape are reported (HMCPSI and HMIC, 2002a).

Police action: successes and failures

A Home Office-funded study (Harris and Grace, 1999) examined the relationship between recorded cases of rape and those resulting in a conviction (500 cases in 1996). In particular, the research was concerned with a change between 1985 and 1997, where the percentage of recorded rapes resulting in a conviction fell from 24 per cent to 9 per cent. This fall had begun before 1985: in 1977 one in three of those accused of rape were convicted (Kelly, 2001: 13). The proportion of reports that do not result in a conviction is called the *attrition rate*. The key findings in the Grace and Harris (1999) study relating to the attrition rate are:

- 25 per cent of cases were no-crimed.
- In 11 per cent of cases no suspect was identified.
- 31 per cent of cases resulted in no further action (NFA) being taken.
- 8 per cent of cases were discontinued by the Crown Prosecution Service (CPS).
- In 7 per cent of cases the accused was acquitted or the case was left lying on file.
- 7 per cent of cases culminated in a conviction for an offence other than rape.

It is apparent that several decisions taken by the police lay behind the attrition rate. Cases involving acquaintances were more likely to be no-crimed. (This would happen if a complainant 'retracts completely and admits to fabrication'.) Sometimes the police conclude that the allegation is false, and choose to believe an alternative version of reality (especially when the victim had been drinking). If this happens the victim might choose to withdraw the complaint, or resign herself to the fact that there will be no further action. On occasion the decision to 'no crime' cases has led to criticism, and there is some evidence that the police have responded to these criticisms, but there is so much variation it is difficult to generalize (Kelly, 2001). Harris and Grace (1999) showed that complaints were withdrawn in one in three cases, while in 15 per cent of cases there was insufficient evidence for the case to proceed to trial.

Cases involving intimates (defined as current or ex-partners) were more likely to be NFA-ed and discontinued by the CPS. Half of the NFA-ed cases were withdrawn complaints, and a third were caused by insufficient evidence. Kelly (2001) argues that there are three main reasons for NFA being taken. First, there is no suspect identified, especially in stranger rape cases; second, the complaint is withdrawn, and third, there is insufficient evidence. This often relates to borderline cases where it is the word of the complainant versus the word of the accused. Many of these cases are referred to the CPS for guidance, and the majority (66 per cent) are dropped (Harris and Grace, 1999). A case was most likely to proceed if the complainant was under 13 years of age, was subjected to violence, and the attacker was a stranger. Stranger rapes are most likely to proceed, but these account for a relatively small minority of all offences.

Detection in rape cases

Only in 15 per cent of cases that were treated as crimes was no suspect identified. The detection rate for stranger rape cases was one in three. Improvements have been made, especially now that DNA testing can produce evidence, but detection rates still remain low. There have been a few studies (e.g. Chambers and Millar, 1983 cited in Kelly, 2001: 19), and these indicate that 31 per cent of victims knew their attacker; 25 per cent of detections were the result of a description given by the victim, and 18 per cent of perpetrators were caught in the act. The remaining quarter of cases involved detective work.

In the Harris and Grace (1999) study, half of all the cases that were crimed and detected were sent to the CPS. The CPS discontinued a quarter of the cases it received. Of the discontinued cases 15 per cent were discontinued on public interest grounds. This occurred mainly in cases where the complainant knew the accused, and it was judged that compelling the victim to testify in court would not be helpful. The remainder were dropped on evidential grounds. Age was related to discontinuation, with cases involving very old and very young victims being the least likely to result in discontinuation.

Two-thirds of cases reaching the end of the process in the Crown courts ended with a conviction, including a quarter for rape/attempted rape. A quarter of those accused were acquitted (usually by a jury). It was found that the severity of the sentence for this crime (a starting point of five years imprisonment) put off juries from determining guilt in cases involving an acquaintance or intimate (Harris and Grace, 1999).

Harris and Grace (1999) concluded that reform was urgently required. In particular better guidance needed to be given to the police to aid them in taking decisions related to no-criming. Calls were also made for an improvement in the quality of medical and photographic evidence. In addition to improved policing methods, it was suggested that there needed to be better support for victims/complainants, especially in the early stages, and that this support could be provided by agencies other than the police. Improved communication was needed between the police and the CPS, and between the police and complainants, and the police would benefit from consulting the CPS more regularly, especially in borderline cases.

A few years later a co-authored report by Her Majesty's Crown Prosecution Service Inspectorate and Her Majesty's Inspectorate of Constabulary (HMCPSI and HMIC, 2002a) identified problems with leadership, victim care and the tracking of cases through the judicial system. More specifically, it said there were insufficient trained police staff to deal with rape, and that the training officers were given did not conform to a national minimum standard. Echoing earlier research, it observed that there are inconsistencies in the reporting and recording of offences. The environment victims experience is not always conducive to making them feel relaxed, safe and secure. The quality of investigation varies significantly, and it often lacks robustness. For example, forensic knowledge varies across the country. There is a lack of continuity in particular cases (that is, links between the police and the CPS). The quality of information the police provide to victims is also patchy.

The outcome of this report was the Rape Action Plan (HMCPSI and HMIC, 2002b), which focused on three main areas:

■ improving the investigation and prosecution of offences
■ improving victim care and victim examination facilities
■ improving the skills of police officers.

In relation to police investigation, the plan stated that the use of early evidence kits (EEKs) should be more widespread, enabling victims to provide urine samples and/or mouth swabs. The plan called for the wider availability of sexual liaison officers (SOLOs). These officers belong to a dedicated team and undergo a comprehensive seven-day training programme. They then look into rape, serious sexual assault, and historical allegations involving men, women and juveniles. The SOLOs have proven to be a good innovation because they act as a single point of contact for coordination, especially in the early stages. They are able to prepare an evidential package for investigating officers, and they provide victim liaison and support, and operational support for other officers (Payley and Clayden, 2005). The police were also required to apply what they had learnt from murder cases to rape cases: for example, ensuring an early response, cordoning off the crime scene, capturing witnesses, and review and quality assurance (HMCPSI and HMIC, 2005a, 2005b).

POLICING RAPE: KEY POINTS

■ The example of policing rape shows quite clearly that many rape victims do not experience a positive outcome from their contact with the police.
■ Many police officers have treated rape victims poorly, and in some instances failed to believe what the victim was telling them.
■ Research has shown that the police do not understand the reality of rape, and the obstacles the police have created put off many victims from coming forward.
■ The police have attempted to improve their sometimes deficient response to this crime.

CONCLUSION

This chapter has introduced the twin concepts of policing and the police. The activity of policing is as old as human society itself. It refers to control of, and surveillance over, various human behaviours and not just crime. Social changes and increased opportunities for crime and disorder occurring in the eighteenth and nineteenth century exposed the limitations of communal policing, and by 1829 a specialized police force was introduced. Initially unpopular, the police were gradually accepted over the course of the nineteenth century and by the end of the First World War broad swathes of the British public, with the exception of the underclass, gave their consent to the police.

The main tasks carried out by the police are twofold: first, crime fighting and law enforcement, and second, peace keeping and order maintenance. The police perform these roles in partnership with other agencies in the statutory, voluntary and private sectors. Although there is a clear framework outlining the roles and responsibilities of the police service, this is not necessarily reflected in the reality of police work.

This chapter has considered two examples of policing where there is a mismatch between what the police are supposed to do and what they actually do. First, the police culture was examined. This culture is shared by the rank and file, and officers at this level operate with a high degree of discretion. Consequently officers do not always observe the letter of the law or the policy guidelines issued by the government and their senior officers. This was shown by reference to the treatment certain minority groups experience on the streets. The final part of the chapter considered the police culture in response to the policing of rape victims, demonstrating that the police do not always treat the women who experience this crime with sympathy and sensitivity.

FURTHER READING

There are many books on the police. *The Handbook of Policing*, edited by T. Newburn (Cullompton: Willan, 2003) is a comprehensive edited collection covering almost all police and policing-related topics. The size of this volume is daunting, and first-year students do not really need this depth and breadth of knowledge, but it will prove to be an indispensable resource to prepare for any assessment on the police.

Several other general and shorter texts introduce the key debates. In particular, R. Reiner's *The Politics of the Police* (3rd edn) (Oxford: Oxford University Press, 2000) is excellent. There are also very useful and informative introductions in B. Bowling and J. Foster, 'Policing and the police', in M. Maguire, R. Morgan and R. Reiner (eds), *The Oxford Handbook of Criminology* (3rd edn) (Oxford: Oxford University Press, 2002), P. A. J. Waddington, *Policing Citizens* (London: UCL Press, 1999), and A. Wright, *Policing: An introduction* (Cullompton: Willan, 2002).

The following websites are also informative:

www.police.uk

www.acpo.police.uk/links/index.html

STUDY QUESTIONS

1. Describe the different meanings of the terms 'policing' and 'the police'.
2. Why was the Metropolitan Police Service established in 1829?
3. Describe the roles and responsibilities of the police service as:
   a) peace keepers
   b) crime fighters.
4. Discuss the main problems with the police culture. Is it necessary to reform the police culture? If not, why not? If yes, how could this be done?
5. Discuss the response of the police service to the crime of rape. What could the police do to improve their performance in this area of their activities?

The Prosecution Process: The Courts and Sentencing

INTRODUCTION

It is in the courts that the administration of justice most visibly occurs. Although the police play a pivotal role in deciding which cases enter this stage of the criminal justice process, a specific set of principles and practices are applied in the courts, which are primarily concerned with balancing the rights of offenders against the needs of wider society and individual victims. However, if ethnicity, class, age and gender are considered this balance is not always struck.

After describing the legislative and policy context, this chapter focuses on the role of the prosecution and the courts in processing individual cases. The courts also perform a major role in sentencing policy, determining whether or not offenders are punished in prison or in the community.

The chapter is divided into four main parts. The first considers the structure and roles of the prosecution process and courts, including the Crown Prosecution Service (CPS). There is then a general overview of the court system, especially the magistrates' courts and the Crown court. The bulk of this part looks at the procedures and principles used in the magistrates' courts. The second part rehearses some of the policy goals and philosophies underpinning sentencing. The policy goals are public protection, punishment, making amends and crime reduction. The philosophies consist of deterrence, rehabilitation, incapacitation and retribution. In the third part the main sentences available to the courts at the time of writing are outlined, as set out in the Criminal Justice Act (2003). Finally there is a short historically informed case study investigating some of the issues raised by gender and sentencing, and the differential treatment experienced by women.

THE STRUCTURE AND ROLES OF THE CPS AND THE COURTS

In this part of the chapter:

- the role of the CPS is outlined and its relationship with the police is briefly discussed
- there is an outline of the court system in England and Wales, including the magistrates' courts, the Crown court, the High Court and the Court of Appeal
- there is a description of the courts and the roles and responsibilities of the players involved in criminal justice
- the procedures followed in the courts are described
- the process of decision making in the courts is outlined.

The Crown prosecution process

It is only in relatively recent times that the police have not been responsible for prosecuting individuals. Since 1986 the Crown Prosecution Service (CPS) has decided whether or not a case should be taken to court so people can be prosecuted. Nowadays the police are only responsible for the investigation of an alleged offence and preparing a case for the CPS. The CPS plays an important role because in most cases it decides whether a person will be charged with a criminal offence, as well as the appropriate charge or charges. The CPS decides whether to prosecute by referring to the Code for Crown Prosecutors. This is applied to consider the facts of a particular case. The police can still determine a charge, but only for cases that are minor and routine.

When the CPS is sent a case by the police, its staff review the case to make sure it is appropriate to go ahead with a prosecution. On receipt of the file a Crown prosecutor reads it to ascertain whether the police have enough evidence against the defendant. He or she also assesses whether it is in the public interest to bring the person concerned to court. Crown prosecutors are required to decide whether a person is to be charged with a criminal offence, and they also determine exactly what the offence should be. This suggests that there are various factors Crown prosecutors must consider before deciding that an offence should be prosecuted in the courts. For example, under certain circumstances it may be possible to consider alternatives to prosecution, such as a caution for adults and a reprimand or warning for juveniles or young people.

The job of the Crown prosecutor is more complicated than this, though, because in criminal cases circumstances may change and the prosecutor must ensure the case is kept under continual review. It is possible that the CPS will decide to change the charges or even stop a case. If it does so, it is necessary for the prosecutor to notify the police. If a case is stopped it might not be done so permanently. Sometimes the police are given an opportunity to gather more information, which may in turn lead to another changed decision.

It is quite clear then that the CPS works very closely with the police, but there is a gap between them as they are completely independent of each other. In the last analysis the CPS has the most influence, because it decides on whether or not to proceed with a case and the nature of the charge.

The court system in England and Wales

In the judicial system in England and Wales there are six types of courts: magistrates' courts, county courts, Crown court, the High Court, the Court of Appeal and the House of Lords. The relevance of the Sentencing Advisory Panel and Sentencing Guidelines Council is briefly mentioned in relation to the Court of Appeal. Each of these players is now introduced in turn.

Magistrates' courts

Just the bare bones of this court are outlined here, as a large part of this chapter considers its workings in some detail. This is the first tier of the criminal court system in England and Wales. Every criminal case starts its life in a magistrates' court, and between 95 and 98 per cent of cases are actually completed there. Indeed a large number of offences, including most road traffic offences, can only be dealt with by a magistrates' court. As well as criminal matters, magistrates deal with family proceedings, gaming licence applications and betting licence applications. There are actually four different types of court:

- adult courts
- youth courts
- family courts
- licensing committees.

These four courts have different jurisdictions and rules of procedure. If the magistrates' court is unable to sort out a particular case it is referred to one of the other courts in the legal system. Two types of magistrates' courts are important in relation to this book: the adult court and the youth court.

The adult court is the court where persons aged 18 and over who are accused of committing a criminal offence appear. These courts also deal with the enforcement of fines imposed on people aged 18 and over. As the name suggests, youth courts deal with children and young persons. These were set up by the 1991 Criminal Justice Act, replacing the old juvenile courts. A 'child' is the term for someone aged 10 or above but who has not reached 14 years of age. 'Young persons' are those aged from 14 to 17. The law states that a child younger than 10 cannot be charged with committing a criminal offence. Magistrates in the youth courts are drawn from a special panel, and at least one of those who hears each case must be a woman. Cases are heard in private, in line with the Children and Young Persons Act (1933) (CYPA), and the press are not allowed to report personal details relating to the offender.

We shall return to the magistrates' court shortly.

The Crown Court

On paper there is one Crown court, but in practice there are a number of Crown court centres distributed throughout the country. This court sets to work on more serious offences (those that rate as indictable or triable either way) for sentence and trial. It takes up appeals from cases heard in the magistrates' court, and passes sentence on cases referred by the magistrates. Judges of the High Court (see below) take up the most serious cases. Circuit judges hear most cases. These are full-time judges appointed by the lord chancellor. They are typically barristers and solicitors belonging to the circuit bench. Recorders also hear cases, and in some instances magistrates may be included. A recorder is a part-time judge, usually with several years' experience as a barrister or solicitor, who arbitrates in the Crown court.

In the Crown court, cases are tried by jury. A jury consists of 12 members of the public selected to hear the trial and determine the innocence or guilt of the defendant.

The High Court

This court is based in London in the Royal Court of Justice, but some county courts may be designated as district registries of the High Court. There are three divisions:

- the Queen's Bench
- Chancery Division
- Family Division.

The High Court considers civil disputes, especially those involving large sums of money or property, libel or slander. The Queen's Bench has a jurisdiction over criminal cases, and tackles original and appellate cases.

The Court of Appeal

There are two divisions in this court, civil and criminal, and the latter, the Criminal Division, is of interest here because it hears appeals from individuals convicted in a Crown court. It is presided over by the lord chief justice. From time to time it is necessary for the Court of Appeal to refer complicated and disputed cases to the House of Lords.

In the 1980s the Court of Appeal started to issue sentence guidelines relating to some offences such as rape, theft, burglary and drug dealing. The purpose of these guidelines is to determine the most appropriate tariff for an offence. The Court of Appeal potentially provides influential guidance, but in practice its function is reactive rather than proactive. In other words, specific cases have to be brought before it before it can issue guidance, and most cases brought to its attention are a result of appeals made by the defence. Consequently the guidance is not based on the systematic application of principles.

The Sentencing Advisory Panel and Sentencing Guidelines Council

Further guidance of the kind mentioned in the previous section has been provided by the Sentencing Advisory Panel (SAP), which was introduced by the Crime and Disorder Act (1998). The rationale for its introduction was to ensure that sentencing was carried out more systematically on the basis of clear guidelines. The SAP reviews the various factors that have a bearing on sentencing, and attempts to create a consistent approach. It then makes recommendations to the Court of Appeal, which the court may accept and recommend to other courts.

The Sentencing Guidelines Council (SGC) was introduced by the Criminal Justice Act (2003). According to Carter:

Each year the Council should issue guidelines that ensure that offences are treated proportionately to their severity, are informed by evidence on what reduces offending, and make cost effective use of existing capacity.

The Sentencing Advisory Panel (which works to the Council) should be given responsibility for independently projecting future demand and should produce evidence on the effectiveness of different sentencing options in reducing crime and maintaining public confidence.

(Carter, 2003: 42–3)

The House of Lords

This is the highest appellate court in the country. Its members are life peers. Any appeals are made to an Appeals Committee, consisting of three peers. If there is a point of law in a Crown court case that either the defence or prosecution considers to be of public importance, the case can be appealed to the Lords. The legitimacy of an appeal is decided on by either the court or the House of Lords, although the final decision depends on what the Lords say. Beyond this there is the European Court of Human Rights at Strasbourg and the European Court of Justice in The Hague.

CRIMINAL JUSTICE AND THE MAGISTRATES' COURTS AND CROWN COURTS

At some point most criminology students are required to visit a magistrates' court, but even if this is not required of you, it is worth making arrangements to see one in action.

With the exception of the youth courts and family courts, magistrates' courts are publicly accessible, and from simply observing the proceedings it is possible to gain considerable insight into the roles of the different players. The brief description below should help those who have not as yet visited a court.

The layout of the courtroom

The size of the courtroom and its décor vary from place to place. No two courts are identical, but there are some typical features. At the very front of the room, usually on a stage, is the magistrates' bench. There must be a minimum of two magistrates sitting for a case, but the norm (and the maximum) is three. The magistrates normally enter the courtroom from a door at the back of the room. They sit behind a desk which separates them, at least symbolically, from the rest of the room.

Immediately in front of but below the magistrates' bench is a desk called the clerk's bench. The clerk to the justices is either a solicitor or a barrister. As well as providing legal advice to the court, clerks have overall administrative responsibility for the courts. The clerk's bench is also normally set slightly higher than the furniture in the rest of the room.

In the centre of the main area of the courtroom there are desks for the solicitors representing the prosecution and the defendant. The solicitors conduct their business from these desks. At each side of the room are two boxes: the dock on one side, and the witness box on the other. The witness box is used for all persons, including the defendant, who give evidence. Defendants who are charged with more serious crimes are placed in the dock for the duration of their trial. Adjacent to the solicitors' desks is likely to be the probation desk. This is where the probation officer representing the defendant sits. This officer is available to represent and provide information about the defendant. Towards the back of the court is seating for the press, who have the right to report all matters in the magistrates' court unless there is a restriction (such as in a family court). There is also a designated space for members of the public, and anyone over 14 years of age is entitled to sit in and observe the proceedings.

The role and responsibilities of magistrates

The lord chancellor, who acts on behalf of the Queen, appoints magistrates, but this follows an initial recommendation by local advisory committees. Magistrates are typically members of the community who have volunteered to assist in the working of the legal system. There are certain expectations about the qualities of the people holding this post, and they must display integrity and understanding. Such qualities must be recognized in them by other people. While there is no requirement for them to have legal knowledge, they must have a breadth and depth of experience and knowledge of life.

Because magistrates are not required to have legal knowledge, they need to attend training to acquaint themselves with the operation of the court and to familiarize themselves with their duties. This begins with observing the court, followed by specific training to ensure that they have sufficient knowledge of the law to follow cases. They also need a working knowledge of the rules of evidence, and an appreciation of the nature and purposes of sentencing. Once magistrates have been appointed they receive regular updating sessions on developments in the law, procedure and practices. In 1990, for example, the Magistrates' New Training Initiative (MNTI) was introduced to ensure magistrates were equipped with the necessary competencies. When magistrates have acquired experience they may receive specialist training so they can chair a bench.

In principle anyone can become a magistrate, but there are some exclusions. Individuals with a conviction for a serious offence, those under certain court orders and undischarged bankrupts are prohibited from sitting. Some occupations make it impossible for someone to become a magistrate: a police officer, a member of the armed forces and a traffic warden cannot do so. No one can become a magistrate on a specific bench if he or she has a relative sitting on the same bench. Some other occupations may also conflict with magisterial duties.

In 2003 there were 28,344 magistrates.

District judges (formerly known as stipendiary magistrates) also sit in magistrates' courts. They are trained legal professionals (solicitors or barristers with a minimum of seven years experience). They usually serve in larger courts in urban areas, and (unlike magistrates) they are salaried. Unlike most magistrates they sit alone, and they tend to take on more lengthy and difficult cases. In 2002 there were 95 district judges.

Magistrates are also called justices, or justices of the peace (JPs). Each magistrate is appointed to a bench serving a defined area. The word 'bench' is used in three distinct senses, to refer to:

■ the team of magistrates sitting in court on a particular day of business
■ the whole group of magistrates in a particular area
■ the actual place where they sit in the court.

In general, magistrates sit as a bench of three. All the magistrates are of equal rank because they are 'approved' following identical procedures. As indicated above, some magistrates receive special training enabling them to act as chair, but all of them have a vote on deciding guilt or innocence. In youth or family proceedings there is a requirement for there to be at least one male and one female magistrate sitting. Magistrates sitting on these benches are also given specialist training.

Court users

Various other people have roles to play connected with a magistrates' court. Amongst the personnel most commonly found there are:

■ court clerks
■ ushers
■ administrative and support staff
■ advocates (prosecuting, defence and duty lawyers)
■ CPS staff
■ police officers
■ probation officers.

Court clerks

The person doing this job gives advice and guidance to magistrates concerning points of law, procedural and practical matters, to assist them in making judgements. A clerk is required to have legal training, and will either be a solicitor or barrister, or hold a diploma in magistrates' law. The clerk also manages the court and ensures that proceedings run smoothly and efficiently. The chief clerk to the justice holds overall responsibility for the day-to-day working of the court, and must be a qualified barrister or solicitor.

Ushers

The duties performed by ushers vary, but a key function is assisting the clerk with the smooth operation of court business. The usher also keeps a register to check who is attending the court (defendants, solicitors and witnesses), in order to keep the clerk informed. The usher is also directed by the clerk to move people and paperwork around the courtroom.

Other court staff

Several departments perform vital administrative and support services but there is no need to discuss them in detail here.

Advocates

An advocate may either be a solicitor or a barrister. Advocates have a duty to both their client and the court. For the client, their duty is to present the case effectively in as convincing a manner as possible. In relation to the court, they are required to administer justice and to guarantee that no attempt is made to mislead the court. Advocates must also have confidence that the information they give or refer to is correct. They should also be assured in their belief that any witnesses they use will give truthful evidence. The prosecuting advocate is instructed by the CPS, since the CPS prosecutes most cases brought before the magistrates' court by the police. The defendant can make either of two pleas, guilty or not guilty. If the defendant pleads guilty, the prosecuting advocate presents the facts of the case and informs the court if there are any previous convictions. If the plea is not guilty, the prosecutor needs to provide satisfactory proof to the court that the defendant did commit the offence as charged. The outcome is entirely dependent on the provision of robust and reliable evidence, based on what witnesses say in the court or from written witness statements.

Defence advocates represent the defendant. They are required to present the facts of the case as effectively and convincingly as possible, to outline any mitigating circumstances to the court, and to make sure that their client is treated fairly. When a defendant pleads not guilty, it is the responsibility of the defence to call on witnesses and to provide written statements in support of its case.

Some defendants arrive at the court on the day of their trial, or have been held in custody, without legal representation. These individuals are allowed to request legal advice from a duty solicitor. This professional is normally a local solicitor who is part of a rota system. This makes local solicitors available on an ad hoc basis to provide services to defendants lacking legal representation.

Police officers

Police officers may be present for a number of reasons, including giving evidence in a trial, accompanying defendants who have been arrested and kept in custody until their appearance in court, and requesting a warrant.

Probation officers

In Chapter 9 it is shown that one of the main roles of the probation officer is to 'advise, assist and befriend' the offender. This is underpinned by a more general intention to help the offender to refrain from offending and to lead a law-abiding life. Most probation work is community based, supervising offenders on community service and probation. Probation officers also supervise people on parole (individuals released from custody early). However, they also perform a crucial task in the courts, where they produce pre-sentence reports, which include information about defendants including their personal and social circumstances (their family background, relationships, employability and financial position). These reports also spell out sentencing options, recommending alternatives to custody such as counselling or treatment.

COUNTY COURTS

This is the setting where civil cases are dealt with (such as disputes between neighbours, small claims, and divorce), as well as family jurisdiction, a role shared with magistrates' courts. The court also responds to insurance matters following traffic accidents.

THE CROWN COURT

This court is responsible for four main areas of work, all of which have a strong link with the magistrates' court.

■ Individuals who are sentenced for a criminal matter in a magistrates' court may appeal against their *sentence*, and it is the Crown courts that respond to such petitions. A circuit judge and two magistrates normally hear appeals. An appeal begins with the prosecution presenting the 'facts' of the case, followed by a presentation from the defence, who set out the defendant's argument, which typically concerns the harshness or unfairness of the sentence. The circuit judge and magistrates then assess the appeal and consider whether it should be upheld or dismissed. There are two possible outcomes to an appeal. If the appeal is accepted, the sentence is reduced accordingly, depending on the nature of the decision. If the appeal is dismissed the original sentence is unchanged, and in some instances the sentence may actually be increased.

■ The Crown court also hears appeals against *convictions* in a magistrates' court. Again these appeals are normally heard by a circuit judge and two magistrates. The main difference from an appeal against a sentence is that the whole case is heard again, but a jury is not involved.

■ The third role also relates to the activities of the magistrates' court, which can commit defendants to the Crown court for *sentence*. This occurs if the magistrates decide that the offence they have tried is too serious to be sentenced by them, and is more appropriately referred to the Crown court. A judge or a recorder who sits with two magistrates deals with such cases.

■ Magistrates may transfer criminal proceedings to a Crown court for *trial* if the offence is indictable. Crown court trials are the responsibility of a judge and jury. On being committed to a Crown court the defendant has the choice of pleading either guilty or not guilty. If the defendant pleads not guilty, it is necessary for a jury to be sworn in. (There is no jury if the defendant pleads guilty.) Once the case begins, each side outlines its case, with the prosecution setting out its side before the defence does so. Witnesses are called by both sides, and cross-examined by the legal representatives for both the defence and prosecution. After the detail of each case has been heard in full, both sides make a closing speech summing up the main points of their argument. At this stage the role of the judge becomes important, because she/he is required to summarize the proceedings and give direction to the jury regarding necessary points of law. The jury is then asked to leave the courtroom, and retire to a separate room where the members discuss the case and decide on the guilt or innocence of the defendant. They return to the courtroom to announce their decision. If they find the defendant not guilty, she or he is discharged, and is free to walk out of the court. If the jury decides the defendant is guilty, the judge passes a sentence.

PROCEDURES: A CLOSER LOOK AT THE MAGISTRATES' COURTS

How does an individual end up being required to attend court as a defendant facing the prosecution for a criminal offence? The main routes to the courts are answering a summons, following an arrest authorized by a warrant, or after an arrest made without a warrant.

Summons

This is a document issued by JP, a justices' clerk or an authorized court clerk. It requires a person to attend at a specific time and place in response to an allegation that he or she has committed an offence or offences. This is known as the 'information'. Issuing a summons is a judicial act, and it is imperative that the person who issues it is satisfied that an offence known to law is disclosed, and that the court has jurisdiction to deal with it. Basically, the issuer needs to be sure that a crime has occurred, and to be satisfied that all is in order.

Arrest

The power of arrest is given by statute or by virtue of a warrant issued by the court. Following the arrest of a person for committing an offence, he or she must either be released on bail or brought before a magistrates' court the day after being charged at the latest (except if it is a public holiday).

Warrant

A warrant is an authority to arrest a person. JPs are often asked to issue a warrant in a case where it is considered necessary to arrest someone for a non-arrestable offence. (No warrant is needed when the power of arrest is given by statute.) The warrant is intended to ensure that the person attends the court to answer the case.

In some instances, the name of a defendant is unknown or there is uncertainty about his or her address. In this case it is not possible to issue a conventional summons, and a warrant is issued instead.

Only JPs are allowed to issue a warrant, and before they do so it is necessary that the information on which the warrant is based is presented in writing and substantiated on oath. This is crucial because the liberty of an individual is at stake. The issuing of a warrant is dependent on the offence being either indictable (including triable either way offences) or punishable with imprisonment. If the name of the accused is not known, a *descriptive warrant* may be issued. As the name suggests, this describes what is known about the suspect, in order that he or she can be identified and served with the warrant. The description must be fairly precise, or a relatively large number of people would be susceptible to arrest.

Jurisdiction

There may be a spatial and temporal limitation to the exercise of a magistrates' court jurisdiction. In the case of indictable offences there is no limit to when a prosecution may be started, but for most summary offences proceedings must begin within six months of the commission of the offence. There are some exceptions to this rule, such as failure to pay national insurance contributions and non-payment of a vehicle excise licence.

An offence is normally dealt with in the geographical area where it was committed. The situation is less clear-cut when an offence is committed in a motor vehicle. In these instances the offence is dealt with in any of the areas through which it passed on the offending journey. Once the geographical jurisdiction has been determined, it is possible to add on other offences (for instance, a summary offence committed outside the court area may be dealt with if the court has a 'local offence' to deal with as well).

Proceedings before the court

Ordinarily, and without fail in more serious cases, defendants must attend the court in person to enter their plea, which will either be 'guilty' or 'not guilty'. At this point the charge is read, and fully explained if appropriate. Defendants then make their initial contribution: that is, they make various further decisions or speeches depending on the circumstances. For example, if a defendant pleads not guilty to an 'either way' offence, it is necessary to decide whether the case should be heard in a magistrates' court or a Crown court, and the defendant is 'put to his/her election': that is, he or she makes this decision. This is more commonly known as the *mode of trial procedure*. It is an often time-consuming but essential part of the process. If the defendant agrees to summary trial (in the magistrates' court, without a jury), the plea is taken formally at this stage. In summary and 'either way' offences, if the defendant pleads guilty, the facts of the case are read out and the defendant is given an opportunity to speak in mitigation. The court may hear evidence on oath, but it does not do so as a matter of course. If the plea is not guilty, a trial takes place and evidence is heard.

If a defendant elects for trial by jury, committal proceedings take place. These are proceedings which confirm that there is sufficient evidence for the case to go to trial. To put it another way, is there a case for the defendant to answer relating to the charges alleged? If the defence agrees to committal without the evidence being considered, the court simply certifies that the documents have been tendered and commits the defendant to the Crown court without looking at the evidence. The defence need not agree to this: sometimes the court is required to assess the strength of the evidence. It may listen to witness statements as part of this process. Crucially, in these circumstances magistrates do not ascertain the guilt or innocence of the defendant (that is the jury's job in the Crown court): instead they decide whether a 'prima facie' case (one that calls for an answer) has been made.

In some instances, court proceedings take place in the absence of the defendant. It is possible in a summary case, if a summons has been posted or delivered by hand to the defendant and the defendant fails to turn up, for the court to proceed without the defendant being present. It is also feasible in some cases for a defendant to choose not to attend, but instead to plead guilty by post, although this only applies to summary offences where the punishment does not exceed three months imprisonment. In this circumstance, the defendant is sent a statement of facts, and/or the written statements of witnesses. This statement is all that the prosecution can refer to in the court. (It is up to the prosecution to decide whether to initiate this procedure.) If the defendant does not choose to challenge the statement of facts or to ask for any other issues to be considered, he or she can sign a written plea of guilty, and the court then decides on the sentence in his or her absence. It is not permissible to plead guilty by phone, and a defendant who chooses to plead not guilty has no option but to attend the court to do so.

In all other cases the defendant is expected to be present. In some circumstances the court enforces the defendant's attendance, by issuing a warrant. This is done in two main circumstances, both of which follow the defendant's initial failure to appear in court when the case is scheduled: first, if the defendant has been given bail, and second, if a summons has been issued to the defendant in person, or the defendant is known to have had the issue of a summons brought to his or her attention. In this second circumstance, a warrant is only issued if the offence is imprisonable, or if after conviction, the court proposes to impose a disqualification (from driving, for example). It is also only done when the court considers that to proceed in the absence of the accused would be inappropriate because of the seriousness of the case.

A fundamental principle: to 'hear both sides'

A fundamental principle of the criminal justice system is the maxim 'hear both sides', which provides safeguards to an accused person. Any deviation from this rule must be explicitly permitted by law. This means that a magistrate is only permitted to hear a summary case in the absence of the accused if notice has been given to the accused, and he or she has had a reasonable opportunity to attend and put the other side of the case. Similarly a magistrate cannot disqualify the accused from driving in his or her absence unless notice of this intention has been served on him or her. The reading of previous convictions is not allowed unless the accused has been served with a copy; however, details of driving licence endorsements on a DVLA printout may be referred to in summary cases in the absence of the accused. The use of witness statements is not permitted unless copies are served in advance.

Likewise, if a guilty plea is expressed in a letter, the court can only judge the case on the basis of the information that the accused has also received. Only the statement of facts or witness statements that the accused received may be read out in court, and the court cannot permit the prosecution to add new information. Accused people have some important rights: they must be kept informed of the charges they face, the date they are to be considered, and when written evidence is used, the contents of it. If those accused attend the court, they are allowed to have their say, but if they choose not to attend, they need to be made aware that they were at least given the chance to do so. However, very occasionally a defendant has a genuine reason for not having known about an impending prosecution, and in these cases the hearing of the case in their absence can be judged unfair. It is then possible to apply to have the case reopened, and possibly heard in front of a fresh bench of JPs.

Decision making

Magistrates take many decisions as they perform their duties. Some are not routine, but there are several types of decision they do undertake routinely.

Bail or custody

If a case has been adjourned (that is, the initial hearing has taken place but the full trial is postponed to a later date), the court may, for more serious offences, choose to either release the defendant on bail (that is, let the person return home until the case is heard) or direct that he or she be held in custody (that is, in prison). (For less serious offences, bail is automatically granted.) The Bail Act (1976) is important here, in particular because it sets forward the general presumption that unconditional bail will be granted in favour of the defendant. Despite this general rule the courts may grant only conditional bail – set conditions on the person's liberty, such as ordering the defendant not to go near a witness's house – or if an exception to the defendant's right to bail applies, order the person to be remanded in custody. Some common examples of reasons for not granting bail are when the court has substantial grounds to believe that the defendant might:

- fail to attend court
- commit further offences
- interfere with witnesses in the case.

In addition if the defendant is alleged to have committed an indictable offence while on bail, then further bail would not be granted. If the accused has committed a more serious offence, such as homicidal rape, and has previously been convicted of a similar offence, then bail would only be granted if there were exceptional circumstances.

Since the 1976 Bail Act there has been growing concern about dangerous offenders who are on bail. For example, the Bail (Amendment) Act (1983) allowed the CPS some rights to appeal against decisions taken by magistrates to grant bail. The Criminal Justice Act (2003) expanded the powers of the CPS so it could appeal against decisions taken relating to all imprisonable offences. Moreover, section 19 of the same piece of legislation made it possible for a suspect who appears from his or her behaviour to be under the influence of class A drugs to be also denied bail.

Mode of trial

As noted earlier, offences that are 'triable either way' may be heard in magistrates' courts or in a Crown court. If there is an indication of a not guilty plea, the court hears representations from the prosecution and then from the defence as to which mode of trial is the most suitable. The magistrates' decision needs to bear in mind the nature of the case, and particularly the seriousness of the offence. Other issues that are considered include the sentencing powers held by the magistrates, or in other words the adequacy of the magistrates' power of punishment. Since Crown courts can imposer stiffer penalties, this can be a reason for sending a more serious case to the Crown court. There may be other circumstances that make the case more suitable for trial in one way rather than another.

The defendant also has the right to claim a trial by jury. For example, if the defendant states that he or she wishes to be tried in the Crown court, the magistrates must send the case there, even if they believe they could otherwise have dealt with it.

Guilty or not guilty

If a defendant chooses to plead not guilty, then a trial must take place, and at its conclusion the magistrates need to decide whether the defendant is guilty. In most cases the so-called burden of proof rests on the prosecution, and it must prove guilt beyond reasonable doubt (the required standard in criminal cases). All defendants are presumed innocent, and defendants are not required to show that they did not commit the offence. Previous convictions are not disclosed to the magistrates until they have ascertained the guilt of the defendant. The decision taken by magistrates will be based on evidence heard from the prosecution witnesses, the defendant and any witnesses for the defendant, as well as the legal arguments from the prosecution and defence and advice from the clerk.

In most cases the defendant pleads guilty, and magistrates then only have to determine the appropriate sentence.

Sentence

Section 49 of the Criminal Procedure and Investigations Act (CPIA) (1996) states that in triable either way cases the defendant is asked to indicate whether he or she is pleading guilty or not guilty. This is normally known as the 'plea before venture' procedure because, if the indication is of a guilty plea, the magistrates go on to consider whether their powers are sufficient to sentence appropriately, or whether the defendant should be committed to the Crown court for a judge to pass sentence.

If a guilty plea is entered, the prosecution presents an outline of the facts of the case and informs the court of any previous convictions. The legal representative acting for the defendant then speaks in mitigation: that is, he or she informs the court of the defendant's view of the offence, and refers to any personal circumstances that might affect the sentence. It is also possible for the magistrates to obtain a pre-sentence report written by the probation service, and if necessary a psychiatric report. Magistrates decide on the sentence by focusing on the offence and by taking into consideration the other information presented to the court, including reports, mitigation, court guidelines, guidance from the higher courts and the advice of the clerk.

THE COURT SYSTEM IN ENGLAND AND WALES: KEY POINTS

■ This section has described the structure, roles and responsibilities of the court system in England and Wales in the early twentieth century.
■ It has outlined in some detail the appearance and layout of the courts.
■ Policy and procedures will change over time, and it is worth checking the Home Office website to see whether and when any changes have occurred.

SENTENCING: POLICY GOALS AND PHILOSOPHIES

In this section:

■ the goals of sentencing are introduced, focusing on public protection, punishment, making amends and crime reduction
■ there is an overview of some popular sentencing philosophies, including deterrence, incapacitation, rehabilitation and retribution.

Policy goals

Sentencing is a contentious and complex activity, and magistrates and judges must take into consideration both the facts of the case (that is, what happened) and the personal circumstances of the offender. Beyond this there are arguably four key considerations underpinning sentencing policy.

First is the issue of *public protection*. Offenders come in all shapes and sizes, and pose various degrees of danger to the public. A shoplifter may be a nuisance but his or her behaviour is not as threatening as that of an armed robber. Even when a serious crime such as homicide is considered, different offenders pose different degrees of risk. Take for example a frail and elderly woman who has killed her husband who was suffering from an acute medical condition such as senile dementia, and a violent drunken man who stabbed to death someone in a pub who accidentally spilt beer on his shoes. Both these people have committed an abhorrent injurious act, but there are clearly major differences between both the offenders and their crimes. Most people would probably agree that it is just to take into account these aspects in passing sentence, and sentencers do indeed do so.

Second, a sentence needs to *punish* the offender in a way that is fair and appropriate. Again, it is likely that a sentence will take into account the age of the offender and his or her motivation. Perhaps the elderly woman committed the murder because she felt – arguably, misguidedly – that she was relieving the suffering of someone she loved. The violent drunk might also attempt to show mitigating circumstances, but it could perhaps reasonably be argued that he showed a lack of self-control and there is no acceptable justification for his behaviour.

Third, in passing a sentence the aim is to make sure the offender *makes amends* for the crime. A sentence should make the person feel sorry for what he or she has done, and the punishment is a method of trying to ensure that as far as possible, the guilty person repairs the damage done. In most instances, the sentence is not necessarily directed at recompensing the victim, since (as noted earlier) the state assumes the status of victim. If a defendant is fined, for example, the money goes not to the immediate victim of the crime but to the state.

Fourth, sentencing policy is part of a more general aim to *reduce crime*, and in particular to reduce reoffending. This is achieved in different ways by different sentences. If defendants are sent to prison, they will not be able to commit more crimes, at least while they are under lock and key. In other words, they are incapacitated (see below). Other sentences may attempt to change people's behaviour, again with the overarching aim of stopping them from committing crime.

Each of these four factors will be on the mind of a sentencer, and their relative importance will vary from case to case. This brings the discussion back to the facts of the case, and the personal circumstances of the criminal. Now we move on to focus on the philosophies underpinning sentencing.

Philosophies

The first three of these philosophies (deterrence, rehabilitation and incapacitation) are consequentialist or reductionist approaches, whereas the fourth, the retributist, is non-consequentialist.

Deterrence

In very simple terms the idea behind this principle is that it is possible to stop people from committing crime by introducing a punishment that puts them off from offending. A common form of deterrence is the development of a punishment that people dread or fear. If people are sufficiently afraid of what may happen to them if they offend and are caught, then, it is argued, they will think twice before acting.

Incapacitation

This covers any measure where an attempt is made to physically restrict a person from offending again. It is not possible legally to incapacitate a person until he or she has been convicted for committing an offence. Various penalties are available to incapacitate offenders, in ways that are either temporary or permanent. Examples include a prison sentence and disqualification from driving. In most cases the penalty is for a fixed period. There are also more permanent measures, and in some parts of the world thieves may have their hands chopped off or are subject to capital punishment (that is, execution). The rationale for the latter is to ensure that a person can never offend again.

Rehabilitation

The aim of this is to return individuals to normality, or those behavioural conventions accepted by most people who conform. Many criminals are seen to be in need of rehabilitation because they are under-socialized, which means that they may not have been taught how to behave appropriately. The causes of their failure to behave properly may be social, biological or psychological factors over which they have little or no control. The method used to try to rehabilitate people depends on what is identified as the cause of their behaviour.

Rather than punishing the offender, the aim is to provide treatment in order that he or she can be helped or cured. The type of treatment will depend on the assessment of the causes of the crime. If the crime is explained in psychological terms, the treatment will focus on the offender's mind, and will consist of therapy (such as cognitive behavioural therapy) or counselling. Biological approaches may also focus on the brain and the production of chemicals such as hormones. Social forms of rehabilitation focus on issues such as education and training, because many offenders lack the basic skills needed to make them employable.

Retribution

The view underlying this is that people should get their just deserts, or the belief that a wrongdoer should be punished because he or she deserves it. Retribution works on the basis of the assumption that every case of the same type needs to be treated alike, so that offenders are treated consistently and with certainty. The punishment may be an end in itself: it shows how much society objects to what the offender has done. Another example is the principle of just deserts. The argument here is that the right punishment is one that reflects the seriousness of the offence, which takes account of the harm caused by the offender and the extent to which he or she was culpable (in other words, his or her motives).

SENTENCING GOALS AND PHILOSOPHIES: KEY POINTS

■ Each of the goals and philosophies outlined above has been significant at one time or another.

■ However, particular goals and philosophies nay be prioritized at particular times.

■ It is also possible for sentencing to consist of a more than one goal or philosophy at the same time.

SENTENCING POLICY: THE SENTENCES AVAILABLE

In this section:

■ there is an introduction to the general sentences available

■ the specific sentences available in the early twenty-first century are outlined, with a distinction drawn between custodial and non-custodial (or community-based) sentences

■ some of the changes to the sentences available after the Criminal Justice Act (2003) are outlined, in particular the emphasis on combining elements of custodial and community-based sentences

■ the differential treatment of young people by sentencing policy is established.

What sentences are available to the courts in England and Wales? The most widely used sentence is the fine, which requires no further explanation; although it is often perceived to be the most lenient sentence as it does not involve the direct deprivation of a person's liberty. Of course, being fined will restrict what people can do, as they will have less spare money in their pocket, but the punishment stops there. Another type of sentence is a community-based sentence, such as restorative justice, where an offender is required to directly make amends to a victim. Last but not least, the sentence that probably comes first to your mind is prison. Imprisonment is presented as the most severe punishment, and is generally used for the most serious offences.

Crimes to which a prison sentence is attached have a maximum term set by Parliament. This means that sentencers cannot impose a sentence of more than a fixed maximum length, even if they personally feel the defendant in front of them has committed a most heinous crime and should be imprisoned for longer. Judges and magistrates are also given other advice, in the form of the sentencing guidelines prepared by the Sentencing Advisory Panel and the Sentencing Guidelines Council (discussed on page 177). These are designed to ensure that there is consistency across the criminal justice system. There would be a perceived, and possibly actual, injustice if certain courts were giving more lenient sentences to defendants for the same offence than other courts. Sentencing guidelines also set fixed minimum sentences for serious repeat offenders, or those people who commit the same crime on several occasions.

In essence, then, sentencers are in the business of determining whether and to what extent a guilty person should be punished and/or rehabilitated. It is also necessary to remember that the sentence may involve neither community-based nor custodial interventions, but rather compensation. And of course, if the individual is found not guilty, no sentence is passed.

Sentencing is now considered in some more detail, paying particular attention to the situation following the Criminal Justice Act (2003).

The Criminal Justice Act (2003)

The Criminal Justice Act (2003) was influenced by the Auld Report (2001) and the Halliday Report (2001), especially the latter. The Act emphasizes deterrence, a greater role for rehabilitation, and the incapacitation of persistent offenders. It is a wide-ranging piece of legislation covering a lot of ground, and the discussion of it here is restricted to the aspects that involve sentencing. It is the first statute that identified the aims of sentencing. In s.142 (1) they are defined as:

(a) the punishment of offenders.
(b) the reduction of crime (including its reduction by deterrence).
(c) the reform and rehabilitation of offenders.
(d) the protection of the public.
(e) the making of reparation of offenders to the persons affected by their offence.

Types of sentence

The fine

This penalty is used by the courts in response to many offences. Most fines are meted out by magistrates, and there are maximums set at five different levels: level 1, £200; level 2, £250; level 3, £1000; level 4, £2500 and level 5:, £5000. The Crown courts also impose fines, but they have no set limits. However, there are practicable limits to the fine imposed, as the amount set needs to be related to the seriousness of the offence and the ability of the offender to pay.

Fixed penalty notices, which are given for less serious offences, such as parking tickets, speeding, graffiti and public disorder, are also a form of fine. Rather than prosecuting an offender in the courts, the requirement is that a fixed sum of money is paid to the magistrates' court. What is interesting about this sentence is that the offence is assumed, meaning that there is no conviction and the offender is not given a criminal record. The person required to pay the order can choose whether to pay the fixed penalty, or contest the case in court, in which case if guilt is established, the penalty is individually determined.

Community sentencing

The aim of community sentences is to combine an element of punishment with a wider aim to change offending behaviour. There may also be an attempt to get the offender to make amends to the victim of the crime. It is a type of sentencing where efforts are also made to help offenders address any personal factors that may cause them to commit crime, such as drug misuse. Community-based punishments have been traditionally been delivered by the probation service, although the Carter (2003) review has resulted in the introduction of the principle of *contestability*, which means that the voluntary and private sectors can bid to provide community punishment.

Community sentences have changed significantly over time, and it is not inconceivable that they will change again. Some of the texts students will use will be out of date as new legislation is passed into law. However, this is not necessarily a problem because at an introductory level it is the broad principles, issues and debates that are most important.

To illustrate the previous points, community penalties are imposed only if the offence(s) committed are sufficiently serious to warrant this type of sentence. The combination of elements in the penalty order needs to be suitable for the offender, and any restrictions imposed need to be in proportion to the seriousness of the offending behaviour. There are some exceptions to these general rules, particularly for persistent minor offenders. If a person who is aged 16 or above appears before the court and has been fined on three previous occasions, it is possible to impose a community sentence. A probation officer must produce a pre-sentence report (PSR), on the basis of which it is decided whether an offender is suitable for an order. In some instances a pre-sentence drug test may be requested.

Community order

The Criminal Justice Act (2003) introduced the *community order*, which is a single generic order to which a range of requirements are attached. For example, an offender may be:

- given a curfew and excluded from certain places at certain times
- supervised in the community
- required to do unpaid work
- ordered to receive treatment for drug and/or alcohol problems
- prohibited from doing certain activities
- required to go to an attendance centre
- ordered to receive care or treatment relating to mental health.

Basically, the aim of the community order is to create a bespoke sentence, where the courts can pick and mix from different elements to make up a specific community order. These changes enable sentencers to make the most of technological advances such as electronic tagging (see Chapter 9) and voice recognition, making it possible to take away an offender's liberty to some degree without imprisoning him or her. The overarching aim is to reduce offending on the basis of a sentence that is tough, and not soft, as community sentences are sometimes perceived to be.

It is useful to identify some of the requirements of this generic community sentence. Not all of the points mentioned below are built into any individual sentence, as it is important that the sentence meets the needs of the offender to ensure that it is effective or that it works. The section below draws on a table produced by Davies, Croall and Tyrer (2005: 305).

■ The inclusion of compulsory and *unpaid work* is a defining feature, along with attendance and supervision. This element of the order is similar to what were known in the past as community punishment orders and community service orders. The offender is required to work for a period of between 40 and 300 hours, and this work must be completed within 12 months. The courts may decide that the offender needs to be electronically monitored. The thinking behind this sentence is to get offenders to repay their debt to the community that was harmed by their actions. An offender is also expected to develop new skills, which are achieved through work placements offered by charities, community organizations and local authorities. In providing these placements, these agencies anticipate that they will benefit from the offender's contribution.

All adult offenders aged 16 and above who have harmed a community, for example through drunkenness, antisocial behaviour or vandalism, can be given this sentence. From time to time this sentence can be used for some serious one-off offences like drink driving and driving while disqualified. An offender may be required to perform tasks such as tidying up a park or removing graffiti, or might have to install crime prevention devices such as security locks. Other offenders may have to work in charity shops. There may also be a focus on providing offenders with new opportunities to acquire practical skills that are applicable in real-work situations, offering preparation for further formal training and employment.

■ An order for *supervision* was previously made under community rehabilitation orders and probation orders. The supervision may last for up to three years, and involve electronic monitoring. The aim is to change offender attitudes and behaviour though rehabilitation. It is believed that an offender who has been rehabilitated is less likely to offend in the future. To achieve this the offender is required to attend a regular meeting with a probation officer. At the outset the meetings are held on a weekly basis, but if the offender makes progress then the meetings become less frequent. Electronic monitoring may also be used.

■ The constructive use of offender time is also achieved through their participation in specific *activities*. This may last for up to 60 days of activities. Compliance may be observed through the use of electronic monitoring. The order may require the offender to make some reparation to the victim of the crime.

■ Any programmes used as part of the order are designed to change the behaviour of offenders, and the offender may be *prohibited from doing various activities at particular times*. For this order to be imposed the probation service needs to present the courts with evidence to show that a prohibition is practicable. As for the other requirements mentioned above, electronic monitoring may be used.

■ There are *curfews*, which as one would reasonably expect typically depend on the use of electronic monitoring. Curfews can last for between two and 12 hours a day, for up to six months. The rationale behind this is both to develop a punishment and to reduce the opportunities an offender has to offend. It is similar to house arrest. The aim is also to protect the wider community from antisocial behaviour. Curfews are used for people where there is no identified need for rehabilitation and supervision. The rationale is to create a structure to give more order to the day-to-day lives of offenders. The hours of the curfew are set at a similar time to when the offending behaviour occurred, which often includes the hours of darkness. The purpose of the order is to coerce people into staying indoors, in most cases at home, for the duration of the curfew.

■ There is *exclusion* from certain areas. Typically with the use of electronic monitoring, a person can be stopped from going to particular place on a particular day or days for up to two years.

■ A *residence requirement* will be included to make sure the offender is traceable. The accommodation must be based on the recommendation of the probation service. Electronic monitoring can be used if necessary keep the offender under surveillance.

■ *Attendance centres* are made available for the under-25s. Attendance is required for between 12 and 36 hours in total, but only up to three hours on any single day.

There are some other interventions but these can only be delivered if the offender gives their consent, such as:

■ *The treatment of mental health problems, drug treatment and alcohol treatment.* These treatment programmes last for a minimum of six months, and the court needs to be satisfied that the offender has a relevant problem.

Compensation

An offender convicted in a criminal court can be ordered to pay compensation. To help the court decide on the scale of the compensation awarded, the victim provides the police with evidence of the losses incurred, including receipts. The police can then pass on this information to the CPS, which in turn processes the form and informs the court. Compensation is not available to all victims, and there are quite strict guidelines. For example, only the following can be compensated for: personal injury; losses resulting from theft of, or damage to, property; losses occurring as a result of fraud; loss of earnings due to absence from work; medical expenses; travel expenses; pain and suffering; and loss, damage or injury caused by a stolen vehicle.

It is the court that decides whether the order is made against the offender. The offender then pays the money into the court, which passes it on to the victim. In deciding to make an order the courts consider offenders' financial circumstances, to make sure they are able to pay. For example, if an offender is of limited means it might be decided that he or she cannot reasonably to pay the amount of the loss immediately and in full, and arrangements can be made for payments in regular instalments rather than a single one-off payment.

A discharge

Although an offender has been found guilty, the courts are able to make an order that discharges him or her. A discharge is made if the court judges that punishment is not appropriate. This may happen following consideration of the personal character of offenders and the circumstances surrounding their behaviour. There are two types of discharge. The first is an *absolute discharge*, where no further action is taken. This is applied for a minor offence, or if the court appearance itself is deemed to have been a sufficient deterrent. Although no action is taken, the offender is left with a criminal record. Second there is a *conditional discharge*, where an offender is released and a note is made of the offence on the person's criminal record. The courts state that no further action will be taken if the offender does not reoffend within a particular time period, which cannot be more than three years.

Imprisonment

The first part of this section discusses some general principles applying to imprisonment. This is followed by an acknowledgement of changes arising from the Criminal Justice Act (2003).

A custodial sentence is the toughest penalty the courts can impose. Prison sentences are limited by the maximum penalty that is available for a particular crime. A person can only be sent to prison if the offence is so serious that no alternative is appropriate. If the offence is of a violent or sexual nature, the court may decide that a custodial sentence is the only or best method of protecting the public. Prison is also used for offenders who have failed to comply with the requirements set out in a community order.

When the courts impose a prison sentence, the length of sentence is the maximum amount of time a person can spend locked up. For sentences less than four years, an offender will be released after serving half of the sentence. If the sentence is for four or more years, an offender can be *considered* for parole halfway through the sentence. The Parole Board can recommend that the person is not released at that point, but the offender will be let out of the prison automatically at the two-thirds point of the sentence. Following their early release prisoners are *on licence* in the community until they reach the three-quarters stage of their sentence.

For some offences there is a minimum sentence. If a person commits a second serious sexual or violent offence the outcome is an automatic life sentence. There is a minimum sentence of seven years imprisonment for a person who has trafficked class A drugs on three occasions. This covers cases where the drugs are being imported, produced and supplied, and those where the suspect possesses them. The maximum sentence is life. A person caught committing domestic burglary on three occasions is given a minimum three-year prison sentence. The maximum sentence is 14 years imprisonment. If a person is found in possession of, or is distributing, prohibited ammunition or weapons, there is a minimum prison sentence of five years. The maximum sentence is ten years imprisonment.

The Criminal Justice Act (2003) made a number of key changes to custodial sentences, including a new mandatory framework for life sentence prisoners in order to make public protection a priority. The most significant and innovative changes affected short-term sentences, and the Act introduced custody plus, custody minus and intermittent custody.

■ *Custody plus* consists of short period in prison followed by a longer period of community supervision. For instance, this includes a prison sentence of between two and 13 weeks, with a period of licence for a minimum of 26 weeks. Thus if an offender was given 12 months imprisonment the maximum time he or she would spend in custody would be 13 weeks. If an offender does time for two offences, the maximum custody time is 26 weeks. This sentence is considered ideal for offenders with drug-related problems. The spell inside can be used for detoxification, and then they are then released into the community, where they are placed under strict supervision to ensure they stay on the straight and narrow.

■ *Custody minus* gives offenders an opportunity to be punished in the community, but if they fail to observe the conditions attached to the sentence, then there is the threat of a prison sentence.

■ *Intermittent custody* refers to a prison sentence that is spread over a longer period. For example, offenders might go to prison at weekends, thus allowing them to continue in employment. This means that a person spends between 14 and 90 days in custody followed by a licence period of from 28 to 51 weeks in the community.

This new approach to sentencing will be introduced into the context of a new approach to managing offenders, the National Offender Management Service (NOMS), which includes both the prison service (see Chapter 8) and the probation service (see Chapter 9).

Sentencing policy is different for young people, and the next section outlines the situation for young people at the start of the twenty-first century.

Sentencing for young offenders

A 'young offender' is someone aged 17 or less who has committed a crime. It is known that the peak age for offending is currently 14, illustrating the importance of early intervention, and the Youth Justice Board for England and Wales is an executive non-departmental public body and the agency responsible for preventing crime among young people.

The sentences available for young offenders are different from those available for the adult population. Overall, custody is used as a last resort. If young people get into trouble by committing a minor criminal offence or antisocial behaviour they can be dealt with outside the courts. The Criminal Justice Act (2003) introduced the youth community order, curfews, exclusion orders, attendance centres, supervision and action plan orders.

Before 2003, for cases involving antisocial behaviour the police and local authority were able to use pre-court orders such as the anti-social behaviour order (ASBO) or child safety orders. If it is a first or second minor offence, the police have to hand reprimands or final warnings. These are used to prevent further offending behaviour and to give support and help as early on as possible.

Young people who are charged with an offence appear before a youth court, and the Crown courts are used only in very serious cases. The sentences a young person may receive are:

■ a discharge
■ a fine
■ a reparation order (for instance, requiring the offender to repair a damaged bus shelter or remove graffiti from a telephone box).

Community punishment can also be used for 16–17 year olds, and they may have to work with the elderly, for example. Those aged 16 and 17 can also be given community rehabilitation sentences, such as a programme designed to address offending behaviour. A curfew order can also be used so the young person stays in a particular place at a particular time, and drug treatment and testing orders are available for people with a drug misuse problem.

There is also a *referral order*, which is doled out to all young offenders (aged 10–17) who plead guilty and are convicted for the first time. Post-conviction the offender is referred to a Youth Offender Panel which considers the best course of action.

Unfortunately from time to time some young people commit offences of a serious nature, such as murder or rape. For adult offenders the minimum sentence is set at 14 years. However, under section 90/91 there is a difference for young people. The case is heard in Crown court and the whole of the sentence is spent in custody, but the Home Secretary sets the release data for section 90 cases, and the release data for section 91 cases is set automatically.

Intensive Control and Change Programme (ICCP)

This offending behaviour programme was introduced in 2003 for offenders aged 18 to 20. It takes 18 hours per week and usually lasts for a year. The programme is targeted at prolific offenders, and is treated as an alternative to short custodial sentences. It is most likely to be aimed at young people who are at a high risk of being sent to prison for less than a year, and for whom the risk of reoffending is assessed as medium to high. In the region of 20 per cent of offenders fall into this category.

The ICCP is delivered by a multi-agency team, including police and volunteers. The 18 hours are filled with a range of activities including education, employment training and mentoring. There is also an element of community-based punishment such as electronic tagging and curfews.

SENTENCING POLICY: KEY POINTS

- Traditionally there are two main types of sentence, custodial and non-custodial.
- Under these two umbrellas there have been a diversity of sentences and orders, and specific sentences are subject to changes of their substance and name or title.
- In the past custodial and non-custodial sentences were seen as separate, but following the Criminal Justice Act (2003) the two may be more closely integrated in a single sentence.
- However, the custodial and non-custodial elements retain their distinctive goals and philosophies.
- It is likely that the available sentences will change in the foreseeable future, and it is necessary to keep up to date with changes. The Home Office website will keep you up to date about reform and change.

SENTENCING POLICY AND PRACTICE: WOMEN'S DIFFERENTIAL EXPERIENCES

In this subsection:

■ the relationship between gender, justice and sentencing is examined
■ the extent to which men and women receive different sentences for equivalent offences is considered
■ an attempt is made to explain differential treatment.

A key principle in criminal justice is that every person is treated equally in the eyes of the law. In other words, personal characteristics such as gender and race should have no bearing on people's treatment. The expectation is that in the legal system, everyone is immune from those forms of prejudice and discrimination existing in wider society. The basic point to be made here is that however fair criminal justice principles may appear, men and women do not enter the courts in equal circumstances, and that this may bear on what happens at the stage of sentencing.

These assumptions are spelt out clearly in section 95 of the Criminal Justice Act (1991) (see Chapter 2), which reminds the judiciary to not discriminate. Unfortunately this request has not always been heard or acted on, and women and minority ethnic groups are in fact treated differently from white men in the courts. For instance, there is evidence to show that while the differential experiences of men and women are complex, females may encounter more punitive treatment than their male counterparts. This has not always been the situation, but certainly since the mid-1990s the rate of increase in the numbers of women being sent to prison is greater than it is for men (Fawcett Society, 2004). To make sense of this Hedderman (2004) has argued that between 1992 and 2000 more women have been dealt with in the courts, but the proportion ending up in the Crown courts (where a custodial sentence is more likely) has not changed. This indicates that more women are being imprisoned not because of the seriousness of their offending, but because judges in particular are treating women with more severity.

For this reason it may be argued that there needs to be more control over judicial discretion, although any changes taking place need not focus on individual sentencers. Why? According to Hedderman (2004), this difference has occurred because the sentencing options available have created a bias in the system that will lead to discrimination.

What is the evidence for this discrimination? An important question is, does the data tell us that differences in sentencing are explained by the gender of the defendant? As with most criminological research the results are not conclusive, and the interpretation of any findings is likely to be ambiguous. For example, although we have just said that women appear to experience harsher punishment, at other times they may be treated with relatively more lenience. It has been found that there are chivalrous attitudes that suggest women should not be sent to prison.

To start making sense of these issues, some commentators argue that male and female defendants experience equal treatment in the courts, and that any differences in terms of sentencing outcomes are caused by factors such as offence type and previous convictions. Kapardis and Farrington (1981) adopt this position, and argue that if a range of variables influencing sentencing are taken into consideration, then the gender of the defendant is shown to be irrelevant. In contrast, the Fawcett Society (2004) shows that relatively more women with fewer convictions than men are sent to prison. This evidence is contradictory, but one of the reasons is that these pieces of research were done at different moments in criminal justice history, and any differences may reflect different policies and attitudes.

Since the 1970s and 1980s, in sentencing policy there has been a shift away from the principle of rehabilitation towards that of just deserts, where it is argued that the punishment needs to be in proportion to the seriousness of the offence. Also, the Criminal Justice Act (2003) stated that sentencers should focus on the offence rather than the offender. In theory this would mean that the gender of the offender is of no significance, and there are consistent sentencing decisions and outcomes. However, the most crucial point is that there *is* a difference, and that this needs explaining.

Carlen (1983) has attempted to account for this bias, in particular when women are treated more harshly. It would appear that those responsible for punishment somehow see female offenders as 'more criminal' than men because in addition to breaking the law they break social rules, particularly the expectation that women should behave themselves. This is especially so for more serious crimes. Cavadino and Dignan illustrate this when they say that 'it seems very likely that some women are effectively punished for deviating from conventional norms, and that the system tends to react to female offenders in a manner which is, in one way or another, imbued with sexism' (2002: 328).

This indicates that women are subjected to the double jeopardy of being a criminal, and a female criminal at that. Other writers like Pearson (1976) do not share this view, and suggest that women are much more likely to be treated leniently than males. Clearly the issue of gender and sentencing is deeply problematic. It is necessary to look more closely at the decision-making process and the factors affecting this.

Explaining the differential treatment of men and women in the courts

Most empirical and theoretical research into gender, crime and justice illustrates that male and female defendants are treated differently in the courts by sentencers. According to Parisi (1982) there are three main theoretical approaches.

- Women receive preferential treatment from the CJS.
- Women receive more punitive treatment from the CJS.
- Women receive equal treatment from the CJS.

Preferential treatment

This approach states that women are treated more leniently than men, demonstrated by the fact that women are more likely to receive a non-custodial sentence than men, and if they are imprisoned their sentence tends to be shorter than men's (Parisi, 1982). Let us examine the reasons for this treatment.

Pollak's (1950) research shows that criminal justice professionals, who are over-whelmingly male, adopt chivalrous attitudes towards women. This is seen as a simple extension of wider social attitudes, where men tend to be protective towards women. For example, when Pollak did his research in the 1940s most judges were men, and they appear to have thought that it was inappropriate to punish women by sending them to a masculine environment, and that female offenders needed protection.

Other researchers have focused less on chivalry and emphasized instead the naiveté of women offenders. Male judges who tend to base their opinions on the women they know, such as their mothers and wives, also hold this viewpoint. The tendency to attribute the qualities of these women they know to female defendants, and therefore to perceive them as innocent, results in relatively more lenient treatment (Parisi, 1982). Steffensmeier (1980) arrives at similar conclusions, and also argues that judges regard women as less crime-prone and less dangerous than men. For these reasons women are less likely to be judged to be in need of harsh punishment.

In addition to these cultural attitudes, it is argued that treating female offenders more leniently than men is more practicable, especially because it is more likely that a woman will be responsible for looking after her family. If a woman with responsibility for a family is sent to prison, the costs of child care often have to be taken on by society (Parisi, 1982). Judges may also be chivalrous because of their assumptions about child rearing, which they may see as a female role. If they were to treat a woman harshly this would also affect her children, because the end result could well be family breakdown.

There are other considerations, including ones that are more directly related to criminal justice. Some judges hold to the view that in comparison to men, women are more responsive to community-based sentences. More than that, they think prison is not the best option for women because of the limited opportunities for rehabilitation (Steffensmeier, 1980).

It is worth acknowledging that there is little evidence to show chivalrous attitudes among female judges. There is not much robust data on this because most judges are men, but there are now similar numbers of male and female magistrates. It would be interesting to learn whether the idea of chivalry is still in existence, and whether this has an impact on magistrates, who are responsible for most sentencing decisions.

Punitive treatment

There are two main reasons for female defendants to be treated more harshly than males. First, Nagel (1981) claims that the likelihood that women who offend will experience harsher treatment is caused by their unfeminine behaviour. This perspective is similar to the chivalry account in the sense that it is underpinned by stereotypical assumptions about male and female behaviour. A popular perception held of women is that 'normal' women are gentle and passive, and that women who offend and do not display these qualities are 'not normal'. This perception is evident for typically female types of crime, but if women commit an offence that is traditionally associated with men, such as violent crime, then they are seen as 'doubly deviant' (Nagel, 1981).

Parisi (1982) provides a second explanation, which is related to the chivalry hypothesis. According to this account women are punished to protect them from themselves. Because women are inherently passive and weak they are not fully in control of the decisions they take, and institutionalization may be seen as a solution to their behaviour.

Equal treatment

A key proposition of this approach is that any differential treatment of men and women is caused by legally relevant and legitimate factors such as offence type and the number of previous convictions a defendant has. In other words, the gender of the defendant is not seen as a significant factor (Parisi, 1982).

Adherents to the view that men and women should be treated equally argue that equality is best achieved if the approach to justice is consistent. There is less concern with the consistency of the outcome (Hedderman and Gelsthorpe, 1997). For that reason, rather than looking at statistical data, which simply shows sentence outcomes, it is necessary to look at other factors leading to that final decision. The various factors specific to the offender need to look at the different circumstances facing males and females.

Although the equal treatment approach provides an invaluable insight into the different experiences of women, it does not take into consideration whether equal treatment results in equivalent effects on both sets of defendants. It is clear that male and female defendants entering the courtroom have different circumstances, and that the impact of a sentence will vary from individual to individual. A woman with children who is given a prison sentence will experience different long-term effects, which are probably more damaging than those suffered by a man in the same position (Koons-Witt, 2002). In short, there is little evidence to support the equal treatment explanation.

Summary

It would appear that sentencers sentence differently according to the sex/gender of defendants, but there is less clarity if an attempt is made to decide whether the treatment of women is harsher or more lenient. Research showing less punitive treatment indicates that the role of women as child carers has influenced sentencing decisions, as the imprisonment of women with children incurs other social and economic costs (Hedderman and Hough, 1994; Pearson, 1981; Parisi, 1982). Other studies have concluded that women experience harsher treatment partly because they break the law but also because they contradict established cultural expectations about how women should behave (Nagel, 1981). Early research supporting the harsher treatment argument (Carlen, 1983; Worrall, 1989) has been given more weight since the 1990s, as female defendants are imprisoned more frequently than men, and women with fewer previous convictions than men seem to be more susceptible to incarceration. The reasons for this are complex, although it is probably not all about a desire to punish women more, but rather because of the lack of alternatives to custody.

CONCLUSION

This chapter has outlined what goes on in the courts, paying particular attention to the key elements of sentencing policy.

FURTHER READING

This chapter covers a number of different areas, and the issues it addresses are covered in much more depth and detail in two key texts: A. Ashworth, *The Criminal Process* (3rd edn) (Oxford: Clarendon Press, 2003) and M. Cavadino and J. Dignan (eds) *The Penal System: An introduction* (3rd edn) (London: Sage, 2002). See also chapters, 7, 9 and 10 of M. Davies, H. Croall and J. Tyrer, *Criminal Justice: An introduction to the criminal justice system in England and Wales* (Harlow: Longman Pearson, 2005), M. McConville and G. Wilson, *The Handbook of the Criminal Justice Process* (Oxford: Oxford University Press, 2002) and U. Smart, *Criminal Justice* (London: Sage, 2006).

As with most areas of criminal justice, policy change is certain, and viewing the following websites will keep you up-to-date with developments:

The Court Service: www.courtservice.gov.uk

Home Office (sentencing): www.homeoffice.gov.uk/justice/sentencing/index.html

Sentencing Guidelines Council and Sentencing Advisory Panel:
    www.sentencing-guidelines.co.uk

Crown Prosecution Service: www.cps.gov.uk

STUDY QUESTIONS

1. Describe the main functions of the:
   a) Magistrates' courts.
   b) Crown courts.
2. Identify the main custodial and non-custodial (community-based punishments) used in the courts.
3. What are the main changes to sentencing policy resulting from the Criminal Justice Act (2003)?
4. Select a news story from a local and a national newspaper that focuses on a criminal trial.
   a) Identify the nature of the offending behaviour (e.g. is the offence indictable, summary or triable-either way?).
   b) Identify the sentence.
   c) Identify the reasoning behind the sentence given (see the section on the goals and philosophies of sentencing, and chapter 11 in Davies, Croall and Tyrer (2005)).
5. In passing a sentence what considerations need to be given to:
   a) deterrence?
   b) incapacitation?
   c) rehabilitation?
6. Write a 200 word précis highlighting the key factors influencing the differential treatment of female offenders in the courts. Visit the Fawcett Society website for additional ideas to answer this question: www.fawcettsociety.org.uk

8 The Prison

OVERVIEW

The aim of this chapter is to provide:

■ a concise history of changing conceptions of punishment and the origins of the modern prison
■ an explanation of the rationale for using prison as a form of punishment
■ a description of the formal structure of HM Prison Service and the prison estate
■ an evaluation of the imprisonment of women and the gender-specific issues it raises
■ a discussion of the over-representation of certain Black and minority ethnic groups in comparison with the White population.

INTRODUCTION

Contemporary discussions of *penology*, or the study of punishment, concentrate on the relative significance of custodial versus non-custodial sentences, or incarceration versus community-based punishments, for reducing crime and the harmful effects of victimization. This chapter outlines the philosophical and practical considerations underpinning the use of prison as a means of punishment. It traces the emergence of the prison as the preferred option for policy makers in Anglo-American societies, and critically considers the arguments for and against this development in policy, in the context of wider changes in society and within the criminal justice system. Racial, gendered, age and class-based forms of discrimination are especially significant for understanding the contemporary significance of prisons.

This chapter introduces the prison as an institution and then focuses on the topic of imprisonment, or the experience of being in a prison environment. The prison exists at the end of the criminal justice system, and people end up there because they have either been found guilty of committing a crime or are waiting for a trial to determine their guilt. However, it is necessary to bear in mind that the imprisonment of a person is based on decisions taken at other, earlier, stages of the criminal justice process. That the prisoner finds him or herself in a prison cell is in part a consequence of the actions and decisions that are either taken or not taken by other agencies. For example, police racism may result in a relatively high proportion of members of minority ethnic groups ending up in prison. Also, as shown in Chapter 7, sexist assumptions have a bearing on sentencing policy.

To gain a detailed understanding of the prison it is necessary to briefly trace its origins and some initial developments. In line with Chapters 6 and 8 this requires us to revisit an earlier historical period, in this case the eighteenth and nineteenth centuries. The prison was very much a product of the Enlightenment, and is seen by some to be an element of modernity, in particular in its 'civilizing process' (Elias, 1982; Lea, 2002). At this stage the philosophical assumptions justifying the birth of the prison are rehearsed. This will involve some discussion of the methods of punishment prevailing in society prior to the construction of prisons. There are other reasons for the emergence of penitentiaries at that time, and these are briefly addressed. The key point is that within a relatively short period of time the prison came to be a feature of modern British society, serving as a stark reminder of where wrongdoers could end up. Indeed there are still prisons built in Victorian times, which are used to accommodate twenty-first century prisoners.

After this historical account of the origins of the prison, the chapter then describes the prison estate, and the key people and departments responsible for its day-to-day running. The final part of the chapter considers the different experiences of female and Black and minority ethnic group prisoners.

A HISTORICAL OVERVIEW OF THE DEVELOPMENT OF THE PRISON SYSTEM

This section:

■ provides a brief history of the development of the prison in modern times
■ outlines some of the main reasons that prisons were built
■ considers attitudes to punishment and how these change over the course of centuries.

By going back to the medieval period and then examining developments up until the latter stages of the eighteenth century, it is possible to clearly identify two functions performed by the prison: first, to keep people in custody, and second, to control and coerce people. The prison was also there to punish, especially for minor criminal offences. In the case of more serious offences, punishment took the form of a physical assault on the human body, and in extreme cases, death. This issue is returned to shortly, but before that let us spend some time focusing on the historical context.

In historical accounts of the modern prison a prominent figure is John Howard. His main contribution to the history of penal institutions was the 1774 Gaol Act, developed in part out of his experiences in a French prison in the late 1750s. He found the conditions there to be appalling, prompting him to strive for change. Similarly, he described the conditions under which criminals were kept in late eighteenth-century England, and although he found some purpose-built prisons in urban areas, the prison environment was more commonly found to be a room in either a castle or a gatehouse on the edge of a town. Prisoners were even detained in cellars in places such as town halls. In many cases prisoners were herded together rather like cattle in overcrowded and unsanitary conditions. Overall there was a lack of regulation, and the custodians frequently abused their power and authority by exploiting prisoners.

Howard was more than an observer of these social conditions, he actively campaigned to reform the system. In 1784 he lobbied for more regulation of prison conditions, including improved sanitary conditions and a change in the moral turpitude (that is, the baseness or depravity) of prison life, for both prisoners and their overseers. Ironically, Howard died from typhoid in 1790 while visiting a Russian military prison.

The early versions of the prison started to change from the late eighteenth century onwards throughout northern European societies, such as England. The appearance of new prisons was related to other broad developments at that time, in particular the establishment of *asylums*. These included mental hospitals, workhouses, industrial schools and reformatories for juveniles (Ignatief, 1978; Foucault, 1977). This was a gradual process, and carried on into the early stages of the nineteenth century. An often cited example of the modern prison is Pentonville, which was opened in 1848. This establishment is often taken to be a 'model' prison (Pratt, 2002). It had 500 cells, each designed to accommodate one prisoner who was detained in silence. Prison life in Pentonville was regimented, and each prisoner followed a daily routine regulated by uniformed staff. These early prison officers were employed by the state. In contrast with the earlier methods of incarceration, punishment was a primary function. However, the punishment inflicted on prisoners was less barbaric than earlier penalties such as the death penalty and torture. Take the following example (of a French punishment) from Foucault.

> On March 2 1757 Damiens the regicide was condemned ... to be taken and conveyed in a cart .... To the Place de Grève, where, on a scaffold that will be erected there, the flesh will be torn from his breasts, arms, thighs and calves with red-hot pincers, his right hand ... burnt with sulphur, and on those places where the flesh will be torn away, poured molten lead, boiling oil, burning resin, wax and sulphur melted together then his body drawn and quartered by four horses and his limbs and body consumed by fire, reduced to ashes and his ashes thrown to the winds.
>
> (Foucault, 1977: 3)

This example puts the emphasis clearly on the physical body, especially the infliction of pain and suffering, invariably in a public setting. This penological approach was gradually replaced by a philosophy of punishment where the focus was on the mind instead of the body. As Cohen (1985: 14) puts it, the mind, not the body, was 'the object of penal repression'. Thus there are two key developments: first, the existence of physical space (in the form of asylums) to accommodate criminals, and second, a new ethos where containment in the prison was preferred above physical harm. The move away from brutal physical punishment towards containment in a prison cell reflected the ascendancy of civilized values, such as rationality, over and above the barbarity of pre-civilized ways of seeing the social world (Pratt, 2002).

At that time there was a view held by some politicians and other agencies, in particular the police, prosecutors and sentencers, that prison was an acceptable method of punishing offenders, but that it should only be used as a last resort. Indeed this assumption underpinned the decisions they took in practice. However, the principles justifying the use of prison, rather like other criminal justice interventions, are prone to change, and the popularity of imprisonment as a sanction varies periodically and in the context of different jurisdictions.

The decision to send offenders to prison is based on many factors. Rates of imprisonment cannot be explained in any simple way by the factors that might reasonably be expected to have most impact on them. Common-sense thinking (see Chapter 1) might lead us to believe that more people are sent to prison as crime rates increase, or in response to different penal philosophies or perspectives on punishment. It may also be assumed that demographic factors play a part in determining prison numbers, so that if there is a relatively high proportion of people in the population in their late teens and early 20s the prison population will expand. Other explanations refer to socioeconomic conditions and the view that the workings of the labour market, for example, and rates of unemployment could affect the use of prison. Among these are what are known as *radical* explanations of imprisonment.

Radical explanations of the functions of prison rest on the presumption that institutions where people are incarcerated are an element of the repressive state apparatus that is used to control particular populations. Drawing on the ideas of Marx, the main premise is that the capitalist system of production is controlled by a ruling and affluent class, and that this class does everything in its power to maintain its dominant position. This is dependent on a system of social control which represses the working classes. The oppression is legitimized through the criminal law, which exist to enable the ruling classes to control the poor majority (Cohen, 1985: 22).

Perhaps the most explicitly Marxist interpretation is in the work of Rusche and Kirchheimer (1968) and Melossi and Pavarini (1981), who argued that it is, in the last analysis, the economy that determines the function of the penitentiaries. These scholars argue that the penal system exists not only to punish people who break the law but also as a method of regulating and continuing the supply of human labour, so capitalism can continue to expand. The prison is a rational method for deterring lower-class crime. Rather than executing criminals, the prison is there to instil fear into the mind of the offender. Above all, when serving a prison sentence the convicted offender was set to work. Inside the prison, work was not a source of profit as it was in the factories in the outside world, but a form of punishment.

All of the above factors are, at least superficially, plausible explanations of why imprisonment rates are so changeable, but there is another key reason: the influence of government and the political elites that govern society. In other words, imprisonment is also a reflection of political choices rather than an outcome of crime rates, penal philosophies, socioeconomic and demographic factors. There are numerous examples of the extent to which imprisonment is a result of political and ideological priorities, demonstrated in due course by the influence of sexism and racism on prison matters.

THE DEVELOPMENT OF THE PRISON SYSTEM: KEY POINTS

■ Early prisons were built to create a more humane and civilized method of punishment, in contrast to the barbarism of corporal and capital punishment.

■ The prison was widely regarded as an effective method of controlling offenders.

■ The use of prison can be justified by appealing to various philosophies and by referring to social conditions, such as high crime rates.

■ Prison may be used to incapacitate and punish or rehabilitate offenders, but whatever the justification, policy makers determine its use as part of the political decision-making process.

THE KEY PURPOSES OF IMPRISONMENT

In the previous section two functions of imprisonment were mentioned. The first – the function of keeping people in custody – operates by making sure justice is realized without problems. For example, suspects may be remanded in a custodial setting before trial to protect the public and actual or potential victims from harm and danger. Another custodial function is the detention of people arriving into the country, who may be held for the purposes of controlling immigration. The controlling function of the prison can be used to exert pressure on offenders to ensure that they conform. The other key function is 'punishment', which is arguably the main reason that people nowadays end up in prison. In other words, the rationale for imprisonment is *punitive*. It is a sanction imposed against individuals in response to the offence for which they have been convicted.

If punishment is the overriding principle of imprisonment, we need to have a clearer idea of what we mean by this. However, there is a lack of consensus about the meaning of the word 'punishment' in the context of custodial penalties. An influential view is that a consequence of being sent to prison is that individuals are punished by losing their liberty and by living in an environment where conditions are harsher than they are in the outside world. Adherents to this perspective base their argument on Jeremy Bentham's principle of 'less eligibility', which suggests that convicted criminals, or those who are detected and prosecuted via the criminal justice system, lose their entitlement to the rights enjoyed by most law-abiding citizens. An alternative view is that the loss of liberty is a sufficient punishment in its own right.

The debate about the relative significance attached to the punitive functions of imprisonment is ongoing. For example, in the 1980s there was a discussion conducted in England and Wales by politicians, policy makers and academics about the extent to which prisons should be either for the treatment and training of offenders, or a form of humane containment. This was to change radically in the next decade, in 1993 when the Conservative home secretary Michael Howard argued that conditions in prison need to be 'austere' and uncomfortable for prisoners. In some ways this can be seen as the opposite of the original intention. There is thus considerable confusion in public policy debates about the purpose of prison, but it does indicate that the uses of imprisonment are dependent on the political values and imperatives of the day rather than prison conditions and crime rates.

THE PRISON ESTATE

In this part:

■ the structure of the prison estate is described, including the institutions that are provided specifically for young people
■ the prison population is calculated
■ some of the experiences of prisoners are outlined.

HM Prison Service

A prison sentence involves the court passing the convict to the Prison Service. Someone who has been convicted of a serious offence could be imprisoned virtually anywhere in the country, whereas criminals who are given relatively shorter sentences tend to be accommodated in their local area. Prison is often used to contain people who are a threat to public safety, and this includes dangerous and violent individuals such as paedophiles. However atrocious the crime a prisoner may have committed, all prisoners are supposed to be treated fairly and with humanity. There is more to prison than taking people out of the equation: there is an emphasis on creating law-abiding people. This may be achieved by encouraging prisons to take part in education or rehabilitation programmes. The thinking behind this is that prisoners with improved social and personal skills are less likely to reoffend on release.

There are 139 prison establishments in England and Wales, which are subdivided into various categories, including high-security prisons, local prisons, closed and open training prisons, young offender institutions (for sentenced prisoners aged 21 and under) and remand centres. Prisons also have different levels of security. Each prisoner is subjected to a risk assessment to determine his or her security category. Risk is calculated on the basis of the likelihood of a prisoner escaping or absconding, and the risk he or she would pose to the public in the event of an escape.

In England and Wales in December 2005, the prison population or the total number of people held in prison was 77,066, and a further 3205 were under home detention curfew supervision (NOMS, 2005). This figure is the highest it has ever been, and since the 1990s it has increased dramatically by some 25,000. The prison population in England and Wales is the highest in Western Europe.

There are various ways of looking at these statistics. First, this figure can be compared with the overall operational capacity of the prison estate. The *operational capacity* is the total number of prisoners who can be held in the existing prison estate. Decisions about operational capacity are taken by area managers, who have to consider factors such as the control and security of prisoners, and whether the prison regime can operate properly. It is not possible to use all the space that is available in theory, and 'usable operational capacity' takes away 1700 places from the full operational capacity by taking into account the complex needs of various types of prisoner. Key factors are sex, age, the security category, conviction status, single-cell risk assessment and the geographical distribution of prisoners in relation to prison establishments (NOMS, 2005). On 9 December 2005 the usable operational capacity was 78,521. This means there were 1455 spaces. Twelve months earlier, on 9 December 2004, the population was 75,284, with a slightly lower usable operational capacity of 77,104. There were 1820 spaces available. So the prison service is near to capacity. It was widely predicted in the spring of 2006 that towards the end of that year there would be 80,000 people in prison.

Before we consider some of the experiences of prisoners, it is necessary to look at the accommodation provided for young people in some more detail.

Young people

There are three main types of secure accommodation for young people: secure training centres (STCs), local authority secure children's homes (LASCHs) and young offender institutions (YOIs).

Secure training centres

These centres are purpose-built to accommodate offenders up to the age of 17. STCs are actually run by operators from the private sector that have been contracted by the Home Office. There are four in England and Wales. They are secure environments designed for vulnerable youngsters who have been given a custodial sentence, and they aim to educate and rehabilitate. They are relatively small in size, and for every eight trainees sentenced there is a minimum of three dedicated staff to address offending behaviour. The aim is to make sure the individual needs of each offender are targeted effectively through intensive supervision. The philosophy of STCs is to educate the trainees through the provision of programmes encouraging their personal development. The trainee is given formal education for some 25 hours per week for 50 weeks of the year. Everything detainees might need during their stay is provided on a single site, including education and training, health care (including dentistry) and specialist services relating directly to offending behaviour. This can involve a contribution from mental health and social professionals.

Local authority secure children's homes

LASCHs are there to concentrate on the complex emotional, behavioural and physical needs of young people. These homes are run on a day-to-day basis by local authority social services departments, although they are governed by the Department of Health and the Department of Education and Skills. The support and services delivered by LASCHs are tailored to the specific needs of youngsters. This is dependent on there being a high ratio of staff to young people, in the context of a small home that typically caters for between six and 40 young people. Some institutions have six staff for every eight young people, others have two staff for every three young people, and there are others where there is one member of staff to two young people. LASCHs are used selectively, and accommodate the most vulnerable offenders, especially those aged 12 to 14, girls up to 16 and boys aged 15 to 16.

Young offender institutions

YOIs are actually run by the Prison Service, and are purpose built to contain 15–21 year olds. The Youth Justice Board uses YOIs, but is only responsible for placing young people aged under 18 in secure accommodation. As a result of this some YOIs accommodate people who are older than those normally found in STCs and LASCHs. The Youth Justice Board has to commission and purchase places for under-18s, and they are detained in separate juvenile wings. The ratio of staff to young people is lower than in STCs and LASCHs, and a higher number of offenders are accommodated.

Inside prison: the rules

On arrival in prison inmates are given an Information Book outlining the rules and regulations. There are different books for male, female and young offenders. All people are in prison because it has been proven they have broken a rule, or they are suspected of doing so, and a number of prisoners continue to break the rules when they are inside. Each year there are over 100,000 offences against prison rules and regulations (Matthews, 1999). Although there is a problem with discipline, most prisoners do not face a disciplinary hearing or adjudication. The types of offences committed are varied, and may include serious offences, such as making an escape attempt or torturing another prisoner, as well as less serious ones like not working properly. When a rule is broken the prison establishment may start disciplinary proceedings and impose a punishment, such as the removal of privileges or confinement to a cell.

Personal officer

Each new prisoner is also supposed to be allocated a personal officer who is there to respond to any questions prisoners have, and to help them if they wish to make a complaint. Because of a lack of resources some prisoners are not allocated a personal officer, but they can seek similar support from the officer who is in charge of their unit or wing.

Although prisoners are denied their liberty and freedom of movement they do have some rights, such as the right to have visitors.

Visitors

Most people held in prison who have not been convicted (that is, those who are waiting for trial) are allowed to see visitors every day, although they can only receive visits for up to one and a half hours per week. Some prisons only permit visits to unconvicted prisoners on three days a week, and in these cases the visit is restricted to one hour. Unconvicted prisoners should be offered the opportunity of at least one weekend visit every fortnight.

Convicted prisoners have fewer privileges, and visitors wishing to see them need to submit a request for a visiting order (VO). This group of prisoners is usually allowed one domestic visit per fortnight, which includes one weekend visit every four weeks. Each visit normally lasts at least one hour. There is an Incentives and Earned Privileges Scheme, though, which may result in a prisoner being allowed longer or more frequent visits.

THE IMPRISONMENT OF WOMEN

This case study:

- examines the significance of gender for understanding imprisonment
- considers the proportion of male and female prisoners making up the prison population
- focuses on the experiences of female prisoners, highlighting a range of issues that impact on women more than men.

Here is another a snapshot. At the end of September 2005 the prison population in England and Wales was 77,807, of whom 4768 were female. There are fewer prisons for women than for men (19 in England, none in Wales, one in Scotland).

So the number of women in prison is significantly lower than the number of men, which might be expected given what we have learnt about the different offending behaviour of males and females (see Chapter 2). The fact that men are more likely to commit crime, especially more serious or indictable offences, provides a plausible and convincing explanation of the relative over-representation of men in prison. We looked in Chapter 7 at the suggestion that women experience discrimination or differential treatment, particularly in their contact with the police service and in the courtroom. However, clearly this discrimination does not result in as many women as men going to prison. But the number of women prisoners has generated considerable concern among academics, and to some degree among politicians too. Why the controversy?

One reason is that there was a 173 per cent increase in the average population of women in prison between 1992 and 2002. The equivalent rise for men was 50 per cent (Home Office, 2004b). Why has the number of women prisoners risen so much more steeply? This requires some further explanation, but first let us consider some other information about female prisoners.

According to the Home Office (2004b), a significant proportion of female prisoners (71 per cent) were given a custodial sentence of less than 12 months. In part, this is a reflection of female offending behaviour: 40 per cent of women received into prison were convicted of theft and handling. While women do commit more serious offences, such as crimes of violence, only 12 per cent of receptions were for this crime category.

These figures are good examples of the danger of relying on statistics. It might be thought at first that compared with the male numbers, the number of women prisoners does not represent a big problem, but the figures on trends tell a very different story, and the figures on types of offence suggest more problems and questions. However, the statistics are only one cause for alarm: other factors, particularly the everyday experiences of women in prison, are arguably a reason for more concern.

Historical context and gender issues

We have already looked briefly at the origins of prisons, but some developments relating to female prisoners need to be highlighted. Separate women-only prisons were not established until the early 1800s, following the campaigning activities of Elizabeth Fry and John Howard. Perhaps the most notorious prison establishment built specifically for women was Holloway, opened in 1902. However, from the 1850s onwards there was a decline in the number of women in prison. This coincided with changes in penological thinking, especially an increased emphasis placed on psychiatry. This trend continued until 1968, when the home secretary announced that women's prisons (principally Holloway) would be redesigned so that they could cater better for the medical needs of women prisoners.

The Criminal Justice Act (1991) has been identified as a landmark piece of legislation because it suggested that imprisonment was not necessarily the best approach in penal policy. The 1991 Act promoted the notion of 'justice', and discussed community-based sentences as an alternative to imprisonment. This type of thinking was relatively short-lived, though, as the 1990s were a decade of punitive rhetoric and action in public policy (with targeting of lone-parent families and Murray's version of the underclass debate). The most telling moment was Michael Howard's 'Prison works' speech, given at the 1993 Conservative Party annual conference, which effectively signalled a U-turn on the 1991 CJA. Not only were ministers talking tough, there was also evidence of women prisoners being handcuffed while in labour.

Conditions in prisons have always been poor – some would argue, necessarily so – but there was an accentuated decline from the 1980s onwards. In December 1995 the chief inspector of prisons, Sir David Ramsbotham, and his Inspectorate team walked out of HM Prison Holloway. They did so because of the appalling conditions found there, including a filthy rat-infested environment overrun with cockroaches, where prisoners were locked in their cells for most of the day (Ramsbotham, 2003). This was followed in 1997 by another damning thematic report from HM Inspectorate of Prisons (HMIP) (1997). Also in that year the High Court ruled that teenage girls must be treated differently from ordinary female prisoners. Because of these problems, the Home Office recognized that gender-specific issues needed to be addressed, and it created the Women's Policy Group in 1998.

Prison reform and women's issues

There are many factors bringing about prison reform, but Carlen (2002a, 2002b) singles out several motivating factors which are common to many different parts of the world. Scandal is a major driver, and there have been several related directly to the imprisonment of women. The prison is also in a position that requires legitimization in response to campaigns. Attempts to reform prison frequently meet obstacles, though, and one problem is 'carceral clawback' (Moffatt, 2002): this refers to ideological values that are mobilized periodically to maintain the prison system as it is, essentially unchanged.

Let us now consider some of the issues currently facing women in prison. Important issues include:

- mental health and self-harm
- drugs
- mothers in prison
- young women in custody
- Black and minority ethnic group females

Many prisoners, both male and female, end up being locked up because of the often difficult social circumstances in which they live, or as a result of their chaotic and disorganized personal lives. There are some gender-specific factors, though, which need to be considered. The 19 prisons used to contain women can be categorized as either closed or open, rather than the four categories used for men. Many of the prisons used to accommodate women were formerly used for men, and thus the facilities are not always appropriate. What is more, there is no separate provision for young female offenders, as there is for young male offenders.

Carlen and Worrall (2005) show that where femininity has been acknowledged women's regimes have been influenced, often informally, by various ideological assumptions about womanhood and femininity more generally. For instance, there is the perception that women who commit crime are in some way 'doubly deviant' because such behaviour goes against the grain of what is expected of their sex. Consequently there is a tendency to treat female prisoners as if they are unwell, and to medicalize and pathologize their behaviour. This indicates that there is a concern for the welfare of female prisoners, although this is largely related to wider attitudes towards the family, based on recognition of women's central role as child carers.

There is a situation therefore where women are not only 'marginal' in numeric terms (because there are fewer of them in prison) but their qualitative experiences are different too. The female prison population consists of fewer recidivists (repeat offenders) and relatively more foreign nationals and minority ethnic individuals than the male population (Carlen and Worrall, 2005). The prison culture is explicitly male, especially the attitudes and beliefs of prison staff. Because most prison officers are men (see Table 8.1), it is not surprising that male officers are present in female prisons, which may make the inmates feel uncomfortable.

Table 8.1 *Gender breakdown of prison staff*

	Men		Women	
	number	%	number	%
Prison officers	19,455	81	4,470	19
Governor grades	1,044	81	248	19
Other grades	1,528	52	10,502	48
Total	22,027	68	15,220	32

Source: Home Office (2004b).

Many women outside prison take on more responsibilities than their male counterparts, especially child care, and this can place a sometimes intolerable burden on their psychological health, the fragility of which is apparent when they are imprisoned. When mothers are sent to prison often young children are left with wider family members, especially grandparents, but some are placed in care as there are no responsible adults available. The masculine bias of the prison culture is also apparent in the education, training and resettlement opportunities available for women. This provision is often based around gendered stereotypes about the types of work 'suitable' for women.

A report published by HMIP (1997) estimated that 20 per cent of women in prison have been in care. This shows that a significant proportion of this population have experienced institutionalization. The reasons for a person to end up in care are complex, but common ones are neglect and abuse. Thus the finding in a survey that 50 per cent of women reported having experienced abuse is perhaps not altogether surprising (HMIP, 1997). Another survey showed that 37 per cent of women had attempted suicide prior to their incarceration (Singleton et al., 1998). Another study revealed the extent of drug use among women in the year before they were imprisoned: 47 per cent said that they had used crack cocaine, and 57 per cent heroin. The comparable figures for males were 28 per cent (crack cocaine) and 35 per cent (heroin) (Home Office Research Findings, 2004b).

Some issues that affect women in general have an even greater effect among minority ethnic females, in particular drug use. Self-harm and mental health also pose dilemmas for the prison service. While this is not obviously a gender-specific matter, there are a range of other issues where the differences between males and females are more apparent. In September 2005 there were 80 females under the age of 18 in custody, and as a group they presented different considerations from their male equivalents. The most significant factor is women's role as parents. Only five prisons have dedicated mother and baby units.

Now we shall look in more detail at some specific issues, including female black and minority (BME) prisoners, drugs, mental health, self-harm, mothers in prison and young female prisoners.

BME prisoners

I have already mentioned the significance of race and ethnicity for understanding the pattern of imprisonment. When we look at both race/ethnicity and gender, it is noteworthy that 29 per cent of female prisoners were from a minority ethnic group, compared with 22 per cent of male prisoners, and of these 24 per cent were classified as Black compared with 15 per cent of the ethnic minority men. There is a degree of minority ethnic group over-representation in the prison population for both sexes, but it is more pronounced for females. Moreover, 20 per cent of women doing time were foreign nationals. (The equivalent figure for males is 10 per cent.) Why is this figure so high? One reason seems to lie in the fact that 75 per cent of the Black women and (in June 2002) 84 per cent of the foreign nationals had been imprisoned for drug-related offences (Home Office, 2004b). If foreign nationals are excluded from the equation, 45 per cent of the Black women in jail had been sentenced for drugs offences, compared with 26 per cent of the White women. This category of offences also featured more heavily than for Black males (of whom 18 per cent had committed drug-related crimes).

Drugs

It is worth exploring the issue of drugs in some more detail. Home Office (2003b) figures show that the pattern of drug use among male and female prisoners is different. This is especially apparent in relation to the use of hard (class A) drugs such as crack cocaine and heroin: 47 per cent and 57 per cent of women prisoners reported using crack and heroin respectively in the 12 months before they were incarcerated. The equivalent figures for men are 28 per cent for crack and 35 per cent for heroin.

A drug habit has a bearing on sentencing outcomes. Many women are, in general, sentenced much more leniently than men, although this is less true for female recidivist drug users and violent first-time offenders (Caddle and Crisp, 1997). Inside prison the levels of drug use are comparable in male and female establishments. Drugs are linked to bullying and intimidation in both environments (Home Office, 2004b). The introduction of mandatory drug testing (MDT) in prisons in 1995 has proven to be more intrusive for female prisoners.

Mental health issues

Many male and female prisoners experience mental health problems, but women prisoners are more likely to have received either support or treatment for a psychiatric problem, including in-patient treatment, before they were sentenced to prison. Functional psychosis is more prevalent among female prisoners and they are more likely to suffer from a neurotic disorder. Mental disorder among women is linked to their relatively high degree of dependence on opiates.

Although women experience more serious psychiatric problems than men, in some respects they are less likely than men to be suffering from a personality disorder. Women appear to be less dependent on alcohol than men, with 38 per cent of women and 58 per cent of men drinking at 'hazardous levels' (NACRO, 2001). Male prisoners are more likely to have poor access to community mental health services, and they use prescribed drugs more commonly.

Closely related to mental illness is the problem of self-harm.

Self-harm

Suicide and self-harm are major problems for the prison service. Even when suicide rates were declining in the wider community for most of the 1980s and 1990s, they continued to increase behind prison gates (HMIP, 1999). An HMIP survey (carried out in 1996, cited in Home Office, 2004b) focused specifically on the extent and prevalence of self-harm among female prisoners, finding that 40 per cent of them either hurt themselves or attempted to commit suicide. There is a close links between these behaviours and a background where abusive and broken relationships are the norm. The rate of self-harm is significantly higher in the remand population, possibly given the uncertainty of this status and the enhanced anxiety this produces (HMIP, 1999).

The reasons for these self-destructive actions are complex and multi-faceted, but

Liebling's (1992) research shows that women are profoundly affected by the separation from their families, more so than by the austere prison regime they inhabit. The ways in which women react and adapt to imprisonment is very different from men, most notably because females tend to internalize their distress and anxiety, whereas men project it outwards, showing their anger through disturbances and rioting. There is an interesting twist and turn on the self-harm issue, as the evidence suggests that self-harm may be treated less as a health problem and more as a discipline problem. This orientation of the prison service may account for the relatively high number of disciplinary cases pursued against women prisoners in comparison with men.

Mothers in prison

A Home Office study (Caddle and Crisp, 1997) looked at the experiences of motherhood of 1766 female prisoners. The sample included 65 per cent sentenced prisoners and 27 per cent held on remand. Of this sample, 1082 (61 per cent) were either pregnant or were already mothers of children aged 18 years or younger. The research revealed that this particular group of women tended to have their children at a younger age than the general, non-custodial, population: 55 per cent of the prisoner sample gave birth to at least one of their children while they were still teenagers. There was also a higher proportion of single mothers in prison than outside. The researchers explored possible linkages between early parenthood and women's past experiences, finding that 73 per cent of women had spent most of their lives until the age of 16 with two parents.

The children of women in prison tended to be young, with 30 per cent and 34 per cent having children aged under five and nine years respectively. Of these children, 71 per cent had been living with their mother before she was sent down, although only 28 per cent lived in a household they shared with their natural father (Caddle and Crisp, 1997). Ten per cent of children were either in care or adopted. For 85 per cent of the children their mother's prison sentence was the first time they had lived separately.

It is possible in some cases for mother and child to be closer together, demonstrated by the existence of mother and baby units (MBUs). There are five of these units, offering approximately 90 places. Given their scarcity, women may have to move farther from their home to access a place in an MBU. While MBUs bring some benefits for some women, other women are reluctant for their children to be in prison (Caddle and Crisp, 1997).

Imprisoning women also has consequences for the behaviour of their children: 44 per cent of women reported that there was a deterioration in the standard of their children's behaviour, while 30 per cent stated that their child became withdrawn. Twenty-two per cent of mothers reported that their children experienced problems with their eating. Thirty-one per cent of the children had to change school. Seventeen per cent of mothers with children aged 10 or over said that their children were 'mixing with the wrong crowd' (Caddle and Crisp, 1997).

The negative impact of all this on the health and well-being of female prisoners cannot be over-estimated. The sense of helplessness resulting from women who are unable to help and support their children is a major cause of frustration and anxiety.

Feelings of depression, loneliness and problems with family and personal relationships are not uncommon. In prisons there are practical difficulties associated with visits, and only 53 per cent of women prisoners had been visited by their children. Finally, the expectation that a woman prisoner would become a lone parent on release increased substantially over the course of a prison sentence: a rise from 34 per cent to 43 per cent (Hedderman and Gelsthorpe, 1997). An outcome of this is that many families are never reunited, so the prison term causes lasting damage beyond the life of the sentence.

Young women in custody

Young women are marginalized within the prison service in both quantitative and qualitative terms. Unlike male prisoners, females aged under 21 tend to be held in establishments that are jointly designated as adult prisons and young offender institutions. The containment of young women in prisons has attracted the interest of human rights campaigners, who are concerned that this policy is an infringement on the civil liberties of young people. Accordingly, a Howard League report, *Lost Inside* (1997), called on the government to uphold Article 37 of the UN Convention on the Rights of the Child and remove young women from prisons. In response to this a court ruling stated that taking young female offenders to an adult prison that was not also a young offender's institution (YOI) was unlawful.

More recently the Youth Justice Board (YJB) has set a goal of removing all females under 16 from prison service establishments. In 2005 the YJB started to develop segregated units within some prisons created specifically for under-18s. The aim of these changes is for prisons to fulfil their obligations to protect young women, as required by the Children Act (1989). While these aims are laudable, the prison capacity is limited and space is increasingly scarce in a highly punitive environment. As well as creating the physical space to accommodate these young prisoners, an additional aim is to provide educational services that are appropriate to that age group, as well as multi-disciplinary services, including stronger links with Youth Offending Teams (YOTs).

There is some research examining the experiences of young female prisoners. One study (Eves, 2004) interviewed 84 young women, including 62 (76 per cent) who were White. Of these young women, 47 per cent had experienced care as they were brought up, and 9 per cent had children. Already it is clear that the experiences of this population mirror those of adult prisoners, confirmed further by the findings that many women (63 per cent) experienced depression on arrival in custody, and that 37 per cent were dealing with the turmoil of coming off drugs. The environment was also found to be hostile, and 41 per cent of the interviewees said that they were shouted at on arrival, further unsettling them. Some of the women reported that they were bullied (13 per cent) and assaulted (21 per cent), adding to their already upsetting and disturbing experiences. To make matters worse nearly half of the interviewees said that they experienced practical problems contacting family and friends. As for adult prisoners, finding a job on the point of release was crucial for reducing the risk of reoffending (Eves, 2004).

THE IMPRISONMENT OF WOMEN: KEY ISSUES

■ Prison is a hostile environment and negative experience for all prisoners.
■ Men and women experience considerable suffering when they are deprived of their liberty.
■ Gender is significant, though, because women experience problems that are particular to them.
■ Mental health affects female prisoners in particular ways.
■ Women have general health needs that are not adequately addressed by a system that was originally designed with men in mind.
■ A major concern with the imprisonment of women who are mothers is the harmful effects of their imprisonment on their children.

BLACK AND MINORITY ETHNIC GROUP PRISONERS

The purpose of this case study is:

■ to see whether different ethnic groups experience imprisonment differently from majority ethnic group members
■ to look at the statistical information on the prison population relating to ethnicity
■ to consider the differential experiences of Black and minority ethnic (BME) group prisoners.

This section considers the treatment ethnic minority prisoners receive, focusing on ethnicity and the prison population (numbers), race relations policy in prisons, and racism in prison. The section concludes by considering some of the reasons that there is a disproportionately high number of African-Caribbean origin (Black) people in the prison population. It is only since the 1980s that there has been any ethnic monitoring of the prison population. However, even before this date various community organizations had highlighted the over-representation of Black people in prison. Ethnic monitoring actually began in June 1984 as part of an attempt to assess race relations in prisons, but it was made a statutory requirement by section 95 of the Criminal Justice Act (1991) (Bowling and Phillips, 2002).

Statistical information about BME prisoners

Home Office (2005c: 87) statistics shows that on 28 February 2003 there were 17,775 BME prisoners. This number accounted for 24.6 per cent of the prison population. This figure was broken down into separate minority groups, revealing that 16 per cent of prisoners were Black, 3.4 per cent Asian, and 4.8 per cent were members of the Chinese and 'Other' minority ethnic groups. The proportion of each of these minority groups in the general population, as counted by the 2001 Census is 2.8 per cent Black, 4.7 per cent Asian and 1.2 per cent 'Other'. A quick glance at these figures shows that Black people are over-represented nearly six times over in the prison population, whereas Asians are under-represented.

Over the years there has been a dramatic increase in the numbers of Black people being sent to prison, and between 1993 and 2003 the number of Black people in prison increased by 138 per cent. The prison population during this period increased for all ethnic groups, but the rate for Black people was greater, as is demonstrated by the equivalent increases for white and Asian prisoners of 48 per cent and 73 per cent respectively.

A significant proportion of the prison population are foreign nationals, including 12 per cent of the male and 21 per cent of the female populations. For the male group, foreign nationals amounted to 4 per cent of the White prison population. The same figures for other ethnic groups are Blacks 34 per cent, Asians 29 per cent and Chinese/'Other' 45 per cent. Clearly a higher proportion of foreign nationals are from visibly different ethnic groups. A similar pattern is evident for women, where 5 per cent of White prisoners were foreign nationals. The equivalent statistics for other groups are 58 per cent of Blacks, 42 per cent of Asians and 47 per cent of Chinese/'Other' (Home Office, 2005c: 87).

The Home Office (2005c: 90) scrutinized these statistics in more detail, showing for example that there were relatively more BME prisoners on remand, especially in the 'Other' category. The reasons for these differences may be related to offence type. For example:

- More Black (37 per cent) and Asian and 'Other' groups (26 per cent) were inside for drug-related offences than were Whites (13 per cent).
- The crime of robbery also shows a higher proportion of Black prisoners (Black 19 per cent, White 13 per cent, Asian 12 per cent and 'Other' 12 per cent).
- If burglary is taken as an example, then it can be seen there are fewer Black prisoners (8 per cent) imprisoned for this offence (compared with 18 per cent of White prisoners). The percentages for 'Other' and Asian prisoners are also relatively small at 7 per cent and 5 per cent respectively (Home Office, 2005c: 90).

Offence type also has a bearing on sentence length, because some offences are likely to receive lengthier custodial sentences than others. For example, 56 per cent of Black offenders were serving a prison sentence of four or more years. The equivalent figures for 'Other' ethnic groups was 50 per cent, and for Asians 51 per cent, whereas for Whites it was 44 per cent. At the less serious end of the sentencing scale, 11 per cent of White prisoners were imprisoned for less than 12 months, compared with 6 per cent of Black prisoners, 8 per cent of Asians and 11 per cent of 'Other' minority groups.

Explaining the disproportionate number of Black people in prison

Clearly race and ethnicity would appear to be of some significance, and Black people in particular are over-represented in the prison population. This could be explained as an effect of racial discrimination, and there is evidence of this at earlier stages of the criminal justice process, especially by the police (Bowling and Phillips, 2002). Hood's (1992) study of sentencing showed that four-fifths of Black men are given a custodial sentence, in line with the seriousness of their offending behaviour and the mode of trial. However, 20 per cent of cases showed evidence of differential or discriminatory treatment. Hood argued that one-third of this 'race effect' is the result of the higher proportion sentenced to custody, and two-thirds is because of the higher proportion of black offenders pleading not guilty, and the relatively long-term prison sentences they received as a consequence of this. Indeed following the publication of the Macpherson (1999) inquiry, which investigated the circumstances surrounding the racially motivated murder of the young black teenager Stephen Lawrence, it was concluded that British society is 'institutionally racist'. However, there are other factors that may explain the prison population, such as the age structure of different ethnic groups, social class, education, employment status and social exclusion.

Race relations policy in prisons

In the 1970s and 1980s some campaigning groups exposed the harsh treatment ethnic minority prisoners experienced, including brutality and harassment. This is hardly surprising given the number of prison officers who were openly racist and belonged to the National Front (the forerunner of the British National Party). There was also evidence that prison officers held stereotypical views of Black inmates, which was evidenced in the reports they submitted to the parole board. Officers also discriminated against Black prisoners when they allocated jobs to prisoners and in disciplinary matters. Officers were not sensitized to religious and cultural needs. In the 1980s the Home Office responded and introduced numerous initiatives to address this problem. The Home Office also 'played down' incidents involving confrontations between Black and White prisoners. If it was not possible to ignore these episodes, then Black prisoners were the cause of the problem and had to be dispersed (McDermott, 1990).

Progress has been slow, though. A recent initiative is Racial Equality for Staff and Prisoners (RESPOND), which called for a review of the complaints procedure, a new investigations strategy, and racial harassment training.

Racism in prison

Genders and Player (1989) reviewed this issue back in the 1980s. Race relations was generally regarded as a non-issue by prison staff. However, there was evidence of staff with racist and stereotypical views of Black inmates (for instance that they were arrogant, lazy, hostile, noisy, had non-British values, and had 'a chip on their shoulder'). These characteristics were sometimes seen to be innate. These were evident on classification forms completed at intake. Blacks are more likely to be disciplined by the book, in contrast to Whites, where more discretion is exercised. Some officers regarded Blacks as biologically inferior and unable to do some jobs or benefit from education (even though African-Caribbean and Asian prisoners were more willing to attend classes than Whites). Asians, by contrast, were seen as model prisoners (polite and hard working), although devious. Officers saw the tendency of particular ethnic groups to stick together as a problem, and wanted the number of ethnic minorities in individual prisons to be limited. Inmates recognized racism, but this was something that was often seen to exist in other prisons. Where there was racial prejudice, this was more likely to be manifest by avoidance rather than through overt conflict. Inmate perceptions about racism amongst staff were mixed and inconclusive. There is also evidence of racist victimization by fellow inmates and prison staff.

While this chapter was being written an inquiry into the circumstances surrounding the death of Zahid Mubarek was published. He was an Asian prisoner who was murdered by his violent cell-mate, Robert Stewart. The inquiry revealed institutional racism to be underlying Mubarek's death, finding evidence of prison officers neglecting vulnerable inmates and incompetence (Home Office, 2006).

Conclusions: the issue of proportionality and representation

- It has been shown that Black people are more likely than Whites to be sent to prison, even when all legally relevant factors are taken into account.
- When Blacks and Asians are sent to prison their sentences are longer than for Whites. For example, Hood's (1992) research in the West Midlands, England, found that Black defendants had a 5 per cent greater probability of receiving a custodial sentence once legally relevant factors had been considered. This would indicate that there is direct discrimination.
- Compared with White people, African-Caribbeans (Blacks) have significantly higher rates of imprisonment.
- Asians, Pakistanis, Chinese and other Asian people have higher per capita rates of imprisonment than Whites. Indians and Bangladeshis have lower rates than Whites.
- Around 1 to 1.25 per cent of the African-Caribbean population is in prison, which is eight times higher than it is for Whites.
- Other ethnic groups lie somewhere between the two poles, although Indians have a lower rate than Whites.
- The per capita rate of Black imprisonment among particular age groups, and the lifetime imprisonment rate, are not yet known. It is obvious, though, that a disproportionate number of Black people have criminal records.
- In prison, minority ethnic prisoners are more likely to discriminated against, suffer abuse and miss out on early release. Black people are stereotyped as violent and dangerous, thus justifying differential treatment (brutality and dispersal). Blacks are more likely to be disciplined by the book, in contrast to Whites, where more discretion is exercised.
- Finally, on release Black people are more likely to meet discrimination as they attempt to find accommodation and work. A vicious circle may begin.

CONCLUSION

The prison is a product of the Enlightenment and prisons were first built, at least in part, to replace more brutal forms of punishment such as torture. Throughout the nineteenth and twentieth centuries the prison population continued to expand, and it is an institution that seems set to stay, although its functions may change once the framework for the National Offender Management System (NOMS) is agreed (Carter, 2003).

Although prisons were initially introduced as a more civilized method of punishing offenders, this chapter has given two examples of injustice by highlighting the differential treatment of female and minority ethnic prisoners. The evidence suggests that these groups are discriminated against, both consciously and unconsciously, and that their respective experiences of prison are far more negative than those of White men. The conditions inside British prisons are poor, with overcrowding being a particular problem. The prison environment is a punishing one in more than one sense, as many people leave prison with inadequate support to get them back on the straight and narrow. The introduction of NOMS, where the plan is to create more integration from the beginning of a sentence to the resettlement of offenders, might address this, but only time will tell.

FURTHER READING

A good starting point for this topic area is chapters 12 and 13 of M. Davies, H. Croall and J. Tyrer, *Criminal Justice: An introduction to the criminal justice system in England and Wales* (3rd edn) (Harlow: Longman Pearson, 2005). The following readings are also essential to gain familiarity with the field: M. Cavadino and J. Dignan, *The Penal System: An introduction* (3rd edn) (London: Sage, 2002), N. Flynn, *Introduction to Prisons and Imprisonment* (London: Waterside Press, 1998), R. Matthews, *Doing Time: An introduction to the sociology of imprisonment* (Basingstoke: Palgrave Macmillan, 1999), and R. Morgan, 'Imprisonment', in M. Maguire, R. Morgan and R. Reiner (eds), *The Oxford Handbook of Criminology* (3rd edn) (Oxford: Oxford University Press, 2002).

There are also a range of websites, with the following being particularly useful.

Prison Service: www.hmprisonservice.gov.uk

Howard League: www.howardleague.org

HM Inspector of Prisons England and Wales:
www.homeofffice.gov.uk/justice/prisons/inspprisons/index.html

STUDY QUESTIONS

1. Why did the prison emerge as a method of social control at the time it did?
2. What are the main functions of:
   a) the prison service?
   b) imprisonment?
3. Describe and discuss the main issues facing women in prison today.
4. Why is there a disproportionately high number of African-Caribbean prisoners?
5. Write a short essay up to 500 words presenting a case for reducing the female prison population.
6. Identify the key problems the prison service currently faces.

9 Probation: Community-Based Punishment and Community Justice

OVERVIEW

The aim of this chapter is to provide:

■ a contrast between custodial punishment (see Chapter 8) and community-based punishment
■ an illustration of the jobs done by probation officers
■ a historical account of the origins of the probation service and the importance of organizational change in the evolution of the service
■ an evaluation of the different value frameworks that have impacted on the activities of the probation service
■ a description of community-based punishment, focusing on drug treatment and testing orders (DTTOs) and electronic monitoring.

INTRODUCTION

The existence of the probation service demonstrates that imprisonment is not the only form of punishment in modern societies. This organization is responsible for the provision of non-custodial or community-based punishments. Chapter 7 referred to sentences overseen by the National Probation Service, and this chapter builds on that by introducing students to the main jobs undertaken by probation officers. Second, the origins of the service are traced from a historical perspective, outlining its main philosophical and professional rationales. Although policy makers and the public tend to express stronger support for the use of prison as the main method of punishment, there is a credible case for using alternative measures provided by the probation service and other agencies. After examining the organization we look at two case studies exploring the use of community based interventions: the drug treatment and testing order, and electronic monitoring.

WHAT DO PROBATION OFFICERS DO?

The function of probation officers has changed very much over time, but in the early twenty-first century the probation officer is responsible for the very broad activity of supervising offenders in the community. This involves work in the courts, especially in writing pre-sentence reports (PSRs) for offenders. As was noted in Chapter 7, probation officers administer the following community-based orders: community punishment orders, community rehabilitation orders, community punishment and rehabilitation orders, and DTTOs. In line with the move towards the National Offender Management System (NOMS), probation officers carry out prison work before and after prisoners are released. For example, offenders are supervised while they are on licence. Further work is done with offenders in bail and probation hostels.

Probation officers are increasingly required to work with victims, particularly through the victim contact work they do with the victims of violent offences. In the run-up to a violent offender being released from prison, the probation officer works with the victim or the family of the victim to prepare them for this outcome. Probation officers have not always done all of these things, and the next section shows how their work, in contrast to that of the police, sentencers and prison officers, has changed dramatically since the nineteenth century.

A BRIEF HISTORY OF THE PROBATION SERVICE

This section:

■ reviews the evolution of the probation service since the nineteenth century
■ shows that the probation service has experienced far more changes to its roles and responsibilities than other criminal justice agencies.

In line with the previous chapters, which focused on the police service and the prison service, this chapter outlines the emergence of the probation service from a historical perspective. Obviously what the organization did two centuries ago has no direct bearing on what the service does today, but it is necessary to assess the extent to which there are persistent themes to aid understanding of the probation service today (May, 1991).The aim is to identify the continuities and how these relate to any changes occurring throughout the criminal justice sector and in society as a whole. When historians study the emergence of any organization they attempt to impose order on what are in actual fact a chaotic set of occurrences. History is about making sense of major developments in human societies with the benefit of hindsight. In contrast to policing and imprisonment, the changes taking place in relation to probation since the 1900s are far more noticeable.

Throughout this chapter key dates in the history of probation are noted. It is quite clear that the philosophies underpinning probation have changed markedly over time, and especially the different criminological theories probation officers utilized in their work with offenders. This is reflected in part by the different types of people who have been employed as probation officers. Also, over time the role of the service has changed, including the people or clients it has had to work with. Many writers refer to four distinctive periods of probation work, beginning in the nineteenth century and ending with the current situation.

The first period runs from the nineteenth century until the 1920s, shortly after the end of the First World War. In that epoch perhaps one of the main organizing principles of probation was developed, specifically its threefold aim to 'advise, assist and befriend'. The second period is from the 1920s to the 1960s. During this period the service was influenced by scientific values and principles, demonstrated by the arrival of case management. The 1960s was characterized by political radicalism associated with the rise of the feminism and anti-racism movements, and this brought about changes in many areas of social life, including probation. Hence there was a third phase (1970s–1990s), where probation acquired a more critical edge. Although the service belonged to the state and the criminal justice system, it challenged the conservatism of the status quo and became radical in its outlook. Finally, the fourth period began in the 1990s and continues to the present day. The defining feature nowadays is the modernization agenda, where the service is under increasing pressure to conform with a policy agenda of a government committed to 'what works', and a preoccupation with risk assessment and risk management.

The nineteenth century to the 1920s

The history of the modern probation service is all about the origins of non-custodial sanctions and punishment in the community, or those penalties used as an alternative to the prison. In the United Kingdom and the United States early probation work focused on the 'medieval common law doctrine of recognisance', which was used as an alternative to harsh penalties (Brownlee, 1998: 63). This may be defined as 'A bond entered into by an accused person before the court to do, or to refrain from doing, some specific act or other, often simply to "keep the peace"' (ibid.). In other words, offenders are bound over to ensure that they do not misbehave, and on the condition that they satisfy this requirement, they avoid a punitive response such as imprisonment.

Before examining what constituted probation in the early days it is necessary to briefly refer to the prevailing approach to penal policy in the Victorian period. In his work on the concept of the penal complex, Garland (1985) identifies two key features. The first point concerns the belief in individualism. In relation to probation, for instance, the emphasis is on individual offenders, and their particular behaviour is explained in terms of their psychological make-up. Second, because attention is fixed on the individual mind in this instance, it can be thought to follow that each person makes a rational decision and moral choice about his or her actions.

Early probation work was mainly done in the courts and surrounding areas. The idea of probation was initially concerned with 'testing' individuals, and was used in relation to juveniles, for example under the Juvenile Offenders Act (1847). The overarching aim was to address the welfare needs of offenders and to avoid punishing them. The principles of probation were later applied to adults, partly coinciding with the appointment of the Police Court Missionary in 1876. In 1887 the Probation of First Offenders Act made it possible for the courts to release offenders 'on probation' to missionaries (May, 1991).

By the turn of the twentieth century there were around 100 of these missionaries, who were actively committed to a religiously motivated but humanitarian cause of caring for offenders, many of whom were amongst the more vulnerable members of society (Vanstone, 2004). However, assistance and support was not provided equally to all, and the police court missionaries did make a clear and firm distinction between individuals who were 'deserving' and 'undeserving'. It is here that the influence of the Church of England Temperance Society was apparent. This philanthropic organization promoted religious values, evidenced by frequent talk about 'saving souls'. A lot of early probation work was oriented towards addressing the drunkenness and alcohol abuse associated with many offenders frequenting the courts. There was purportedly a strong link between drinking and fecklessness, including criminality. The view was that if offenders were educated about the dangers of alcohol and encouraged to refrain from using it, their behaviour would improve. This was also seen to be a better alternative than simply punishing offenders (Brownlee, 1998).

In essence the work done by the missionaries was seen by the courts to be useful because they could sometimes supervise the perpetrators of relatively minor offences rather than their being sent to prison. This early probation work was eventually recognized by the state, partly for humanitarian reasons, but also because it would reduce public expenditure on imprisonment. By 1907 there was legislation, and the Probation of Offenders Act (1907) was introduced. Probation was now an 'order' of the court rather than a sentence, and was therefore not a punishment (Nellis, 2003). Probation now had a statutory basis, replacing the principle of 'recognisance'. The Act also resulted in the payment of officers, many of whom were volunteers, but they still lacked training and there was no centralized control over their activities. A few years later the Criminal Justice Act (1925) was passed into law, requiring every court to appoint a probation officer. These officers also carried out welfare and civil work, such as matrimonial and child care cases, right up until the 1980s.

The 1930s–1960s: professional casework

Over the course of these four decades the value framework and the organizational structure of probation changed. The largely evangelical and voluntary work described in the previous section disappeared, and according to May (1991) the role of probation officers was more therapeutic in orientation. Understanding of offending behaviour was based on an appreciative stance towards the principles of positivism, especially psychological variants. The causes of crime were thought to be psychodynamic, or to be found in the individual psyche or mind. Because of this adherence to positivism it was assumed that offending behaviour could be treated in the same way that medical professionals treated sick people. Moreover, probation officers were extremely confident that any interventions they applied to individual offenders would lead to a change in their behaviour.

At the same time there developed a closer affinity between probation and social work, and especially the values of social work permeated probation work. Subsequently, probation was increasingly oriented towards welfare values, especially the goal of rehabilitation. These changes are clearly related to an expansion of probation activity. For example, in 1908 there were 8000 probation orders, in 1933 there were 19,000 orders, and in 1943, 38,000 orders.

Most people working in probation were direct entrants, although some initial training began in the 1930s, and this signified the growing professionalism amongst probation staff.

In the aftermath of the Second World War (1939–45), probation became more centralized, different probation areas were coordinated, and there were clearer management structures. There were arguably four organizing principles shared by all probation officers at that time, expressed in a statement issued by the United Nations in 1951 (cited in Brownlee, 1998). First, care was taken to ensure that offenders were suitable for interventions delivered by probation officers. In other words, offenders were selected according to preset criteria. Second, attached to probation orders was a conditional suspension of punishment. This means that offenders will not be punished on the condition that they satisfy the requirements set out in an alternative to a punitive sanction. Third, probation needs to involve an element of personal supervision, and fourth, such supervision must involve guidance or treatment to address the factors surrounding offending behaviour. Overall, probation was court-based, paternalistic and authoritarian (May, 1991).

The 1960s–1990s

All through these years probation underwent profound organizational and legislative changes, and the values of probation work were redefined in response to theoretical and ideological developments. As far as organizational changes are concerned, a landmark event was the publication of the Morrison Report (1962, cited in May, 1991), which among other things made a social work ethos more explicit in probation practice. There were also calls for further training to ensure probation staff possessed qualifications. By 1966 the role of probation included aftercare.

The Probation and After Care Service Act (1967) led to a change in the nature of the relationship between probation officers and magistrates. In particular, probation officers were given more say in explaining the relationship between the offender's social background and his or her offending behaviour.

In the 1970s there was a spate of legislation affecting the probation service, including the Criminal Justice Act (1967) and the Children and Young Persons Act (1969). The Criminal Justice Act (1972) created more roles and responsibilities, and resources, for probation officers, including:

- community services
- day training centres
- money payment supervision orders
- suspended sentence supervision orders
- deferred sentences
- probation hostels.

To respond effectively to these and other organizational and legislative changes there was a massive expansion of personnel involved in probation work. There was also recognition that the skills required by staff were different, and there was an increase in the number of graduates recruited into probation, demonstrated by the requirement for certified professional qualifications. In the 1970s new entrants to the profession were required to take social work training such as the CQSW, which became the DipSW in 1989. As the diversification of tasks continued unabated throughout the 1980s, there were pressures from the centre, or the Home Office, to assert more control over probation staff. For example, the introduction of a Statement of National Objectives and Priorities meant that increasingly central government prescribed the jobs that probation officers should undertake.

There were also major developments in theoretical criminology and thinking in policy circles. The 1960s and 1970s were the heyday for Marxist thinkers (Taylor, Walton and Young, 1973) and labelling theorists (Becker, 1963). The contribution of these thinkers to criminological theory is examined in Part Four, but we can note here that they drew attention to the negative and harmful effects of state agents on offenders. They saw the probation service as a coercive organization concerned with regulating the workless classes and maintaining the interests of the state and ruling classes. Probation officers, like all criminal justice staff, were in the business of applying labels to stigmatize powerless groups in society.

Further damage was done to the reputation of the probation service as a result of the publication of an analysis of the impact of probation interventions on offenders, especially the rates of recidivism or reoffending. Contrary to the optimism of probation officers who considered their interventions to be bringing benefits, especially the rehabilitation of offenders, the opposite was actually the case. As Martinson (1974) put it, 'nothing works'.

It is clear then that probation practice and ideas about probation were in flux, and there was much debate about the value and status of probation work. During this period the probation service was professionalized but at the same time the organization was politicized, and disputes were widespread. In essence most of the debate focused on whether the primary task of probation officers was to care for or control offenders. In other words, is probation about rehabilitation or punishment?

The 1990s onwards

A key turning point was the 1991 Criminal Justice Act, which was underpinned by the principles of just deserts and proportionality. This piece of legislation was introduced to reduce the expanding prison population by diverting all but the more serious offenders from custody. The 1991 Act imagined an enhanced role for probation, and the service was required to provide punishment in the community for those who were not given a prison sentence. Probation became a sentence of the court, and imposed restrictions on the liberty of offenders. Throughout the 1990s the probation service was increasingly influenced by the Home Office, suggesting that probation was becoming more centralized. The 1992 National Standards were revised in 1995, 2000 and 2002, and in 1996 probation training was removed from the social work profession. This change signalled a shift away from social work to law enforcement, and also made probation officers more directly accountable to the government and indirectly to the taxpayer. The probation service was now an arm of the criminal justice system. This tendency to centralization took another turn in 2000 when the Criminal Justice Act created the National Probation Service (NPS). The result was the creation of 42 probation areas, which shared their boundaries with the police areas in England and Wales.

In the 2000s the workload of the probation service has increased mainly because as well as administering community punishments, it works more and more with the prison service, as well as with victims of crime. Nowadays probation is no longer seen as an alternative to punishment, but a punishment in itself. Also, under three successive New Labour governments covering the period between 1997 and 2007 the negativity of Martinson's (1974) finding that 'nothing works' was rejected. The probation service was required to satisfy the requirements of the NPM and provide value for money. To say 'nothing works' was a sign of failure and defeat. Instead the 'what works' agenda was promoted, and the probation service was placed in a position where it had to demonstrate the effectiveness of its attempts to reduce reoffending and rehabilitate offenders.

The work of the NPS was also brought more into line with other criminal justice agencies as a result of the Crime and Disorder Act (1998). This so-called joined-up working is described in more detail in the next chapter. It is clear that probation officers in the twenty-first century are not expected to 'advise, assist and befriend' offenders but rather to enforce the law, protect the public, reduce offending and rehabilitate existing offenders.

In 2003 the coming of another Criminal Justice Act (2003) and the publication of the Carter Report meant further change to the probation service. As well as the new generic community order, new proposals suggested that a new framework was required for offender management, the National Offender Manager Service (NOMS) (Home Office, 2004c). This organization was to be headed up by a chief executive, charged with the responsibility for punishing offenders and reducing offending behaviour. In other words, this chief executive would be responsible for all offenders, breaking down the silos of the prison and probation services. The target was the end-to-end management of offenders, who would be given either a custodial or non-custodial sentence (Carter, 2003).

THE HISTORY OF THE PROBATION SERVICE: KEY POINTS

- Like all institutions the probation service has changed over time but the changes it has faced are more pronounced.
- The service has strong links with the social work profession, and traditionally its orientation towards offenders has been one of care rather than control.
- Over time the effectiveness of probation service work with offenders has been found to be wanting, and the organization has come under pressure to improve its performance.
- Towards the end of the twentieth century the original social work ethos of the probation service was replaced by an emphasis on offender management.

To explore the diverse activities of the probation service and community-based punishment in some more detail there follow two case studies, one looking at drug treatment and testing orders, and one that examines a study of electronic monitoring.

DRUG TREATMENT AND TESTING ORDERS (DTTOS)

In this case study:

■ the DTTO, a community sentence, is discussed
■ this sentence is situated in the context of the probation service and the work it does with other agencies
■ there is an overview of some evaluations of the effectiveness of DTTOs.

The DTTO was established by sections 61–63 of the Crime and Disorder Act (1998), and is administered by the probation service. In this section the DTTO is first contextualized. Why was it introduced when it was, and what was the underlying rationale for its introduction at that particular moment? It is therefore necessary to focus on relevant aspects of the policy-making process in the area of penal policy. Some evaluations of the impact and effectiveness of DTTOs are then reviewed.

Context

The DTTO was introduced by a New Labour government and presented as a 'flagship' initiative to tackle drug-related criminality (Barton and Quinn, 2002; Crow, 2001), which was costing taxpayers in the region of £1.5 billion per annum (Falk, 2004; Turnbull et al., 2000; Turner, 2004). The problems the DTTO was intended to address were not new. In particular it focused on the social and economic costs incurred by drug use, such as acquisitive crime.

The DTTO is a high-tariff sentence, and can last for between six months and three years for offenders who are aged 16 and above (Bean, 2002; Falk, 2004; Turnbull et al., 2000). Basically this order requires the offender to receive treatment either as part of or in association with another community sentence. The order is managed and enforced by the probation service. Any defendant for whom the recommendation for a DTTO is made must show to the courts clear evidence that he or she is 'dependent on or has a propensity to misuse drugs' (www.homeoffice.gov.uk/docs/dttguid.html). A significant feature of the DTTO is that any individual who undergoes the order must give his or her consent to entering the programme. The court also needs to be satisfied that the defendant is likely to be committed to the goals of the programme, and that he or she will benefit from what is an expensive sentence (Turnbull et al., 2000).

The DTTO represented something of a departure in penal policy, inasmuch as that the legally enforceable treatment of offenders who are dependent on drugs was relatively rare. The medical profession and criminal justice agencies were both sceptical about relying on legislation, in particular the use of coercive approaches to the treatment of drug dependency (Carnwath and Smith, 2002; Turnbull et al., 2000; Unell, 2002). However there was legislation in place which provided for an element of treatment, specifically section 1A (6) of the Criminal Justice Act (1991), which gave the courts the power to include treatment as one of the conditions attached to a probation order. However, as Turnbull et al. (2000: 1) indicate, the probation service did not use this power to a significant extent. The reason for this was that neither sentencers nor probation officers were particularly aware of the availability of this option, largely because of the lack of Home Office guidance. There was also an ideological reason for probation officers' resistance, particularly because this piece of legislation involved a degree of coercion. This went against the grain of the probation service mission to 'advise, assist and befriend'. As always there were also concerns about the cost of the treatment and who would foot the bill (Unell, 2002).

Following the Criminal Justice Act (1991) the political economic context in which the probation service operated soon changed, most notably following the then home secretary, Michael Howard's Conservative Party conference speech, which launched the 'Prison works' policy and added to the populist and authoritarian law and order agenda of the Conservative government of that day. The probation service was required to abandon its social work values and to focus instead on adopting a tougher approach, especially towards the increased numbers of individuals characterized as users of 'hard core' drugs (Barton, 1999; Bean, 2002; Turnbull et al., 2000). This was also driven by the influence of the 'War on drugs' in the United States. While New Labour, the architects of the DTTO, was elected to govern in 1997, the agenda was clearly set by its predecessors (Carnwath and Smith, 2002; Turnbull et al., 2000). Tony Blair, the New Labour prime minister (1997–), when he was shadow home secretary in opposition to Michael Howard had coined the phrase 'tough on crime, tough on the causes of crime', which was clearly a reference point in strategies oriented towards drug-related offenders (Barton, 1999).

While New Labour did not curb increases in the numbers of people sent to prison, it did recognize that imprisonment is not always the best way of dealing with the problems presented by drug misusers, and also that the prison environment can often worsen drug dependency amongst inmates. The DTTO was introduced to counter the worst excesses of mass imprisonment, but the government was careful to avoid any accusation that it was a soft option for drug abusers (Turnbull et al., 2000). For example, it was necessary to ensure the credibility of the order with the public, but principally among sentencers. Subsequently the Home Office emphasized that the DTTO was an intervention that would be effective in relation to high-risk cases, and that the 'testing' requirement was sufficiently punitive. DTTOs were used as a method of dealing with defendants who would usually have been given a custodial sentence (Turnbull et al., 2000: 37).

As such, the DTTO is intended to be punitive, and can be seen as an example of enhanced social control or 'net widening' (Cohen, 1985) and declining confidence in rehabilitation. However, there is also an emphasis on 'what works', and renewed belief in evidence-based treatment (Raynor, 2002; Turnbull et al., 2000). Clearly because enforced drug treatment is relatively novel there was a lack of robust evidence to justify its application, but several reasons were given for expecting it to succeed. First, the DTTO is well managed. Second, it was argued that targeted and supervised programmes can be effective. Third, there was an assumption that coercion may be used to engage high-risk offenders in treatment programmes. Fourth, there is clear potential to reduce drug-related offending (Falk, 2004; Hough and Mitchell, 2003; Rumgay, 2001).

Digging deeper into the research literature, there is a pessimistic view that coercion can cancel out rehabilitation. However research by Hough and Mitchell (2003: 41) suggests that coerced treatment is not necessarily any less effective than treatment entered into voluntarily, and that those who are coerced into treatment stay on programmes for a longer period. There was also evidence to show that such treatment is more likely to work if it is part of a community-based sentence rather than being attached to a custodial sentence (Underdown, 2001). Although the DTTO is concerned with rehabilitation, it is necessary to remember that it is an intervention to reduce crime, and that this should be done as effectively, efficiently and economically as possible. For this reason the probation service has to work by paying close attention to the values of the NPM to show that the sentence is delivered, and above all that attendance and completion rates are both high (Loader and Sparks, 2002; Underdown, 2001).

The DTTO is a clear example of joined-up thinking concerning a problem with multiple causes and effects. Drug misuse is clearly related to acquisitive crime, for example, and there is a clear connection between criminal justice and health and well-being. It is logical, therefore, for health and criminal justice professionals to work in partnership and for there to be a multi-agency response (Barton, 1999; Unell, 2002). Partnership approaches to tackling drugs are fraught with difficulties, not least because they raise questions about the relative significance attached on the one hand to 'care' or rehabilitation, and on the other hand to 'control' and enforcement functions. To put it more simply, professionals from the medical world will perceive drug use differently from probation officers. Thus, health and criminal justice concerns may not be incompatible but they are potentially difficult to reconcile (Bateman, 1999; Carnwath and Smith, 2002). To illustrate this, agencies that provide treatment in the National Health Service (NHS) and the voluntary sector have opposed the DTTO as 'an instrument of court' because there is the danger that criminals may be prioritized above non-criminals waiting for similar treatment (Hough and Mitchell, 2003: 46). Another objection is that many defendants who enter into the DTTO are only doing so because it is an seen as an infinitely preferable alternative to being given a prison sentence (Bateman, 1999; Unell, 2002).

It is quite clear that the probation service has to confront the interests of various professional groups with different responsibilities, and to attempt to find some middle ground between the extremes of enforcement and treatment. Health policy, at least in principle, is about responding to need, whereas criminal justice policy is, in the last analysis, about ascertaining the guilt or innocence of defendants and treating them appropriately (Bateman, 1999; Rumgay, 2001). Rumgay describes these contradictions and tensions well: 'in the Drug Treatment and Testing Order ... the technology and skills of drug treatment have become conflated with those of law enforcement, leading to ambiguity of purpose, with a potentially damaging impact on interagency collaboration' (2001: 128).

This quotation raises profound questions of an ethical nature about attempting to integrate strategies and techniques of control and treatment (Turnbull et al., 2000). Probation officers regard the DTTO as a community sentence and therefore their responsibility. In preserving their professional interests probation officers may attempt to sideline health and drug workers at certain points of the delivery programme. There are other rubbing points surrounding the issue of disclosure of information about clients. Furthermore, there are questions about the primacy that should be attached to requiring clients to abstain from use, and about whether interventions should be focused on harm reduction (Barton, 1999; Turnbull et al., 2000). To give a concrete example, there is a tendency for probation officers 'to work with high caseloads'. Medical professionals are more likely to limit the number of clients they will see

(Turnbull et al., 2000). An outcome of these different professional cultures is a degree of unevenness in the delivery of the DTTO, depending on the professionals managing it. Consequently, the quality of the programmes varies significantly. This not only affects clients but also does not instil confidence in sentencers. As Falk (2004: 403) puts it, a 'mixed message' is given 'to courts whose co-operation and commitment to the process, which was variable to start with, is essential to ensure that orders are made'.

Evaluations/evidence

What do initial evaluations of DTTOs tell us? There was an initial pilot study undertaken before the DTTOs were rolled out nationally (Turnbull et al., 2000). The pilot areas included Liverpool, Croydon and Gloucestershire. The results of this study show a complex situation regarding the effectiveness of the orders. In these three geographical areas it was found that there was a reduction in the use of drugs, and that less money was spent on them: the pre-DTTO figure was £400 per week; the post-DTTO figure £25. It would also appear that there is some evidence that offenders completing the order were less involved in acquisitive crime (Bean, 2002; Cavadino and Dignan, 2003; Turnbull et al., 2000; Turner, 2004). Further research was commissioned to interview individuals who had completed the DTTO six months and two years later. Clients who completed the DTTO were shown to be less likely to be reconvicted (53 per cent) than those who did not complete their order (91 per cent) (Turner, 2004; Turnbull et al., 2000). The positive message here must be put into context, though, because the overall retention and completion rates on the DTTO are low. Under a third of the offenders who were given a DTTO as part of their sentence completed the programme, meaning two-thirds did not (Parker, 2004; Turnbull et al., 2000). In response to these relatively poor results, supporters of the DTTO argued that this was attributable to the kind of 'teething problems' encountered by many novel policy innovations. Other studies have by and large corroborated the findings of the pilot studies (Turner, 2004; Hough et al., 2003; Cavadino and Dignan, 2003; Falk, 2004).

Before these results were received, let alone appraised, by the government a decision was taken to roll out this sentence nationally. Unsurprisingly this roll-out lacked clear strategic planning, and there was also evidence showing the clear lack of a consensus (Bean, 2002; Falk, 2004). It was highly likely that there would be problems with its implementation, and as Falk remarked, 'vast and worrying inconsistencies in terms of assessment, sentencing and practice have emerged both within and across areas in England and Wales' (Falk, 2004: 398). The lesson to be learnt from this is that if the government had exercised some patience and waited for the research evidence, many of these difficulties could have been avoided. If the government had waited a little longer, the questionable quality of treatment programmes and the failure of programmes to match offender needs and appropriate treatment services would all have been preventable (Falk, 2004).

Another emergent problem with the DTTO was identified by the National Association of Probation Officers, which highlighted a number of unintended consequences, arising as a result of the managerialist emphasis on measuring performance against targets. This gave probation officers negative incentives, and it was envisaged that officers would select offenders in the low-risk category because they were more likely to complete an order and boost the credibility of the DTTO (Cavadino and Dignan, 2003; Turnbull et al., 2000).

Some practitioners have questioned certain aspects of the DTTO, in particular the tests administered to find out whether a defendant has breached the conditions attached to the order. It is argued that the test is based on a flawed understanding of the problems facing drug abusers, not least the high risk of an individual relapsing and drifting in and out of problematic drug use. The expectation that an individual will be able to come off drugs in just a few weeks is unrealistic. This has been cited as one of the reasons that there is such a high attrition rate, with many offenders withdrawing from and not completing the programme (Turnbull et al., 2000). It has been recommended that sentencers and the professionals delivering DTTOs need to be more realistic about what they aim to achieve. A concerted effort should also be made to make sure offenders feel that they can meet the targets set as part of the sentence. This raises yet another tension for all involved in DTTO work. There is a clear case for flexibility to respond to the pitfalls just mentioned, but offenders also need to be given the impression that the order is based on consistent principles and is ultimately enforceable. If this balance is not attained, the sentence will be seen as a soft option and not sufficiently punitive (Falk, 2004; Turnbull et al., 2000; www.probation.homeoffice.gov.uk).

So far a lot has been said about the stumbling blocks associated with the implementation of the DTTO. However most of the teams charged with its management have overcome these problems. Moreover, there are examples of good practice coming to light (Falk, 2004; Hough and Mitchell, 2003; Turner, 2004). There is still a dearth of robust evidence to show that DTTO programmes are an unqualified success, but resources are being ploughed into their continuation (Falk, 2004). The government's updated drug strategy of 2002 made it clear that there should be a 100 per cent increase in the number of 'problematic drug users' participating in treatment programmes by 2008. In addition the usage of DTTO was widened to include a range of other potential beneficiaries, including treatment for offenders convicted for less serious offences offered as part of a 'lower-intensity DTTO' (Falk, 2004). To drive this forward the Drug Interventions Programme supported this community sentence in order to maintain its integrity.[1]

Update

The Criminal Justice Act (2003) passed into law the community order in April 2005. This led to the replacement of the DTTO by the drug rehabilitation programme (DRR). This has been introduced in response to the perceived risk of providing too much treatment for less serious and less prolific offenders who have been exposed to a 'high-intensity' DTTO. The aim of the DRR is to 'bring about a change of approach, matching treatment to need and using other requirements, such as unpaid work, to restrict liberty' (www.probation.homeoffice.gov.uk/files/pdf/pc55.pdf).

The National Standards for the DTTO have also been subjected to review by the National Probation Directorate and National Treatment Agency because it was suggested that the standards actually undermined retention rates. Accordingly, the proposals were revised so there was more flexibility to enhance the management of the order (Hough and Mitchell, 2003; www.probation.homeoffice.gov.uk).

This case study has shown that the DTTO, if completed, provides an opportunity for the most vulnerable and socially excluded offenders to find a way out of their drug-dependent lives and to reform their characters in the eyes of potential employers, as well as their family and friends. It is a mechanism that may divert offenders from custody and direct them towards a structured programme to address their drug misuse. The intended consequences do not always materialize, largely because of implementation problems. It is necessary that these difficulties are addressed to ensure the order works more effectively.

ELECTRONIC MONITORING

This case study:

- provides an historical overview of the usage of electronic monitoring (EM) as a community-based punishment
- considers EM in the context of wider criminal justice policies
- notes more recent technological innovations
- assesses the evidence stating that EM is effective.

This case study traces the emergence of tagging or electronic monitoring (EM), a method of keeping offenders under surveillance in the community. It shows how this technology, originally developed in the United States, was exported to the United Kingdom. The take-up of the tag, or 'magic bracelet' (Whitfield, 2001), was gradual, but now it is an important element in crime reduction. Also, the technology behind this type of surveillance is becoming increasingly sophisticated, signalled by the use of satellite tracking systems and voice recognition technology. The apparent effectiveness of EM is then assessed.

Electronic monitoring: a historical overview

Electronic tagging is nowadays widely used as a method of keeping convicted offenders under surveillance, although it did take some time for this technique to catch on. The origins of the principle of tagging, at least in Britain, can be traced back to the turn of the twentieth century, when convicts were marked with indelible ink. Wherever they moved this physical marker stayed with them, rather like the electronic devices did some 70 years later. A more tangible link is the concept of tracking, practised in the United States in the 1970s, which was a method enabling correctional agencies to maintain supervision over individual offenders. This was done in the community and was seen in some ways as an alternative to custody or prison. This form of supervision, along with night curfews, made location-specific observation possible, and it became an important feature of community-based supervision (Nellis, 2004b).

The first time an electronic 'tag' was actually used was said to be in 1964 in Massachusetts. It was soon recognized that this was potentially a useful technique for controlling behaviour as part of a wider system of surveillance.

EM has two historical trajectories, one American and the other British. In the United States, Judge Jack Love was the first figure to advocate the use of EM. The well-known myth is that the idea of EM was taken from the *Spider-Man* comic, where the superhero was shown being tracked through a transmitter attached to his wrist. Love was inspired by this technology, and used his imagination to apply it to the reality of criminal justice policy making, specifically the idea that tagging could be used on petty criminals rather than sending them to prison where they would share a cell with a habitual criminal. Prisons were also overcrowded and proving to be expensive, and a huge burden for taxpayers. EM offered a perfect solution.

The initial reception to EM was somewhat sceptical, and it was not employed widely, being used most in New Mexico and Florida. It was further developed over the years and used in other parts of the United States, and soon caught the attention of the British government, although not without the help of an influential individual who campaigned for its adoption in the United Kingdom.

This was Tom Stacey, a journalist, prison expert and one-time convict who campaigned to raise the profile of EM in the 1970s. Stacey drew attention to the apparent failures of penal policy to reform and rehabilitate offenders at that time, and saw EM as an alternative approach. In 1982 he founded the Offender Tag Association (OTA) to promote his personal vision of its potential uses. According to Stacey, the tag device 'Would allow the offender to have a regular, lawful life, earning his[2] living within a defined area .... And with such irksome conditions as might encourage him to mend his ways' (1989: 59).

When Stacey originally voiced these views back in the late 1970s and early 1980s they were in some senses ahead of their time, and the government did not share his enthusiasm and optimism. By the end of the 1980s the government was more willing to listen, especially when the Home Office came under fire because of the size of the prison population.

Electronic monitoring and criminal justice policy

The Conservatives eventually introduced tagging and EM, and the main aspiration was that its use would, in Whitfield's words, 'reduce the use of custody without increasing risk to the public, [and] avoid the stigma of prison' (1997: 81). Clearly the aim was to reduce the use of imprisonment, but the first experiments were related to those on bail and not convicted prisoners. The media response, and the reaction of sceptical politicians, was critical. Despite these negative perceptions a white paper, *Crime Justice and Protecting the Public* (Home Office, 1990) demonstrated that the government was committed to using EM for the purpose of curfews. The home detention curfew (HDC) was introduced by the Criminal Justice Act (1991). It was 'designed to ease [the] transition of prisoners from custody to community' (Dodgson and Mortimer, 2000 cited in Stone, 2002: 159).

The introduction of the HDC resulted in widespread opposition, and the probation service was not slow in objecting to EM. Its resistance actually led to the government having to use private security companies to deliver EM. This initial experiment with the EM technology was relatively short-lived, and Michael Howard (then Conservative home secretary) cast into doubt one of the influential rationales behind its adoption in 1993, when he made his 'Prison works' speech. In short, the government reversed the 1991 Criminal Justice Act, which called for less use of prison and greater reliance on community-based punishments. As an example of the latter, EM was not seen as effective in the context of a more punitive approach to crime.

EM was not abandoned altogether in 1993, and there were periodic debates about its usefulness, although it was not until New Labour was elected in May 1997 that it came back into favour. The first home secretary under that new regime, Jack Straw, was keen to change the status of EM by mainstreaming it rather than treating it as an experiment. Indeed Straw argued that EM was 'the future of community sentencing'. The probation service was still resistant, since the use of surveillance techniques for the purposes of control went against the grain of the 'social work' ethos at the heart of probation philosophy and practice (Nellis, 2004a). New Labour ignored these concerns and promoted EM as the best alternative to custody, making England a leading advocate in Western Europe.

This quotation illustrates New Labour's attitude towards EM:

> We need a service better able to take forward new national strategic developments. New technologies offer opportunities for services to be delivered in new ways and more cost-effectively. For example, electronic monitoring can provide a cheap and effective means of imposing tighter supervision on offenders; of imposing discipline on chaotic lives; of reintegrating offenders more effectively into society; and an inescapable means of detecting breaches of court orders. A new service needs to embrace such technologies and to incorporate the opportunities they offer into their strategies for confronting and impacting on offending behaviour, thus making better and more focussed use of probation core competencies and skills.
>
> (Home Office, 1998b: 8 cited in Mair, 2001: 168)

In 1999 New Labour gave a new impetus to the HDCs initially introduced under section 12 of the 1991 Criminal Justice Act. As a sentence the curfew order may last for up to six months, and controls the offender's movements for a period of between two and 12 hours per day. This order was extended to include 10–15 year olds in February 2001, and EM was also an element of a bail scheme piloted in April 2002 to target 12–16 year olds. Individual supervision and surveillance programmes (ISPs) also included the application of EM as part of curfews and attempts to rehabilitate young offenders. Between January 1999 and February 2004, 144,000 offenders experienced EM.

Ongoing technological innovations

Further developments are being planned, and British policy makers are intent on following the US approach. For example, the Correctional Services Review has called for preparations to be made for the arrival of satellite tracking using a piece of technology called global positioning systems (GPS). The Home Office (2004c: 6) remarked that GPS will 'be an increasing feature of correctional services in the future'. This was only introduced in Britain after examining carefully the evidence supporting its application in the United States. Policy makers in Britain judged that there needed to be firm evidence that satellite tracking was effective by looking at its relative successes and failures before actually implementing it.

The usage of EM has been further extended to monitor non-criminal groups such as failed asylum seekers (*Guardian,* 10 March 2006). In March 2006 the Home Office stated that it planned to use EM following a pilot scheme in Scotland and trials in Liverpool and Croydon. This resulted in 150 asylum seekers being tagged, with an additional 260 being required to report their whereabouts to immigration services by telephone (*Guardian*, 14 March 2006). The aim is to tag all adult asylum seekers arriving at immigration screening service units, with the exception of victims of torture or human trafficking. The rationale for this is to avoid adding further to a 'backlog' of failed asylum seekers who may have up to an 18-year wait before they are deported (*Guardian*, 14 March 2006). The use of tagging would reduce the costs of detention, as well as providing a more humane method of monitoring people than locking them up.

As well as conventional EM devices, voice recognition technology has been used. This technology can recognize a person's voice even if he or she attempts to sound like someone else and even taking into account the effects of smoking and colds. According to Tony McNulty, an immigration minister at the time:

> We can get to a stage where [voice recognition] software will pick up your voice almost as distinctively as DNA can. It is early days but it could be a part of a portfolio of reporting conditions. For example, we might require somebody to ring in three times a week and then the fourth time they must go to meet somebody.
>
> (*Guardian*, 10 March 2006)

Surveillance technologies have not replaced the human touch, but the advances achieved since the 1970s are impressive. However, is EM effective – or in plainer English, does it actually work?

Does EM work?

Nellis (2003) warns that there has been a 'dearth of effectiveness research'. There are various ways of assessing whether EM has been effective, and this section focuses on four measures: cost, punishment, rehabilitation and reoffending. Before looking at these factors in more detail, we shall examine the first trials using EM. In 1989 EM was tested out in three sites, Nottingham, Newcastle and South London. The participants were on bail. The trial was based on monitoring 150 offenders over a six-month period in these three cities. The results were not positive, and confirmed the findings of the Richard Hart case. (Hart was the first offender to be tagged in the United Kingdom, but the tag failed to work properly on 15 occasions (ibid.).) Whitfield (1997: 19) also outlines a case in Nottingham where a defendant who was only ten minutes into his curfew took off his tag and absconded. Perhaps not surprisingly the media picked up on this and publicized widely the perceived deficiencies of EM. Since then there is other evidence to show it has been successful, even if the success is not unqualified.

The next section draws on a number of areas identified in Nellis's work, including:

■ cost
■ punishment

- rehabilitation
- reoffending
- effectiveness.

Cost

This can be measured in various ways, but whenever the cost of any policy is considered the basic costs will always include physical and human resources. The cost of manufacturing, distributing and maintaining EM technology is the physical cost, and the implementation and administration of EM is the human cost. Policy evaluators will also consider other types of cost, such as savings made elsewhere.

As was mentioned above EM was introduced, in part, as a policy of *decarceration*, or as an alternative to prison. Because the economic cost of keeping a person in prison is high, it makes sense to seek out cheaper alternatives, and EM did just this. Stacey (1989) has argued convincingly that an offender is able to move outside prison, albeit in a controlled manner, in a way that is cost-effective. Dodgson et al. (2001) show this with the following figures. At the turn of the twenty-first century the annual cost of tagging an offender was £2,000, while it cost a minimum of £24,000 a year to keep someone in prison. The saving per annum from using EM was estimated to be in the region of £36 million, freeing up that money to be spent elsewhere.

However, Whitfield (2001) has questioned the view that EM has reduced the prison population, and argues that its main use has been in the HDC.

Punishment

Nellis (2004a) indicates that EM is, at least in principle, a less punishing form of punishment than imprisonment. However it may be regarded as a more severe method of community punishment than other types of non-custodial penalty, in the sense that most types of community penalty require the compliance of the offender. EM involves the imposition of much stricter sanctions against the offender, who is required to be in a specific place at a specific time. An offender's compliance with a sanction can be checked with ease using a computer. Since administrators can easily identify breaches of the conditions, they can respond quickly to them.

I have mentioned early probation officer resistance to the introduction of EM, but over time this antipathy softened, and eventually many employees in the profession considered it to be an effective penalty for several reasons. This is important as the supervisory role of probation officers is essential for ensuring the completion of tagging programmes (Whitfield, 1997). Many offenders also lack stable home lives and support networks to help them through the sentence. For that reason, regular contact between the probation officer and the monitored person is essential, for developing rapport and to make sure the offender remains focused on conditions such as drug treatment or anger management (Nellis, 2004a).

EM avoids the stigma attached to a prison sentence, and was preferred by offenders partly because it gave them more of an opportunity to reflect on their behaviour than is likely in a potentially overcrowded prison environment. It also meant offenders did not lose contact with their families, and made it feasible for them to keep their jobs (Walter, Sugg and Moore, 2001; Nellis, 2002).

Rehabilitation

The pioneer of EM in Britain, Tom Stacey, argued that EM was a sound method of rehabilitation because it encouraged a sense of personal responsibility, which is often taken away from offenders in prison. Contrary to the arguments of some sceptics EM is not a soft option, because the restrictions offenders experience limit their freedom of movement and association, as well as giving them space for critical reflection on their past and present behaviour. It also gives them scope to anticipate how they will conduct themselves in the future (Nellis, 1991). Walter et al. sum up some of the rehabilitative goals of EM: 'It can give people breathing space, if they are forced to stay in and behave slightly different for a period of time, then it forces them to take a look at different ways of operating' (2001: 3).

If offenders are locked up in prison cells, their reflections are likely to be less critical as they take place in the company of other offenders, with the outcome that they become more criminally minded, thus giving credence to the view that 'prison serves as a reservoir for future crime' (Hurd cited in NACRO, 2001). EM has also been used to ensure offenders attend treatment programmes (Sugg, Moore and Howard, 2001). Given the numbers of people monitored electronically this capacity to rehabilitate is a novel opportunity.

Because offenders are at home rather than in an impersonal prison environment, rehabilitation and behaviour change are arguably more achievable, as EM can reinforce family values. Indeed, Whitfield (1997) has gone so far as to say that tight-knit family units are more or less a prerequisite for the success of EM, especially if contact with supervisors is intermittent. It is also possible for offenders to stay in employment for the duration of their punishment (Black and Smith, 2003), and this saves them the difficulty of finding a new job when they have a criminal record.

Reoffending

There are various ways of measuring reoffending, and the timescale used to measure it is significant. Research has shown that trials carried out between 1995 and 1997 showed an 80 per cent completion rate. The introduction of the HDC showed a 95 per cent completion rate (Dodgson and Mortimer, 2000). Two per cent of subjects reoffended and 1 per cent were returned to prison (Dodgson et al., 2001). Curfews are a powerful tool because they can target particular types of offending at particular times, for example either in the day or at night. Offending that can be tackled in this way includes alcohol and drug-fuelled crime, driving offences, property crimes like burglary and shoplifting, and public order offences. In addition to reducing opportunities to commit crime, it is possible to target certain categories of criminal, such as young people, by separating them from the potentially negative influence of their peers.

Despite the limited evidence of some success, Gendreau et al. (2000) identified an increased recidivism rate of 5 per cent.

The use of EM for released prisoners has proven to be beneficial as it provides enhanced supervision, making resettlement much easier in what is often an uncertain and chaotic time. For instance, there is scope for diverting offenders from particular situations where they are more likely to drift or be pushed back into offending.

There are various arguments to show that EM has had a positive impact and that in some instances it can claim to be effective, but this does not mean EM is without problems. Arguably the main problem is the tendency for some tagged criminals to reoffend. The media is not averse to highlighting such cases, as they are deemed newsworthy. Nellis (2004a) illustrates this with the example of Elias Cachetti, who stabbed a teacher after taking off his tag. It turned out that he had previous convictions for threatening behaviour, mugging, drug dealing and vandalism, and the judge who sentenced Cachetti described him as being particularly violent. The lesson to be learnt is that just because someone is tagged it does not mean that he or she is unable to commit crime.

There are other problems, too, such as the limits of risk assessment, labelling and stigmatization, and the impact of EM not only on the offender but also on his or her family. The decision to tag an offender is based on the calculation of the risks that a person poses to him or herself and the wider community, in terms of the seriousness of the offence and the likelihood of the person reoffending (Kemshall, 2003). A risk assessment is, in the last analysis, a prediction of how someone is going to behave, and without a crystal ball it is not realistic to expect this to be completely accurate. Although the probation officers responsible for such assessments more often than not get it right, mistakes are made, as in the Cachetti case (Nellis, 2004a). This all depends on the knowledge probation officers have of the offenders in front of them, as well as the risk assessment tools they are equipped with.

Howard Becker's (1963) key concept of *labelling* (see Chapter 11 for more details) is helpful for understanding another difficulty with EM. Use of the tag, like any other penalty, gives offenders a label that stigmatizes them. The visibility of the tag marks the person as an offender, which sustains a sense of social exclusion. The family of the offender may also experience stigma and a sense of shame if the tag their son or daughter is wearing is visible to visitors to their home (Nellis, 2002). Family members are also likely to have other negative experiences. In particular, it creates a prison within the home, where the parents and/or partner of the offender are under at least some informal pressure to act as supervisors. This is something that they are not trained to do, nor may they be willing to act in this capacity.

When EM is used against sex offenders, such as paedophiles, to keep them away from places such as schools where they may watch children, this does not overcome the fact that they may offend in the home instead. Similarly offenders could be tagged as a result of a violent crime they have committed against someone in a public place. The tag can be used to take them away from similar situations, but their violent tendencies might be displaced to the home where the victim may be a family member (Nellis, 2004a). Extreme care needs to be taken when attempting to assess the success or failure of EM.

Another issue falling under the effectiveness subheading relates to who is responsible for the delivery of EM. In many areas of the criminal justice sector some services are provided by the private sector, and EM is no exception. To date EM has been the responsibility of the probation service, but because this agency initially assumed a critical standpoint to the technology, and also because of arguments relating to cost and efficiency, private-sector providers such as Securicor, Serco Geografix and Group 4 have been used. These private companies have all been involved in monitoring and working alongside the probation and prison services. In reality the private and public-sector agencies have not always liased properly and worked together in partnership. There is very little sign of an infrastructure or communications system to integrate the probation service with profit-making organizations. There are other tensions, especially the different interests of private commercial companies, whose bottom line is making profit. It is not in the interests of these outfits to publicize breaches and non-compliance. The assumption that the public sector is less efficient than the private sector is also not always supported by evidence, and Serco Geografix supposedly monitored one individual who offended on a multiple basis while tagged.

Anticipating the effectiveness of future developments in EM

The arrival of GPS and voice recognition technologies undoubtedly opens up a range of new and exciting surveillance opportunities. In an article in *The Times* (20 July 2004 cited in Nelly, 2005: 131), Davies discussed the merits of the government's aim to place 5000 prolific offenders under surveillance, drawing attention to the use of tags and satellite tracking as a method of creating a prison environment, albeit without the bars. Under such conditions attempts would be made to rehabilitate offenders and, at the same time, to reduce the number of criminals who reoffend. However, Davies issued a caution, stating that there was limited evidence to support the claim that technology can be used to prevent crime. In actual fact, electronic monitoring could 'encourage' rather than 'deter' criminals. This appraisal recognizes the benefits but is also ambivalent inasmuch as it highlights possible drawbacks and unintended consequences.

It would appear that tracking and tracing offenders and where they go will be made far more straightforward. It should be a more reliable method of ensuring offenders attend and complete any treatment programmes that are a condition of their sentence.

Other developments are occurring, some of which would not look out of place in science fiction. Bright (2002) has highlighted the use of micro-chips to put paedophiles under surveillance. These chips are used to monitor the heart rate of a sex offender: if there is evidence of raised blood pressure staff monitoring the chip will be alerted to the possibility that the offender might about carry out an attack. Civil liberties campaigners who regard this as an infringement of individual human rights have addressed the consequences of using this technology, but there is clearly the potential here for enhanced monitoring and control of a dangerous group of offenders.

ELECTRONIC MONITORING: KEY POINTS

■ EM now has a high profile in the criminal justice system.
■ It belongs to a repertoire of approaches to crime reduction, and has given sentencers a wider range of sentencing options.

■ Since its introduction in the United States and the United Kingdom there have been failures, glitches and teething problems, but many of these have been ironed out.

■ The technology behind EM has also developed at a rapid pace, and it seems to be set to continue to do so. What is science fiction today soon becomes a fact tomorrow.

■ Perhaps the most compelling argument for EM is its cost-effectiveness in comparison with imprisonment. EM can reduce the prison population and provide a different form of punishment, which protects the public, creates safer communities but also does not necessarily produce the damaged people who leave prison.

■ Finally, EM offers new opportunities for combining punishment and rehabilitation.

CONCLUSION

In comparison with the other criminal justice agencies we have discussed, the roles and responsibilities of the probation service have been transformed the most. These changes have been described in some detail in this chapter. Since the nineteenth century those bodies carrying out probation functions and the probation service itself have had to strike a balance between caring for and controlling offenders. The main change is the transformation of probation from a social work profession to a criminal justice profession.

On some occasions in the history of the service the priority has been rehabilitation, whereas at other times punishment is more dominant. At the moment the National Probation Service is mainly involved in law enforcement and ensuring that its activities are effective. It needs to show that what it does works in terms of rehabilitation and resettlement. The accountability of the NPS to the Home Office does not seem set to change, as the centre increasingly determines the orientation of the service. Finally, the NPS works more and more in partnership with other criminal justice agencies, especially since the 1998 Crime and Disorder Act, which is discussed in detail in the next chapter.

FURTHER READING

The probation service is in the midst of restructuring as part of the creation of the NOMS, so the policy framework and functions of the service are likely to change, and students should be aware of this. However it is still important to be aware of the history and past developments in the service.

As a starting point a key reading is Chapter 14 in M. Davies, H. Croall and J. Tyrer, *Criminal Justice: An introduction to the criminal justice system in England and Wales* (3rd edn) (Harlow: Longman Pearson, 2005). Key issues are covered in the introduction to G. Mair (ed.), *What Matters in Probation?* (Cullompton: Willan, 2004) and in A. Worrall, *Punishment in the Community: The future of the criminal justice system* (Cullompton: Willan, 2004). Older texts that provide excellent coverage of relatively recent events in probation include I. Brownlee, *Community Punishment: A critical introduction* (Harlow: Longman, 1998) and D. Whitfield, *Introduction to the probation service* (2nd edn) (Winchester: Waterside Press, 1998).

These websites are invaluable sources of information:

Probation Service: www.cjsonline.gov.uk/working/homeoffice/probation.html

National Offender Management Service (NOMS): www.probation.homeoffice.gov.uk

STUDY QUESTIONS

1. Describe the main changes that have taken place in the probation service since the nineteenth century.
2. What were the main functions of the probation service in the 1990s?
3. What are the main functions of the probation service in the 2000s?
4. Discuss the contribution the probation service has made to address offending behaviour.
5. Describe the rationale behind DTTOs and the effectiveness of this intervention.
6. Discuss the uses of electronic monitoring and its impact on controlling offenders in the community.

10 Multi-Agency and 'Joined-Up' Approaches to Criminal Justice Policy

---

OVERVIEW

The aim of this chapter is to provide:

- ■ an explanation of the relevance of joined-up approaches to tackling crime and disorder
- ■ an account of the emergence of joined-up approaches in government thinking and policy
- ■ a description of the Crime and Disorder Act (1998) and the cross-departmental policy framework designed for joining up government and multi-agency working.
- ■ a discussion of the linkages between crime policy and social policy, focusing on health, education and housing as examples.

INTRODUCTION

For many years academics, politicians and practitioners in the field of criminal justice have argued that individual agencies cannot effectively reduce crime and disorder if they do not work together. Moreover, there is the view that criminal behaviour can only be addressed by looking beyond the criminal justice system to the wider society, including a host of statutory as well as voluntary and private agencies. The causes of and solutions to crime are dependent on recognition of the complex linkages between institutions and processes at macro and micro levels. In England and Wales, for example, there have developed so-called 'joined-up' thinking and policies to reduce crime and disorder, and create safer communities. The chapter outlines the structure of these ideas and practices, and assesses their impact and effectiveness.

More specifically, this chapter shows how crime reduction and community safety strategies are 'joined up', or connected, with policies intended to promote social inclusion. The idea of 'joined-up' government is based on the assumption that the causes of, and solutions to, social exclusion are multi-dimensional and cut across government departments.

A wide range of agencies and organizations are therefore involved in any response to social exclusion. It is a holistic approach to policy making that seeks to overcome departmental compartmentalization within government and its departments. The aim is to create an institutional framework and set of mechanisms which facilitate the development of cross-departmental networks to respond to interrelated problems. For example, in the early 2000s the working of the following departments could be 'joined up':

- Home Office
- Department for Education and Skills (DES)
- Department of Health (DoH)
- Department for Work and Pensions (DWP)
- Department of the Environment, Food and Rural Affairs (DEFRA)
- Department for Transport (DoT)
- Department for Trade and Industry (DTI).

Each of the agencies working within the criminal justice system is now required to work with other agencies belonging to the welfare state to address reduce crime, create safe communities and create a more inclusive society. In order to learn how this is done it is necessary to consider seven broad areas, which are split here into two sections. The first six areas all fall into the first section:

- the legacy of five successive Conservative governments for social policy (1979–97)
- the shift of emphasis in social policy and crime policy, signalled by the first New Labour government (1997–2001) pledge to be 'tough on crime and tough on the causes of crime'
- the main principles underpinning 'joined-up' government at central and local levels
- the aims and objectives of the Social Exclusion Unit (SEU)
- the main provisions of the Crime and Disorder Act (CDA) (1998) and other relevant legislation, including the relationship between the central government's (Home Office) Crime Reduction Programme (CRP) and local crime and disorder reduction partnerships (CDRPs)
- the relationship between the CDA, the CRP, the CDRPs and the SEU.

Finally, in the second part of the chapter there are three case studies examining the relationships between social policy, crime reduction and criminal justice. The three topics are health, education and housing. Each case study consists of a brief history of the policy area, which is then linked to crime and disorder. The policy response of the first New Labour government (1997–2001) is then discussed.

THE LEGACY OF THE CONSERVATIVE GOVERNMENTS

I have written elsewhere (Crowther, 2000a, 2004) that between 1979 and 1997 the issue of poverty did not attract much attention from four successive Conservative governments, despite intensive activity on the part of the anti-poverty lobby. A closer analysis of debates about poverty soon reveals that there are two distinct perspectives. On the one hand, there are behavioural accounts, which explain the poverty and criminality of individuals in terms of their perceived moral and psychological flaws. On the other hand, structural versions suggest that the material and social circumstances that surround individuals may explain, albeit not excuse, their offences.

During the early to mid-1990s the idea of an underclass was in circulation in political and media discourse, to describe a section of the poor who had become detached from mainstream society, in their behaviour rather than their structural location. The central argument was that the provision of welfare and the legacy of the permissive 1960s had created an idle, immoral, state-dependent and ultimately criminogenic underclass. This was also associated with a rise in lone-parent households, crime and disorder. Neoliberal commentators such as Charles Murray (2000) refused to accept that the actions of the underclass were in any way an effect of government policies, but claimed instead that they were caused by individual personal deficiencies. There was no shortage of counter-argument from academics who suggested that some measure of structural change was necessary, particularly the redistribution of income from the rich to the poor, but they lacked a sympathetic audience among politicians, the media and the electorate.

The election of New Labour on 1 May 1997 led to several changes (Lister, 2004). Tony Blair, the prime minister, made an important speech on the Aylesbury Estate, Southwark on 2 June 1997 which changed, at least at a rhetorical level, what the Conservatives had said and done in social policy and criminal justice policy. In his address Blair pledged that the government would confront the problem of an underclass 'cut off' and excluded from mainstream society. He referred to unstable families, welfare dependency, crime, drugs and alienation. Blair added, 'millions have simply dropped out of society, forming alternative systems of living and language ... that is the threat if we do not stop the break-up of society' (Blair, 1997, cited in Cook, 2006). As was noted in the introduction, the Social Exclusion Unit (SEU) was set up by the end of that year. This unit focused on social problems from a joined-up perspective, and set up 18 policy action teams. The SEU published reports concerning homelessness, neighbourhood renewal, school exclusion and truancy, teenage motherhood, and 16–18 year olds who were not in training or employment.

The concept of social exclusion has a long history in European social policy, but it did not enter into political discourse until the mid-1990s. According to Levitas (1998), there are three discourses on social exclusion:

- a redistributionist discourse (RED) developed in British critical social policy, whose prime concern is poverty
- a moral underclass discourse (MUD) which centres on the moral and behavioural delinquency of the excluded themselves
- a social integrationist discourse (SID) whose central focus is on paid work: in brief, it refers to myriad social problems and their multiple causes.

In modern Britain, discourses on social exclusion tend to overlap with discourses on poverty, particularly Townsend's (1979) notion of 'relative poverty', but rather than a focus solely on the distributional (RED) aspects of poverty and deprivation, its relational aspects attract more attention.

In contrast to its Conservative predecessor in government, New Labour stated quite unequivocally that 'It would also be a mistake to tackle crime as if it is only a matter arising from the criminality of individuals or families.' In other words, the causes of social problems are multifaceted and are found not solely at a behavioural (MUD) level, but also at a structural level. However, some aspects of the behavioural version are still in place. The government stated that it did not share the old (as opposed to the New) Labour commitment to equality and the redistribution of income, underpinned by social rights for individual citizens. The new mission statement was equality of opportunity, married with personal responsibility for one's behaviour and social obligations. For example, in terms of internal affairs:

> the principal aim of the Home Office is to build a safe, just and tolerant society in which the rights and responsibilities of individuals, families and communities are properly balanced and the protection and security of the public are maintained.
>
> (cited in Crowther, 2000b)

This indicates that New Labour is departing from the party's traditional emphasis on the rights of citizens as a prerequisite for the creation of the good society. Instead of rights, individuals are to be given opportunities, mainly work, and it is their duty and responsibility to take these up. Thus government policies concentrate their attention on social exclusion, rather than poverty as such, and social inclusion will only be achieved by changing the way citizens behave, the redistribution of opportunities in schools and the labour market (SID), instead of giving people extra income.

The original remit of the SEU was to encourage cooperation between government departments, local authorities, voluntary agencies, private financiers from the business sector and the wider community, to develop anti-poverty policies. Its efforts will be concentrated on:

> groups who are in poverty, lacking the means to participate in the economic, social, cultural and political life in Britain: ... 5 million people in workless homes; the three million on the nation's 1 300 worst council estates; the 150 000 homeless families and the 100 000 children not attending school.
>
> (cited in Crowther, 2000b)

These issues are also placed in the context of the government's anti-crime and disorder strategies.

THE LEGACY OF THE CONSERVATIVE GOVERNMENTS: KEY POINTS

- During the period in which the Conservatives were in government there was evidence of a growing underclass and social exclusion.
- New Labour was elected to government in 1997 and made a commitment to address the multiple problems linked with social exclusion.
- This framework is described in the following section.

THE CRIME AND DISORDER ACT (1998): THE *JOINING-UP* OF CRIME POLICY AND SOCIAL POLICY

It is the aim of this chapter not to summarize all aspects of the Crime and Disorder Act (1998) (CDA), but to focus on its main provisions regarding crime reduction. The relevant sections are 5–7, 17 and 116.

The CDA includes a statutory framework for police, local authorities and other interested agencies to establish anti-crime and disorder partnerships which will set out the main priorities, objectives and targets of community safety plans. This framework is derived from a basic problem-solving structure that is designed to create effective crime prevention and community safety strategies. National guidelines laid down by the government are modified at a local level to meet the needs of specific localities.

In the first instance, local police commanders (known as 'directors of intelligence') and the chief executives of local authorities (councils and districts) conduct crime and disorder audits within given geographical territories. The rationale of these audits is to produce information about the scale of, the impact on, and cost of each crime and disorder-related problem for communities. This information will enable the participating agencies and groups to discover which problems they share in common, and the ways resources may best be deployed to resolve them. The participants are police and local authority departments, such as housing, education, youth services, planning, environmental health and highways. The other parties include community safety partnerships, health authorities, probation committees, victim support, and local community groups, racial equality groups, cultural associations, chambers of commerce/business groups and regional transport networks. There are no typical partnerships, and there is considerable variation from area to area. Each partnership has different core and peripheral members, and the participating agencies perform different functions in order of their importance.

The Home Office identified three key groups in an example of a possible local crime and disorder reduction partnership: the partnership group, publicly accountable bodies and working groups.

Partnership group

Assistant chief constable (police)
Chief probation officer
Chief executive local authority
Director of social services
Director of education
Voluntary sector
Transport
Magistrates

Publicly accountable bodies

Police authorities
Health authorities

Elected members of local authorities
Probation committee

Working groups

Street robberies working group
Car crime working group
Domestic burglary working group
Anti-social behaviour working group
Racial harassment working group

Each partnership was required to formulate crime reduction strategies with clear aims and objectives. In a sense the CDA has formalized many of the pre-existing informal networks, philosophies and mechanisms associated with partnership and inter-agency work and community safety partnerships. The aim was to get the police, local authorities and local people to join forces to work together to rebuild communities by addressing complex social problems in communities. Crucially, the legislation provided a framework for tackling social problems, but ultimately change would be brought about by the commitment of the individuals and communities involved.

The CDA contained no detailed prescriptions for the agenda for these partnerships or the structures needed to deliver them, but instead advocated 'maximum flexibility'. The rationale for this approach is that the people who live and work in specific areas are in the best position to identify problems and to propose how they should be addressed. The stress is on building on existing structures of coordinated activity, such as multi-agency partnerships, at county, district and borough levels to tackle single, specific and local problems. These should be brought together to avoid duplication and unnecessary competition for scarce resources.

Crime and disorder are not actually defined in the CDA, but burglary, racially moti-vated crime, witness intimidation, fear of crime, domestic violence and repeat victimiza-tion are all designated as requiring special attention. However, there are potential rubbing points because various other players had outlined other priorities prior to this legislation. Her Majesty's Inspectorate of Constabulary (1997), for example, listed the 'key policing objectives' and 'key performance indicators' for the police as responding to violent crime, burglary, working with the community and emergency response. These were again acknowledged in the next report, but it was added that there were no specific priorities, and although these objectives were still important, police performance, espe-cially value for money (VFM), would be evaluated in terms of overall crime reduction. However, special attention would be given to multi-agency strategies which tackled youth crime, took action taken against drugs, and created partnerships that cracked down on general crime and disorder problems at a local level.

A diverse array of tactics will be used, which involve working with families, chil-dren and schools to prevent young people from becoming offenders. These duties cut across the different government departments and focus on social exclusion, school performance, drug-related crime, economic regeneration and the promotion of family life. This is in accord with the view that the causes of crime include poverty, poor housing, poor parenting, associating with delinquent peers, poor school performance and persistent truanting. These strategies fit into the context of the government's wider strategy, and form part of the statutory partnerships (both at local and national levels) designed to take comprehensive action against crime and its causes. The investment of resources is intended to be based on evidence of what actually works rather than unfounded assumptions about what is effective, and the performance of each initiative is to be evaluated.

THE CDA: KEY POINTS

- The CDA created a framework for dealing with crime and disorder that involved a range of agencies beyond the criminal justice system.

CRIME AND DISORDER REDUCTION PARTNERSHIPS

Now we need to examine more closely the mechanisms involved in New Labour's joined-up policy framework. The mechanism used to deliver joined-up approaches to crime reduction and social exclusion is crime and disorder reduction partnerships (CDRPs). The ideas underpinning this concept have been around for a long time even though the terminology is relatively new. The Morgan Report (1991) put the idea on the agenda of policy makers. Since then the meaning of the term has been contested, but for our purposes a Home Office definition is useful. Community safety is:

> an aspect of quality of life in which people, individually and collectively, are protected as far as possible from hazards or threats that result from the criminal or anti-social behaviour of others, and are equipped or helped to cope with those that they do experience. It would enable them to pursue and obtain the fullest benefits from, their social and economic lives without fear or hindrance from crime and disorder.
>
> (Home Office, 1998a: 7)

Community safety refers not just to crime and unlawful activities but also to 'chronic' social conditions brought about by antisocial behaviour, such as low-level disorder and incivilities which cause people to fear for their own safety. This feeling may be real or perceived. Community safety has a wider meaning, though, which is of relevance to social policy as defined in Chapter 5. It includes a range of protective functions provided nationally and locally, some of which are concerned with more than crime and disorder: for example, drug abuse and drug dealing, racial harassment and hate crime, tackling social exclusion, consumer protection, household safety, road safety, fire prevention, mental health and public health. Crucially, it is recognized that these problems are interrelated, concentrated in the same geographical areas and require a 'joined-up' set of responses and solutions. However, it should be noted that the main focus is on crime and disorder, which indicates that in some instances social policy may be being displaced by crime policy.

As was noted above, prior to the CDA there was no statutory requirement for national and local governments to introduce community safety strategies. It is now a 100 per cent police responsibility and 100 per cent local authority responsibility. Councils and other partners have now conducted crime and disorder audits, involving community consultation, to gain an understanding of local determinants and local solutions to crime and disorder. This knowledge is being applied to implement local crime reduction strategies and to build safer communities. As this is a relatively new set of measures for dealing with local crime and disorder problems, the future is very uncertain and there are a range of potential problems which may make this task difficult.

The promotion of community safety requires a range of competencies:

- an understanding of the diverse needs of individuals affected by crime and disorder, particularly their ability to deal with its consequences
- making the effects of crime and disorder tolerable without threatening privacy, liberty, quality of life and increasing social exclusion
- supporting victims of crime and reassuring those who fear crime
- making people aware of the objective risks posed by crime and disorder-related problems.

If CDRPs are to work there needs to be:

- proper consultation of the community and a strong partnership with the different sections of that community
- strong partnership arrangements
- flexibility and partnership.

The Crime Reduction Programme

In July 1998 the government introduced a new Crime Reduction Programme (CRP). This is an example of an 'evidence-based approach' to policy making in field of crime reduction.

Evidence-based policy is based on understanding a specific problem, its causes and the likely impact of any policy interventions. More than that, this approach to policy making is dependent on evaluations of interventions to find out which policies are effective, or 'what works' and under what circumstances. The findings of these evaluations are then fed back into the policy-making process as examples of good and best practice. It is important that the evaluations are appropriate assessments of specific interventions.

According to Paul Wiles (1999), director of research at the Home Office Research and Statistics Directorate, evidence-based or evidence-led policy altered the relationship between the government, policy making, research, evaluation and the development of programmes. This is an unusual innovation because before 1997 it was unusual for the government to refer to evidence obtained from scientific evaluations of existing policy and practice. Instead, it often acted 'on the hoof' by prioritizing short-term political goals, such as maintaining a lead in the opinion polls, instead of sound policy based on research evidence. (Examples are Michael Howard's 'Prison works' campaign launched at the 1993 Conservative Party conference and the 1997 election campaigns of both the Conservatives and New Labour, who tried to out-tough each other on the issue of zero tolerance policing (ZTP).)

The main aim of the evidence-based approach is to strengthen the relationship between policy interventions and evaluations of these strategies and initiatives. In particular, evidence is not just used to introduce a programme but is also gathered and evaluated as part of its development. Thus policy formulation, implementation and the ideas and knowledge derived from research or evaluations are inseparable. Evidence is used to decide where resources will be invested in order to have an effective long-term impact on crime. Thus the CRP is intended to use available resources prudently, initially to slow down but eventually to curb the long-term growth rate in crime.

The CRP was concerned with five broad themes, with varying degrees of relevance to social policy.

- working with families, children and schools to prevent young people from becoming offenders in the future
- tackling crime in communities, particularly high-volume crime such as domestic burglary
- developing products and systems that are more resistant to crime
- more effective sentencing practices
- working with offenders to ensure that they do not reoffend (Home Office, 2000: 59).

These initiatives are required to tackle crime and its causes, including its structural or social, and individual or behavioural, causes. However, each programme has to be 'cost-effective', provide 'value for money' and be evaluated according to its effectiveness, efficiency and economy. Initiatives currently include burglary reduction, targeted policing, tackling school exclusions, the installation of CCTV systems in high-crime areas, improving the information available to sentencers and tackling domestic violence (Home Office, 2000: 59).

Crime Reduction Task Force

The CDRPs and the CRP are coordinated by the Crime Reduction Task Force, which includes representatives from police forces and local and central government. The task force supports, advises and guides the local CDPs/CDRPs and regional crime reduction directors by giving them a national focus. For example, guidance may be given in relation to target setting, the best ways of involving different agencies and the development of good practice. Also at a regional level there are regional development agencies (RDAs) that coordinate multi-agency initiatives, joining up central government, local authorities and local people to regenerate communities.

The question is, what effects do RDAs have on the local delivery of area regeneration packages? In principle, health trusts, the Employment Service, the Benefits Agency, the police, businesses and local people could all become involved in regeneration projects. The aim is to design strategies that link the objectives of different departments.

JOINED-UP APPROACHES TO CRIME REDUCTION: KEY POINTS

■ The idea that crime cannot be tackled effectively by the criminal justice system alone can be traced back to the Morgan Report (1991).

■ New Labour placed joined-up and cross-departmental approaches to tackling crime at the centre of its policy framework.

■ The Crime and Disorder Act (1998) has had a tremendous influence on crime and public policy.

SOCIAL POLICY, CRIME REDUCTION AND COMMUNITY SAFETY

This section examines the relationship between criminal justice and the following areas of welfare and public policy:

■ health
■ education
■ housing.

Health policy and crime

The aim of this section is to:

■ provide a historically informed overview of key debates in health policy
■ explore the relationship between health policy and crime policy
■ consider the extent to which joined-up thinking and practice has occurred in the field of health care.

Key issues and debates in health policy

Back in the 1980s the Black Report (1980: see Townsend and Davidson, 1992) identified structurally generated inequalities in the distribution of ill-health and life expectancy throughout the population. In short there was a lack of equality in access to available care and quality of care. There was also a lack of equal treatment for equal cases: in other words, people suffering from the same malady received different treatment. The report discussed the multiple causes of these problems, and in contrast to many other reports written at that time focused on the social rather than medical or clinical causes of ill-health. However, on the whole the Conservative government at that time denied that there was any link between general ill-health and inequalities in other areas of social policy (such as poor housing, educational under-performance, un- and under-employment and the inadequacy of social security benefits). The findings of the report were rejected, and instead of talking about inequalities in health the Conservatives used the more anodyne term 'health variations' and argued that the 'health of the nation' was largely dependent on individual lifestyles (Ham, 2004).

In the run-up to the 1997 general election and beyond, the New Labour approach to the NHS was low-key and continued along similar lines to the Conservatives, in terms of both its structure and financing (Jones, 1998). Although New Labour had made a promise to abolish the internal market, the structure of the NHS consisting of purchasers and providers was largely unchanged. Instead a number of pilot projects were introduced to find a new system for commissioning health care to substitute for GP fundholding.

The emphasis was on realizing managerialist objectives – including economy, effectiveness and efficiency – through a reformed bureaucratic structure. The New Labour government was also committed to sticking to the spending plans of its Conservative predecessor, and ruled out increased expenditure for the foreseeable future, in light of NHS debts which amounted to £200 million. Moreover, in supporting the private finance initiative (PFI) the government indicated its acceptance of market disciplines and the injection of private capital into the public sector (Moran and Simpkin, 2000). Additional savings were to be made by clamping down on fraud within the NHS, specifically by doctors, dentists, pharmacists and insurance companies. The funding of longterm care for the elderly, or 'greying', population was also an important issue, as was the enhancement of medical technology which led to a rise in demand (Ham, 2004).

The most significant development, though (which has a direct impact on criminal justice) is that all government departments were required to place health on their agendas, and for it to be a part of their policies. Cross-departmental links were established between the NHS and departments including the Department of the Environment, Transport and the Regions (DETR), the Department of Education and Employment (DEE) and the Department of Social Security (DSS), to respond to interwoven issues such as poverty, poor housing, educational underachievement, pollution and discrimination against minority groups.

Thus many of the issues addressed in the Black Report (Townsend and Davidson, 1992) resurfaced, and it became acceptable to acknowledge the relationship between health and social exclusion. Health inequalities are to be addressed through interventions in social, economic and environmental areas by different welfare, statutory, voluntary and private agencies. However, the policy framework and fiscal constraints within which New Labour are working are broadly similar to what they inherited from their Conservative predecessors.

An independent inquiry into health inequalities, written by Sir Donald Acheson (1998), also showed that a wide range of influences have an effect on people's health, including lifestyle and community factors as well as living and working conditions. For example, there is a correlation between relatively high levels of mental health problems (ranging from depression to suicide) and job insecurity or low pay.

A New Labour government white paper, *The New NHS: Modern, dependable* (1997) set the tone for the New Labour response, by recommending a multi-disciplinary response to social exclusion and by requesting reports on varying patterns of exclusion in urban and rural settings. A 1998 green paper, *Our Healthier Nation*, highlighted the linkages between bad health and access to social and health services, and various aspects of social exclusion, including community safety. The paper contains recommendations for the creation of 'healthy settings' in the workplace and in schools to promote health. There were also proposals for a contractual relationship between the government, local agencies and communities, setting out how to improve health.

An important initiative was the introduction of health action zones in 26 localities to tackle health inequalities, deprivation, poverty and social exclusion. The membership of these partnerships includes NHS agencies, local authorities, community and voluntary groups, and local businesses. The aim is to make health care more responsive to local needs by improving the range of services available in local health centres and by providing more complex treatment in regional hospitals (DoH, 2003).

In tackling health inequalities New Labour has recognized the need for careful targeting of the services the government provides, and that there is not a simple gradient from the top to the bottom. The simple redistribution of resources from those at the top to those at the bottom is not seen as the best way forward. This view rests on the assumption that it is not absolute but relative income levels that have more influence on health inequalities. In other words, the issue is how wide or narrow the gaps in income distribution are in relative terms. It is how people perceive their relative poverty that influences their health, especially the ways in which such perceptions lead to stress, frequently resulting in ill-health (Ham, 2004).

In July 2000 the government published *The NHS Plan: A plan for investment, a plan for reform* (DoH, 2000). This report contains some far-reaching recommendations. In particular, there is a plan for sustained increases in funding to create a service that is designed around the patient. The founding goals of the NHS are still valued but it was argued that the practices needed to be changed: investment needed to accompanied by reform. As part of this modernizing project power will be devolved from central government to local health services. Among the significant points contained in the plan is the recommendation for a 'national inequalities target' which will target the main causes of ill-health in deprived communities: 'poverty, lack of educational attainment, unemployment, discrimination and social exclusion'. Again, a cross-departmental approach is the mechanism for formulation and implementation of policy intended to:

- increase and improve primary care in deprived areas
- introduce screening programmes for women and children
- step up services to stop people smoking
- improve the diet of young children by making fruit freely available in schools for 4–6 year olds.

The NHS plan proposes that health authorities will need to formulate strategies involving other services. For example, the work of health action zones could be integrated with other local action zones to consolidate links between health, education, employment and other factors contributing to social exclusion (Moran and Simpkin, 2000). The NHS will play a part in the Government's *National Strategy for Neighbourhood Renewal* (Cabinet Office, 2001). The abolition of child poverty and the expansion of Sure Start are also important (Weinberger, Pickstone and Harrison, 2005).

Health policy and criminal justice

The links between these two areas are explored here in relation to, first, drug misuse and drug-related criminality, and second, violent crime.

Practitioners in the sphere of criminal justice have known the relationship between health and crime for some time, especially in connection with mentally disordered offenders. The Reed Report (Reed Committee, 2002), for example, called for this group to be diverted away from the criminal justice system towards the appropriate health services. Increasingly improved access to health services for certain groups will in the long term contribute to community safety by reducing the risks individuals pose to themselves and others (Home Office, 2005e).

Health is now considered more central than it has been before, demonstrated by the involvement of health authorities and primary care trusts (PCTs) in CDRPs. There are several examples.

- Drug abuse and drug-related crime require multi-agency strategies, involving a broad range of interventions by professionals in health, criminal justice and education.
- Community health surveys have identified fear of crime as an important factor which has a bearing on health.
- Violent crime has a deleterious effect on individuals and their health, especially domestic violence and sexually motivated offences.
- Mental health is also relevant, as the failure of the policy of care in the community has implications for community safety and security (as shown in a white paper, *Modernizing Mental Health Services: Safe, sound and supportive* (HM Government, 1998b)).

In the Home Office (1998a) guidance given to crime and disorder partnerships, the importance of the NHS to crime reduction and community safety was acknowledged. The universality of NHS provision means that, in principle, its services are available to all citizens and should meet individual health needs.

In coming into contact with individuals from all social backgrounds, health service professionals may detect certain types of crime such as domestic violence, and especially repeat victimization. It has been documented that victims of domestic violence are likely to contact NHS staff before other agencies, such as the police (Humphreys and Stantley, 2006). GPs, nurses in accident and emergency (A&E) departments and health visitors may be the first to hear about cases of domestic violence. These practitioners are now receiving training on how to detect a problem, counselling and encouraging victims, whenever the victim feels it is possible, to report an offence to the police.

Alcohol and drug misuse are not only the key factors leading to criminal activity, but also have implications for the health of offenders. Behaviour modification strategies may be used to treat individuals whose actions are influenced in some way by substance abuse (Bennett and Holloway, 2005; Dingwall, 2005).

Some mentally ill people are predisposed to commit mainly trivial offences (Hodgins, 1993). Improved cooperation between the police and hospitals may have improved the system of care, control and treatment provided by these and potentially other agencies (Stone, 2002).

A priority in the New Labour campaign to be 'tough on crime and its causes' is to nip offending behaviour in the bud. Most of this work takes place in the spheres of education, employment and training. However, there is evidence that behaviour disorders found in young children as young as 2 or 3 years old may lead to serious problems later in life, including antisocial and criminal behaviour. Psychologists, health visitors and family therapists can set up parent support groups to support and counsel parents, advising them on the best methods of coping with their children's behavioural disorders. Such support groups have also been useful to help adult prisoners to adapt to family life when they have served their sentence.

Violent crime

The NHS is an important player in multi-agency partnerships contributing to the reduction of violence, the investigation, detection and prosecution of more violent offenders, and referring more victims to support services, such as Victim Support.

A&E units often come across victims of violence who have not reported their victimization to the police, which puts workers in this sector in a good position to respond to violent crime. A&E staff may, for example:

- Encourage people to report the crimes of which they are victims to the police.
- Carry out a risk assessment in order to anticipate the likelihood of future harm.
- Exchange information with other agencies. For instance, information about the places where alcohol-related offences occur can be passed on to police licensing officers.
- Work with the police to prevent crime on hospital premises, maybe including national casualty department violence surveillance. Problems such as vandalism of NHS buildings are part of a wider problem which brings the health service into contact with the police and crime prevention agencies. Violence in the workplace is also an issue. The Health and Safety Executive has found that nursing staff are particularly vulnerable to physical and psychological injury.
- Work with voluntary agencies.

However, some offenders may not benefit from these moves, and may remain excluded, as there are some groups, especially drug addicts, who avoid the NHS, and others whose behaviour can seem bizarre may be made to feel unwelcome at a GP's surgery or in an A&E department.

The NHS also works with social service departments, particularly in the area of child protection (Children's Services Plan). Mental health is also important, particularly the community care plan.

Drugs and drug-related crime

This is a concern for all members of society, and the inter-agency response to these problems reflects this (Bean, 2002, 2004). In 2000 there were 200,000 problem drug misusers, with more than half this number coming into contact with treatment services. The Home Office set targets to:

- reduce by 25 per cent in 2005 and 50 per cent by 2008 the proportion of people aged 25 who report that they use class A drugs

■ increase the number of problem drug misusers in treatment by 66 per cent (2005) and 100 per cent (2008).

Drugs misuse has strong links to social exclusion, not only in relation to health, but also through the New Deal, Neighbourhood Renewal and crime reduction, in particular the work of youth offending teams (Home Office, 2005e).

The responses of multi-agency teams, which include police, local authorities and health authorities, as well as representatives from the probation service, the prison service and HM Revenue and Customs, are coordinated by drug action teams (DATs), which in turn are guided by the advice on drugs-related issues given by the Drugs Reference Group (DRG). DATs are non-statutory organizations which play a pivotal role in implementing and monitoring the government's national ten-year drugs strategy (Home Office, 1998b) at a local level.

The national strategy makes a connection between drug misuse and:

■ offending amongst socially excluded groups, such as the unemployed, the under-trained and under-qualified and those who play truant
■ property crime, especially burglary, theft of and from motor vehicles, and shoplifting, mainly for offenders to subsidize their drugs habit
■ young people aged 16–25.

The strategy seeks to provide services to help people live more healthy lives by:

■ reducing antisocial behaviour caused by the use of drugs
■ disrupting the market for illegal drugs
■ educating young people about the harm caused by drugs misuse, preferably in order to prevent them from using drugs in the first instance
■ setting up the National Treatment Agency (accountable to the DoH) for improving the services available to treat drug users from health and other agencies
■ addressing alcohol misuse.

HEALTH POLICY AND CRIME: KEY POINTS

■ Health policy is central to the welfare state and is central to the lives of everyone in society.
■ Increasingly crime is seen to be related to health policy.
■ Tackling drugs misuse is a key area where health and criminal justice agencies can work together to care for drug users and control drug-related social problems.
■ Violent crime is widespread in society, and its effects sometimes impact on the health service, because patients are the victims of violence and/or violent patients assault hospital staff.

EDUCATION POLICY AND CRIME

This section of the chapter:

■ outlines government policy on education from a historical perspective
■ identifies links between educational policies and criminality, focusing on truancy and school exclusions.

There are many continuities between the Conservatives and New Labour in education policy, such as the continuation of educational reform based on deregulated marketized and privatized initiatives at all levels. New Labour's initial commitment to Conservative Party spending limits also illustrates this. The structures of the education system and forms of governance are also unchanged (David, 1998). Despite this, the New Labour slogans 'Education, education and education' and opportunities 'for the many, not the few' signalled something different (Clyde, 2004).

In its 1997 election manifesto New Labour pledged to:

■ abolish the nursery education voucher scheme, and return the responsibility for funding nursery education to local education authorities (LEAs)
■ reduce class sizes in primary schools
■ improve standards of literacy and numeracy
■ introduce home–school contracts for effective learning
■ provide homework centres for schoolchildren
■ deal with troublesome students, with new management training schemes for head teachers (Labour Party, 1997).

After the election a New Labour white paper, *Excellence in Schools* (HM Government 1997), set out its policies for early childhood and compulsory schooling. A theme running throughout the white paper is the importance of a partnership approach, embracing not only schools and teachers, but also parents, families and communities. The six policy principles were:

■ Education will be at the heart of government.
■ Policies will benefit the many, not just the few.
■ The focus will be on standards in schools, not the structure of the system.
■ Intervention in underperforming schools and celebration of the successful.
■ Zero tolerance of underperformance.
■ Government working in partnership with all those committed to raising standards (David, 1998).

Standards in primary and secondary schools were to be raised by the introduction of LEA education development plans and Ofsted inspections. The principles of the modern comprehensive system were to be extended to all secondary schools, via 'education action zones' and the National Grid for Learning. Levels of educational achievement were raised by family learning schemes and home–school contracts. National guidelines for homework and work-related learning were drawn up. Finally, there were partnerships between schools, LEAs and the Department for Education and Employment (DfEE, formerly the Department of Education, and subsequently renamed the Department for Education and Skills, DfES), among others, to raise standards.

Above all, education and training policies are intimately related to employment policies, and therefore are crucial for tackling various forms of social exclusion (Walton, 2000). There is also some evidence that there is a connection, perhaps not causal, between education, poverty and crime. The main aim is to raise levels of educational participation and achievement by removing the barriers to both of these factors, principally by addressing wider problems of structural inequality, and individual and institutionalized discrimination. The rationale underlying this is to respond to the rapidly and continually changing need for new skills by employers. Education and training are the key mechanisms for providing well-educated and well-trained individuals equipped with the necessary skills for labour market participation and ultimately social inclusion (Clyde, 2004).

In the context of New Labour policy emphasizing the importance of 'lifelong learning', the provision of education covers a range of age groups and types of student, and has unique policy implications (Field, 2005). The main concern here is with those aspects that have a direct impact on criminal justice, for example, truancy and school exclusions. The focus therefore is on the young. However, our knowledge about what happens later in life is also an important justification for concentrating on young people under the age of 16. Research shows that those who did better at school learn more at work. In particular, key or 'basic' skills such numeracy and literacy are essential for most jobs. If an individual is lacking these skills, he or she will find opportunities for work to be few and far between (Clyde, 2004).

Individuals who either stay away from school or are excluded from school because of their unruly behaviour are more likely to under-achieve, and this leads to disaffection and cumulative disadvantages when they enter the world of work. These people are also more likely to commit petty crimes, and in some instances they embark on criminal careers. There is often a vicious circle which leads to school exclusions, beginning with the perception that, for many reasons, certain individuals have low expectations of their schooling, and their teachers in turn have low expectations of them. Those students who are perceived in this way sometimes internalize these beliefs, and this results in growing disaffection and culminates in impoverished aspirations (Walton, 2000).

It should be clear from this outline that there are a number of relevant factors, including individual responses, the attitudes of teachers, and the effects these have on levels of participation and achievement. In the background there are also family circumstances and parental attitudes to education. In some instances, especially in the case of African-Caribbean males (a group with a disproportionately high number of exclusions), 'institutional racism' may lead to discrimination and differential treatment. Also potentially significant may be policies implemented under previous governments, such as the Education Reform Act (1998) which widened parental choice, and the influence of market-led initiatives like school league tables. Schools that score highly are more likely to attract pupils from a middle-class background, and the schools in the lower regions of the tables tend to be left to working-class children whose parents are less interventionist and demanding. Bearing in mind the complex and multi-dimensional causes of the problem, any solutions must also operate on a number of levels, including the individual, institutional and wider policy contexts.

Truancy and school exclusion

Truancy is a major problem, and a social exclusion report (Social Exclusion Unit, 1998) said that 1 million students truant each year. In 1995/6 it counted 12,500 school exclusions. Nationally most exclusions are of children from secondary schools (aged 10–14), with a sizeable minority from the youngest age group (10–11 year olds). Young people who are excluded later on their school careers (those aged 15 and 16) seldom return to full-time education.

The individuals and groups most predisposed to truancy and exclusion include:

- those of a low socioeconomic status
- certain minority ethnic groups, especially African-Caribbean boys
- children in lone-parent families
- young people in care
- young offenders
- boys in general
- children whose parents are disadvantaged and live in rented property, particularly social housing
- those pupils whose early participation in education is low (which sets a pattern for later life)
- pupils with relatively low levels of attainment and achievement.

Social exclusion therefore arises from a number of factors, but most importantly it is low participation and achievement that results in increased risks of unemployment, especially long-term unemployment. This is exacerbated by structural changes in the labour market, including:

- a decline in the availability of unskilled jobs
- the expansion of low-income jobs
- the lack of on-the-job training for the remaining low-skill jobs.

These problems may have an effect on psychological well-being by undermining individual motivation, independence and confidence. It is well known that literacy is associated with more positive attitudes.

New Labour policy

The Social Exclusion Unit (1998) report on truancy said that the target was to reduce school exclusions by a third by 2002. Improved attendance would raise attainment levels and provide more opportunities in later life. This was to be achieved by introducing home–school agreements and making students – and their parents – more aware of their responsibility for attending school. There was a 'zero-tolerance' crackdown on truancy. Numeracy and literacy problems were addressed alongside a review of the National Curriculum to see how it might disadvantage certain groups (Wright, 2005).

Under the Conservatives the main aim of policy in this area was to ensure that the British economy was competitive in the global marketplace. New Labour did not deviate from this policy, but also accepted that social exclusion was a problem and that this may be caused by the workings of the economy. There are a range of policies, some for adults and some for young people, but a main concern is with those not in education, training or employment: the so-called 'zero-status generation'. The plan is to create more inclusive mechanisms through increasing participation and the provision of equality of opportunity. This should not be confused with equality of *outcomes*, which is something altogether different.

One response was education action zones (EAZs), which are multi-agency organizations formulating local solutions to local problems. The EAZs coordinated and formalized partnerships in many ways, such as education and business partnerships, to strengthen links between prospective employers and potential future employees. EAZs also promoted mentoring and parental involvement in school activities. School buildings are used not just by the school but also for other statutory and voluntary agency activities. Schools also make use of libraries and leisure centres to carry out extracurricular activities (Walton, 2000).

New Start was introduced for the disaffected and drop-outs. This is a multi-agency approach involving the careers service, schools, further education (FE) institutions, training and enterprise councils (TECs), local authorities, the youth service and voluntary organizations. The aim is to motivate young people, to support them, help them develop skills and provide opportunities for work experience. Different, individually tailored packages aim to achieve this (Ofsted, 1998).

Status zero

Rather like truants and the individuals excluded from schools, this group refers to those who are not in education, employment or training. They possess low qualifications, and tend to belong to groups of low socioeconomic status, live in social housing, be in care, have learning difficulties and/or be of African-Caribbean origin.

The Social Exclusion Unit: 'bridging the gap'

The aim is to foster a more inclusive society by extending and widening the provision of education and training until the age of 18. There is talk of 'graduation into adulthood'. This needs to be combined with other policies.

Problems

The National Curriculum, educational testing and league tables all emphasize the importance of high skills, and effectively lead to informal social exclusion because some already excluded groups lack the skills to participate in this competitive system. The pressures of this system have also reduced the time teachers have available for pastoral activities and for supervising extracurricular sporting and social activities. This can bring staff–student relationships under strain. There is evidence of this in some deprived multi-ethnic communities, where inter-ethnic conflict is played out in classrooms and playgrounds. The pressures on teachers' time and energies are such that they do not have sufficient resources to deal with this problem in any other way than by excluding pupils.

EDUCATION AND CRIME: KEY POINTS

■ Education policy has been examined because educational achievement is regarded as a solution to social exclusion and related problems such as crime.
■ It has been shown that factors such as truancy and school exclusions may place already vulnerable young people in further danger of being criminalized.
■ Increasingly it is recognized that education and crime policy need to be better integrated to respond to some of the causes of crime.

HOUSING AND CRIME

In this section:

■ there is a short historical account of housing policy
■ there is consideration of the relationship between housing, crime and criminal justice.

Housing has not been high on the agenda of the New Labour government even though this area of social policy is beset with difficulties, including an estimated 0.5 million homes that are unfit for habitation and 0.5 million in need of repair. According to some commentators there is also need for a 100–200,000 new homes in the social housing sector (Malpass, 2005).[1] The expansion of owner occupation has resulted in good-quality local authority housing being sold off, and relatively poor council properties being reserved for the socially excluded. The failure of the 'right to buy' policies in some areas of the country, and various forms of social exclusion in the local authority and private rented sector, have led to an explosion in the number of housing benefit recipients (Balchin and Rhodes, 2002).

When the New Labour government was elected it seemed to be committed to continuing Conservative housing policies by other means. Rather than subsidising the construction of new homes, the government gave subsidies to various groups to cover a proportion of housing costs (such as housing benefit, HB). In 1999 HB accounted for 10 per cent of the welfare budget. The government at that time proposed to replace HB for low-income tenants with a tax credit system, because HB was hard to administer and encouraged fraud. It acts as a disincentive to work and adds to the poverty trap. For example, unemployed people in receipt of HB faced a marginal tax rate of 95 per cent if they took up jobs (Liddiard, 1998).

Even though New Labour passed a bill allowing the release of £5 billion of banked capital receipts for housing investment by modifying Treasury rules, investment on social housing fell by £2.1 billion in 1999/2000. This amounts to less than half the total sum spent by the Conservatives (Hawtin and Kettle, 2000).

Housing is interrelated with social exclusion in other spheres of social policy. For example, poor living conditions (such as overcrowding) have an adverse influence on education, particularly on the ability of children to focus on their studies. If a child's home is damp and cold, this may affect his or her health and school attendance record. Ill-health and educational under-achievement also impact on the ability of individuals to take up opportunities in the labour market. The pressures on parents bringing up children under these difficult circumstances may cause mental health problems. Add to this the tendency of some employers to look at the postcode on job applications in order to identify 'bad' estates and neighbourhoods, and the linkages between housing and myriad forms of social exclusion are clear (Hawtin and Kettle, 2000).

Housing is not just about 'bricks and mortar', but influences the ways in which people are included in the wider community. Safe, secure and affordable housing improves people's chances of a fulfilling personal life, especially for those who belong to a 'nation of homeowners'. Owner occupiers used to be supported by mortgage tax relief (which was abolished in April 2000) but council tenants have been penalized. Margaret Thatcher (the Conservative prime minister, 1979–90) changed the housing finance structure, resulting in the government reducing its subsidies to local authority housing. As a result council tenants not on housing benefit subsidize those who are: in 1999 the Treasury received £700 million from council tenants, and in 2000 £850 million (Malpass, 2005).

Social housing is located in certain geographical areas, especially where there is high unemployment and a lack of jobs. In addition, in 1997 110,000 households were made homeless. The availability of social housing has been narrowed and restricted to those most in need, in particular those on low incomes and in receipt of welfare benefits (two-thirds of households in social housing receive state benefits). Social housing is used more for young households and the elderly than for two-parent families with children.

Currently the housing market is divided into two polarized sectors, the owner-occupied sector and a residualized state sector. We can divide up the state sector further: for instance, identifying 'problem estates' which are 'difficult to let'. Poverty, unemployment, high child densities, high crime and empty properties are all features of these areas. Those who can afford to move away, primarily the employed and economically active, do so (Hawtin and Kettle, 2000).

It has been estimated that there are up to 3 million households on the 1300 'worst' housing estates. Significantly 'worst' is defined in terms of crime, rather than disrepair and the lack of demand for boarded-up properties in some abandoned communities (Murie, 1998). Falling demand is also caused by changes in the labour market, as people move away from areas when old industries and factories close. This pattern is not confined to the inner cities, but is also found in peripheral areas on the edge of cities.

Those living on the worst estates have limited mobility, especially in London and the south-east, where affordable land and property is out of the reach of some people. Likewise movement from the north to the south is made difficult because property prices in the south are prohibitive (Malpass, 2005).

However, it is not just council tenants who experience high levels of deprivation and exclusion. Poverty is also present in owner-occupied households. Some ethnic minority groups and the long-term ill are two examples. These residents may live on or close to the 'worst' estates, but they may not be visible to the authorities. Moreover, some people living in social housing who might be described by the authorities as excluded do not perceive themselves as such (Hawtin and Kettle, 2000)

Ideas of neighbourhood safety might appear to be inclusive, but this is not necessarily so, as the case of care in the community demonstrates.

Estate-based policies

Tenure is an indicator of deprivation, and most programmes focus on the 'worst' estates. Estate-based policies propose to tackle exclusion in areas of where there is a lot of social housing on two fronts: first, through mixed tenure, and second, through regeneration.

Mixed tenure

Many policy makers hold the view that the more poor people there are in an area, the more likely it is that problems will persist. For instance, if there is a lack of employed people in an area, there are few role models and networks to enable individuals to get into work. This may be redressed by trying to ensure that all estates contain both employed and unemployed people. Similarly, there have been calls to ensure that there is a mix of single-parent and two-parent families, and of owner occupiers and tenants.

Regeneration

Under the SEU 'Neighbourhood Renewal' scheme and the New Deal, £3 billion was made available for regeneration. There were 18 action teams (with long-term aims and objectives for 10–20 years), and £800 million was spent on the New Deal for communities to regenerate 20 of the country's 'worst' council estates by improving housing and economic opportunities, mainly for employment. Although there are local variations in what is delivered, there is a national framework.

The Urban Task Force made 105 recommendations. One proposal was to set up designated urban priority areas, giving local authorities and regeneration partners an opportunity to apply for special packages of grants to improve housing and for neighbourhood renewal. Another suggestion is to establish urban regeneration companies to coordinate the work of local authorities and registered social landlords (RSLs) in the delivery of policy. Housing regeneration companies will be enlisted to undertake regeneration of poor and substandard housing. The Urban Task Force claimed that RSLs should provide the lead agency. Inclusion was intended to be achieved by improving participation in community initiatives such as the management and maintenance of properties.

A predicted outcome is that if the worst-off estates are targeted other deprived estates will be neglected, which means that many estates in poor inner cities and the excluded in other types of tenancy will not benefit.

Housing, crime and criminal justice

Murie (1998) shows that crime is also associated with housing tenure and is especially concentrated on some council estates. The Home Office's British Crime Surveys have shown consistently that households in council tenure are twice as likely to be burgled as households in owner occupation. The risk of victimization is even higher in areas with a relatively high proportion of council houses and tenants living in poverty. By contrast, on better-off council estates and in areas with mixed housing tenure the risk of being burgled is significantly lower. The fear of crime is also greater on poorer council estates. Quality of life issues, in particular vandalism, graffiti and noisy neighbours, also concern residents on council estates more than residents with other types of tenure. There is also a perception held by victims on council estates that offenders live in the same area, and that both offenders and victims are equally deprived. Indeed offenders living in socially excluded communities are most likely to commit burglaries in either similar areas or places that are worse off than those in which they live. Thus there is a correlation between the proportion of known offenders in certain areas (the offence rate) and the rates of victimization, and these rates are highest on council estates. It is a similar story for violent crime.

These developments can be explained to some extent by the changes referred to earlier. Traditionally council estates were inhabited by the respectable working class and characterized by social cohesion and stability. Crime was largely absent. High-crime areas were found mainly in the declining and dilapidated private rented sector of the housing market. These areas were deprived, disorganized and had a high turnover. Increasingly, as many of these areas were demolished deprived groups such as lone parents and the unemployed were moved into council accommodation. Thus the make-up of council estates changed. First, there emerged two types of council tenant and estate, namely the 'rough' and the 'respectable', which influenced the allocation policies of housing managers and resident perceptions. Second, large sections of the respectable or affluent working class are now owner occupiers (as a result of the right to buy), while the most deprived three-quarters, those sometimes labelled as 'rough', are left behind in council or social housing which is of less good quality (Murie, 1998).

These processes result in social exclusion because choice of housing is largely based on income and job security. The less choice individuals have, the more likely they are to be accommodated in the least desirable houses. Moreover, the exclusion of residents on council estates is compounded because of the lack of well-funded services and accessible jobs. Consequently they become isolated and trapped on low incomes in deprived and declining areas.

The outcome is increased polarization between conditions in council and owner-occupied areas, not only in the condition of housing but also in the behaviour of some residents. For example, crime is often a response of young people in poor areas. As many youngsters grow older they also grow out of crime, but in the most excluded neighbourhoods, because there are few opportunities for employment and social mobility, their criminal careers extend into their 20s and sometimes beyond.

Council housing is not the only type of tenure associated with social exclusion and crime. Many offenders lead chaotic lives, for example. For a variety of personal reasons offenders may live in temporary housing such as hostels, or on a short-term basis with family and friends. This lack of permanence increases an offender's sense of insecurity. A significant number of offenders are homeless.

The policy response to housing and crime

Tackling the many different types of social exclusion and crime in the area of housing is dependent on 'joined-up' approaches. CDRPs and their crime reduction strategies are multi-dimensional, involving situational and social measures (Pease, 1997). Situational measures are concerned with issues of design, security and defensible space. The view is that crime can be designed out of estates through the use of locks and bolts and improved street lighting. Social measures are concerned with community development and the management of properties as well as people. Work now being carried out by community safety partnerships is based on many of the informal partnerships recommended in the Morgan Report (1991), and on inter-agency working and planning. Many initiatives have been implemented throughout England and Wales in response to sections 5–7, 17 and 116 of the CDA (1998), but Home Office research carried out in the 1990s on the Priority Estates Project (PEP) provides some useful reference points (Pease, 1997).

Foster (1993) shows that PEP examined the impact of estate and housing management on crime and community life, focusing on regeneration policies which address economic and environmental decisions. The main measures were based on inter-agency partnerships and related to:

- design
- addressing disorder by raising residents' care and concern for their communities
- cultivating positive views of estates amongst residents
- increasing resident and housing officials' control over their communities.

PEP did produce some benefits, but many problems were unresolved. The research showed that the impact of management was minimized by developments caused by changes external to specific estates, such as population change, social instability and social heterogeneity. Crucially, resources were an issue. Estates require more of a social mix, and there were attempts to create stability and to keep the number of empty properties to a minimum. This is partly dependent on allocation policies, but the lack of investment in social housing and the use of what housing there is for the most deprived mean that this is not likely to address social exclusion. More information about issues of empowerment, capacity building and citizenship is required (Foster, 1993).

The Crime and Disorder Act (Home Office, 1998a) had consequences for housing, and RSLs were given the capacity to ask magistrates to issue antisocial behaviour orders to restrain persistent offenders.

Exclusion in social housing involves a tension between need and managerial control. There are powers in place to eject those responsible for antisocial behaviour such as crime, vandalism, drug abuse and prostitution, but it is difficult and expensive to make residents with dependent children homeless (SEU, 1998).

The reasons for exclusion from local authority registers are varied. Only a minority are for antisocial behaviour. Most are for rent arrears among the poorest and those least able to managed their finances. This has been extended to debt and rent arrears in the private sector too. There is insufficient evidence to assess whether exclusion is the best way forward.

Homelessness

The denial of access to social housing may result in homelessness. In 1997 there were 165,790 homeless people. This figure is based on rough sleepers. However, there are also 'unofficial homeless' who live in squats and other short-term living arrangements (such as lodging with relatives and friends) (Balchin and Rhodes, 2002).

The 1996 Housing Act made local authorities responsible for providing temporary accommodation for the homeless for up to two years if no alternative accommodation could be found. After two years there was no additional duty to provide a permanent home. This period during which local authorities made some kind of provision was therefore an uncertain one for the individuals involved (Malpass, 2005).

Homelessness limits contact with education and health services. Subsequently the homeless may be economically, psychologically and socially excluded from local communities, either because they lack the necessary security to obtain a job or as a result of ill-health. Children in homeless families tend to fall behind in their education. Homelessness is therefore not just a symptom of social exclusion but a cause of it too (Dean, 2006).

Youth homelessness is also proving to be an intractable problem because individuals leaving care who are aged under 21 are not a statutory local authority responsibility, and accordingly can be denied access to social housing. Reductions in housing benefit for the under-25s may also have an effect. The problem is exacerbated for the young poor, who are generally lacking income and the skills and experience necessary to maintain a home.

To address homelessness the SEU called for a multi-agency approach, the Homeless Action Programme. This coordinated local anti-homelessness strategies at regional and local levels. The broad strategic aims are to prevent homelessness from occurring in the first instance, and where that is not achieved to help the homeless into permanent homes. The next task is to ensure that they do not become homeless again.

The Rough Sleepers Initiative attracted £145 million to help local authority partnerships address the problem in London, with the aim of reducing the number of rough sleepers by two-thirds by 2002. Although the New Labour government has talked about creating opportunities for inclusion, there is a tough-talking, zero-tolerance rhetoric when it comes to clearing beggars off the streets and into hostels.

Housing allocation policies

A green paper published in 2000 called for further 'joined-up' working to allocate housing to address both need and homelessness. Inter-agency work could look beyond immediate need, and dedicate resources to preventing young people and victims of domestic violence from becoming homeless. However, competition between different agencies for scarce resources and different definitions of need make this problematic. In some areas there is simply not enough accommodation (Malpass, 2005).

Excluded groups

Minority ethnic groups

A disproportionately high number of young ethnic minorities, particularly Black people, become homeless. This subgroup are also more likely to be low paid or unemployed and live in deprived areas. Overcrowded housing is a specific problem for Bangladeshis. These problems are overlain by discrimination, institutional racism and racist violence.

Local authority allocation policies limit the mobility of some ethnic groups. Local authorities are not always responsive to the specific needs of ethnic minorities. Black people are also sometimes excluded from housing management and participation in tenants' federations. In the private sector different criteria are applied for assessing mortgages from Black people. It is notable that most deprivation is found in council houses, but there are relatively fewer ethnic minorities in that sector. If most attention is devoted to social exclusion in the council sector, there is the danger that the exclusion of some minority ethnic groups will be understated.

In short, there appears to be systematic exclusion from good-quality housing for many ethnic minorities. Frequently their choices about housing are related to fear of rejection and harassment rather than economic considerations.

Gender

Households headed by women, mainly lone mothers, are another disproportionately large group in council housing. This reflects the allocation policy, which is based on need. Women who find themselves homeless and have children are deemed to be in greater need than those without children. However, the impact of the diminished investment in social housing has been felt keenly by single women, and in some instances this explains why they are housed in inadequate and inappropriate accommodation, or end up homeless. There is also a link between single mothers, access to housing and their status in the labour market, because of dominant attitudes about the family structure. Men have more job security, earn more and are more likely to be the head of household in owner-occupied property.

The number of households in the social rented sector headed by single mothers varies from city to city. In some regions there is relatively little social housing, and in these instances lone-parent households may be more prevalent in other tenure types. Again, if policy focuses on targeting council estates, some groups may miss out, and attention should be diverted to single-parent households in all tenures.

Participation and inclusion

Tenant participation has been couched in terms of stakeholding, citizenship, partnership participation and empowerment. The intention is to adopt user perspectives (bottom-up), not just the perspective of service providers, in order to enhance tenant control and to maximize their involvement in decision making. For instance, the Housing Investment Programme considers evidence of tenant participation before giving out housing subsidies.

HOUSING AND CRIME: KEY POINTS

- Most crime occurs in a particular place, and for some offences where people live is a good indicator of their vulnerability to crime.
- Socially excluded housing estates are particularly susceptible to high rates of crime.
- Policies have been formulated to tackle crime on particular housing estates.
- Success in tackling crime and social exclusion can only be achieved if all agencies from the housing, criminal justice, education and health sectors all work together.

CONCLUSION

Since the late twentieth century criminal justice policy in England and Wales has become more joined-up, in the sense that criminal justice agencies now work alongside other government departments. The chapter has shown that the first New Labour government (1997–2001) set in train a set of reforms that encouraged the criminal justice and welfare agencies to work together to tackle crime and social exclusion in the areas of health, education and housing. The chapter has described what ought to happen, and over the next few years the effectiveness of joined-up policy should become more apparent.

FURTHER READING

This chapter has described the crime reduction agenda in the early twenty-first century. Given the emphasis on joined-up approaches to tackling crime, disorder and connected social problems, surprisingly there is not a single introductory text that examines cross-departmental working. However, there is a significant literature focusing on crime reduction, community safety and social exclusion. Recommended further reading is D. Cook, *Criminal and Social Justice* (London: Sage, 2006), A. Crawford, *Crime Prevention and Community Safety: Politics, policies and practices* (London: Longman, 1998), G. Hughes, 'Crime and disorder partnerships: the future of community safety', in

G. Hughes, E. McLaughlin and J. Muncie (eds), *Crime Prevention and Community Safety: New directions* (London: Sage, 2002) and K. Pease, 'Crime reduction', in M. Maguire, R. Morgan and R. Reiner (eds), *The Oxford Handbook of Criminology* (Oxford: Oxford University Press, 2002).

STUDY QUESTIONS

1. Describe the main components of the Crime and Disorder Act (1998) and outline how it ensures that different agencies work together to tackle crime and disorder.
2. Define social exclusion, and describe its relationship with crime and disorder.
3. Discuss the main features of crime reduction and community safety initiatives.
4. Describe the relationship between crime, disorder and the following areas of public policy:
   a) health
   b) education
   c) housing.

PART FOUR

Theories
of Crime

11 Theories of Crime I: The Individual and Crime

OVERVIEW

The aim of this chapter is to provide:

- an explanation of the main features of theories of crime that focus on the individual
- an understanding of individualistic approaches belonging to the classical school, where the emphasis is on free will and the rational human actor
- an appreciation of individualistic approaches where the focus is on the influence of biological and psychological factors
- an overview of the various models available for explaining the relationship between criminality, the individual and society
- an overview of individualistic approaches.

INTRODUCTION

Many theories of crime have centred on the individual, ranging from those emphasizing the human subject as a free agent (such as classicism and rational choice theory) to ones that suggest individuals are driven to commit crime by their innate characteristics (such as biological and psychological positivism). The first part of the chapter considers the nineteenth-century legacy, including classicism and positivism. The second part introduces a selection of psychological perspectives. The third part revisits classicism, with a focus on right realist, control and rational choice theories. At the end of this section labelling theory is addressed. This is a unique perspective on the individual offender which does not have a strong fit with either classical or positivist approaches. This prepares for the next chapter, which is dedicated to macro-level theories. The chapter uses various examples from the existing literature, and towards the end reflects on the policy implications of these different theoretical approaches for the criminal justice system.

THE INDIVIDUAL AND CRIME

This section:

■ introduces a range of approaches used to explain crime by focusing on the individual offender
■ identifies two broad approaches, positivism and classicism.

This chapter concentrates on those criminological theories that focus on the individual offender. This is arguably the most obvious starting point for any criminological theory, because if offenders did not exist there would be no crime and no need for a criminal justice system. Moreover, it is the offender who is responsible for committing an offence, and offenders need to be held accountable for their actions. If any sense is to be made of criminal behaviour, then logically it is necessary to look closely at its source. Indeed this is exactly what the pioneers of criminology did in various works published from the late eighteenth century onwards (Hopkins Burke, 2005).

However, taking the individual criminal as the starting point there is not a single explanation but a diverse range of competing theoretical arguments and perspectives. For example, *classical* approaches to criminology, which are described in much more detail below, argue that individuals are capable of free will and that they consciously choose how to behave. In other words, crime is a choice. This view is very popular today, and if you scan the pages of any tabloid newspaper you will read accounts of crime in which the offender is accused of being at worst evil and at best feckless and idle (Jewkes, 2004). The message behind the headlines is that criminals are responsible for their own actions, and that they alone are culpable or blameworthy.

Writers belonging to another school of thought, known as *positivism*, have focused on those ways in which biology influences human behaviour, whereas others have focused on the psychological factors associated with criminality. Positivism holds that to a certain extent crime is 'in the genes', and psychological theories suggest that crime is 'all in the mind'. The view here is that individuals lack self-control because innate forces over which they have no, or very little, control determine their actions. Criminals such as violent psychopaths may still be described as evil, but there is a tendency to view them as sick and in need of treatment to rehabilitate them and return them to normality. These are examples of biological and psychological positivism.

Although these are crucial elements of such accounts, they are of course rather crude over-simplifications. For example, another important debate concerns the extent to which human behaviour can be said to be caused by the functioning of the mind, or the brain and body. In other words, are individuals' actions determined by their biology or their psychology? The answers to this question are varied, and while some research evidence would suggest behaviour *is* determined by one of these, most thinkers recognize that the causes of individual behaviour are complex and may include elements of both. Others plausibly argue that the environmental and social context is important too, and that human action is not just driven by psychological and biological variables. Indeed there are also some sociological explanations of criminality which are based on looking at the individual at a micro level. Rather than finding the cause of crime in the offender and his or her inner physical or psychic make-up, attention is turned to the individuals surrounding the offender, such as police officers, who arguably turn individuals into criminals through stereotyping and labelling (Becker, 1963).

In the remainder of this chapter:

■ The origins of criminological theory are excavated, beginning with classical approaches and following up with biological and psychological positivism. Some examples of these different approaches are then outlined.

■ We then return to the classical tradition, which was reinvigorated in the twentieth century in the form of neoclassicism and approaches such as right realism, rational choice theory, routine activities theory and control theory.

■ Following that a sociological perspective (labelling theory) which takes the individual and society at a micro level is discussed. The chapter ends with a discussion of the relative pros and cons of approaches that focus on the individual.

CLASSICAL CRIMINOLOGY

This approach focuses on the individual who exercises rational choice and exercises free will. 'Classical' criminology is a term, like many others, that has been used in retrospect to refer to a range of ideas which were not formulated into such an explicit perspective at the time (Garland, 1997: 15–16). Rather, subsequent criminologists have imposed an artificial coherence on disparate ideas, especially those belonging to Beccaria (1764, cited in Young, 1981). Beccaria is primarily responsible for the classicist perspective, which rests on four assumptions.

The first assumption is that the human subject is rational and can exercise free will. In other words people are able to reason and think about what they are going to do before they actually do it. Taken to its logical extreme, this view suggests that each person is faced with a range of choices about how to behave, and is free, within the limits of rationality, to act as he or she sees fit. An offender is therefore someone who does not exercise the self-discipline we are all capable of, or who deliberately chooses to break the law.

Second, classicists argued that the basis of social order was a 'social contract'. This viewpoint stood in stark contrast to the ideas of the philosopher Thomas Hobbes, who described human society as 'war against all', where individuals competed with each other for scarce resources. Instead, classicists argue, the government effectively (not necessarily literally) produces a social contract, outlining key principles stating what is and what is not acceptable behaviour, and on the whole those in the society cooperate and adhere to these guidelines. This view is also associated with the *utilitarian* principles put forward by Jeremy Bentham, who argued that society should be organized in such as way that there is 'the greatest happiness for the greatest number'. Each person should be free to do what he or she wants, as long as his or her actions do not interfere with the everyday happiness of others. Another related idea is the 'pleasure–pain principle', which suggests that people prefer pleasurable to painful experiences, but they are prepared to experience some pain if the pleasure following this pain is great enough to make up for it.

Third, classicism has strong links with the political philosophy of *liberalism*, which argued that as far as possible individuals should be personally responsible for their own lives, and that the role of the state should be kept to a minimum.

Fourth, crime and disorder are seen as 'infringement[s] of a legal code', and are defined as such within the legal process, 'that is by the due process of law' (Young, 1981: 259). This assumes that the legal and criminal justice system (the police and courts) both operate in a way that is consistent and logical, so each offence is dealt with in the same way. To ensure that the law is observed, punishment exists as a deterrent to put people off from offending again in the future. The punishment meted out is meant to be consistent rather than severe. Moreover, any penalty must be in proportion to the seriousness of the offence, so the punishment fits the crime. This is the principle of 'just deserts'. Above all, the imposition of punishment needs to be swift and certain (Beccaria, 1963).

Although Beccaria's (1963) work proved popular, the classical approach did attract some powerful criticisms. Above all it was criticized for its extreme rationalism, because it did not taken into account individual differences and the fact that some people, such as children and the mentally ill, are less capable of thinking and behaving rationally than others. In particular, it did not recognize that some people do not have much opportunity to exercise free will, because they are constrained or restricted in what they think and do. However, the themes addressed by this model have not disappeared, and in the twentieth century classicism re-emerged in other forms such as rational choice theory and routine activities theory.

POSITIVIST CRIMINOLOGY

This approach suggests that criminals (like other people) are not free to decide how to act, but that their behaviour is determined by their biological or psychological make-up. This is also referred to as the *predestined actor* approach (Hopkins Burke, 2001). As was acknowledged in Chapter 3, this school of thought is characterized by an emphasis on the use of scientific methods to understand the nature of the social world, rather than a reliance on theological explanations. For example, Adolphe Quetelet applied various statistical techniques to interpret national crime statistics. In doing so he discovered a consistent relationship between recorded crime patterns and particular social and demographic factors, leading him to conclude that crime was caused by social organization (cited in Muncie et al., 1996).

However, it is perhaps the work of the biological positivists Lombroso and Ferri that has attracted most attention from students of criminology. Lombroso's book, *On Criminal Man*, published in 1876, is widely regarded as the first attempt to produce a 'science of the criminal'. Lombroso is famous for arguing that there is a relationship between physical characteristics and criminality. In essence, he argued that criminals' actions are biologically determined, and as a result they should be regarded as suffering from a pathological condition, or illness. He was influenced by Darwin's (1968) theory of evolution (see Chapter 2), and argued that criminals are lower down the evolutionary scale than law-abiding citizens. The word used to describe these evolutionary throwbacks is 'atavistic', and he believed criminals could be identified by their sloping foreheads, large ears and long arms.

Criminals were divided into four sub-groups. Some criminals were 'born' that way, and were readily identifiable by their atavistic features. Others were classified as 'insane', because they were mentally ill, suffering from epilepsy, or mentally deficient as a result of alcoholism or other addictions. 'Occasional' criminals were those who committed offences if they were given an opportunity to do so, thus indicating there was a degree of choice in what they did, although Lombroso argued that they were born with particular traits that made them behave in this way. Finally, some criminals were motivated by passions, such as anger, love and jealousy. This work was based on basic statistical techniques, although the scientific credibility of Lombroso's research has been questioned because of its simplicity (Hopkins Burke, 2005). Essentially, however, the argument was that criminals were sick and in need of treatment to reha-bilitate them. As a result of this, indeterminate sentences were proposed, which means that offenders were held in an institution until there was evidence that the treatment had cured them.

Although Lombroso's research is frequently subjected to ridicule, some of his later work did consider other factors such as the weather and immigration. Ferri took up these themes and his *biological positivism* considered the interaction between three factors: the physical (such as race, and where a person lives), individual (such as sex and physiology) and social (culture) (Hopkins Burke, 2001: 56). Although these other factors were brought into the equation, the prime influence was still thought to belong to biological factors, thus this explanation too tends towards biological determinism. A problem with this is that human consciousness is disregarded, and as a result it oversimplifies causation.

Biological theories of criminality have continued to be influential. For example, in the early twentieth century the Eugenicist movement had considerable influence. This system of thought referred to poor people in terms of their biological and hereditary defects, as the 'biological dregs of the population' (Wootton, 1959: 99). In the words of Barnes, the Eugenicist movement formulated:

> a programme for the gradual improvement of the race by deliberate modification of the relative fertility of various groups in society. The eugenic programme, which was most readily justified if evolution was a predictable process, amenable to gradual redirection by cumulative effects of continuing small-scale interventions, was one manifestation of the reformist, interventionist strands of thinking associated with the rising professional middle class.
>
> (Barnes, 1977: 60)

At a later date the movement reappraised its position, and psychological factors replaced biological ones in its explanations. To address the problem of poverty and its associated pathologies, it was argued that household maintenance, personal relationships and mental health required improvement (Wootton, 1959). Poverty was therefore caused by serious defects amongst poor people.

Wootton has criticized the reasoning behind the eugenicist arguments. She argued that:

> We reach the near tautological conclusion that the proof of the psychopathic personality or emotional immaturity of a problem family is to be found in part at least in the characteristic behaviour which merits its inclusion in this class. Yet none of these labels – low intelligence, emotional immaturity or psychopathic personality – can have any meaning except in terms of criteria which are themselves independent of the behaviour they are invoked to explain.
>
> (Wootton, 1959: 62)

Other biological explanations have not been discredited altogether. For example, aggressive behaviour may be influenced by the brain and genetic factors. It is generally accepted now that people in whom parts of the frontal lobe of the brain do not function properly lack inhibition and behave impulsively. Perhaps the most well-known example of the influence of biological factors is the link between testosterone and aggression. Because male animals, and humans, produce more of this chemical than their female counterparts, they are typically more aggressive and violent. Interestingly, the general consensus is that testosterone does not lead to aggressive behaviour in isolation from other external influences, and testosterone production can be reduced as a result of stresses in the external environment. Other research has explored the links between the production of serotonin (an organic compound found in human tissues, especially the brain) and violent crime. People who produce relatively low quantities of serotonin are more likely to have an aggressive personality, and accordingly an inclination to be violent (Bartol and Bartol, 2005).

POSITIVIST CRIMINOLOGY: KEY POINTS

- ▪ Early individualistic accounts suggested that criminals were different from most people.
- ▪ Early interpretations of crime tended to suggest that criminals were sick and in need of treatment to cure them from their malady.
- ▪ The view that criminal behaviour was genetically or biologically determined continued into the twentieth century, as was demonstrated by the Eugenicists.

PSYCHOLOGICAL EXPLANATIONS OF CRIME

Now we introduce some psychological explanations of crime, paying particular attention to psychodynamic and learning theories, especially the contribution of Eysenck. In this section:

- ▪ some psychological explanations of crime are introduced, including approaches that focus on the personality and cognitive development
- ▪ learning theory is also discussed.

Personality and crime

This section introduces some basic information relating to psychological theories of crime. Such approaches are recognizable because they attribute the causes of criminal behaviour to mental processes that develop as individuals interact with their families and the rest of society. The aim here is to simply provide some flavour of a small selection of psychological approaches, in particular psychodynamic theory, cognitive development theory, several variants of social learning theory, and Eysenck's trait theory of personality.

Psychodynamic theories

Psychological theories of crime begin with the view that individual differences may make some people more predisposed than others to commit criminal acts. The relevant differences may be personality characteristics or biological factors, or may be related to social interaction.

Psychoanalytical theory, as developed by Sigmund Freud (1961), concentrates on the personality structure and its influence on human behaviour. Psychoanalysis is based on the assumption that all human beings have natural urges and drives, some of which are buried in the subconscious and unconscious. All humans have criminal tendencies built into their unconscious. For example, there are drives making people aggressive and jealous, and these urges may become manifest in the form of violent and/or property offences. Human beings are not left to their own devices, though: they are exposed to *socialization*. This occurs during childhood, when most children learn to control their inner drives. However, those people who become criminals experience difficulties during their childhood and are not socialized effectively.

Freud (1961) suggested that a common factor accounting for criminal behaviour is a child who fails to identify with his or her parents. Because the child is not properly socialized, a possible consequence is a personality disturbance resulting in antisocial behaviour. These impulses may be directed inwardly or outwardly, depending on the nature of the disturbance the person experiences. The person who displays this disturbance outwardly becomes a criminal, whereas if it is channelled inwards the behavioural response is *neurotic*.

Cognitive development theory

This alternative approach draws attention to the ways in which people organize their thoughts, and the bearing this activity has on their morality. For example, morality is something that is learnt over time, but if moral development is impeded in some way, there is a greater likelihood that a person will offend. An example of this approach is Kohlberg's (1976) theory of the processes associated with moral reasoning.

Kohlberg identified three levels of moral reasoning. The first level of moral development takes place during middle childhood, once children have experienced their initial socialization. This stage is called the 'pre-conventional level', and at this juncture moral reasoning is not based much on intellectual reasoning but is instead based on children being obedient and observing the wishes of their parent(s) or guardian(s). The main motivation behind this obedience is the avoidance of punishment. Towards the end of middle childhood a person reaches the second level, known as the 'conventional level' of moral development. In comparison with the first level, children at this stage are far more capable of reasoning and are able to comprehend the expectations that their family and significant others have of them. The third level of moral development, known as the 'postconventional level', is a transition taking place during early adulthood. At this stage individuals are able to go beyond social conventions by consciously exercising choices about how they behave. At this stage individuals are in a position where they may value the rule of law and perceive the criminal justice system as legitimate. However, as adults they have the capacity to bring about change in their environment, and they may see various ways of changing the existing social order in order to reform and improve society.

According to social development theory the deviant or criminal is a person who does not progress through these three different levels. Because criminals do not pass through each of these phases their moral development is arrested and they are likely to become delinquents.

Learning theory

Certain aspects of behavioural psychology, which holds to the view that human behaviour is learnt, influence learning theory, which argues that behaviour is learnt largely as a result of the consequences of people's actions. For example, people will either be rewarded or punished for particular types of behaviour, and this will have a direct influence on their learning. The consequences of a particular action may result in 'external reinforcement' (Bartol and Bartol, 2005): that is, acquiring something desirable such as money or social status. Most people will behave in ways that make them likely to attain these ends. People's behaviour can also be reinforced 'vicariously' (Bartol and Bartol, 2005), which means they see the behaviour of another person being reinforced and learn from that cue. Finally, some people regulate their own behaviour with reference to their own regulatory mechanisms. On the basis of these insights some learning theorists argue that psychologists can either reduce or prevent deviant behaviour by removing the rewards attached to a particular type of behaviour.

Variations on the theme of learning theory were used to explain the factors causing human aggression by Dollard et al. (1939). This work attempted to use elements of Freudian psychoanalysis, and the outcome was the frustration–aggression hypothesis. The basic point of this theory is that if people become frustrated, then their behaviour will be aggressive, and conversely if they behave aggressively then they will be frustrated. Dollard et al. (1939) agreed with Freud that aggression is instinctual or innate, but deviated from Freud in their argument that frustrating situations and events will only arouse an aggressive response. This psychological explanation has been adopted and adapted by various theorists.

For example, another idea that is very similar to Dollard et al.'s is the *displacement of aggression*. Gross (1992) has put forward this this approach to account for those times when people direct their aggressive feelings not towards the cause of their aggression, but rather at another target. For example, a parent tells off a child, and he (or she) takes out his anger and frustration on a younger sibling, because he is too small and vulnerable to vent his frustration against its cause, the adult. Miller (1941) revised the frustra-tion–aggression hypothesis by arguing that frustration *can* bring about aggressive behaviour, but there were other possible responses to it that are certainly not aggressive, such as depression and lethargy.

Basically, these different revisions suggested that there is no absolute causal or deter-ministic link between frustration and aggression. In a similar vein, Berkowitz (1962) argued that if a person is frustrated the response might be not aggression, but rather anger. For this anger to be turned into aggression it is necessary for certain signs or cues to exist. There might be signals in the environment, for example, that stimulate aggression.

Learning theory, intelligence and crime

According to Wilson and Herrnstein (1985) there is a link between intelligence and crime. They explore the relationship between these two phenomena in their *constitu-tional learning theory*, a perspective drawing on social learning theory, which is inte-grated with biological factors. They start with the simple premise that all human behaviour is related to gains and losses. For example, if people decide they have some-thing to gain from stealing from or physically hurting another person, and that behaving in this way will outweigh the pain caused by the punishment they might receive, they will go ahead and commit the crime. This type of argument is similar to classicism, but Wilson and Herrnstein bring in two other important variables that contribute towards criminality, 'time discounting' and 'equity'.

Time discounting takes account of the time at which the reward or punishment is received, as the name suggests. It allows for the possibility of immediate rewards and delayed punishment being attached to offending behaviour. Offenders are also claimed to consider the time it would take to gain the reward they achieve by offending through legal means. Wilson and Herrnstein suggest that some people are more willing to defer their gratification or wait for what they want than others. Those who are less likely to defer their pleasure are much more likely to become involved in offending behaviour. The second variable, equity, refers to an offender's sense of fairness. If offenders judge that they have been treated unfairly in society, their offending is a method of making sure they experience some form of justice.

These factors mainly concern the ability of individuals to rationalize what they do, but Wilson and Herrnstein also argue that there are constitutional factors that have a bearing on criminal behaviour. For instance, people have different levels of intelligence as well as a different physiological make-up. (By this it is meant that some people are more likely to be physically aroused by certain stimuli than others.) These factors will have an influence on how a person assesses the pros and cons of behaving in a particular way. Thus the degree of physical arousal people experience will influence the extent to which they are conditioned. If a person finds it difficult to associate negative outcomes with committing crime, it is unlikely that they will be deterred from offending behaviour.

The importance of the human constitution is also illustrated by the point Wilson and Herrnstein (1985) make about impulsive behaviour and low intelligence. They claim that children who lack intelligence and do not receive adequate socialization are at the highest risk of becoming offenders. The thesis that there is a link between low intelligence and crime has proven to be a compelling theoretical explanation of criminality, especially for conservative criminologists. For example Herrnstein and Murray (1994) controversially argued that there is a link between IQ (a measure of intelligence) and race. There would appear to be some evidence to back up the claim that low intelligence and crime coexist, demonstrated by the skills deficit many prisoners have. However, there is no evidence to show a *causal* link between intelligence and crime. If there is a correlation or an association but nothing more than that, it would cast doubt on the theoretical validity of this approach.

Eysenck's theory of personality

Eysenck's (1964) writings on crime were intended to be a general theory of crime, explaining the reasons that certain individuals commit crime and others do not. His explanation did not consider social conditions such as social class and poverty, concentrating instead on the biological foundations of the human personality. One of Eysenck's major contributions was his explanation of the factors causing neuroticism: he argued that this was linked to the level of arousal in the nervous system. There is therefore a degree of influence from biological components in this account, but Eysenck did distance himself from any crude form of biological determinism. He was much more interested in examining the criminal personality, and was therefore making an attempt to combine biological and individual variables.

Eysenck was particularly interested in the nature of the interaction between the social environment (often in the form of socialization) and the human nervous system, or a person's neuropsychological make-up. The theoretical point he was making was that people are not predestined to commit crimes (as Lombroso originally suggested) but that the autonomic or central nervous system of the criminal is different from that of non-criminals in some significant ways. Some people have nervous systems that are more reactive or sensitive to stimuli than others, and this makes them more excitable and less able to exercise self-control.

Arguably Eysenck's most important contribution was his identification of certain personality traits or types. He argued that some of these predisposed people towards crime more than others. These personality traits are intrapsychic variables distinguishing people from each other. The traits he identified are actually measurable and can be quantified, and Eysenck used them as the basis for various personality inventories, like the Eysenck Personality Questionnaire-Revised (EPQ-R). When Eysenck (1964) started work on his explanation of crime he identified two dimensions to the personality. The three dimensions are extroversion (E), neuroticism (N) and psychoticism (P) (Eysenck, 1977). Hollin (2002: 152) describes how these three dimensions sit on a 'continuum'. Eysenck (1977) opines that whilst most people in the general population sit in the middle there are a relatively small number of individuals who sit at either extreme (i.e. they are 'high' or 'low'). For example:

- Extroversion includes at the high end extroverts. The people fitting into this category are impulsive sensation seekers. At the low end of the scale are introverted people who tend to keep themselves to themselves.
- Neuroticism includes at the high end people who are anxious and irritable and at the low end of the scale people who are calm or chilled out.

■ Psychoticism also includes a range of characteristics but such people are more difficult to describe, and display characteristics such as a liking for solitude and physical aggression.

We shall return to these issues shortly after expanding what Eysenck had to say about human personality.

Eysenck (1964) claimed there were 'four high order theories of personality'. One higher-order factor is general intelligence or 'G'. This was not treated as particularly significant, and there are stronger influences on behaviour. The other order theories are psychotism, extroversion and neuroticism, which together are referred to as PEN. Extroversion is a personality trait that makes a person need a comparatively high amount of stimulation, whereas neuroticism refers to the arousal levels of the autonomic nervous system. Out of the three elements of PEN, most attention is given to extroversion and neuroticism.

To deepen our understanding of Eysenck's contribution to criminological theory it is necessary to look more closely at his theorization of the personality structure, and in particular at the factors identified as part of his personality inventories.

Extroversion is a reflection of the basic functions of the central nervous system, including the brain and spinal cord. Neuroticism is an effect of the functioning of the peripheral nervous system (that is, the nerve pathways outside the central nervous system). There is no relevant mechanism in the central nervous system for psychoticism. Eysenck has found that two-thirds of people score in the average range, demonstrating that they have stable personalities. These stable people are known as *ambiverts*. Those who score at the ends of the ranges are arguably less stable. It is now necessary to look more closely at the characteristics of Eysenck's personality traits (1977).

Extroversion

The biological make-up of extroverts means they seek high levels of stimulation. Typically they are impulsive, sociable and constantly seeking excitement. They lose their temper quickly, and can be aggressive and unreliable. They are talkative and seen as typical party animals For example, they will take drink and drugs for excitement and stimulation in order to avoid boredom. There is a strong link between this kind of risk taking and antisocial behaviour, such as crime. Since as was mentioned above, people with neurotic personalities tend to be risk takers with antisocial tendencies, a criminal is most likely to be a neurotic extrovert.

Introversion

Introverts tend to be rather reserved and quiet, keeping themselves to themselves. They avoid change and uncertainty, and tend to prefer their own company, avoiding groups. They tend to be reliable and ethical in their conduct, so these people can be expected to be less likely than average to commit crimes.

Ambiversion

People in the mid-range exhibit elements of both introversion and extroversion, but they avoid the extremes of these personality types.

Psychotism

The cause of psychoticism is hormonal: it typically involves over-production of testosterone in combination with low levels of the enzyme monoamine oxidase and the neurotransmitter serontin. Those people who fall into this category tend to be cold, cruel, insensitive, unemotional and lacking fear. These characteristics are found most often among hard-core and habitual offenders.

Eysenck's (1964) ideas have attracted considerable critical attention, and while the details may be flawed they are a good example of the kind of reasoning psychologists use to explain crime.

PSYCHOLOGICAL EXPLANATIONS OF CRIME: KEY POINTS

■ Psychodynamic theories identify the cause of offending behaviour in the human personality and the workings of the brain.

■ Crime is explained in terms of factors such as the socialization and cognitive development of children.

■ Eysenck's account focused on the relationship between the neuropsychological make-up of the offender and the external environment.

THE INDIVIDUAL AND 'CYCLES OF TRANSMITTED ANTISOCIAL TENDENCY'

A distinctively criminological approach drawing on psychology is found in the work of the Cambridge Institute of Criminology, whose researchers are still conducting a longitudinal study, which commenced in 1961, of a group of young males born in a socially deprived area of London between 1951 and 1954. This research is underpinned by the hypothesis that there is something called a 'delinquency cycle', and that there are 'cycles of transmitted anti-social tendency' (West and Farrington, 1977). The key point is that antisocial behaviour and crime are transmitted from generation to generation within families. As the researchers put it, the:

> Findings harmonize most readily with those criminological theories that attribute the importance of individual temperament and individual social learning. They do not negate, but they do lend much support to those theoretical models, which neglect individual character and circumstances in favour of exclusive concentration of external forces.
>
> (West and Farrington,1977: 159–60)

The latest analyses of this data found that 41 per cent of males had been given a criminal conviction – excluding motoring offences – between the ages of 10 and 50. It was found that the average conviction career lasted between the ages of 19 and 28. During this period the average number of convictions was five per offender.

When the children were aged between 8 and 10 a number or risk factors were identified that predisposed them towards offending later on in life. Family criminality and poor parenting were important, as was poverty, educational under-achievement and risk-taking behaviour. Clearly all of these factors are closely related to individual temperament. The importance of temperament and age combined is clear because the males who began their criminal conviction careers the earliest also offended more in later life. For example, the males who started their criminal careers between 10 and 16 years accounted for 77 per cent of crimes resulting in convictions.

Among the sample used for this study there were 7 per cent of offenders who were defined as 'chronic' offenders, and these were responsible for nearly half of the offences recorded in this study. The conviction careers of this group of criminals lasted from age 14 to 35 years.

The lessons to be learnt from the Cambridge research are that adult offenders tend to be antisocial when they are young. The recommendation made is that crime prevention starts at a young age, focusing in particular on housing, drugs and alcohol, employment and aggressive behaviour.

CLASSICISM REVISITED

In this section:

■ the focus is on some of the numerous attempts to reinvigorate the classical criminology of previous centuries
■ these approaches are shown to share in common an assumption that the individual is rational and exercises freedom of choice.

The ideas of Beccaria may have been challenged but they have never really disappeared, and they have continued to influence a range of criminological theories which place the individual at the centre of the analysis. For example, the thesis of *right realism* has been defined as neoclassicism (Wilson, 1983). This approach argues that the positivists are wrong to attempt to look for the causes of crime by referring to biological or psychological variables. The reason crime occurs is that individuals have free will and the capacity to choose how they act. The decision to commit crime is a moral choice, although Wilson recognizes that the choice is not easy for all people because humans are weak and fallen creatures. Because of this it is the role of government to decide on and enforce morality. Morality alone is not sufficient, though, and if the government is to control crime it is necessary for there to be punishment. Penalties exist as a deterrent, the aim being to get potential offenders to consider the pain of being caught, and for this consideration to outweigh any pleasure they may gain. Most people will be deterred from offending by the threat of an adequate punishment, but for those individuals who are not deterred, incapacitation is a possible solution.

Control theory

In contrast to the theories described so far in this chapter (and those covered in Chapters 12 and 13), this perspective asks a very different question. Instead of attempting to explain the reasons people commit crime, the focus of control theory is on the methods used to *control* crime (Hirschi, 1969). The novelty of this approach is demonstrated by the rather simple question it asks: 'Why do people *not* commit crime?' This is diametrically opposed to the question most other criminologists ask. It is taken as a given that people will look out for opportunities to offend, and if the chances of being caught are negligible, they will go ahead and do it. It is also recognized that there are many possible motivations, including financial profit, the status that goes with crime and the pleasure and enjoyment of committing crime. The main insight offered by control theory is that people are more likely to offend if there is a lack of controls to inhibit or constrain them. This apparently common-sensical and obvious statement was attractive to policy makers because potential practical solutions were clear to see, and there were no attempts to over-theorize offending behaviour.

The origins of control theory have been traced back to Hobbes and Durkheim. In *Leviathan* the philosopher Thomas Hobbes (1561) was preoccupied with the problem of social order, asking why human beings obey the rules of society. Hobbes concluded that fear holds most people in check, and hence is a powerful influence on their behaviour (cited in Strauss, 1936). Durkheim (1970) argued that humans have needs and desires that are natural, but are restrained through socialization. In periods of dramatic social change people often lack adequate mechanisms of social control. Hirschi (1969) is a well-known control theorist, and his major contribution to criminological theory is his assertion that a delinquent is most likely to offend if his or her bonds or attachments to wider society are either 'weak or broken' (1969: 16). Hirschi argued that there were four main types of social bond: attachment, involvement, commitment and belief. We shall briefly examine each of these in turn.

'Attachment' is based on social-psychological reasoning and theories of socialization. It is used to explain how childhood and youth are important periods, in particular because of the ties young people have with their parents, schoolteachers and fellow pupils. Throughout this phase people are socialized, or taught how they are expected to behave and the costs of refusing to conform to these expectations. If children form strong attachments, the pressure they feel to conform is greater than if they are uninterested in and disengaged from others in their immediate social environment. Those with weak attachments are more likely to be deviant.

'Involvement' may be seen to have links with attachment in the sense that it suggests that normal individuals become so immersed in the ties and bonds in conventional society that deviance is never really considered an option. 'Commitment' means there is a reason to remain involved because an individual has a stake in society, such as studying for educational qualifications which are likely to lead to a decent job later in life. 'Belief' refers to the acceptance of prevailing social values, and is again likely to be possessed by those who have been effectively socialized in early childhood (Hirschi, 1969).

Empirical work has lent some support to Hirschi's thesis, and self-report data shows that there is a correlation between the high attachment of young people to their family and school, and low delinquency (Gottfredson and Hirschi, 1990).

Wilson (1980) applied Hirschi's ideas in a study of parental supervision of school-children and the impact this has on self-control amongst young people. The study was carried out in a socially deprived area of Birmingham, and introduced the notion of 'chaperonage' to describe how parents look after their children. It was found that where there was chaperonage and 'strict' moral standards children were less delinquent. For example, if parents monitored who their children associated with and placed restrictions on what they did, delinquency was reduced. Although the focus of this study was on the individual children and parents involved, it did suggest that poor parenting skills are often related to pressures beyond people's personal control, such as unemployment and poor-quality housing.

A version of control theory was also produced by Ron Clarke, who played a pioneering role in the development of situational crime prevention techniques throughout the 1980s. The main points of situational crime prevention were rehearsed in Chapter 10. The theoretical insight Clarke (1980) offered was to show how crime can be prevented by removing the situational opportunities to commit crime, or to be more accurate, to limit such opportunities for committing crime. Clarke's (1980) ideas were the theoretical underpinning for a range of crime reduction measures, including *target hardening*. This refers to attempts to make items that could be stolen or vandalized more difficult to steal or damage. For example, the use of better and more locks on personal property could reduce the situational opportunities for thieves and burglars. Clarke also recommended the use of technological fixes such as closed-circuit television cameras (CCTV) as a method of controlling offending behaviour. Oscar Newman's (1973) notion of 'defensible space' was also influential. By using target hardening and surveillance it is possible to ensure that geographical areas are less vulnerable to crime. Ideas that crime could be designed out of shopping malls or housing estates are indebted to situational crime prevention.

Clarke's ideas were built on in Clarke and Felson (2004), whose contribution is, in many ways, another reinvigoration of nineteenth-century classical approaches. Rather than focusing exclusively on the rationally minded offender, the focus was shifted slightly to consider the everyday circumstances surrounding offenders and what they do. However, the rational choice of the actor is still treated as the most important factor. The main advance made by *routine activities theory*, as it came to be called, was to show that the probability or likelihood of offending was influenced by the interaction of three variables in any given time and place. The three factors are a likely offender, a suitable target and the absence of a capable guardian.

This theory warrants some further attention. The first part of the equation is the most obvious: without a person or persons who have the will and capacity to commit a crime, in most instances a crime will not happen. However determined people are to commit a crime, they need an opportunity, hence the suitable target. For instance, a burglar might see an open window or a door ajar, and be encouraged by this to enter a house. More committed burglars might be carrying tools to help them break in and enter, but there still needs to be a target that is 'burglerable'. In crimes of interpersonal violence, offenders tend to choose to attack someone they feel they can inflict more damage on than the victim can return. Finally, the theory rests on the assumption that if a capable guardian is present, the opportunity and will to commit crime can be reduced. This guardian can be a person such as a police officer, a security guard or even a passer-by. The guardian may also be a physical object, such as a CCTV camera: in short, anything that stops or reduces the likelihood of an offence taking place.

This perspective has several practical implications. First, it shifts the responsibility for reducing crime away from the state to the individual and community. Everyone can invest in the necessary hardware to protect their property, and because offenders are assumed to behave rationally, people can anticipate what they might do. Second, this approach emphasized the use of technology in crime prevention, ranging from new locks and bolts to CCTV. Third, the approach highlighted the importance of risk assessment for predicting where and when offending will take place. For example, a car park lacking adequate lighting, CCTV and staff would be considered a higher risk than a car park benefiting from all these factors.

CLASSICISM REVISITED: KEY POINTS

■ In contrast to many criminological theories, control theory examines the reasons that people conform and do not offend.
■ Control theory shows that the bonds and attachments people have (or lack) explain their engagement in criminal behaviour.
■ An influential theoretical approach falling into this category is rational choice theory and routine activities theory, which suggest that a crime occurs if there is a motivated offender, a suitable target and the absence of a capable guardian.

SOCIOLOGICAL EXPLANATIONS OF THE CRIMINAL INDIVIDUAL

In this section individualistic approaches which focus on the individual in a social setting are outlined.

Unlike the other theoretical explanations reviewed thus far in this chapter, the next theory does not take for granted the existence of crime or the offender. The American sociologist Howard Becker (1963) introduced labelling theory to show how people are not offenders until they are labelled as such. Back in the 1960s Becker attempted to explain the processes leading up to the definition of some behaviours as criminal, and to account for why other people were not defined as deviant. In other words, he asked why only certain people are labelled as deviants. In contrast to both classical and positivist perspectives, labelling theorists are not the least bit interested in identifying the criminal mind or a criminal gene. In actual fact they do not look at the offender at all – or to be more accurate, their stance is that offenders only exist when that status is applied to them by another person. Taken to its logical extreme this means criminality is not an innate characteristic, nor is offending behaviour a rational choice taken by offenders themselves.

Becker's main contribution to understanding the relationship between the individual and crime is that it is not so much what a person does that is of theoretical significance, but rather the social *reaction* to what someone does. However, once human actions have been defined as deviant, that identity can influence not only individual self-perception but also future behaviour. In Becker's own words:

> Deviance is not a quality of the act the person commits, but rather a consequence of the application by others of rules and sanctions to an offender. The deviant is one to whom that label has successfully been applied; deviant behaviour is behaviour that people so label.
>
> (Becker, 1963: 9)

So labelling theory considers the reactions of people, and the impact of their responses on the creation of crime and deviance. Once a person has been identified as a criminal, maybe as a 'thief' or a 'paedophile', he or she then tends to be segregated from society, hence the title of Becker's (1963) book, *Outsiders*. A person who is outcast as a result of labelling may then associate with other outcasts. From then on the label sticks, and those to whom the label is attached may continue to live up to it.

SOCIOLOGICAL EXPLANATIONS: KEY POINTS

■ Labelling theory shows that individuals do not have criminal personalities, but rather than criminals are the product of social reaction.

CONCLUSION

The individual offender is centre stage in criminological theory, and this chapter has introduced a range of theoretical approaches that explain criminal behaviour with reference to the individual human subject. It began with a brief resume of the origins of criminological theory, showing that on the one hand, there are theories that argue individual behaviour is determined or influenced by biological or psychological factors. On the other hand, individuals are conscious beings with an ability to act as they choose. These might appear to be diametrically opposed views, but in fact they are not difficult to reconcile: theorists tend to recognize the interplay of biological, psychological, and social or environmental factors. However, any criminological theorist will attach most significance to one of these factors.

A shortcoming of theories that focus on the individual is that there is no acknowledgement of the influence of wider structural or socioeconomic factors on human behaviour. Chapter 12 addresses this imbalance, but it is shown that individual human subjects do not disappear from view. Rather they are free to act as they wish, but not under material social circumstances of their own making.

FURTHER READING

There are many introductions to criminological theory, but one of the most accessible is R. Hopkins Burke, *An Introduction to Criminological Theory* (2nd edn) (Cullompton: Willan, 2005) (see chapters 2, 4, 5, 6, 9 and 15). Also see chapters 1 and 2 of D. Downes and P. Rock, *Understanding Deviance: A guide to the sociology of crime and rule breaking* (3rd edn) (Oxford: Oxford University Press, 1998), and J. Muncie et al., *Criminological Perspectives* (London: Sage, 1996).

STUDY QUESTIONS

1. Identify the main features of classical criminology.
2. Describe the main points of early positivist criminology.
3. Discuss the suggestion that criminals choose to behave in the way they do.
4. Summarize the contribution psychologists have made to criminological theory.
5. How useful is:
   a) control theory for explaining crime?
   b) labelling theory for explaining crime?

12 Theories of Crime II: Society and Crime

OVERVIEW

This chapter aims to provide:

■ a brief introduction to theories of crime which emphasize the influence of society, or social factors, on criminal behaviour
■ a discussion of a selection of sociological explanations of criminality
■ an overview of the concept of anomie and debates about social disorganization and crime
■ a description of subcultural theory
■ a description of radical and critical criminology
■ an assessment of the contribution of left realism to criminological theory, and criminal justice policy and practice.

INTRODUCTION

Another tradition in criminological theory holds the view that criminal behaviour needs to be understood in its wider macro or structural context. These theories incorporate explanations which argue that social forces are deterministic (sociological positivism) and other more nuanced accounts that take into consideration the relationship between structure and agency (such as subcultural theory and left realism). There are many examples of these ideas being applied to explain particular aspects of offending behaviour.

The chapter begins with the work of Emile Durkheim, one of the founding fathers of the social and human sciences. Although he was not a criminologist, Durkheim did refer to crime in his studies (unlike the other two founders of sociology, Marx and Weber). A key concept Durkheim left behind was *anomie* or normlessness, and this idea was developed and applied in the work of the American sociologist Robert

Merton. His classic study of anomie is a reference point for criminologists today. Similarly the publications of the Chicago School are important, in particular for the suggestion that crime is related to geographical factors such as the form of urban areas. It was argued that social disorganization, similar to anomie, was more prevalent in poor communities.

Another important school of thought emphasizing the influence of social factors on crime is subcultural theory, a body of work which explores the relationship between the social structure and the agency of, or choices exercised by, individuals, especially young working-class men. This work suggests that structural factors provide the context but individuals 'drift' in and out of crime at particular moments in their lives.

The work of radical criminologists, such as *left idealism*, is then introduced. This contribution is indebted to the ideas of Marx inasmuch as this explanation of crime is based on an understanding of the distribution of economic and political power in capitalist societies. The final part of the chapter considers the important contribution of *left realism*. This perspective, developed out of left idealism, attempted to build on a range of criminological theories, including an emphasis on individual agency and on structural factors. It is also a general theory, which in contrast to many of its predecessors examines both the offender and the victim, and the relationship between the two.

ANOMIE AND SOCIAL DISORGANIZATION: DURKHEIM, MERTON AND THE CHICAGO SCHOOL

In this section:

- key ideas developed in the nineteenth and twentieth centuries are examined
- attention is directed to the macro level and structural influences on human action.

Perhaps the most important characteristic of the type of sociological explanations mentioned above is that they are not particularly concerned with the individual human subject. Rather they are interested in the organization and development of society as a whole. To apply this argument to crime, they are not interested in the individual criminal in separation from broader patterns of crime, delinquency and deviance. Moreover, the distribution of crime is explained in relation to wider social, economic and cultural structures. Many sociologists are interested in examining the changes occurring in these structures, and their bearing on the occurrence of crime, especially property offences.

Many sociological accounts are influenced by a positivist understanding of human behaviour, of the kind outlined in the previous chapter. However, in contrast to Chapter 11, here we consider whether crime is caused by forces external to the individual, rather than the factors inherent to individuals such as their psychological or biological make-up. The positivist influence is also demonstrated by the commitment to investigating crime by drawing on a range of qualitative and quantitative methods (see Chapter 4). Perhaps the most influential concept in sociological variants of criminological theory, at least in the early days of the discipline, is anomie.

Anomie

As you may already know, Emile Durkheim (1970, 1984) is seen as the founder of the discipline of sociology. He is perhaps best known for his apparently bizarre claim that crime is not only a 'normal' and acceptable feature of everyday society, it is also actually functional. How can this be the case? To respond to this question it is necessary to briefly rehearse the key assumptions figuring in Durkheim's science of society.

Durkheim is an example of a *structural functionalist*. This perspective describes society as a set of institutions (such as the state, the financial sector, the criminal justice system, church and family) which are interrelated and work together. All of these organizations tend to operate or function together because there is a high degree of consensus and they all share the same norms and values. These shared beliefs are known as the 'collective conscience', which ensures that there is harmony in social relationships. Durkheim argued that crime is functional for society because whenever a crime is committed it brings the members of a community together to express their disapproval of the offender. Crime actually helps to define the boundaries of acceptable and unacceptable behaviour. This is further demonstrated through the punishment of an offender.

While societies are for the most part orderly, from time to time there is 'social disorganization', when shared norms and values come under threat, and in some instances there is normlessness or anomie. Anomie is therefore a form of social disorganization, and is most acute during transitional periods in societies. For instance, Durkheim (1984) described a shift from societies based on 'mechanical solidarity' to those based on 'organic solidarity'. Mechanical solidarity is his term for the social arrangements found in agrarian or rural and pre-industrial societies. Such societies are relatively small and well organized, and are normally held together by shared religious beliefs. As a result of industrialization and urbanization profound economic and social changes occurred throughout the nineteenth century, and the bonds associated with mechanical solidarity were weakened. Consequently, there was social disorganization resulting from excessive individualization or egoism. Under these conditions some individuals became unhappy and committed suicide (Durkheim, 1970). The logic of Durkheim's arguments can be extended and applied to explain high crime rates and increased social disorder. Although anomie causes serious anxiety and uncertainty, it eventually leads to the restoration of order and a new set of shared norms and values. The existence of the criminal is functional because it brings people together to express their rejection and condemnation of this behaviour.

Anomie has also been applied to describe less profound social changes, particularly by Robert Merton (1938) in his work focusing on American society in the first few decades of the twentieth century. His overriding aim was to investigate the relationship between the social structure, anomie and crime rates. Merton not only drew on Durkheimian ideas, he also developed a new concept of *strain*. An important theme for Merton is the relationship between the social structure and the value system in the United States. Merton stated quite clearly that values are not inherited by individuals but are learnt from the wider culture. To use Merton's words, his work is a study of the strain between 'cultural goals' and the 'institutional means' available to realize these goals (Merton, 1938).

In the early stages of the twentieth century an important value system was the 'American dream', which suggested that everyone in that society was in a position where if they worked hard enough they could become rich. Society was structured in such a way that hard work was rewarded with material success, and this opportunity was open to all. Experience has made it apparent that not everybody realizes the American dream, and most would argue that this is not merely a result of their not trying hard enough: although in theory the United States is an open society, the reality is rather different and economic opportunities are not distributed equitably. The argument is that because the goals set by the American dream remained distant and elusive for many people, this gave them an 'acute state of anomie', which became manifest in the form of 'strain'. There is a feeling of strain because there are too many obstacles in the way of people, stopping them from achieving their aspirations.

Merton argues that people sign up to the 'cultural goals' attributed to the American dream in different ways, but the most important point he makes, at least as far as criminological theory is concerned, is that the 'institutional means' available are different for different people. More specifically, individuals adapt in various ways to the strain of having their opportunities blocked. There are five modes of adaptation: conformity, ritualism, retreatism, rebellion and innovation. You may feel that the cultural norms in Europe are a little different from the American dream, but Merton's categories can be applied in other cultural contexts too.

Conformity

This is the form of adaptation by individuals who accept the cultural goals and strive to achieve them through legitimate institutional means. The typical conformist has supportive parents, worked hard at school and on leaving college as a young adult entered the world of work. The work ethic established during their years in education enables these people to achieve success at work. It is quite likely that you and your tutor fit this profile: but perhaps you will identify more with the next mode ritualism, which includes certain elements of conformity.

Ritualism

Ritualists tend to tacitly accept the cultural goals even though they are not in a position to achieve them fully. Such individuals may be comfortable with their lot and just go through the motions at work. Other ritualists take great pleasure in carrying out mundane and routine tasks without seeking financial rewards.

Retreatism

Every society includes people who for whatever reason do not subscribe to the dominant social values and do not make any sustained effort to realize the conventional goals. The retreatist is likely to withdraw from conventional social life and look for 'ways of escaping reality', through the use of drugs or dropping out of the 'rat race', for example. While retreatists who use illegal drugs are committing a criminal offence, criminality is not the main motive behind their behaviour. Rather it is an attempt to avoid the full responsibilities of adulthood, which are taken on board by most people.

Rebellion

The rebel's adaptation to both the cultural goals and institutional means is to question the authority of social norms. Rebellion involves the rejection of the American dream, and like the retreatist the rebel does not buy into the goals of wider society. In contrast to the retreatist, rebels actively question and reject the goals of the capitalist system, possibly through an engagement in political protest. The activities of anti-capitalist protestors are an example. Perhaps a better example is the behaviour of the young 'suicide bombers' who appear to have been responsible for the explosions that took place in London on 7/7 (7 July 2005). Arguably it will never be possible to be certain what motivated their acts, but much of the media-led commentary suggested they were rebelling against the social values of modern Britain. Their act of rebellion was also directed against the perceived 'Islamophobia' of the British state, and showed their lack of faith in the institutional means available for expressing their discontent and resentment (Spalek, 2002).

Innovation

This is perhaps the most interesting adaptation for the criminologist. Innovators recognize and accept the cultural goals but also recognize that they are likely to be thwarted in their attempt to realize them, maybe because of their social background and educational failure or under-achievement. The traditional route for realizing the American dream, including hard work at school and the striving for a well-paid job, is not open to innovators, so if they wish to make money and enjoy the trappings of financial success they need to identify different means to achieve this. In other words, they must be innovative and creative, which may lead them in the direction of delinquent and criminal behaviour.

Most criminals are innovators in the sense that they adapt to the strain they experience by creating their own route to success. Say a young man wants a brand new pair of the trendiest designer trainers. These can cost (at 2006 prices) at least £100. If he is jobless, or in work but poorly paid, and does not have rich parents who are happy to buy them for him, he is unlikely to be able to afford the trainers without saving up for several months. If the sense of strain is strong, he might look for alternative, quite possibly illegal, methods of getting hold of them. He could steal a pair from the shelves of the local Foot Locker or JJB Sports, or if he feels the security precautions in place make this too risky, he could steal money, or goods that he can sell for cash on the 'black market'. This is an example of how a consumer society, where products are advertised as being essential for anyone who wants to fit in with their friends, places considerable pressure on people. This can lead them to reject the conventional route to realizing their aspirations, and the criminal behaviour resulting from this may result in 'social disorganization', such as fear of crime in wider society.

Theoretical implications of anomie

Merton's contribution quite clearly rejected individualized explanations of crime, where the emphasis was on the innate characteristics of criminals. Perhaps his most enduring contribution is the detailed explanation of the links between socio-economic change at the macro level of society and crime rates. One problem with a simple argument that poverty causes crime is the evidence that crime does not necessarily decrease during periods of economic prosperity (Box, 1987). Merton's thought is still found relevant by some criminologists today, but there are also criticisms of it.

The notion of adaptation suggests that Merton is willing to accept that individuals make choices, so their decision to offend could be seen as one they make of their free will. However some less sympathetic observers have accused Merton of sociological positivism, because he suggests that the behaviour of the individual social actor is to a degree predetermined by structural constraints such as economic conditions. Criminal or delinquent individuals are seen to hold values and beliefs that constrain or determine their behaviour. There is a more general criticism too. Is the value system underpinning the 'American dream' universal? Is it realistic to apply Merton's theory to the UK context, for example (Downes and Rock, 1998)?

Chicago School: crime and the city

This body of work was produced in the 1920s and 1930s by a group of sociologists working at the University of Chicago, including two prominent researchers, Robert Parks and Ernest Burgess (Farris, 1967). These writers focused on the social environment, particularly in urban areas, and on how environmental factors had an influence on crime. Their main contribution was the notion of the 'zone of transition'.

Rather like natural scientists, Parks and Burgess likened the city to a laboratory, although in this instance it was a social laboratory (Parks, Burgess and McKenzie, 1925). Social scientists were able to use different methods of research to study the complex interconnections of city life. The physical environment of the city was described as consisting of a series of zones which reflected the wider social structure. These researchers identified five zones: (1) the central business district; (2) a zone of transition from business to residence; (3) working-class homes; (4) middle-class homes; and (5) commuter residences. Zone 2, the 'zone of transition', was a poor and deprived geographical area where social disorganization was rife, including high concentrations of crime and disorder.

Shaw and McKay (1969) subsequently used quantitative and qualitative research methods to explore the nature of crime in the 'zone of transition'. They used court statistics going back some 30 years to investigate the relationship between crime and changes in the urban environment. The research was complemented by ethnographic research, where the researchers went out onto the streets to observe the behaviour of people in their own environment. On the basis of the data gathered, Shaw and McKay (1969) found that there was social disorganization resulting from a breakdown of formal systems of authority in schools, and in the influence police officers had over people. Most of the disorganization was found amongst young people, and it also appeared that there was a decline in the influence of parental authority over young people, and adult authority more generally. Thus there was a strong link between the social characteristics of the zone of transition and the behaviour of people in those areas.

Some of the insights provided by the Chicago School were put into practice, for example in Shaw and McKay's (1969) Chicago Area Project of 1934. This created opportunities to regenerate socially deprived areas, largely by encouraging local residents to set up their own initiatives to tackle crime and disadvantage: for example recreation programmes, community pride schemes, mediation services and the employment of 'street-credible' workers.

Criminologists in the UK adapted the work of the Chicago School to understand patterns of delinquency and the relationship between behaviour and place in Croydon (Morris, 1957). This research showed that local authorities deliberately housed particular tenants on two run-down council estates in Croydon, and that those estates then became known as criminal areas. In the spirit of the Chicago School the research shows the link between place and criminality.

INTERIM SUMMARY

Some sociological theories recognize the centrality of social structure for understanding and explaining crime. A commonly cited example is Durkheim's notion of anomie. Attention is directed to those social forces that determine or at least influence human behaviour, rather than biological and psychological drives. Sociologists draw on qualitative and quantitative research methods, and their research is informed by an aspiration to inform criminal justice agencies that any response to crime and delinquency needs to look beyond the individual and recognize the influence of social, cultural and economic conditions within society.

The work of the Chicago School proved to be highly influential on the thought of another key criminologist, E. H. Sutherland, and his idea of 'differential association'. Sutherland (1947) draws on learning theory to account for the processes individuals go through in committing a crime. Perhaps the crucial point about differential association theory is that criminal behaviour is seen as a product of general needs and values found in wider society. However, these general needs and values cannot fully explain crime, because the same needs and values also produce non-criminal behaviour. For example, making money may be part of a criminal enterprise but money is made for other reasons that are not criminal.

In more detail, Sutherland argued that offending behaviour is learnt by interacting with other people. His theory is largely based on the communication occurring in the context of intimate personal groups such as the family or peer groups. The processes through which people learn to commit crime are similar to the processes through which they learn about any other type of behaviour. For people to learn how to commit a criminal act they need to be shown the techniques used. However, criminal behaviour is not transmitted in any straightforward way because all individuals have different attitudes and beliefs underpinning their drives. The factors motivating their behaviour and the justifications they use will also vary. Above all each person considers legal codes in light of his or her inner motivations and drives.

A criminal is seen as a person who has a strong belief that the criminal law does not apply to him or her, hence the person's deviance and criminality. In Sutherland's (1947) own words, 'a person becomes delinquent because of an excess of definitions favourable to violation over definitions unfavourable to violation of law'. There is considerable variation in people's different forms of association and involvement in crime, in frequency, duration, priority and intensity. Frequency here is the number of occasions on which a person commits a crime, and duration describes the length of the period a person is involved in crime (perhaps months or years). Priority concerns the importance attached to crime in relation to other types of behaviour, and intensity is all about the strength of feelings associated with crime and the extent to which such feelings take over a person (Sutherland, 1947). Overall, then, Sutherland argues that people learn how to become deviant but they need to define a situation as appropriate for breaking the law.

ANOMIE AND SOCIAL DISORGANIZATION: KEY POINTS

- The notion of anomie has been used to explain crime in contemporary society.
- Merton focuses on the strain experienced by some people if they are not able to satisfy their material aspirations.
- Although Merton emphasizes the centrality of social structure, individual behaviour is not seen as absolutely determined, as individuals have the capacity to adapt in several ways to the external social environment.
- The Chicago School highlights the influence of environmental factors on criminal behaviour. Certain geographical areas are disorganized, and it is in these areas that most crime occurs.

SUBCULTURAL THEORY

In this part:

- the notion of subculture and its utility for explaining crime is explained
- some of the criticisms of this approach are also considered.

Another body of work also published in the mid-twentieth century was subcultural theory. The American influence is also strong here, although it proved to have an influence on thinking in the United Kingdom too.

Subcultural theory is unashamedly sociological in its concern with the question of order, and the means through which societies are organized in structural and individual terms. Like all criminological theory this perspective belongs to a specific period in time, namely the 1940s and 1950s. It is a theory that drew on past theories, and has also informed theories in contemporary society. Full respect is given to the concept of anomie and the argument that inequalities in society produce problems that sometimes generate delinquent solutions, especially among socially deprived groups.

The main contribution of subcultural theory can be summarized as showing that the actions of an offender or delinquent are influenced, albeit not caused, by a belief in an alternative value system to that found in mainstream society.

An influential thinker within the subcultural tradition is Albert K. Cohen, who coined the phrase 'delinquent subculture' (1955). Cohen's contribution encouraged criminologists to look for the conditions or factors accounting for the emergence of new cultural forms. If a group of people are struggling to come to terms with or adjust to pattern values and behaviour, such as conforming to the rules laid down by authority figures like police officers or school teachers, these people interact and together create a different or alternative culture. Cohen argued that that the lower classes rejected dominant middle-class values, largely because that dominant culture was hostile towards them. For example, teachers and police officers may discriminate against and reject lower-class people. There are parallels here with Merton's (1938) notion of 'anomie', but Cohen (1955) preferred the concept of 'status frustration'.

Social groups, often in the form of gangs, were seen as operating collectively and according to different value systems from those shared by most of society. Over time these gangs created a 'reaction formation', in which the attitudes and beliefs of dominant groups offer a collective solution to restricted opportunities. Subcultural theory is different from anomie and conventional strain theory in another respect, because it sees there as being various methods of attaining status. The delinquent subculture is not exclusively concerned with economically motivated behaviour, and members of such gangs could achieve a high status because of aggressive or violent behaviour. In other words, status was attained as a result of a range of actions that were not purely related to profit seeking.

Cloward and Ohlin's (1960) theoretical contribution attempted to combine Merton's adaptation of anomie with Sutherland's (1947) 'differential association' theory. According to these thinkers there are 'push' and 'pull' factors that explain why someone commits a crime. This tension explains why human behaviour changes over time, and also to some extent the transmission of delinquency across the generations. Their main contribution is recognition of the existence of the availability of illegitimate or illegal opportunities (comparable to Merton's legitimate opportunities), which create an 'illegitimate opportunity structure'.

At about the same time, Miller (1958) also discussed the relationship between the lower social classes and delinquent subcultures. He argued that gang membership is synonymous with a culture consisting of six concerns. A defining feature of a delinquent subculture is *trouble*, and gang members should not shy away from this. It is integral to gang life, where non-conformity to dominant middle-class values is highly valued. Gang members need to assert their *toughness* in order to maintain their status amongst peers and to challenge or frighten off those who do not belong to the gang, but especially authority figures like the police. Membership of a gang is also dependent on *smartness*, and an ability to be streetwise, demonstrated by the aptitude of members to think ahead of outsiders. Miller also argued that gang membership was partly inspired by a quest for *excitement*, something that cannot be found in the humdrum and everyday reality of school and low-paid jobs. The people in gangs tend to view their position as an outcome of *fate*, and something over which they have little control. Their social circumstances determine their day-to-day experience and the actions they are able to take to establish control over social world. Although there is a sense that members of the subculture have little influence over their destiny there is also the view that membership gives them *autonomy*, and freedom on the streets from the day-to-day constraints imposed by school, low-paid jobs or jail.

There is clearly a bias in this account towards American society, but British academics have also made a contribution to the subculture literature. Downes (1966), for instance, found that groups of young people saw delinquency as something that happened in their lives, but that it was not a way of life. More than that, Downes did not find any evidence of organized subcultures like those found across the Atlantic. Rather than a 'reaction formation' (Cohen, 1955), the behaviour of young people was about 'dissociation' from middle-class values. As a result of this, the lives of working-class children tended to provide a self-fulfilling prophecy: they accepted their social position, rather than challenging the status quo through the formation of street gangs.

Hargreaves (1967) arrived at a similar conclusion in his work on under-achieving pupils. He found that these pupils tended to adhere to the ideas described by Cohen's (1955) subcultural thesis, but their deviant behaviour was not necessarily criminal. Instead their deviance was directed at the notion of the ideal pupil, demonstrated by their copying, cheating and being rowdy. Hall and Jefferson (1976) also drew on subcultural theory to account for the rise of a 'counter culture' within the middle class, reflected by the hippy and student movements in the late 1960s and early 1970s. These emphasized cultural values that resisted affluence and consumerism. Other youth cultures include teddy boys, mods, rockers, skinheads and punks (Pearson, 1983; Cohen, 1980).

Some criticisms of subcultural theory

A problem with subcultural theories is that they tend to assume that the dominant middle-class culture – from which the subculture deviates – is in actual fact stable and homogeneous. In other words, there is a view that there is a single set of middle-class values which does not change substantially over time, but there is insufficient evidence that this is the case. Also, subcultural theory does not pay sufficient attention to human consciousness and its influence on social action. In other words, there is too much attention on the influence of social structural factors. This is sometimes called sociological determinism, something recognized by Matza (1969), who argued that individual behaviour is neither completely free nor totally determined.

Matza (1969) formulated what is known as an *appreciative criminology*, and is renowned for his concept techniques of neutralization. A key point of this contribution is that the delinquent or criminal is not fundamentally different from the non-criminal or non-delinquent person, so it rejects some of the arguments of subcultural theory. Criminals are not set apart from conformists because of any biological or psychological differences, or because they are weak-willed and susceptible to social pressures. In other words, the delinquent is to all intent and purposes and for the most part likely to behave conventionally. In his study of young people or juveniles Matza argued that most people recognize the rule of law. It is not possible to offer a foolproof and waterproof prediction of which people will commit crime. However, Matza does suggest that young people are more likely to deviate from the norm because of peer pressure. Whilst they may agree deep down with middle-class values it is not 'cool' to show this to their peers. Indeed, like Cohen (1955), Matza (1969) argues that young people in particular (though not exclusively) can be quite fatalistic, and they perceive themselves as being 'objects and effect' rather than 'subject and cause'. In other words, part of the experience of being a young person concerns the denial of full responsibility for your own actions. Because young people are driven by forces beyond their control, or at least the perception that this is so, they drift in and out criminal behaviour.

Matza's (1969) theorization of the causes of crime recognizes that delinquency is simply a status, but it is a status that is not just attached to a person because the person is a role player. People's behaviour may be determined but only up to a point, as they are conscious social actors who make choices. Thus social actors employ techniques of *neutralization*, which are used by people when they break the law. Although lawbreakers believe in the law, from time to time they will conveniently forget this belief so they can carry out a deviant act. After acting in this way they will attempt to justify what they have done.

Matza makes four points. Delinquents will express *guilt* when they have broken the law. They will say how much they *respect* law-abiding people who conform to social norms. They will have clear ideas about the types of person they can legitimately *victimize*. Finally, in essence the delinquent is subject to similar pressures to comply with and obey the rules as the *conformist*. These factors are associated with the techniques of neutralization, of which there are five.

The denial of responsibility is the first neutralization technique. Here offenders say 'It was not my fault', and argue that they offended because of circumstances beyond their control. They were pushed and pulled and could do little to stop themselves. Second, delinquents deny the injury and harm caused by their actions. For example, a shoplifter may justify her actions by saying, 'I stole from the bank or a major retailer because they can afford it. The company is worth billions and they are insured anyway.' Third, the delinquent can deny the victim by claiming that the victim in some way deserved what happened. Fourth, some offenders condemn the condemners by claiming that the authority that is critical of them is as bad as them. The view is that the condemners are hypocritical. Finally, many offenders appeal to higher loyalties. While they may have broken social rules, they argue for instance that 'I had to do it for my mates.'

Numerous criticisms have been directed at Matza's contribution, and there is disagreement amongst criminologists concerning the applicability of his ideas. Hirschi (1969) has called for a further refinement of the idea, by asking whether criminals neutralize their criminality before or after they offend. If it is the former, it questions the utility of Matza's idea. However, this is difficult to prove either way because Matza's work is rather abstract.

SUBCULTURAL THEORY: KEY POINTS

■ Subcultures are the collective adaptations of groups who are excluded from or who do not buy into the values of the dominant cultures in society.

■ Many subcultures are a reaction and solution to the frustrations of everyday life.

■ Subcultural theory is not without its problems, and the concepts of drift and techniques of neutralization have been used to compensate for some of these problems.

RADICAL AND CRITICAL CRIMINOLOGY

Another school of thought looks at the social causes of crime, and this can be found in the work of scholars who were inspired by the ideas of Karl Marx, although Marx himself never really talked about crime. This section:

■ outlines a number of approaches that are indebted to the sociology of Karl Marx

■ considers the relevance of social class for understanding criminal behaviour.

This section introduces the main tenets of early radical and critical criminological perspectives, focusing on theoretical developments occurring throughout the 1960s and 1970s, particularly conflict theory and the 'new criminology', or what would later be known as left idealism (Taylor, Walton and Young, 1973). It is shown that the emergence of this work coincided with political developments in the field of criminal justice policy. At this time criminal justice professionals were losing their faith in the rehabilitative ideal, or the belief that criminals could be reformed. For example, rehabilitation programmes were subjected to critical scrutiny, and it was suggested that 'nothing works' in penal reform, as demonstrated by the numbers of offenders who reoffend after undergoing treatment (Martinson, 1974). At the same time there were calls for decarceration (the release of people from prison) and non-interventionist approaches to crime. The main contribution of radical criminology is that it illustrated how law and order are closely related to power (Chambliss, 1975; Sellin, 1938).

The origins of radical and critical criminology can be traced back to the work of conflict theorists, such as Turk (1969) and Quinney (1977). The radicals were highly critical of positivist accounts of crime. Radical and critical criminologists are indebted to the ideas of Karl Marx (see Chapter 2), especially his argument that capitalist societies are ridden with conflict over issues surrounding ownership and control. Marx's core thesis, as we explained earlier, is that the ruling class own the means of production and are in a constant battle to maintain their status in society. A central argument is that capitalism is *criminogenic*, or is a cause of crime. The ruling class exercises power to maintain and deepen inequality between the main social classes. One method of doing this is the 'process of criminalization' (Turk, 1969), which explains how particular groups are 'labelled' (Becker, 1963, ch. 11) as criminogenic or crime prone. In capitalist societies the legal system acts as a coercive force to maintain social order by criminalizing the behaviour of the working classes. An example of this is the work of Cohen (1979).

In an interesting article, Cohen (1979) concentrates on the gradual changes which transformed the nature of police–community relations in Islington, North London, between the 1870s and 1920s. Policing in the nineteenth century was based on antagonism between bourgeois law and proletarian street cultures, often involving violent confrontations between the police and the policed. After the First World War (1914–18), the nature of this relationship altered as a result of the restructuring of class relations and the labour market, and changing patterns of consumption. These factors led to the creation of a new political economy of policing. One of the emergent trends during this period was a reduction in the level of violence, which was achieved through a process of 'urban pacification'.

Cohen also argues that structural processes led to the gradual disappearance of the street cultures found in the nineteenth century. This was also related to the substitution of the rough lower working class with a skilled aristocracy of labour. In effect, the old working class divided into two: skilled workers who were incorporated into the labour market, and the unskilled and the young, who remained unincorporated into the world of work. Increased economic opportunities and trade union membership coincided with the respectable working classes' acceptance of a police presence in their communities. This happened unevenly and some male youths continued to clash with the police, but this was on a much smaller scale in the 1920s than in the 1870s. This, in part, was also a consequence of changes in the pattern of policing.

To expand on an issue covered in Chapter 6, the police perform a combination of 'expressive' and 'repressive' roles. On the one hand, they provide community and welfare services, and on the other hand, they are law enforcers. The repressive role is more formalized, because as an arm of the state apparatus the police can legitimately use force. These sometimes interlocking and sometimes conflicting functions generate friction. To illustrate this, Cohen describes how police officers are expected to enforce the law without favouring one group above another, exactly in the same way as the judiciary. However, if the principles underlying formal legal rationality are treated as statutory norms and applied as rigidly on the streets as they are in the courts, there would be mass arrests. Thus, to minimize the obvious difficulties that would arise if every law were enforced, including the threat to public order, police officers exercise discretion. In Cohen's words:

> While statutory norms were still routinely enforced in the centre, in the new heartlands of the working class city they were increasingly used only as an emergency measure, to justify the last resort of physical repression. In their place, a system of informal, tacitly negotiated and particularist definitions of public order were evolved which accommodated certain working class usage of social space and time, and outlawed others.
>
> (Cohen, 1979: 131)

The main issue, therefore, is the effect of changes to the labour market on working-class communities, particularly the extent to which the divide between the 'rough' and 'respectable' is forged. The respectable had a stake in society, whereas the 'rough' did not. However, the police managed to negotiate a notion of 'public propriety' which was acceptable to the 'respectable' majority.

Jefferson (1990) draws on Cohen's theoretical arguments, and applies these to explain the 'hegemonic crisis' that followed the economic recession of the mid to late 1980s. The restructuring of the labour force led to the creation of 'the new lumpen'. At the same time police powers were being increased and the service was increasingly unaccountable to the public it served. Moreover paramilitarism led the police to exercise their legitimate use of force to maintain public order. Jefferson argued that this is especially so in areas:

> In which sections of male, especially male, especially black youth and militant dissidents of all kinds – pickets, demonstrators, etc. – figure prominently with whom the preferred negotiated approach – the 'unwritten system of tacit negotiation' – has never been properly established or has broken down. This breakdown may be fairly temporary, in the case of say a particular industrial dispute, or, in the case of some highly alienated groups – Afro-Caribbean youths, for example – apparently irrevocable.
>
> (Jefferson, 1990: 41)

It should be apparent that so far most attention has been directed at the poorest groups in society. Radicals also discuss the 'crimes of the powerful'. For example, 'left idealists' have argued that the activities of criminal justice agencies, such as the police, tend to reflect the interests of the state and ruling class. For this reason the police target working-class communities and street crime. In doing this, writers such as Sutherland (1938) suggested that the authorities were neglecting the problem of 'white-collar crime', a category of offences committed overwhelmingly by professionals at work, such as fraud. In addition there was 'corporate crime', or those offences committed by corporations or big businesses. Crimes such as embezzlement and corporate neglect are examples of offences that are potentially very harmful and damaging, and yet largely ignored by the state (Box, 1983).

RADICAL AND CRITICAL CRIMINOLOGY: KEY POINTS

■ In contrast to structural functionalists such as Durkheim and Parsons, radical and critical criminologists contend that society is made up of different social classes that are in conflict with each other.

■ Rather than concentrating on criminal behaviour there is an attempt to examine the 'process of criminalization', which may be driven by the mass media, which influences public perceptions of crime.

LEFT REALISM

In this section:

■ the origins and main features of left realism are outlined

■ this holistic theoretical approach is shown to bring together in a single account the victim and offender with the reaction of the state and wider community.

This section outlines a significant and ongoing development in criminological theory, beginning in the 1970s: in particular, the movement from left idealist to left realist criminology. Left idealism was discussed above, but left realism is an integrated theoretical perspective comprising the concepts of relative deprivation, marginalization and subculture. Its major contribution is the 'square of crime', a model used to explain the causes of crime with reference to the state, offender, society and victim (Young, 1992, 1999).

There are two things to note about the relationship between left idealism and left realism. First, left idealism preceded left realism: the former was developed in the 1970s and the latter in the mid-1980s. Second, although traces of the former remain in the latter, it offers a more sophisticated and rounded explanation of crime.

Left idealism focused primarily on the capitalist system of production, in particular its criminogenic properties and qualities. Following the logic of other Marxist arguments, the law and legal system is regarded as a coercive instrument that maintains the prevailing social order, which is achieved mainly by criminalizing the working class and their culture. Left idealism argues that the only solution to crime is to overthrow the capitalist system and create a socialist society where fairness and justice replace greed and individualized competition (Taylor, Walton and Young, 1973).

Just over ten years later, left realism largely replaced left idealism (Young, 1992; Lea and Young, 1984, 1993). Left realism is a rich and complex body of work but there are three main contributions.

First, left idealists argued that the oppressed working classes engaged in crime as a form of rebellion and also to redistribute capital by stealing from the upper and middle classes. Lea and Young (1984, 1993) argued that their earlier explanation had romanticized working-class crime because the poor did not steal from the rich, like Robin Hood did, to distribute their stolen goods to poor communities. Instead, most crime was intra-class, meaning that the poor stole from other poor people amongst the working classes.

Second, left realism was developed to offer a less simplistic explanation of crime. Left idealism had highlighted the law and criminal justice system as oppressive forces stigmatizing and labelling the working class as criminal. In short, the emphasis was on the state and its capacity to criminalize powerless groups. Left realists argued that such an account neglected the significance of victims, and by looking exclusively at the reaction to crime paid insufficient attention to the action or the crime itself.

Third, left realism emerged because of wider changes in society, especially in the political and economic culture. In 1979 there was a general election, which led to a Conservative government under the leadership of Margaret Thatcher. There was nothing unusual about this because the Conservative Party had more or less dominated party politics for most of the twentieth century. However, the 1979 general election result stands out from many others as far criminologists are concerned because for the first time in a British election campaign, law and order was prioritized as a number one issue. The Conservatives at that time detected widespread and deep-seated anxieties about crime and disorder, and showed that crime blighted the lives of all, but especially the working classes. The Conservatives alleged that Labour was not taking crime seriously.

In response to these three factors some left-idealist criminologists, mainly those who were generally supporters of the Labour Party, revisited their ideas, possibly because they acknowledged the Conservatives had a point. More than that, the

Conservative government adopted the main tenets of a criminological perspective known as 'right realism' (Wilson, 1983), which (as was shown in Chapter 11) held individuals to be responsible for crime.

The right-realist explanation of crime informed policy makers and researchers at the Home Office, where in the 1980s there was little interest in identifying factors such as poverty as a possible cause of crime. This would have contradicted government policy. Rather than looking at poverty and inequality, attention was directed at reducing opportunities for crime through measures such as situational crime prevention (see Chapter 10). Young was critical of this approach to criminology, and labelled it pejoratively as 'administrative criminology' (Young, 1999).

Left realism stands in stark contrast to many earlier theories of crime because it aspires to integrate several theoretical explanations. There are three main explanations, involving 'relative deprivation', 'marginalization' and 'subculture' (Lea and Young, 1984, 1993). Each of these is examined in turn.

What is relative deprivation? Taking the second, and key, word, deprivation refers to the lack of something such as income or a particular commodity. It has been established, for example, that if people do not have enough money to buy food they are more likely to steal to ensure their survival. Obviously being denied of material goods does not automatically lead to a person committing crime, but it is arguably much more likely. 'Relative deprivation' is a slightly more complicated idea, and recognizes that in modern British society absolute deprivation is relatively rare, but despite this crime rates are still high. If one of the main causes of crime is less evident, why do so many individuals commit crime? Relative deprivation is all about perceptions and expectations. There are some connections here with Merton's (1938) 'strain theory'. For example, in a consumer society there are certain goods or products desired by many people, including those who can legitimately purchase a commodity and those who cannot. Even if people cannot afford a product it does not follow that they will not desire it or expect to own it. Some individuals still consider what they cannot expect to rightfully own to in some way 'belong' to them, and therefore they obtain it illegally by stealing it. Thus there is no physical need to be satisfied, but rather an emotional or psychological desire.

'Marginalization' is another key concept. A clue to the meaning of this idea can be found in the prefix 'margin'. If you open a notepad on the left-hand side of the page there is a margin removed from the main body of the page. In society there are individuals and groups who do not fit into mainstream society and who are pushed into the margins. This marginalization may be economic, political or social. To be economically marginal means that people are either on the edge of the labour market or in a low-paid job, and are not able to participate as fully in everyday social life as those people in secure and adequately paid occupations. Political marginality occurs when people do not vote, either because they are denied the right to vote (such as young people under the age of 18 and prisoners) or they refuse to vote because they feel the political parties do not represent their interests (as do many members of ethnic minorities and the poor). Social marginalization normally results from the two types mentioned previously, where people are not able to participate in those activities enjoyed by most people.

The third idea, subculture, also links with relative deprivation and marginalization. A subculture is a smaller culture within the main culture. Culture is a big idea, and there is a lack of agreement about what counts as culture, but for our purposes it can be defined as a way of life informed by a set of attitudes, beliefs and values. For instance, there is a specifically English culture, and while it is not feasible to explain what it consists of here, we can all appreciate that there are certain things the English do and believe that the French or Australians do not.

Rightly or wrongly there are certain traits typically associated with particular national cultures. A subculture is a part of a main culture, but no more than a single element within it. In criminology the subcultures that receive particular attention are deviant groups who either commit crimes, or are thought to do so. In the 1970s it was the mods and rockers (Cohen, 1980), in the 1980s it was football hooliganism (Armstrong, 1998), and today it is the antisocial behaviour of the 'yob culture' intertwined with the so-called 'hoodies' and 'chavs' (Cook, 2006). In contemporary societies there are many subcultures, and there is a tendency for street styles from the United States to be adopted and adapted on the streets of the British towns and cities. It should be noted that not all subcultures are criminogenic, but a significant number are. They are, by definition, deviant from the parent or host culture.

The most significant and enduring contribution made by left realists is the 'square of crime'. At each corner of this box are four interrelated factors: the state, society, the offender and the victim.

The state

The structure of the state was identified in Chapter 5. The most important components in the square of crime are the criminal justice agencies and the political system. The police, the courts, prison and probation services are all formal agencies that have prime responsibility for identifying and responding to crime and criminality. Each of these agencies all plays a part in labelling individuals and groups as offenders. Increasingly each of these agencies, with the exception of the prison service, has to respond directly to the needs of victims of crime.

The offender

This part of the square of crime makes a distinction between two types of offender, individuals and corporations. Thus left realism does not lose sight of left idealism and its interest in corporate and white-collar crime, but the individual criminal, who is typically a working-class male, is central too. This corner of the square is occupied by an individual who is identified as a criminal, or engaging in behaviour recognized and classified as criminal. Any examination of the offender asks fundamental questions about crime and the criminal: who, what, why and when?

Society

The position of the state is pivotal in relation to the offender because it has the formal powers to deal with all aspects of criminality. Society is also important in several ways. First, crime occurs in a given social context, and social circumstances are important for finding out the causes and consequences of crime. Second, society is also a mechanism of control. In contrast to the state this control is informal, and is provided generally through what is called civil society, which consists of structures such as the family, peer groups and youth clubs. The criminal justice system is there as a deterrent for would-be criminals, but for it to work effectively it is necessary for social networks to back up wider social values and respect for the rule of law.

Victims

Rather like the left-realist view of the offender, this theory sees the victim as either an individual or a group. Basically, a victim is a person or group of people experiencing the harm caused by crime or criminality. There is also attention given to the many factors that either encourage or prevent victimization. An important legacy of left realism is that considerable attention is given to the vulnerability of the victim.

The square of crime therefore offers a multi-dimensional image of crime, including its many causes and consequences. It is in essence a framework for understanding crime based on an appreciation of complex social relationships. In contrast to previous theories the focus is much broader and holistic in its attempt to provide a more balanced explanation of crime and criminality. It is a dynamic model looking at the interplay between:

- the state and society
- the state and the offender
- the victim and the offender
- the offender and society.

The state and society

The state is clearly part of the society, but for left realists the two are separate in the sense that the state is a formalized and bureaucratic system with the legitimate power to coerce and restrict the liberty of lawbreakers if it is thought necessary. In most democratic societies the state does not have the capacity to exercise these powers arbitrarily and without checks and balances, such as the legal system. However, its influence is such that it does have a monopoly of the powers of criminal justice agencies. Recognition of these powers is never taken for granted, though, and the criminal justice system is situated in a social context. Society needs to give its consent to the activities of the state and the rule of law, to ensure their legitimacy. More importantly, though, the state cannot take on board absolute responsibility for dealing with offenders and victimization. It is necessary for social institutions in civil society, especially schools and families, to prevent crime through socializing and educating young people. Indeed since the Crime and Disorder Act (CDA) (1998) (see Chapter 10) there has been a requirement for all the main social institutions, even those that do not belong in the criminal justice system, to be actively engaged in crime reduction.

The state and the offender

This social relationship concerns the relationship between individual offenders and the state at all stages of the criminal justice process. While the state has several significant powers, such as the powers to make an arrest, prosecute, sentence and punish an individual, the state must also respect certain rights and safeguards. For example, as was shown in Chapter 5, the police cannot arrest an individual without good reason. Throughout the prosecution and sentencing process the state requires the Crown Prosecution Service (CPS) and courts to produce robust evidence and to prove beyond all reasonable doubt the guilt of the accused. When convicted offenders are punished they experience many deprivations, such as loss of or limits to their freedom, but prison officers cannot abuse their powers by torturing inmates, however heinous the crime they may have committed. The state is also required to protect some offenders, such as convicted sex offenders, from vigilantism.

The victim and the offender

Most criminological theories have concentrated more or less exclusively on the offender without considering the interaction with the victim. By focusing on the interplay between these two actors it is possible to obtain a fuller and more detailed picture of the causal and motivational factors behind offending behaviour in relation to different types of victim. The circumstances and processes will vary from crime to crime and person to person. In some instances the offender and victim will come into contact in a public space (as in a street robbery) and in others in a private setting (as with domestic violence). The demographic characteristics of the offender and victim may also be significant. At all times, though, the victim is more vulnerable than the offender is because the victim lacks formal rights within the criminal justice system.

The offender and society

All offenders belong to society, however unpopular their behaviour, but there are different ways of thinking about this interplay. Some critical and radical criminologists such as left idealists perceive offenders to be the victims of their social background and experiences, such as discrimination in the labour market, which are seen to account for, if not justify, their involvement in crime. For such thinkers punitive attitudes held by wider society do little more than stigmatize and demonize offenders, culminating in further marginalization and perversely, more offending. Other commentators hold the view that offending behaviour victimizes wider society by increasing levels of fear and anxiety. Left realists advise that offenders can never be considered separately from the social context they inhabit, as crime relates not only to what the offender does – the action – but also to how it is perceived by others – the reaction.

The contribution of left realism

What kind of contribution has left realism made to criminological theory? Perhaps one of its most salient contributions is that it offers a dose of realism to theorizing, and crucially for developing criminal justice policies. It served as a constructive response to right realism and its domineering influence in policy-making circles throughout the 1980s. Another practical benefit resulting from the intervention of left realism is that these commentators were among the earliest critics of the British Crime Survey, which certainly in its early days was an example *par excellence* of 'administrative criminology'. In Chapter 3 the notion of the 'statistically average victim' was mentioned. Left idealists argued that Home Office attempts to dismiss or assuage public anxieties about crime by presenting figures to downplay the risk of victimization were seen to be misleading if crime surveys were undertaken locally, rather than being based on a sample selected from the entirety of England and Wales. For example, the Islington Crime Survey (Jones, Maclean and Young, 1986) showed that some groups presented as relatively immune from crime in the BCS were in fact vulnerable in some deprived areas at a local level. Women and elderly people are two examples. Local crime surveys informed policing practice and crime prevention policy in local communities, and also offered crucial insights for feminist criminologists (see Chapter 13).

Left realism also had a bearing on the criminal justice policy developed by New Labour when it was in opposition during the final years of Conservative rule, and also when it was elected to power in 1997. Left realism provided New Labour politicians with a conceptual framework for linking crime to social exclusion, illustrated clearly by Tony Blair's statement 'tough on crime, tough on the causes of crime', which became manifest in the multi-agency and joined-up working enshrined in the CDA (1998). The recognition of the necessity for localized governance was also a legacy of left realism.

LEFT REALISM: KEY POINTS

- This complex theoretical framework has had a profound influence on criminological theory as well as government policy.
- Left realism recognizes the reality of crime and the need for radical solutions to address crime and its causes, hence Tony Blair's phrase 'tough on crime, tough on the causes of crime'.
- Left realism provides a multi-dimensional framework for understanding crime, which focuses on the interactions between the offender, the victim, the state and wider society.

CONCLUSION

The theoretical contributions in this chapter have continued to contemplate the individual offender, but in contrast with Chapter 11 the emphasis has shifted to the external influences on human behaviour. Early criminological theories illustrated the ways in which structural factors either determine or have an influence on human behaviour. It has been found that an over-reliance on macro-level structures, especially by Marxist criminologists, is inadequate, and human agency has been recognized, principally in the form of subcultures.

The final section of this chapter moved on to consider left realism. This has proven to be an influential approach mainly because it synthesizes different elements of criminological theory to describe the relationship between the offender, the victim, the criminal justice system and wider society. Although this perspective has advanced criminological thought, and has had an impact on criminal justice policy and practice, some critics have argued that it has not done enough to accommodate the differential experiences of women and minority ethnic groups. The following chapter takes on board these criticisms, and reviews some ideas associated with deconstructive approaches.

FURTHER READING

The best place to start is chapters 7, 10 and 16 especially of R. Hopkins Burke, *An Introduction to Criminological Theory* (Cullompton: Willan, 2005). Also read the more demanding account in R. Rock, 'Sociological theories of crime', in M. Maguire, R. Morgan and R. Reiner (eds), *The Oxford Handbook of Criminology* (Oxford: Oxford University Press, 2002).

The Sage Dictionary of Criminology, edited by E. McLaughlin and J. Muncie (2nd edn) (London: Sage, 2006) provides concise summaries of the main theories covered in this chapter. These are not sufficient by themselves but each entry will get you started. Use the references at the end of each entry to deepen and broaden your knowledge and understanding.

STUDY QUESTIONS

1. Define anomie, and consider the use of Merton's adaptations (such as ritualism and innovation) for explaining both property and violent crimes.
2. Discuss the potential relevance of subculture for explaining crime in contemporary society.
3. Describe the main points of Matza's neutralization techniques.
4. Outline the main points of radical accounts of the class dimensions of crime and crime control.
5. Write down the main similarities between the ideas of strain theory and relative deprivation.
6. What is left realism, and what does it tell students about the:
   a) state?
   b) offender?
   c) society?
   d) victim?
7. Compare and contrast the main features of criminological theories that focus on individual and social influences on criminal behaviour.

13 Theories of Crime III: Critical and Deconstructive Perspectives

OVERVIEW

This chapter aims to provide:

- a short account of the contribution made by scholars who are critical of the criminological theories outlined in Chapters 11 and 12
- illustrations of a range of critical accounts
- an appreciation of theorizations of gender, focusing on the impact of feminist and masculinist perspectives on criminality
- an appreciation of theoretical works focusing on race and racism
- a discussion of postmodernity and its significance for understanding crime control, with a particular emphasis on the concepts of risk and surveillance.

INTRODUCTION

This chapter assesses the contribution of the criminologies of modernity discussed in Chapters 11 and 12 in light of critical and deconstructive approaches to the study of crime. Since the late 1970s many scholars have subjected the criminological literature to extensive criticisms, including feminist, anti-racist, poststructuralist and postmodern perspectives. This rich, diverse and complex literature does not altogether jettison the more traditional concerns of criminological theory, but pushes to the forefront of analysis issues such as discourse, surveyance and risk.

Thus far in this part of the text the focus has been on what are essentially sociological, and to some extent, psychological explanations of crime and disorder. Many of the assumptions made about society and human beings in these approaches are underpinned by the values of the Enlightenment and the project of modernity. In other words, accounts of criminal behaviour are based on a set of core ideas and principles developed throughout the eighteenth and nineteenth centuries. Moving into the twentieth century the contributions outlined in Chapters 11 and 12 remained influential, and much of this work was inspired by the so-called 'founding fathers' of social science, Durkheim, Marx and Weber. For psychology the key figure is Freud. Social and human science, including criminological theory, is still coming to terms with the ideas of these seminal thinkers. Their thinking influences all of the theoretical explanations of crime examined thus far, either directly or indirectly.

In the latter half of the twentieth century many of these approaches, especially the criminological theories covered in Chapter 12, were subjected to several criticisms by critical and deconstructive approaches. Critical perspectives have focused on the issue of power, in particular the use of power by dominant social groups to subjugate and marginalize other communities, including women and minority ethnic groups. Deconstructive approaches require students to question everything that that they might take for granted in criminological theory. Accordingly, terms such as 'crime', 'the law', 'the offender' and 'victim' are all treated as problematic. Likewise the concept of 'justice' is treated as a problem. Basically, as the word deconstruction implies, it is necessary to take apart and unpack such ideas, especially by focusing on the discourse, or words and language, used to explain criminal behaviour and its control.

The rest of this chapter is split into four parts:

- The contribution of feminism to criminological theory is considered.
- Theories that focus on the relationship between masculinities and crime are outlined.
- The contribution of anti-racist writers who have highlighted the fundamentally flawed nature of mainstream theories is also discussed.
- Some deconstructive approaches including postmodernism and poststructuralism are introduced.

FEMINIST CONTRIBUTIONS TO CRIMINOLOGY

In this section:

- the contribution of feminism to criminological theory is discussed
- some of the applications of feminist theory to criminal justice policy and practice are highlighted.

A student of criminology in the twenty-first century is almost certain to encounter the ideas of feminist scholars at some stage of their studies, although it is possible that a minority of teachers will treat feminism only as an add-on at the end of core modules. Although feminism is still relatively peripheral in the criminologies of modernity, the situation now is much better than it was in the early 1960s when feminism was virtually unheard of in most criminological circles. Although the situation improved somewhat from the late 1960s onwards (Heidensohn, 1968), mainstream criminology is still frequently characterized as 'malestream' criminology (Cain, 1990).

The word 'feminism' is arguably misleading because there is not a single feminist approach, but rather a diversity of perspectives. This diversity has developed gradually since the late eighteenth century, following the publication of *A Vindication of the Rights of Woman* by Mary Wollstonecraft (Wollstonecraft and Mill, 1929). Over the last 220 years or so feminist thinking has had a profound influence on the social sciences and criminology, although its influence on the latter did not occur until the final third of the twentieth century. Accordingly we shall:

- briefly trace the origins of feminism, highlighting some of its different perspectives and highlighting its relevance to the study of crime
- outline a selection of feminist critiques of criminological theory
- assess the impact of these critiques on contemporary understanding of the operations of criminal justice.

A brief history of feminism – what about crime?

The work of Wollstonecraft (Wollstonecraft and Mill, 1929) is of central importance to the human sciences because she made explicit the issue of sex and gender, drawing attention to the differential treatment of men and women, and particularly the discrimination women experienced at the hands of men. This work made an invaluable contribution to the 'first wave' of feminism, or what was eventually called liberal feminism, in the early twentieth century. The causal factors underlying the inequitable status of men and women were not located in biological differences but in social relations. Gender differences were seen to be explicable in terms of the different social roles performed by men and women, and it was claimed that women were denied certain resources and experiences enjoyed by men. Accordingly, inequalities and discrimination could be addressed through social reform, and liberal feminists have focused their attention on achieving change through legislative change and education.

The overarching aim has been to equalize opportunities for men and women in all areas of social life, especially in the world of work but in other areas too. For example, the Sex Discrimination Act (1976) was introduced to outlaw discrimination. Basically liberal feminists have attempted to reform society so that discrimination against women and the lack of equality between men and women is reduced. The positive impact of liberal feminism on social relations between men and women cannot be denied, including the sphere of criminal justice, as is evidenced by the higher numbers of female police officers and changes in policies regarding male sexual violence (see Chapter 6).

However, the second wave of feminism – commencing in the late 1960s and gaining momentum throughout the 1970s onwards – questioned the essentially reformist agenda of the first wave. This so-called second wave comprised many voices saying different things about the experiences of women, but they shared at least three features in common.

■ They were united in the view that liberal feminism was not radical enough, in either theoretical or practical terms. For example, how could the persistence of rape and the flawed police response be explained?

■ Writers in this wave also made problematic the male-centredness of the social sciences (for instance, why did criminology focus mainly on men?).

■ Most crucially, they explained differences between men and women in terms of power relations (so the question is, why do men dominate society?).
(Daly, 1998)

There were differences of emphasis too, reflected by the emergence of distinctive although sometimes overlapping feminist perspectives, including:

■ radical feminism
■ Marxist and socialist feminism
■ anti-racist feminism.

It is not possible to do justice here to the subtle differences between these perspectives, and only the key points are discussed.

Radical feminism parted company with the first wave by arguing that women were oppressed by a system known as patriarchy, or the 'rule of the fathers'. Men are the dominant sex and male power is exercised to oppress women. For example, the law and the criminal justice system work in such as way that women are fundamentally disadvantaged. The law is man-made and written to reflect male interests and culture (Smart, 1977). The effect is that women are oppressed and controlled by men in both the public sphere (such as the law, the state, culture) and the private sphere (such as the family, home and sexuality). In criminology the focus has tended to be on violence against women, especially sexualized violence (Radford, Friedberg and Harne, 2000; Hester, Kelly and Radford, 1996; Brownmiller, 1975), an area where the law was felt to be inadequate. Radical feminists are not just preoccupied with ideas, and they have engaged in action to address male oppression, illustrated by their creation of Women's Aid and the Rape Crisis Federation. This point is expanded later on in this section of the chapter.

Other feminist perspectives, such as *Marxist* and *socialist feminism*, accept to varying degrees that patriarchy is still influential but they place much more emphasis on social class and economic influences on gender relations. In short, adherents to Marxist and socialist approaches focus their energies on the sexual division of labour and the competitiveness of the capitalist system of production. Women are oppressed by men within the family, for example, but this as essentially an effect of capitalism rather than the malevolence of male power. For traditional Marxists the solution to this state of affairs is social revolution bringing about a communist society. However, socialist feminists have argued that the working class and labour movements have built into them male interests which operate at the expense of female concerns, so women are oppressed as a result of capitalism and class relations as well as by men or through patriarchy.

As well as considering sex and class, Black or *anti-racist* feminist writers have argued that Black and other minority ethnic women are oppressed on the grounds of their race. Consequently Black women may be oppressed by White women, as well as by patriarchal and class-based social structures. The result is that there are hierarchies of oppression arising from the interplay or intersection of gender, class and race (Daly, 1998; Daly and Maher, 1998). An appreciation of race underpins the work reviewed in Chapter 8, where the experience of minority ethnic women in prison is touched upon.

A selection of feminist critiques of criminology

There are many different feminist theories, and a few examples of their relevance to criminological theory have been given, but these illustrations need expanding. Although the origins of feminist social science can be traced back to the early twentieth century it took much longer for the discipline of criminology to take this on board, and it was not until the late 1960s that a few lone highly critical voices were audible (Heidensohn, 1968).

At various stages in this book, especially in Chapter 2, it has been shown quite clearly that most offenders are male and that masculinity is probably the best indicator of criminality. Women commit less crime than men and also commit fewer serious offences. Moreover, females generally 'grow out' of offending earlier than their male counterparts, and their criminal careers, if they have them at all, are shorter. Significantly, when females do offend, such as in girl gangs, while there are differences female offenders do share some things in common with their male counterparts (Burman, Batchelor and Brown, 2001).

However, before the arrival of feminist critiques the focus on male criminality was treated as unproblematic, and the differential offending of women was not acknowledged, let alone investigated. Back in the late 1950s Wootton (1959: 32) commented on the fact that women seldom offend, observing that criminologists chose to ignore this simple fact. She added that the neglect of this issue was surprising because the criminal justice system would be much smaller and the 'prisons empty' if males acted more like females.

Thus it would appear that that the relatively small number of female offenders was seen as a sufficient justification for their omission and neglect. Feminist criminologists have not attempted to turn this fact on its head, but rather have tried to question the tendency of criminology to be 'gender-blind' (Walklate, 2004). More crucially, Smart (1977) has argued that criminology has not only failed to look at women, but when it does women are treated stereotypically.

The gender-blindness of criminology has a long history, traceable back to the early days of the discipline. Positivist criminology tacitly accepted that the offender was male, but some criminologists did explore female offending. Those who did regarded the female offender as someone who was abnormal and acting against expected types of behaviour. Moreover, as pointed out in Chapter 7, women who commit crime are perceived to be 'doubly deviant'. Biological positivists, introduced in Chapter 11, maintain that the lower rate of female offending can be attributed to their biological inferiority, especially in their mental capacities. Females were less inclined to become involved in crime because of their lower intelligence and lack of passion.

The most notable contribution is that of Lombroso and Ferrero (1895/2004). This research, drawing on Darwinian evolutionary science, was conducted in the last decade of the nineteenth century, and based on visits to police stations, prisons and asylums. The researchers compiled a record of the physical features and sexual behaviour of female criminals, concluding that the female offender is more dangerous and cunning than the male offender. In addition they suggest that 'as a double exception the criminal woman is consequently a monster' (Lombroso and Ferrero, 1895/2004), which had the effect of dehumanizing those women who commit crime.

Similar themes were taken up by Pollak (1950) in his positivistic analysis of the factors driving women to commit crime. Pollak talked about female offending behaviour that was 'hidden', arguing that women are inherently deceitful, a claim supported by their proclivity to commit undetectable crimes. He argued that women were as likely as men to commit crime but they committed different types of crime. The crimes women committed were related to their social role, which at the time he was writing was mainly confined to the domestic setting and their caring role as wife and mother. The offences they committed were made possible by this role but also concealed by it, hence the oft-cited example of women poisoning their husbands.

Pollak (1950) also widened his discussion to explore the treatment of women in the criminal justice system. It was suggested that because of their deceitful nature women were able to persuade police officers and court officials that they were passive and law-abiding. As a result criminal justice professionals adopted 'chivalrous' attitudes to protect women from the punitiveness of the system, resulting in more lenient treatment. The result of this is that women were treated less harshly even though in practice their criminality probably deserved harsher treatment.

Sociological positivists also failed to address female crime. For example, Merton's (1938) adaptation of Durkheim's theory of anomie does not address women's offending. Merton's elaboration of anomie does not mention women, and he does not provide evidence to back up the claim that all women share the goal of monetary success, and if they do that their adaptations are the same as or similar to those of men. Subcultural theories also have nothing or very little to say about female offending, indicating that the main concern for women is with interpersonal relationships. As far as differential association theory goes, women have less contact with pro-criminal influences.

Heidensohn (2002) has shown that control theory may explain the relative rarity of female offending because of men's and women's different degrees of attachment, involvement, commitment and belief (Hirschi, 1969). Heidensohn (2002) shows how these are related to the different roles men and women are socialized into, especially the extent to which women are constrained by the domestic role, as wives and mothers for example. In this setting they are expected to carry out certain control functions (such as disciplining children), although this type of work is largely done on behalf of men. Many married women are also confined to the private sphere, where they become isolated and alienated from the public sphere of the workplace. If they enter the world of work, male power is also evident there. The outcome of this is that women are controlled by their roles and their interactions with men to the extent that they have little time and space to engage in crime.

On the whole, traditional criminological theories say very little about women and girls, and to all intents and purposes they are invisible. Feminists have exposed the male-centredness of theoretical criminology, which in itself is a major contribution. Most significantly, as is made clear in the next subsection, feminist theory or theories have brought about changes in criminal justice policy and practice. However, some feminist writers have questioned the need for women to become involved in criminology.

The impact of feminist critiques on criminal justice

Some feminists have attempted to develop a theory of female offending, most notably Adler (1975), who argued that feminism has emancipated women from the oppressiveness of male-dominated power structures and that in consequence they have more freedom to offend (Chesney-Lind and Pasko, 2004). However, the evidence reviewed in Chapters 2 and 7 suggests that female offending has not increased significantly relative to male offending.

Given that crime is essentially a male activity, and the intellectual problems associated with the discipline of criminology, there is a view that there is no such entity as a distinctive feminist criminological theory. Developing one is made more difficult by the diversity of perspectives or feminist theories, and the relative significance these theories attach to the Marxist category of class and the concept of race. It should also be noted that Carol Smart (1990) has more recently argued that it is not necessary to create a feminist criminology, and that feminists have nothing to gain from criminology. In her view, criminology is a positivistic enterprise concerned with responding to the research agendas of various governments, who give little or no attention to the theoretical insights produced by criminologists. Furthermore, Smart claims feminists have other more interesting and important tasks ahead of them than engaging with criminology.

In spite of Smart's persuasive argument, other feminists have persevered with criminology to consider the diverse experiences of women as offenders and practitioners. Carlen (1989, 2002c), for example, has shown the relationship between the stereotypes produced by the powerful about female offending behaviour. This work can be used to show how the state and criminal justice system can marginalize and demonize female offenders without looking at the socioeconomic circumstances influencing their criminal behaviour.

Other research has focused on the treatment of women throughout the criminal justice system. Chapters 7 and 8 demonstrated some of the influences that have a bearing on the sentencing of women, and the markedly different experiences of women in prison. Feminist theory underpins much of the work, highlighting the lack of an appreciation of the specific factors affecting females in general and female offenders in particular.

Some feminist work has also exposed the difficulties faced by female victims of sexual violence when they enter the courtroom to testify against the person who assaulted them. It has been shown that some women face 'secondary victimization' when they are cross-examined by the defence, especially when the character and sexual history of the victim is discussed as a mitigating factor for the defence (Zedner, 2002; Spalek, 2006).

There is also a body of literature pioneered by Heidensohn and Brown (Heidensohn, 2003; Brown and Heidensohn, 2000), who have drawn attention to the complex ways in which police work is gendered. Although there are more policewomen now than ever before, women police officers continue to experience structurally generated discrimination and disadvantage in an organization where the culture is influenced to a significant degree by masculine ideals and values. This has been most apparent when looking at women officers and their career progression. Silvestri (2003), for example, provides a detailed account of gender and police leadership, and how female police leaders and managers behave differently to women officers, in comparison with how female officers are treated by male officers amongst the junior ranks. Her work also explains how senior officers are able to overcome some of the barriers put in place by male officers. Although some inroads have been made through the agency of female police officers, there is still powerful structural constraint – especially a sexist police culture – inhibiting career progression.

FEMINIST CONTRIBUTIONS TO CRIMINOLOGY: KEY POINTS

- ■ Traditional criminological theory has taken it for granted that 'the offender' is male. Female offenders are regarded as abnormal and 'doubly deviant'.
- ■ Feminist theories – there is more than one – have critiqued the male-centredness of criminological theory and highlighted the structured inequalities between men and women.
- ■ Some feminists have argued that feminist criminology should be abandoned and that the inclusion of a feminist perspective is not particularly useful.
- ■ Feminist theory is not armchair theorizing and has been of practical use to improve the lives of women.

MEN, MASCULINITIES AND CRIME

This section:

- ■ explains the emergence of criminological theory focusing on men and masculinity
- ■ considers the impact of the second wave of feminism on understanding the involvement of men in crime
- ■ focuses in depth on the seminal work of Connell and his concept of gender relations
- ■ describes some attempts to apply Connell's ideas to explain crime.

It is quite clear then that men, or to be more accurate males, are responsible for the bulk of offending behaviour. As well as their committing quantitatively more offences, the evidence, however limited it may be, shows that there are qualitative variations in the types of offence men and women commit. Male violence, for example, manifests itself in many different forms, including warfare between nation states and power blocs, such as the US/UK alliance on a global stage (Cohen, 2000), corporate crime (Beirne and Messerschmidt (2005) and the turf wars fought on the streets of ethnically divided communities. Men also occupy a dominant position in relation to women, evidenced by the extent and prevalence of domestic violence and rape. It has also been emphasized that these statistical facts have not been adequately explained by many criminologists. The feminist critique of criminological theory rehearsed above has pointed out that implicitly 'malestream' theorizations of offending behaviour are if not fundamentally flawed, at least deeply problematic.

Some male criminologists have taken on board the 'transgression of criminology' by feminist scholars (Cain, 1990), as well as the emergence of empirical evidence exposing men's participation in the subordination and exploitation of women in interpersonal and sexual relationships.

Of particular relevance to this section are a group of male writers who are coming to terms with the insightful contribution of various 'second-wave' feminists to criminology. As well as feminism there is the influence of a small but growing body of work that focuses explicitly on men, and masculinity or masculinities. The scholarly outputs of men writing about the criminality of men fall into two broad categories, the sociological and psychological. Two things need saying about these perspectives. First, at least in criminological circles, the two are not mutually exclusive and there is some articulation between them, and second, more has been written from a sociological perspective, largely because criminology, or at least the way it is studied in Britain, is more sociological in its conceptual and methodological orientation.

Related to this second point is the fact that one particular individual, the sociologist Bob (R. W.) Connell (2002), has had a major and enduring influence on thinking about men and masculinity. Connell's modernist – macro-level, materialist and structural – sociology, which is informed by a wealth of empirical evidence drawn from various areas of social life, has been the starting point for all criminologists working in this area (Jefferson, 1997). An important influence on Connell's thinking is Marx's analysis of capitalism, but rather than developing a class analysis, he shows how the gender order is also a product of capitalism, and in the current climate that includes globalizing capitalism. Connell's work is especially interesting because he takes on board feminism, although he does not accept certain radical accounts arguing that male dominance and patriarchal structures are monolithic and absolute. Masculinity may be intertwined with power and authority, furthering heterosexual and specific class interests, but it can be challenged and is changeable. In short, masculinity appears in different forms in different cultural and historical contexts.

Connell has numerous critics but they are in a sense in an inescapable position of having to respond to the agenda he has set (Jefferson, 1997). Although Connell's thinking has not been jettisoned, his work is at the heart of the confused state of play in studies of men, masculinity (or perhaps rather masculinities) and crime. For these reasons his contribution is reviewed in some detail, followed by an exploration of one of his most sympathetic critics and occasional co-author, Messerschmidt (1993, 1997, 2000, 2004), who has made considerable inroads into this muddied area.

Connell and 'gender relations'

Sociological accounts of gender include variants where the focus is on social identities or identity categories (in this context, men and women), and relational approaches like that advanced by Connell in his explanation of masculinity (2000, 2002). Perspectives relying on a notion of identity, such as biological theories, identify pre-existing and separate categories for men and women, who are polarized into dominant and dominated groups. Sometimes men/males and women/females are seen as two entirely separate and opposed groups, but research has shown that males and females are similar in more ways than is widely acknowledged, and that differences amongst males are as pronounced as those between males and females (Messerschmidt, 2004). A further problem with this categorical approach is that there is insufficient appreciation of power and diversity within a particular category: for instance, the homophobic violence heterosexual men direct towards homosexual men. This suggests that not all men are equally dominant in social relations, opening up a wider debate about gender hierarchy and gender injustice.

For Connell 'gender relations' are relational: that is, they occur as a result of social interaction between men and women, rather than deriving from the static categories of men and women. There is no attempt to explain sex and gender in terms that are reducible to bodily sex or reproduction. Rather than focusing on particular categories of types of people, 'gender relations' are based on a set of social practices belonging to a 'structuring process' creating gender regimes. For instance, the life histories of men's lives constitute social structures. According to Connell there are hierarchical relations connecting particular gender groups who compete with each other in the pursuit of material advantage. Rather than men and women existing in separate groups, they are connected through specific social mechanisms. The outcomes of these different competitive struggles are variable, and all men do not necessarily subordinate all women.

It is important to look beyond a simple opposition of males and females. Men and women and their varied material interests are practices carried out in many different historical, cultural and institutional contexts. Connell's macro-level analyses of these issues show that although there are changeable structural hierarchies and multiple masculinities, men are in a dominant position overall because of something called 'hegemonic masculinity'. This concept, based on Gramsci's (1971) notion of hegemony, suggests that a certain form of masculinity – one amongst many – is valued more highly than others at a particular time and place, and this in turn legitimizes the social domination of masculinity.

Hegemonic masculinity is not so much about groups and interests as a socially dominant ideal of manhood. This ideal, backed up by effective authority, encourages men to see the dominant ideal of masculinity as something to which they aspire. This task is far from straightforward because forms of hegemonic masculinity change over time in cultures and even within subcultures. Jefferson (1996a) illustrates this well in relation to risk taking among young men, where excessive drinking, drug consumption and predatory violence are a form of hegemonic masculinity in a particular milieu.

In addition to 'hegemonic masculinity', Connell's (1987) discussion of gender is based on three main structures, which in turn are based on Mitchell's (1971) structural model. Mitchell wrote from the perspective of radical feminism, but Connell adopted and adapted her ideas to consider gender relations with particular reference to masculinity. Connell describes three structures: power, work and cathexis.

- *Power* refers to authority, control, coercion and violence.
- *Work* refers to the division of labour and production.
- *Cathexis* refers to sexual and emotional relations.

In all his work Connell considers these three structures, and to a lesser degree he has taken on board postmodern thought, illustrated by his use of the concept of 'symbolism' and allusions to language and sign systems. However, Connell's work is ultimately embedded in a materialist conception of the social world where postmodern sympathies are out of kilter.

Thus far it has been established that masculinity forms part of a hierarchical relationship in any gender regime. Crucially there are multiple masculinities rather than a singular version, but there does tend to be White, heterosexual and class-based dominance. The last point is important, because dominant forms of masculinity are acquiring global significance, such as the so-called 'transnational business masculinity' (Connell, 2000), which stands against gay masculinities, as well as those forms of masculinity that are marginalized by race, ethnicity and imperialism. Connell's analyses investigate men from different social classes and ethnic groups and men of different sexual orientations, and show that there are a multiplicity of relations between gender, class and sexuality. However gay men are marginal for most of the time, a salient point given that this group of men is a beneficiary of the 'patriarchal dividend'.

Connell's work is not without weaknesses, but by drawing attention to the historical specificity of particular gender orders he shows how macro social institutions generally benefit men even though there is considerable variety in men's placements in this order.

Arguably four insights of Connell's thinking are of particular value to criminologists. First, Connell (2000) has consistently shown in his study of masculinity that it is not simply a case of looking at men on the one hand and women on the other hand. Women may adopt masculine attitudes, so masculinity is not something linked exclusively to men and the male body. Connell makes this point when he states that 'Unless we subside into defining masculinity as equivalent to men, we must acknowledge that sometimes masculine conduct or masculine identity goes together with a female body' (2000: 16) Thus criminality associated with women and girls is not unrelated to masculinities.

Second, masculinity is not static and changes over time and place. Masculinity is context-bound and influenced by prevailing institutional cultures and structures. Third, gender needs to be seen as part of a relational process, where there is diversity and difference not only between genders but within them too. There is no single masculinity but multiple masculinities. The fourth and final point relates to multiple masculinities and the consequence that there are no clear-cut and fixed identities. Despite this there are ideal types of masculinity that sustain hierarchical relations, especially patterns of male dominance. For instance, hegemonic masculinity exists because there are elite-type or powerful groups who provide moral and cultural guidance and leadership to maintain the status quo, which is buttressed if necessary by coercion.

Connell's work has been considered here at some length, which may be rather surprising as he has not focused on crime and criminal justice in any depth, but it was necessary because his work informs the work of Messerschmidt (1993, Connell and Messerschmidt, 2005). Messerschmidt shows that attempts to accomplish a masculine identity make reference to idealized versions of a dominant masculinity. This ideal is an unobtainable aspiration for many boys and men in different settings, such as at home, at work and school. Messerschmidt (1993) is concerned with recognizing a diversity of masculinities, for example by looking at youth crime and its interconnection with wider structural inequalities. He shows how masculinities are related to power and the division of labour in the context of class and race relations.

In line with critical, radical and left-realist criminologists, Messerschmidt (1993) draws attention to those groups marginalized and excluded from labour markets, but rather than arguing that these factors push men into crime, he describes how men who cannot access economic and material resources commit crime as a method of 'doing masculinity'. Collison (1996) also uses this kind of reasoning in his investigation of the links between consumption, drugs markets and masculinities. In underclass-type communities which are awash with visual images of the affluent society and where the chances of obtaining wealth and material goods are all but blocked, the drugs economy is a way out. More than that, the behavioural response to these conditions sometimes involves predatory forms of masculinity, inspired at least in part by media narratives. Respect is no longer gained through graft, but by an extended week of pleasure in a space that is liminal and chaotic. The physical demands of labour and the cogent images of masculinity it provides, which were so closely related in the world of work, become enmeshed with the reality of, and semi-fulfilled fantasies about, criminality in the workless society (Collison, 1996: 14).

The suggestion that crime is a form of gendered social action that creates opportunities for the maintenance of privileged forms of masculinity is shared by Byrne and Trew (2005) in their research into offenders' perceptions about their own behaviour and orientation towards crime. They found that a positive orientation to crime – that is, a greater willingness to offend – was more prevalent among their male than their female respondents.

A strength of Messerschmidt's work is that he draws attention to different offences and how men in different classes and ethnic groups define their experiences of crime differently. For example, White working-class masculinities will be markedly different from Black masculinities because of the groups' different experiences of labour markets. The nature of the criminal response of these groups will also vary, as will the nature of the masculine response, although the celebration of toughness and physical power is likely to be present.

Final comments

These essentially structural accounts have been questioned through Collier's (1998) studies of embodiment and the 'sexed body' and Jefferson's (1997) innovative psychosocial approach. Jefferson in particular questions the structural determinism found in some explanations of masculinity and crime. His important contribution (1997) is indebted to psychoanalysis. For instance, some of his work has focused on individual cases such as the former world heavyweight boxing champion, Mike Tyson (Jefferson, 1996b). Tyson was imprisoned for the rape of Desiree Washington, and this was followed by the decline of his status as a champion and his psychological disintegration. Some commentators explained Tyson's life in terms of his class (working) and race (Black), but Jefferson's analysis considers the ambivalence in Tyson's psyche. On the surface he was a huge and powerful man, although this concealed a more troubled personality. This is apparent in Jefferson's account of his transformation from 'a little fairy boy' to a 'complete destroyer', which shows how the biography of this sportsman was full of contradictions.

Jefferson (1996b) shows Tyson as a young man who had a lisp and who lacked the physique he later acquired as a result of years of graft in the gymnasium. Tyson became 'Iron Mike' by splitting off, or rejecting, his own perceived deficiencies and projecting the resulting violent feelings toward his opponents in the ring. In other words, Tyson's life cannot be explained in terms of structural factors alone, and psychological factors are important too.

MEN, MASCULINITIES AND CRIME: KEY POINTS

■ Feminists have argued that criminology is male-centred, and the work reviewed above continues to focus on males. However this body of work is informed by the feminist critique of malestream criminology.

■ The work of Connell has been particularly influential, especially his study of gender relations.

■ Connell's structural analysis focuses on three structures, power, work and cathexis, to demonstrate the development of something he calls 'hegemonic masculinity'. This shows how male power is applied in different social settings to maintain masculine dominance.

■ Messerschmidt has drawn on Connell's work to show how men 'do' masculinity in relation to crime.

■ Structural accounts of men, masculinities and crime are not without their limitations, and Jefferson has suggested that a psychosocial perspective is also important.

RACISM AND ANTI-RACIST APPROACHES

This section builds on the material in Chapter 2 to consider the concept of racism and its theoretical significance for understanding crime. This concept has a long history, but it took longer to emerge than the ideas of race discussed in Chapter 2.

We do not need to consider the origins of the notion of racism here, but it might be useful to offer a definition. Racism is:

> those discourses that signify phonotypical or genotypical characteristics, creating a system of categorization, onto which negative/positive attributes, are applied in a deterministic manner. This system of categorization can be used to exclude groups in the process of allocating resources and services.
>
> (Singh, 2000: 36)

Above all the concept of racism shows how the differential treatment of minority ethnic groups, such as the disproportionate number of African-Caribbeans who are sent to prison, is justified.

Thus racism refers to those ideas and practices that result in the differential treatment of people because of their biological or culture differences. Basically, racism suggests that a particular group of people are inferior, mainly because of the way they look and the qualities or attributes associated with that appearance. These differences are seen as biologically determined, fixed and unchanging. This means that races are seen as natural features and unalterable. Phenomena such as colonialism lay bare how racism operates, although the term was not explicitly recognized by many in the colonial era of the nineteenth and early twentieth century.

It is necessary at this point to outline various attempts by criminologists to theorize racism.

■ It is worth noting that racism may be manifest in what individuals think, say and do. Some individuals view people with a different skin colour than their own as inferior, and they express that belief in their thoughts and/or actions. This is sometimes called *individual racism.*

■ There is also a view that organizations and their activities discriminate against particular racial groups. The emphasis is less on what individual people say and do, and more on the discriminatory activities of an organization, such as the police service. This is called *institutional racism.*

Racism works in many ways, including verbal insults, intimidation and physical violence (including murder). The most extreme case is genocide. The perpetrators of racism can be individuals, groups of people, government agencies and nation-states (Bowling and Phillips, 2002; Cohen, 2000).

While social scientists continue to find evidence of racism in all societies, it should be pointed out that the usefulness of concept of race has been questioned. Indeed natural and social scientists have rejected the existence of any biological basis to the categorizing of people into racial groups. They have shown that races only exist as a social construct, and as such there is nothing natural or unchanging about race. Despite this race is still treated as if it is real, which is theoretically significant. Take Allahar's observation:

> Biology and race became independent variables that explained the rate of social advancement and economic progress ... but as the historical roots of racism disappeared, racism did not. Rather, new racist ideas have evolved all the way from classical antiquity, utilizing the images of medieval thought and colour symbolisms of Christianity to inform discriminatory practices right into the modern period. For although races are socially imagined and not biologically real categories, human beings continue to act as if they were real; and as long as they do so, race becomes real in its consequences.
>
> (Allahar, 1993: 52)

Thus, despite the rejection of the category of race, racism continues to be identified as a problem, and citizens and policy makers continue to refer to race in their day-to-day work. There has been a subtle change, though, and 'race' is now used interchangeably with the concept of ethnicity. This is problematic too.

To see people as having a particular ethnicity or belonging to an ethnic group does not avoid the problem of racism, and notions of inferiority and superiority do not disappear altogether. For instance, Anthias (1990) shows how race is used interchangeably with race and biological factors, possibly functioning as a 'signifier of an immutable and deterministic difference' (Anthias, 1990: 23). Thus 'in much theoretical or everyday discourse "race" and ethnic categories are used as equivalent' (Anthias, 1990: 20). These categories are situated in relation to the notion of *ethnos*:

> The hallmark of this set of phenomena is inclusion and exclusion, difference and identity; the construction of entities, on the one hand, by way of some notion of a historical point of origin or essence and, on the other, the collective difference from the other .... Race has no analytical validity in its own right but is a social construction with its own representational, organizational and experiential forms linking it ontologically to the wider category of ethnos, which provides its analytical axis.
>
> (Anthias, 1990: 21–2)

Thus, socially constructed categories of race and ethnicity are employed to describe social groups in terms of essential characteristics, bound together by a sense of shared origin or *ethnos*. Although Anthias's (1990) work has much to offer, it is important to keep in mind Allahar's comment above, so much so that I shall repeat part of it: 'Although races are socially imagined and not biologically real categories, human beings continue to act as if they were real; and as long as they do so, race becomes real in its consequences' (1993: 52).

To put it another way, the perception that there are races guides social action. Holdaway makes a similar theoretical point in his work on the racialization of British policing:

> Race is a term with no validity attached to it by natural scientists. It has nevertheless been found that 'race' is a social category and criterion which police distributes services and other resources. An environment of 'racialized relations' is enacted by taken for granted routines of police work. The mundane then has a significance that extends beyond its taken for granted character.
>
> (Holdaway, 1996: 204)

This means that race is meaningful for individuals and groups involved in policy making.

There is also a phenomenon known as the 'new racism'. Rather than using skin colour to describe a group as inferior, discrimination is based on cultural differences, which are seen to make an ethnic group problematic. In this way social customs such as language, domestic life and religion may be chosen to target a group and label them as inferior or problematic.

According to the logic of the 'new racism', ethnicity is seen as something fixed and immutable, as race was once seen to be. To illustrate this, in British society the 'new racism' suggests that there is a unified culture and shared sense of history and sense of belonging. All British citizens are members of a nation-state and it is this common and shared national identity that makes them gel into a whole. Gilroy (1987) has shown that the British culture and ethnic identity is characterized as White. Adherents to the 'new racism' would show that traditionally there were no Black people in this country and that various social problems such as crime and disorder have arisen in British society because non-White people pose a threat to the integrity of the dominant White culture. Black groups, even if they were born in Britain, are seen as outsiders who do not belong to the nation-state. What tends to happen is that majority ethnic group unites to protect its ethnic identity by describing the ethnicity of minority ethnic groups as 'Other' (Gilroy, 1987).

These theoretical contributions have been applied in myriad ways to show how the criminal justice system is racist. A relatively recent example is Macpherson's definition of institutional racism as the:

> collective failure of an organization to provide an appropriate and professional service to people because of their colour, culture or ethnic origin. It can be seen or detected in processes, attitudes and behaviour which amount to discrimination through unwitting prejudice, ignorance, thoughtlessness and racist stereotyping which disadvantage minority ethnic people.
>
> (Macpherson, 1999: 6.24)

This quotation is important for several reasons, not least because Macpherson's point was accepted by the government of the day. Anti-racist writers such as Gilroy (1987) had argued for many years that the criminal justice system functioned in a discriminatory fashion, but the state had largely ignored these claims. However, certain elements of the theoretical work of anti-racists were interwoven into this definition, which proved to be an influential touchstone in criminal justice reform.

RACISM AND ANTI-RACISM: KEY POINTS

■ Racism is the attempt to identify individuals and groups as inferior on the basis of physical or cultural markers of difference.

■ Racism may be manifest as either individual racism or institutional racism.

■ Theorizations of racism have demonstrated that the criminal justice system has operated in ways that are racist.

■ The publication of the Macpherson inquiry indicates that certain aspects of anti-racist theory underpin public policy.

CRITICAL CRIMINOLOGY AND SOCIAL DIVISIONS: GENDER AND RACE

The previous section has outlined critical approaches to the understanding of the criminal justice system. Both feminists and anti-racists have shown how powerful groups – either men or the White majority – oppress and subordinate women and minority ethnic groups through the legal and criminal justice systems. These theoretical insights have proven to be influential by drawing attention to social injustice, and have brought about changes. However, racism and sexism are resistant to change, and there is still much to be pessimistic about.

POSTMODERNITY, THE POSTMODERN AND CRIME

There is another set of theorists who have argued that social change is very difficult, especially in the context of postmodern society. Developments such as the risk society and the surveillance society are further reasons to be sceptical about the capacity of critical criminologists to bring about further change.

In this section:

- it is explained what is meant by postmodernity and the postmodern
- some theories that have been described as postmodern are introduced
- there is a discussion of two other important concepts, risk and surveillance.

The idea of the postmodern has provoked considerable debate across a range of academic disciplines including philosophy, sociology, cultural studies and literary criticism. For example, the notion of the postmodern has also been used in the arts, especially in painting, architecture, cinema and literature. It is via these areas of study that postmodern and poststructuralist theories have influenced criminological theory, although in a rather roundabout way.

Unlike the other theories addressed in Chapters 11 and 12, as well as the critical perspectives discussed in the preceding section, the impact of postmodern thought has on mainstream criminological thought is rather limited. This is not because postmodern perspectives are not useful. Rather it is because they are novel, but above all it is a result of the lack of any concerted effort to apply such thinking to solve practical problems in real-world settings. Also, as will be made clear, there are some more philosophical reasons why postmodern theories may well be of limited utility for criminologists.

Let us start once again with some definitions. The prefix 'post' means after and beyond, so the discussion is about after-modernity and what comes after the modern. In Chapter 11, modernity was described in the context of the Enlightenment, as the period where scientific ideas usurped religious beliefs. Modernity was the age of reason, characterized by industrialization, economic growth and a general commitment to social progress. For some commentators, such as Giddens (1999), human societies are still in the era of modernity, albeit this phase can be thought of as late modernity. However, others have argued that by the last third of the twentieth century there was a move *beyond* modernity, towards a condition that has been called postmodernity (Lyotard, 1984). If this is the case, what are the theoretical implications?

Postmodernism subjected to powerful criticism traditional Enlightenment values such as reason and progress. Lyotard described reason as a *metanarrative*, and the postmodern as 'incredulity towards narratives'. Taking this further, ideas like justice, fairness and truth are also metanarratives. Basically, postmodernism is an attack on traditional values and the view that there are universally relevant value frameworks. It is argued that there is no set of higher rational principles to judge values and knowledge, and all that remains is a plurality, or many different, but equally legitimate, sets of values. It is not longer possible to appeal to the overarching principles of justice and truth because they do not exist. Anyone who speaks of truth and justice can only do so in a particular local context, and what is said is not necessarily transferable to other contexts. This leads to fragmentation, individualization and diversification. Postmodern theories also question the use of categories such as class, race and gender. Often when students start to think in this way it makes thinking about the administration of criminal justice quite difficult.

However, Hopkins Burke's (2001) account of transition from modernity to postmodernity and its bearing on crime is very clear. The next section is an overview of his ideas.

Modern societies are mass societies characterized by:

- mass production and mass consumption
- organized labour
- the welfare state
- full employment.

These factors are part of what in England became Beveridge's welfare state. Such societies are characterized by moral certainty and the relevance of grand theory for explaining the workings of societies. For example, liberalism, conservatism and socialism are all grand theories, albeit using different terms and concepts, and there is an assumption by adherents that they can be used to solve all problems in society. These grand theories or meta-narratives are said to represent the interests of mass groups or social classes, which are often seen in terms of a conflict of interests between capital and labour. Political parties on the left and right offer competing explanations of the solutions to this conflict of interests. In modern societies this is typically seen to require the continuation of the profitability of capitalism together with 'cradle to grave' welfare provision.

So although there are conflicting interests there has been considerable social consensus. Many social scientists have asked how this consensus was possible. One answer is that it was achieved through the institutions of civil society (the church, educational organizations and so on), and also through the police targeting non-respectable sections of the working – and under – classes.

The maintenance of this consensus has become even more problematic because modern societies are becoming increasingly fragmented and diverse. For example, in the economic sphere mass production-line technologies have been replaced with flexible working patterns and a flexible workforce, and in the political sphere, the old distinction between left and right is no longer relevant as neither end of the spectrum adequately represents the interests of diverse groups and their interests (industry, finance, small business, the unemployed, sexuality, the environment and so on).

The postmodern political economy is complex and morally ambiguous. There are a range of different but equally legitimate perspectives. In contrast to modernity, where there are universal principles, truths and values, postmodernity recognizes that there are many different discourses and different people with different interests. Rather than absolute truth and values there are relative truths and values. This means there are multiple realities, so the meaning of morality is less clear-cut and more ambiguous. This relativization of values has consequences for politicians and policy makers, as few of the diverse views and interests in wider society are easily accommodated by traditional political parties of either the left or right. Politicians and policy makers have to respond to ambiguity and attempt to build support by referring to a range of groups and interests in relation to many different issues.

To illustrate the relevance of postmodernism Hopkins Burke (2001) examined crime and the postmodern condition in the contemporary United Kingdom. It is necessary to consider:

- relatively recent changes in the political economy (1960s–2000s)
- changes in crime trends (1960s–2000s)
- social-scientific explanations of these changes.

The relationship between crime and unemployment is nowadays often treated as axiomatic. However, in earlier historical periods when there was high unemployment (such as the 1930s) crime rates were remarkably low. The poor may have been poor but they were honest and respectable. Communities had strong bonds and shared moral values. Since the late 1950s onwards crime has increased, which coincided with a breakdown of respectable values. This breakdown was arguably because of the relativism of postmodernism, where 'anything goes' and there has been a dissipation of moral certainty. To address this, the police need to confront lawbreakers and contribute to a wider strategy aiming to restore moral certainty. This would be difficult. Why?

Traditional working-class cultures are dead (we now live in a postindustrial society), and the old moral values exist no longer. The twenty-first century is an age of moral ambiguity and cultural diversity. The police and other players that lead strategies intended to restore moral certainty will experience problems. Traditional working-class cultures belonged to a simpler age when communities were all very similar and the degree of conformity was much higher. There were also fewer opportunities to commit crime (everyone was poor and the pressures to conform were greater). This was the era of what Durkheim called 'mechanical solidarity'.

Following the Second World War, and particularly in the 1950s, there were widespread changes in society. The consumer society developed, with a more highly educated, sophisticated and affluent citizenry. Individuals were able to escape from the uniformity and conformity of old communities. There was more diversity, and people had very different and more individualized experiences. Individuals enjoyed more freedom and choice. This fits with Durkheim's notion of 'organic solidarity'.

The most significant change since the 1950s has been increased prosperity, but this has not been shared equally because:

- skilled workers have all but disappeared and their jobs been replaced by 'McJobs': simple, low-status and disposable
- there has been an increase in the number of double income (cash-rich/time-poor) households
- a relatively high proportion of lone parents are trapped in poverty
- the experience of poverty is qualitatively different in the twenty-first century from how it was in the twentieth century.

Poverty was once experienced by whole communities, whether people were in or out of work. Now those in work are much better off than those out of work. However, those out of work are not as stoical as their counterparts in the 1930s. They do not accept their lot, and aspire to possess the commodities enjoyed by other people.

These factors can perhaps explain the dramatic increase in crime from the mid-1950s onwards. This needs to be situated in the context of the shift towards a postmodern society, which is diverse, fragmented, affluent but unequal. The following factors are also significant.

- There are more opportunities to commit crime (that is, more stealable goods).
- There has been a declining significance for informal social controls (such as family, for instance in the disappearance of two-parent families in some excluded communities).
- There has been a disintegration of traditional working-class culture, which has been replaced by the fragmentation/individualism associated with the shift towards an entrepreneurial society (involving more and more moral ambiguity). The consequence is unlimited aspirations and pervasive anomie.
- Working-class culture was traditionally recognized as focusing on productive capacities, but now the focus is on consumption (especially among the youth). As there are fewer opportunities for employment, attachment to subcultures becomes increasingly seductive. These are not confined to the excluded, and individuals from all social backgrounds drift in and out of deviant activities (especially drug misuse).

To summarize these disparate issues, increased prosperity has benefited broad swathes of the citizenry in postindustrial and postmodern society. The poor are not as poor in absolute terms as they were in the 1930s, but they experience their poverty in qualitatively different ways (Hopkins Burke, 2001)

The contribution of Foucault

A key postmodern thinker is Michel Foucault (1977), who shares Lyotard's (1984) 'incredulity towards metanarratives'. Foucault's contribution has been referred to as 'poststructuralist', which means he rejects the social structures identified in the work of Marx, Weber and Durkheim and the personality structure identified by Freud. More than that, as a poststructuralist Foucault concentrated mainly on *discourse*. This idea deserves some more attention.

Many postmodern and poststructuralist thinkers reject the view that there is an external reality, and claim instead that social relations are expressed through language. 'Discourse' refers to everyday talk and speech, but Foucault uses it in a different sense, as a way of talking about the rules and protocols used in language. Discourse is about the relationship between power and knowledge, and the social construction of meaning. All social relations are a product of discourse and power/knowledge relations. Thus a discourse is a product of a particular context, and its meaning is localized and contextually specific. The basic point is that society is not a product of the social structure or individual psychology, but of language. This is a rather abstract theory, but some of Foucault's ideas have been used by criminologists. These are sometimes called Foucauldian approaches. We shall look at two examples: first, the politics and economics of the risk society, and second, surveillance and the panopticon.

Foucauldian paradigms: the politics and economics of the risk society

The influence of Beck's *The Risk Society* (1992) on the social sciences cannot be overstated, and Foucauldian criminologists have readily absorbed his key observation that risk society has replaced social class. These approaches consider relatively recent changes in crime control and its practical orientation towards the poor through a range of discursive and political rationalities. For example, strategies of risk assessment and risk management embedded in the logic of actuarial justice have been used to segregate the hazards presented by an unruly underclass (Feeley and Simon, 1994; Ericson and Haggerty, 1997). Other analysts (referred to below) draw on the literature of *governmentality* (Dean, 1999). Here the focus is on the workings of politically constituted, differentiated and hybridized networks of statutory, voluntary and private agencies. In contrast to radical or Marxist criminologists, proponents of the governmentality approach argue that these networks do not reflect the unitary interests of elite-type groups such as the bourgeoisie. However the police force sometimes mobilize themselves in order to impose sovereign control over given territories and specific social groups, some of which may be socially excluded (Stenson and Edwards, 2001: 74).

Feeley and Simon (1994) have focused on the concept of *actuarial justice* to explain innovations in crime and control in the United States. Actuarial justice is contrasted with liberal conceptions of justice belonging to the Enlightenment project of modernity, which are concerned with establishing the guilt, responsibility and obligations of individual suspects and offenders as part of a more general aim to reform and reintegrate them into society. Towards the latter stages of the twentieth century the usefulness and viability of this objective was questioned. Actuarial justice is less attentive to either the rehabilitation or the punishment of individuals, and is preoccupied with devising 'techniques for identifying, classifying and managing groups assorted by levels of dangerousness' (Feeley and Simon, 1994: 173). Justice is no longer individualized, but determined by assessing and managing the risks and hazards presented by 'groups' and 'aggregates' such as 'permanent-marginal' underclass-type populations.

As for other Foucauldians, the issue of social class is not at the forefront of Feeley and Simon's (1994) analysis, but what it does show is that some groups of offenders, for instance sex offenders, share characteristics that give a predisposition to specific types of behaviour. With regard to this group of offenders, risk assessment and management have been defined by the Probation Service: the former is 'an assessment carried out to establish whether the subject is likely to cause serious physical or psychological harm to others' and the latter an 'action taken to monitor a person's behaviour and attitudes, and to intervene in his/her life, in order to prevent them harming others'. The 'desired outcome' of 'risk assessment' and 'risk management' is 'public protection' and enhanced security (HM Inspectorate of Probation, 1995 cited in Hebenton and Thomas, 1996: 434).

The production of 'knowledge for security', and dissemination of this knowledge, or 'communications about risk', are prerequisites for 'knowledge-for-security' (Hebenton and Thomas, 1996: 428, 431). The creation of security is reliant on both, hence the term 'security through knowledge' (ibid.: 439). For example, the police service survey and monitor populations to produce knowledge, which may be applied in the context of risk management strategies to regulate specific categories of suspects or offenders (Ericson, 1994: 161 cited in Hebenton and Thomas, 1996: 432).

In principle, intelligence systems are in place to store the data used to inform and harmonize the policy responses of the different agencies involved in community safety and crime reduction (Hebenton and Thomas, 1996: 435–6). In practice the attainment of security through 'risk management' is far from simple, as local intelligence systems are not adequately equipped to actively assess, monitor and keep track of all offending groups. Furthermore, multi-agency networks coexisting along the police–policing continuum (the police, education, probation) are rarely coordinated.

Ericson and Haggerty (1997) develop similar ideas in their characterization of the police as 'information brokers' who collaborate with other organizations such as welfare organizations and insurance companies to identify the crime risks imposed on society, in order to control and govern crime. They process and reproduce knowledge for security through systems of information technology, bureaucracy and surveillance. They then refer to prudential and actuarial models to calculate and measure the risk of particular behaviours and the scale of harm or loss they cause. The application of scientific knowledge enables different expert groups to classify, target and exclude deviant populations.

However, there would appear to be fundamental problems with this type of analysis because risk is not always calculable (this is the *prudential paradigm*), and all knowledge of risk is finite and entangled with ignorance and uncertainty (Beck, 1992). Police officers operate with different risk management strategies in relation not only to traditional and specialized police activities such as investigative techniques and styles of detective work, but also to a wider range of policing activities they carry out with multi-agency partnerships. Crawford (1997) suggests that actuarial principles are invoked when agencies amass crime data, which is in turn used to inform crime prevention and community safety initiatives in specific geographical territories, such as incapacitation and community-based punishments.

Such representations of risk are over-coherent and too systematic. Ericson and Haggerty (1997) have conceptualized an ideal-typical model of risk assessment and management, instead of considering how different strategies are combined in many different ways, producing hybrid forms of risk management. In other words, models of risk found in policy documents are not implemented straightforwardly as they come into contact with traditional police practices and procedures, as well as more novel policing techniques and strategies found along the police–policing continuum. The pure conceptions of risk imagined by policy makers are thus hybridized in practice.

Surveillance and the panopticon

According to Fussey (2005), Foucault's usage of Jeremy Bentham's notion of the *panopticon* has been used to assess the use of surveillance in society (Coleman, 2004; Webster, 2004). Another thinker has adapted Foucault's thesis by inverting the 'panoptic gaze' to develop the concept of 'synoptic surveillance' (Mathiesen, 1997).

Many criminological discussions of surveillance have drawn extensively on Foucault's interpretation of the panopticon (Haggerty and Ericson, 2000; McCahill and Norris, 2002; Coleman, 2004; McGrath, 2004). We shall define what is meant by the panopticon and panoptic surveillance, then explore the relevance of this idea for examining surveillance.

A panopticon is in the literal sense a building: a prison in which all the prisoners can be viewed from one central point. Bentham designed a panopticon, but his designs were never put into practice.

Earlier in the chapter Foucault's critical stance towards the Enlightenment was sketched. According to Foucault, modernity could be characterized as a disciplinary society where power could be found everywhere. Foucault used *capillaries* as a metaphor to show that power, like blood, flowed throughout the whole body. In other words, power works rather like a network. It is in fact a 'carceral network', which performs a recycling function. As Foucault puts it, it 'takes back with one hand what it seems to exclude with the other' and 'it saves everything, including what it punishes' (Foucault, 1977: 301).

To extend the metaphor, the disciplinary power in the main social institutions such as asylums, factories, schools and prisons also operated in wider society (Foucault, 1977). Foucault expressed this like this: 'we have seen that, in penal justice, the prison transformed the punitive procedure into a penitentiary technique; the carceral archipelago transported this technique from the penal institution to the entire social body' (Foucault, 1977: 298).

One commentator has remarked that Foucault's discussion of discipline can be understood in terms of a 'trialectic of power' linking power with knowledge and space (Soja, 1996: cited in Koskela, 2003: 295). On the basis of this Foucault argued that society is observed relentlessly by a disciplinary system. The word 'observation' is key, and it is here that Bentham's notion of the panopticon is referred to explicitly. The panopticon was used in such a way that individuals were faced with the permanent threat of being under surveillance, and this acted as a deterrent to ensure they did not deviate. This surveillance was essentially a threat, as people would not know whether they were actually being watched. The principles of the panopticon are used throughout society, and are part of the transformation of punishment described in Chapter 8. Instead of inflicting physical torture on criminals as was done prior to the Enlightenment, the panopticon encouraged individuals to regulate themselves. Because surveillance is ubiquitous in disciplinary societies it is anticipated that crime may be prevented by people administering a form of self-deterrence.

Although these changes occurred in the eighteenth and nineteenth centuries, Fussey (2005) shows their relevance in contemporary societies. Indeed various scholars have noted a theoretical connection between the panopticon and the use of CCTV (Lyon, 1994; McCahill, 1998; Norris and Armstrong, 1999), and panoptic principles have also been advocated to varying degrees (Fyfe and Bannister, 1996; Reeve, 1998; Staples, 2000; Fox, 2001). Reeve, for example, argues that:

> there is a possibly more negative and potentially sinister aspect to the monitoring gaze of the camera. This is something clearly reminiscent of what Foucault ... has described as the disciplinary society, in his use of the metaphor of the panopticon as a device of total surveillance in a rationally organized society.
>
> (Reeve, 1998: 71)

It would appear therefore that Foucault's discussion of the panopticon has become an element of accounts of CCTV. Yar (2003) has reviewed Foucauldian accounts of surveillance, and suggests that the panopticon has been understood in three main ways. First, it has been understood in terms of 'qualified applicability', which means some writers may have their doubts about its usefulness but they recognize that the panopticon is at least of some significance (e.g. Norris and Armstrong, 1999). Yar (2003) observes that other theorists do not recognize the panopticon because the conditions for panopticism are no longer in existence. Deleuze, for instance, is of the view that disciplinary institutions are no longer relevant in postmodern society. Third, according to Yar (2003), there are other commentators who have refined Foucault's notion of the panopticon and applied it differently. Poster (1990) has talked about a 'superpanopticon', which is a method of processing information in databases.

Gandy's (1993) work identifies a 'panoptic sort' to explain the methods used to place consumers under surveillance. This is important because information about consumers is actually a commodity. For example, retailers have access to the profiles of consumers to find out about how they shop. This is not directly relevant to criminology but it is a potentially useful idea because a 'panoptic sort' can use information to facilitate the identification and classification of people. In the commercial world this information can be sold to interested parties. Likewise this information could be gathered and disseminated in a similar format throughout the criminal justice sector.

Now let us explore in more detail the extent to which the idea of the panopticon is useful for describing surveillance. Foucault's theorization of the panopticon is a common reference point in explanations of surveillance, but it has not always been taken on board without some criticism. Perhaps the most problematic aspect of Foucault's idea is the suggestion that surveillance is universal, or that it can be found everywhere. This assumption was critiqued by Norris and Armstrong (1999), who showed that not all groups are placed under surveillance, and that CCTV is used to target particular sub-populations such as a socially excluded underclass. This observation can be applied to the discussion on actuarial justice (see page 355), which tends to classify particular groups as more risky and dangerous. Rather than operating universally, power functions in a differentiated way to protect certain groups from other groups.

There are other criticisms of the panopticon metaphor, and it has been suggested that as a metaphor the panopticon is somewhat deficient because surveillance is only feasible in the specific environment in which it is applied and not beyond it (Norris and Armstrong, 1999; McCahill, 2002). Lyon (1994) has argued that Foucault's implication that the panopticon effectively reduces society to a prison cell is over-simplistic. This argument is elaborated by Boyne (2001), who argues that the panopticon is all about total control and that this cannot happen in many modern societies because citizens do not lived in fixed places, and this makes continual observation difficult. Boyne (2001) adds that even in a total institution like the prison where movement is restricted, panoptic technologies cannot guarantee the compliance of all inmates. If they could, there would not have been examples of prison riots.

If the example of CCTV is investigated in more detail, it is clear that even though there are cameras there is still the need for physical intervention by police or security guards if a person breaks the law. In other words, people do not discipline themselves just because the cameras are there. Indeed it is also quite possible that a person is not aware that the cameras exist. Thus the panoptic surveillance offered by CCTV is just one disciplinary mechanism.

On the whole, there is a fair degree of scepticism about the utility of the notion of the panopticon for explaining surveillance in wider society. In defence of Foucault (1997), his description of how the techniques of surveillance used in closed institutions like prisons are applied throughout wider society is interesting, but the influence of the panopticon is not all pervasive. However, Foucault was arguably describing general patterns and developments, and he likened the panopticon to a dream building. For example:

> [it] must not be understood as dream building: it is a diagram of a mechanism of power reduced to its ideal form; its functioning, abstracted from any obstacle, resistance or friction, must be represented as a pure architectural and optical system: it is in fact a figure of political technology.
>
> (Foucault, 1977: 205)

Mathiesen (1997) has attempted to develop Foucault's theory of the panopticon with his conception of 'synoptic surveillance'. The point he takes from Foucault is that the panopticon involves a few people watching many. Mathiesen (1997) inverts the logic of this argument by asserting that contemporary society is what he calls 'a viewer society', where it is the many watching the few. In the world Foucault described the panopticon was used by those responsible for social control over controlled populations. In the world Mathiesen describes the general population is able to observe the more powerful. To give a concrete criminological example, this is evident in the Rodney King case, where the beating of King by Los Angeles Police Department (LAPD) officers was broadcast on television. A similar recording was made of a later police assault on another man, Donovan Jackson, in an adjacent area.

So it may seem that Mathiesen (1997) is rejecting Foucault's (1977) theory of the panopticon. This is not actually the case because Mathiesen suggests that the *synopticon* and the panopticon actually complement each other. The surveillance offered by the panopticon and the media coverage made possible by the synopticon are both forms of power. In Mathiesen's own words:

> News from these parts of the panopticon – news about prisoners, escapes, robberies, murder – is the best pieces of news which the synopticon... can find. Inside the synopticon ... the material is purged of everything but the purely criminal – what was originally a small segment of a human being becomes the whole human being – whereupon the material is hurled back into the open society as stereotypes and panic-like, terrifying stories about individual cases.
>
> (Mathiesen, 1997: 231)

In other words, it can be argued that the synopticon reinforces the punitive features of the panopticon.

Mathiesen's argument also differs from Foucault because he claims that disciplinary functions are more likely to be exercised from the synopticon rather than via the panopticon. For example, he argues that people observed as part of a general system of surveillance like the panopticon may change their outward behaviour, but their attitudes inside may be unchanged. In accord with this, Mathiesen argues that it is our initial reception of information which shapes our attitudes, and 'directs and controls or disciplines our *consciousness*' (Mathiesen, 1997: 230; emphasis in original).

In sum, Mathiesen's idea of the synopticon does revise Foucault's theory of the panopticon, and he builds on it by looking at the relationship between the media and surveillance.

POSTMODERNITY, THE POSTMODERN AND CRIME: KEY POINTS

- Postmodernity refers to the historical period that superseded modernity.
- There is a debate about whether there is a postmodern period, but there is certainly doubt and declining faith in the Enlightenment project of modernity.
- Postmodernity is characterized by uncertainty and moral ambiguity.
- New ideas have been introduced to explain society and crime, such as risk and surveillance.
- Postmodern theories adopt a relatively extreme stance but they do offer some insights into the complex workings of criminal justice institutions.

CONCLUSION

This chapter has shown how criminological theory has been forced to adapt to broader social changes in late modern or postmodern society. Critical writers have highlighted the failure of mainstream, or 'malestream', criminology to address the issues of race and gender. The theoretical work undertaken by anti-racists and feminists has transformed the discipline of criminology, although they have not gone far enough for some commentators. Criminological theory has also been influenced by postmodern thought, demonstrated with reference to the notion of risk society and ideas about surveillance.

FURTHER READING

To understand the debates covered in this chapter the following three texts are useful. First, on race, see B. Bowling and C. Phillips, *Racism, Crime and Justice* (Harlow: Longman, 2002). For discussion of gender issues see S. Walklate, *Gender, Crime and Criminal Justice* (2nd edn) (Cullompton: Willan, 2004). Use the index of R. Hopkins Burke, *An Introduction to Criminological Theory* (2nd edn) (Cullompton: Willan, 2005) to find a discussion of postmodern influences. Also see the *Sage Dictionary of Criminology* edited by E. McLaughlin and J. Muncie (London: Sage, 2006) for concise definitions.

STUDY QUESTIONS

1. Define the main features of feminist criminology.
2. Describe the key points of anti-racism.
3. Describe the nature of crime in postmodern society.

Conclusions and Summary

This book has covered a lot of ground in a relatively short space, but I hope it has provided a useful introduction to a complex field of study. The final part of this conclusion summarizes the general contents of each of the four parts in the main body of the text, indicating how best readers can build on this introductory knowledge. Those reading for a degree in criminology will find that in the later years the areas covered in this text are frequently revisited, but it is necessary to focus on each issue in far more depth and detail. The information provided in this book will be fleshed out by specialist modules, but it should remain useful as a reference source.

Before we reflect on the contents and identify how they might be relevant to readers in future, let us highlight some emergent themes. The key themes running throughout this book are the criminal justice system and policy, crime data and methods of data collection, and theory. One crucial point that must be made is that the subject matter of criminology and criminal justice is live and dynamic, and that the past will play a part in shaping whatever is in store in the future. There will be some continuity but changes will be noticeable too. Despite this continuity, perhaps the only real certainty is change. This is especially so with regard to the criminal justice system and criminal justice policy, which is responding to an ever-changing external environment. Changes will occur as a result of:

- new types of offending behaviour being recognized
- old types of offending behaviour being carried out in different ways
- existing behaviours being perceived differently.

The permanence of change can be seen by considering global or worldwide developments, in particular terrorism and technological innovations such as the Internet and the mobile phone.

CHANGES IN CRIME AND CRIMINAL JUSTICE

Terrorism

The world is an exciting place, but one that is also full of risks that policy makers must tackle. At the moment the major threat to the global social order would appear to be terrorist activity resulting from political instability and conflict between various forms of religiously determined extremism. Terrorism is a crime that has not been considered in this book, largely because criminologists are still attempting to come to terms with the implications of the current situation. However, governments and policy makers are addressing this phenomenon on a daily basis. It has placed new demands on the police and security services, which were not particularly well equipped to respond to suicide bombers.

Terrorism is not new, but since the explosions on 9/11 and 7/7 the nature of the threat posed by, and the *modus operandi* of, terrorists has changed drastically. The response of the British government has been to create new legislation giving the police and criminal justice system more powers to tackle this problem. For example, the length suspects can be detained under PACE (1984) has been deemed unsatisfactory for dealing with terrorism. This raises debates about civil liberties and the need to safeguard the rights of suspects. It is likely that terrorism will become more significant for criminologists in the future. This is not the only area of change, though.

Internet crime

Since the mid-1990s another area of change in criminal justice policy has been related to technological innovations. For example, the Internet has created many opportunities to bring people together from different parts of the world and unite them in a global communications network. In the past few years policy makers have had to respond to new hazards, including the use of the Internet as a site for the sexual abuse of children. The manufacture, distribution and supply of pornographic images of children on the World Wide Web is disturbing in itself, but it is important to be aware that at some stage real sexual abuse has occurred somewhere in the world. Internet paedophiles might commit their offence in a hotel room in Manchester, but its visual record can be viewed in places as far apart as London, England and Melbourne, Australia.

The emergence of this crime created new jobs for the police service, which traditionally had not investigated virtual crime. Police in England and Wales also had to cooperate with the police in other parts of the world where policing methods were different. There were new challenges for legislators, who had to draft laws to respond to this type of offending, resulting in new sentences and punishments. Because Internet paedophilia occurs in various parts of the world, it is necessary to be aware that different jurisdictions deal with this crime in different ways, and the sentencing frameworks may be underpinned by different philosophies and rationales. Basically, new crimes result in criminal justice agencies developing new policies. As well as this, the criminal justice system needed to form new alliances with experts in the information technology field.

Other criminals interested in identity theft and fraud have embraced the Internet. Many people now use the Internet to do their shopping, and give personal details online to retailers and banks. To all intents and purposes this is a secure and safe way of carrying out financial transactions, although some innovative offenders have been able to exploit this technology by obtaining credit card details and indirectly money. The police and courts react to this type of offending, but the financial services sector have had to take some responsibility for tightening up security.

Mobile phones

At a more mundane level it is only since the late 1990s that there has been mass owner-ship of mobile phones. Again, these were identified as a good thing, enabling people to keep in touch with each other in ways that they had not done previously. There is a negative side to their use, though, demonstrated by the problem of mobile theft. The inbuilt cameras led to a craze known as 'happy slapping', where someone would assault another person and have the attack recorded on a friend's mobile.

These illustrations show how new types of offending behaviour may be recognized (such as 'happy slapping') or how old types of offending behaviour are carried out in different ways (such as the sexual abuse of children, and terrorism). There is also some evidence that existing behaviours are being treated differently. The reclassification of cannabis (described in Chapter 1) is one example, and another is antisocial behaviour, where previously non-criminal behaviour has been criminalized (see Chapter 3).

It is therefore clear that criminal justice policy has had to change in the last ten years in response to new crimes. It is more or less certain that further changes will occur in the near, mid-term and long-term future. Predicting what those changes may be is an inexact science. However, you might find it interesting to write down some ideas in the back of this book and revisit them later to see how good your predictions were.

There are also continuities in policy, and to a degree these are more noticeable. The core functions of the police, court and prison services all remain essentially unchanged. The probation service underwent major changes throughout the twentieth century, and recent developments are aiming to redefine its identity alongside the prison service.

Continuity amidst change

To demonstrate this point in some more detail, the police service continues to deal with the crimes it has responded to in the past, including robbery, theft and burglary. The detection rate for some of these crimes remains low, although not as low as it is for rape and other forms of sexual violence. It remains high for serious violent crimes, such as murder, despite tragedies like the unresolved murder of Stephen Lawrence. The police may face new and ever-evolving crimes in 2006, including those mentioned above, but the essential features of police work, including the prevention and detection of crime, remain unaltered.

In 2006 the government proposed to restructure the police force in England and Wales, by regionalizing and reducing the number of forces. This plan was shelved, in part because of the resistance demonstrated by the existing 43 constabularies.

Despite the significant changes in sentencing policy the functions of the courts are largely unchanged. The weight attached to sentencing philosophies and rationales changes across time and space, but the job done in the courts in the meting out of fines, community-based penalties or custodial sentences endures. The probation and prison services may be reconfigured into NOMS but their core jobs are likely to remain similar to what they are now.

Perhaps one of the most enduring themes in criminal justice policy is the need for joined-up thinking and practice. Since its introduction by New Labour in 1997 joined-up approaches have come to be found in almost every area of criminal justice. This started with the Crime and Disorder Act (1998) and the crime reduction partnerships bringing together the police, local authorities and other interested parties. The Carter Review and the Criminal Justice Act (2003) refer to seamless sentencing and seamless punishment.

So far changes in the criminal justice system have been discussed in light of novel as well as more familiar crime problems. Criminologists can get carried away with looking for the new, however, and it is necessary to keep a watchful eye on those things that do not change.

Crime data

In order that change and continuity can be monitored it is necessary to access relevant data. The changes in policy also have an impact on the methods of criminological inquiry. At the moment there is an almost unimaginable wealth of information about crime. Various types of data can be obtained readily from government websites, such as the Home Office. The police, court, probation and prison services also have websites that make available all types of data about their day-to-day operations and the work they do with regard to suspects, offenders and victims. Local authorities and the voluntary and private sector also produce web-based information about crime. Add to this the fictional and factual representations by the mass media, and there is potentially a recipe for confusion. At times there is arguably information overload, but the data out there is an invaluable source for students of criminology.

Although crime data is burgeoning, the research methods used to gather it remain largely unchanged. It is worth acknowledging that during the period in which New Labour were in power, Home Office officials expressed a preference for quantitative data. Although this book has not covered the subject, all criminologists need to know how to produce and interpret statistical data.

If you are studying criminology, you may be given an opportunity to do some original research, which will involve your collecting some primary or secondary empirical data. Primary data is original material gathered either through interviews or by designing and distributing a survey. Secondary data is material that has been produced by someone else, such as the Home Office's British Crime Survey. Students can use this data and interpret it in light of their personalized research question. It is worth noting at this stage, though, that many universities and colleges are aware of the risks involved in doing research. This is especially important in criminology and criminal justice because of the sensitive nature of the subject matter. For that reason it is improbable that students will be allowed to do research that involves gathering primary data, and specifically they will not be permitted to interview offenders or victims of crime. For that reason many students will base their research on secondary data, including theoretical materials.

Theory

Criminological theory is as susceptible to change as the other domains of criminology and criminal justice. The introductory overview of theory in this text is partial and very selective, and there has been no opportunity to mention the work of some major contemporary writers. However the basic features of the three distinctive theoretical perspectives outlined in Part Four should provide a framework within which to understand and critically assess the work of criminologists of all kinds.

Theoretical work focusing on the relationship between crime and the individual, and crime and society, provides a rather traditional way of seeing and explaining crime. The third perspective – the critical, radical and deconstructive – takes issues with these traditional theories and dismisses them as being dated and inadequate for explaining contemporary criminality. Despite the differences between them, criminological theories exist to explain in one way or another:

- offending behaviour
- the experiences of victims of crime
- the work of criminal justice agencies.

The point about criminological theory is that it can be used as part of an attempt to explain particular criminological problems. It may or may not offer a persuasive account of offending, and this is something that a theorist needs to judge. For example, Merton's theory of anomie is not particularly useful for explaining Internet paedophilia, and those working in this area will need to either adapt it or seek another theory. It may be that a new theory is developed, but this will start from an existing explanation of crime, such as rational choice theory.

So far some themes relating to the criminal justice system, criminological data and theory have been identified. The final part of this chapter summarizes the contents of the four main sections of the book, and identifies what is in store later for those studying for a degree in criminology.

A SUMMARY AND THE WAY FORWARD

Part One of the book started by discussing the concept of crime. It described several methods of defining crime such as common sense, including personal experience, the popular press (mass media), political power, and practical and professional perspectives. However, the book adopted a legal definition of crime as the violation of a written code or the law. A key point about this definition of crime is that what counts as a crime changes over time. This was demonstrated with reference to legislation on homosexuality, stop and search, and drugs. These examples suggest two things: first, that the law changes in response to changing social conditions and attitudes, and second, that there is a gap between the law in writing and the law in action, largely resulting from the use of discretion. This has consequences for citizens who come into contact with the criminal justice system, especially the police in their gatekeeping role.

New legislation comes into effect continually, and this book cannot reasonably predict what it will comprise. However the policy implications of any piece of legislation can be assessed by considering:

- the reasons it was introduced
- its impact on criminal justice agencies
- its impact on the wider citizenry.

The legal definition of crime is just one possible way of defining the concept, and many criminologists argue that it is rather limited in its focus. Later on the book has suggested some alternative perspectives, and demonstrated that law enforcement policies are applied differentially against women and men, and majority and ethnic minority groups. A student of criminology needs to consider a range of different definitions of crime, and select relevant approaches. Whichever perspective is chosen, it needs to be justified.

In Chapter 2 two key actors in the criminal justice process were introduced, the offender and the victim. This chapter described some of the elementary features of the concept of the offender. The reasons that people offend were not discussed at this stage, but some of the consequences of committing crime were identified. Most crimes involve a victim, and this chapter introduced victimological perspectives to account for people's diverse experiences of victimization. Although the criminal justice system has traditionally focused on detecting, prosecuting and punishing offenders, the victim has recently been given more recognition. In the last analysis, though, criminal justice is essentially about a dispute between the individual offender, the state and the rule of law.

Different people experience criminal justice in many different ways, both individually and in wider groups. It was argued that social divisions are important factors for understanding criminal justice. Social class, race/ethnicity, gender and age are all highly significant when it comes to understanding the differentiated patterns of offending behaviour and victimization. Most offenders and victims are found in the lower social classes. There is clear evidence of differential patterns of offending and victimization with regard to race and ethnicity. Sex and gender, as well as age, are also key determinants of offending behaviour and victimization. Criminological research has shown that most offenders are young working-class males. Victimological studies indicate that crime affects everyone, though certain groups are more prone to becoming victims of particular offences. Whenever you consider a particular crime and the criminal justice system's response, it is always necessary to think about social divisions.

You may go on to study different factors influencing offending behaviour and victimization. Drawing on the theoretical material in Part Four, it should be possible to consider, for example, the reasons that people commit burglary, and to recognize not only that there are various explanations of burglary, but that different explanations can be used in relation to various offences.

Any study of criminology at more than an elementary level must consider in depth the significance of social divisions such as gender and race, in the light of feminist and anti-racist theories. You may need to consider explanations, and not just descriptions, of the relationship between the victim and offender. You could find that the perspective of left realism provides you with an illuminating reference point.

The first part of the book introduced some research evidence and crime data, but the second part considers this in a more systematic fashion. Chapter 3 identified some of the most widely used sources of the data, the recorded crime statistics collated by the police and the British Crime Survey (BCS). This data is published by the Home Office and is easily accessible via the Internet. Much of this data appears in a statistical format, and in very general terms the BCS has shown that there is between three and four times more crime than is reported to and recorded by the police.

Some of the BCS data has been subjected to further analysis to provide a basis for considering issues such as the experiences of crime victims. This data is more qualitative, and gives an insight into the subjective factors behind the crime statistic (which is arguably an objective fact). The Home Office is not the only source of quantitative and qualitative information about crime, and criminologists have undertaken studies focusing on crime problems of national and international significance. There are also many studies of crime problems in local contexts, and I referred to a piece of basic research I was personally involved in.

This introduction to the different sources of data can be built on by considering in more depth the strengths and weaknesses of different sources of data. You should also look at the appropriateness of particular data sources for answering specific questions. As well as being able to identify sources of data, criminologists need to have the ability to interpret and apply the information.

Chapter 4 then explored the research methods used by criminologists to gather data. Research methods are a core issue to all students of the social sciences, and those studying in this field will need to build on this basic introduction. The scope of this chapter was limited to describing some of the tools criminologists use to find out about crime. It retained the distinction between quantitative and qualitative data employed in the previous chapter, and discussed the different approaches used to gather information.

The methods used by qualitative researchers include interviews and ethnographic approaches. This type of data provides an insight into people's perceptions about criminological matters, and more generally into the strategies they use to make sense of the social world. Quantitative researchers are interested in gathering statistical information, and in addition to using the sources identified in Chapter 3 they design surveys to gather numerical data. Quantitative research is influenced by positivism, and the assumption that it is possible to identify causal influences and predict human behaviour. Thus there is a range of methods used to collect crime data, but they are all required to show that the material gathered is valid, reliable and representative of the population studied.

Chapter 4 was descriptive, and students will need to acquire the ability to explain why particular methods are appropriate for answering particular research questions.

Part Three described the main features of the criminal justice system. Before looking at each of the agencies, the chapter introduced the wider context in which it is embedded. It is suggested that the criminal justice system is an integral part of the welfare state, and Chapter 5 described the state and its different components. In addition to this context the chapter introduced the concept of justice, and explored the role of legislation, in particular the Police and Criminal Evidence Act (1984), which is intended to ensure that the police treat suspects fairly. Although justice is an important consideration, the chapter showed that in more recent times other value frameworks are becoming influential in criminal justice policy, especially managerialism, or the new public management (NPM).

At the start of the criminal justice system or process are the police, who perform a gate-keeping function. This organization is the most researched, and also attracts the most attention from the media. The police have many roles and responsibilities, but these tend to fit into two general categories, crime fighting and peace keeping. The police force has carried out these tasks since its formation in the nineteenth century, and the police perform essentially the same tasks now as they did almost two centuries ago.

After describing the structure and organization of the service, Chapter 6 considered the mismatch between what the police are supposed to do in principle and what they actually do in practice. The concept of police culture was used to illustrate how rank and file police officers frequently deviate from what is expected by police managers and policy makers. Police culture also sustains stereotypical ideas about certain social groups such as the underclass, the working classes and minority ethnic groups. This chapter also evaluated the police's response to sexual violence against women. Among other things this example of police work challenges common-sense views that the police always detect the offender.

Chapter 7 then moved on to consider the prosecution process and the courts. The cases that end up in the courts have been through the filters of the police and Crown Prosecution Service, and as the example of the police's activities in relation to rape shows, a significant number of reported cases do not get to the courts. The work of the courts is extremely important because it is in this setting that the administration of justice occurs most explicitly through sentencing. The chapter described in some detail the structure and functions of the courts system, focusing mainly on the magistrates' and Crown courts.

The philosophical assumptions underpinning sentencing and the main sentences were outlined, drawing a distinction between custodial and non-custodial sentences. The rationales for sentencing are complex and sometimes confusing, and this is reflected in sentencing policy and its outcomes. Some of the contradictions of sentencing were investigated by looking at the treatment of female offenders by sentencers. As was pointed out in Chapter 2, certain social groups are treated differently on the basis of social divisions, and to a point these differences can be explained as a consequence of discrimination and stereotyping.

The outcome of appearing in court as an offender may be a discharge or a fine, but the most widely researched sentences are imprisonment and punishment in the community. Chapter 8 outlined the emergence of the prison from a historical perspective, arguing that this institution was introduced primarily to punish offenders. Prisons were also seen as an alternative to more barbaric forms of punishment such as torture, although prison reformers over the centuries have criticized the inhumane conditions of prison life. The rationales used to justify locking people up have also changed over time, and there is a tension between punitive and rehabilitative functions.

Drawing on the UK experience, the chapter showed that the prison population is now the highest it has ever been. Among other things this has led to prison overcrowding and a general sense of crisis in the prison service. The chapter then explored the very different experiences of female and minority ethnic group prisoners. Overall their experiences are much more negative than those of White men, and their treatment is generally of a harsher nature.

In the 2000s the government decided that the work of the prison service needed to be brought more in line with the National Probation Service. The idea was to create the National Offender Management Service (NOMS) so there was a strong connection between sentencing and resettlement. In short, the aim was to create more coherence and continuity in sentencing and penal policy. This also raises the issue of contestability, which in this context implies competition between potential providers of offender management services in the statutory, private and voluntary sectors. At the time of writing the logistics of these new arrangements had not been confirmed, so the book focused on the prison and probation services as separate, albeit related entities.

Accordingly Chapter 9 provided an overview of the origins and evolution of the probation service. This organization has changed the most since its inception, beginning as an agency that cared for offenders and evolving into one that is now more controlling and punitive in its orientation, hence the phrase community-based punishment. Indeed there was a view that the probation service offered a soft option for offenders, and in more recent times the organization has repositioned itself to make it appear tougher. The chapter considered two examples of punishment in the community, DTTOs and electronic monitoring. The structure of the prison and probation service may have changed by the time you read this text but the principles discussed will still be live.

Chapter 10 revisited some of the issues and debates addressed in Chapter 5, especially those concerning the welfare state. The focus was on joined-up approaches in criminal justice policy, which have made explicit the links between welfare and criminal justice agencies. The passing into law of the Crime and Disorder Act (1998) made it a statutory requirement for the police to work with local authorities and a range of agencies in other fields such as health, education and housing to reduce crime and disorder. After describing the CDA framework some examples were given of the achievements of joined-up policies designed to tackle crime and social exclusion in the areas of health, education and housing. It is still too early to tell how effective these joined-up strategies have been, but it would appear that the CDA resulted in a change of approach.

All the chapters focusing on the criminal justice system are essentially descriptive. If and when you move beyond this introductory level, it will involve making a comparison between what a particular institution (such as the police service) is supposed to do and what it does in practice. In a sense, students should dig beneath the surface of the formal structure to assess what is actually happening. Each chapter in Part Three attempted to do this in the case studies, although these accounts were relatively superficial inasmuch as they described a situation rather than attempted to explain it. Consequently many questions were left unanswered and some were not even asked.

The fourth, and final, part of the book, introduced criminological theory. Chapter 11 explained the purpose of theory, and outlined the origins of criminological theorizing. In the nineteenth century there emerged two conflicting perspectives, classicism and positivism. Classicism focuses on the individual offender as a rational being who is free to choose how to behave. In short, people commit a crime because they want to, although they may consider the possible pain they would experience if they were caught. Positivists argue that the offender is a product of his or her biology, psychology and/or social environment. The basic premise is that people are not in full control of their actions because they are driven to some degree by inner or external dynamics. Although this dispute was initiated in the nineteenth century it continues to be debated to this day. Accordingly after this general overview of the beginnings of criminological theory, Chapter 11 focused on explanations of crime that place most emphasis on the individual. It referred to various sociological and psychological perspectives, some suggesting that offenders are driven by their innate characteristics and others claiming that the criminal is an autonomous subject.

While Chapter 11 touched on some sociological variants of criminological theory, the following chapter summarized those theories that argue criminal behaviour is influenced by the wider social environment. Most of Chapter 12 assesses structural explanations, and their suggestion that socioeconomic factors such as social class determine or influence human behaviour. However, other theories within this broad approach recognize that individuals do exercise some self-control and choice, as is illustrated by their ability to create subcultures that deviate from the dominant culture in mainstream society. In the last analysis, though, society exerts more of an influence and ultimately conditions its members' behaviour.

Chapter 13 was very critical of the approaches to theorizing covered in the other two theoretical chapters. Feminist criminologists, for example, have argued that criminological theory did not make explicit the fact that most offenders were male. This was taken for granted but feminists have problematized this fact. They have also shown that wider inequalities between men and women are reflected in criminal justice policy, where women are discriminated against and subsequently disadvantaged. The empirical evidence provided in Chapters 6, 7 and 8 backs up this theoretical claim. Similarly, anti-racist theorists have shown how racism operates to stereotype minority ethnic groups. Finally, criminological theory has been criticized by postmodern commentators. Postmodernity refers to a complex set of ideas, but the key point is that the universal values of modernity (such as justice) are no longer seen as relevant: we live in uncertain times characterized by moral ambiguity. The social divisions of class, gender and race are no longer significant as identity is individualized. The outcome is fragmentation and chaos, and the emergence of different processes in crime control. This was illustrated with reference to the notions of risk and surveillance.

As was noted above, many key thinkers have not been included in the discussion in this book, but if you continue your criminological studies they will become familiar to you. Above all, as you study in more depth you will need to consider how to apply criminological theories to explain particular criminological problems. There will be a requirement to identify a theory or theories that are relevant to the questions you are attempting to answer. It is quite likely that single theories (such as labelling theory) will provide some solutions but not others. Theories are there to be used, but sensibly, in order to make sense of particular criminological problems.

Notes

INTRODUCTION

1 This case study is based on references initially gathered by Kate Bevin (2006) for the purpose of her undergraduate dissertation.

CHAPTER 1, DEFINING CRIME AND STUDYING CRIMINOLOGY AND CRIMINAL JUSTICE

1 To be fair, Paddick did say that that the portrayal of Brixton as 'some kind of dangerous, lawless, wasteland' is 'another gross exaggeration' (*Guardian*, 2 July 2002).
2 NCIS was launched in 2000 as the key provider of criminal intelligence to national and international bodies, to enable them to disrupt the manufacture, distribution and trafficking of drugs (see http://ncis.co.uk).

CHAPTER 3, UNDERSTANDING CRIME DATA I: SOURCES OF INFORMATION

1 The 1982 and 1988 surveys also included Scotland, but with those two exceptions Scotland and Northern Ireland have separate surveys.
2 The place where the research was carried out has been anonymized and a fictitious place name has been adopted.

CHAPTER 5, THE CRIMINAL JUSTICE SYSTEM AND ITS PROCESSES

1 In short, *laissez-faire* economics refers to a society in which workings of the economy and society are left alone without government interference. This is the total opposite of the welfare state set up by Beveridge as described earlier in this chapter.

CHAPTER 6, THE POLICE: GATEKEEPERS TO THE CRIMINAL JUSTICE PROCESS

1 Rape is defined as 'sexual intercourse where a man knows that a woman is not consenting or is reckless as to whether or not she is consenting'. Since 1985 this has also been applied to incidents where the victim is a man.

CHAPTER 9, PROBATION: COMMUNITY-BASED PUNISHMENT AND COMMUNITY JUSTICE

1 The Drug Interventions Programme (formerly the Criminal Justice Interventions Programme) has been instructed to support access to treatment under the community sentence, in order to ensure that the delivery of DTTO performance targets are not threatened (www.probation.homeoffice.gov.uk).
2 Note the gender of the offender. The assumption was that it would be a man.

CHAPTER 10, MULTI-AGENCY AND 'JOINED-UP' APPROACHES TO CRIMINAL JUSTICE POLICY

1 The social housing sector includes housing owned, let and managed by local authorities and registered social landlords (including housing associations, local housing companies and housing action trusts).

Glossary

Accused The person who is suspected of committing a particular criminal offence.

Acquittal What happens when a person is found not guilty in the courts.

Adversarialism It is presumed by the prosecution in England and Wales that a person is only guilty of committing an offence if there is evidence to prove his or her guilt beyond reasonable doubt.

Anomie Emile Durkheim used this concept to describe the normlessness brought about by social change. Robert Merton used it to explain the means individuals use to satisfy the needs they cannot satisfy legitimately.

Antisocial behaviour Behaviour that is not necessarily criminal but disorderly and causing people to be fearful.

Arrest The lawful detention of a suspect, typically by a police officer.

Attorney General This person looks after the Crown Prosecution Service (CPS), the Serious Fraud Office and HM Revenue & Customs prosecutors.

Bail A suspect or defendant may be released before a case is concluded on the condition that he or she returns to the police station or court at a later date. Failure to return may result in a sanction or punishment.

Barrister A professional lawyer who acts as an advocate in the courts.

Bench The team of magistrates sitting in court on a particular day of business, the whole group of magistrates in a particular area, or the actual place where magistrates sit in the court.

Beyond reasonable doubt The required standard of proof in criminal cases.

Biological positivism The view that criminal behaviour is influenced by physiological factors.

British Crime Survey A Home Office survey that focuses on crime victimization throughout England and Wales. This measure of crime complements the recorded crime statistics produced by the police.

Burden of proof In most cases the burden of proof rests on the prosecution, which must prove that a defendant is guilty beyond reasonable doubt.

Capital punishment The sentence also known as the death penalty.

Chicago School A number of researchers writing at the University of Chicago in the 1920s and 1930s, who argued that criminal behaviour is related to environmental and geographical factors.

Circuit judge A full-time judge appointed by the lord chancellor. Circuit judges are typically barristers and solicitors belonging to the circuit bench.

Class (social class) Refers to a person's occupation or what he or she does in the world of work. There is also a close relationship between a person's job and his or her income and wealth.

Classical criminology, or classicism A theory in which offenders are viewed as rational creatures who choose to commit offences. They may be deterred or put off from committing crime by the threat of punishment.

Clerk to justices A solicitor or a barrister who provides legal advice to the court and has overall administrative responsibility for the courts.

Code for Crown Prosecutors The policies and procedures guiding the working of the Crown Prosecution Service (CPS).

Cognitive development The development of attitudes and beliefs that people hold about the world.

Committal This occurs at the pre-trial stage and refers to those cases that are transferred from the magistrates' court to the Crown court for sentence or trial.

Common law The law that is created on the basis of decisions taken in the courts. Note the difference between this and statutory law (see *statute*).

Community safety The general well-being of a community, where crime and other threats to security are addressed.

Compensation A penalty requiring the offender to reimburse the victim for his or her losses.

Conditional discharge When the courts mete out this sentence no further action is taken for the current offence on the condition that the offender does not reoffend within a specified time period. Failure to comply with this condition results in another penalty being imposed.

Conflict theory The theory that powerful groups in society, such as the ruling class, define crime and regulate it to maintain their own material interests.

Control theory The theory that crime is committed by people with weak bonds and attachment to the wider society.

Conviction When a person is found guilty in a criminal court.

Crime Law breaking or the violation of a legal code.

Crime control model The thesis that the overriding aim of the criminal justice system is to arrest, charge, prosecute and sentence criminals as efficiently and effectively as possible. The guilt of the offender is taken for granted, rather than being seen as something to be proven beyond reasonable doubt.

Crime prevention Methods of stopping crime from occurring (see *situational crime prevention*).

Crime reduction Methods of cutting the number of crimes committed.

Criminal justice agencies The police, crown prosecution, court, probation and prison services.

Criminal justice system The joined-up working of the criminal justice agencies (see above) in the wider context of the state and society.

Criminology The study of crime, including its causes and reduction.

Critical criminology Criminology that takes the stance that society in general and the criminal justice system in particular is oppressive and discriminates against minority groups, such as ethnic minorities and women.

Crown court This is the court where trials on indictment are heard in front of a judge and jury.

Crown Prosecution Service This agency is responsible for the prosecution of most criminal cases.

Curfew Offenders given this type of sentence are required to be in a particular place at a particular time.

Custody A prison sentence or the detention of a suspect by the police.

Custody minus An offender is given an opportunity to be punished in the community but if he or she fails to observe the conditions attached to the sentence there is the threat of incarceration or imprisonment.

Custody plus Consists of a short period in prison followed by a longer period of community supervision.

Dark figure Offences that are not reported to the police as well as those they do not record.

Defence Representation of the defendant.

Defendant A person at a trial who has been accused of committing a crime.

Determinism An explanation of criminal behaviour that assumes offending is strongly influenced by social, biological or psychological factors that are beyond the control of the individual.

Deterrence A sentencing principle underpinned by an assumption that it is possible to stop people from committing crime by introducing a punishment that puts them off from offending.

Differential association theory The theory that people commit crime because their orientation towards law breaking outweighs their commitment to observing the rule of law.

Discharge Those occasions when sentencers in the courts take no further action against a suspect.

Discretion The selective application of legislation or policy.

District judge A trained legal professional (a solicitor or barrister with a minimum of seven years experience), who usually serves in larger courts in urban areas, and who is salaried. Unlike most magistrates, district judges sit alone, and tend to take on more lengthy and difficult cases.

Diversion Attempts to keep offenders outside of the criminal justice system.

DNA A nucleic acid in which genetic instructions are encoded in a way that is unique to an individual. Found in evidence such as blood, hair and bodily fluids that can be used in criminal investigations.

Doli incapax Literally, 'incapable of crime'. A phrase that describes children who are not legally responsible for their actions.

Due process In contrast to the crime control model, this model takes the stance that the criminal justice system must prove beyond reasonable doubt that the accused is guilty. Criminal justice agencies must observe all the rules and procedures to safeguard suspects.

Electronic monitoring The use of technological devices, such as electronic tags, to monitor the movement of offenders.

Ethnicity The culture, attitudes and beliefs of a particular social group. This is sometimes used interchangeably with *race* (see below).

Ethnomethodology A sociological approach that focuses on the individual social actor and his or her attempts to produce meaningful social interaction with other social actors.

Evidence Material and information gathered by the police to present to the Crown Prosecution Service and eventually to the courts. It may include victim and witness statements and physical evidence such as samples that provide *DNA*.

Feminist criminology Approaches which highlight the differential and inequitable treatment of women in society.

Fine A sentence of court involving a financial penalty.

Gender The socially constructed categories of male and female.

Guilt In criminal cases this needs to be established beyond reasonable doubt.

HM Inspectorate These bodies carry out reviews of criminal justice agencies to ensure that their service is delivery is efficient and effective. For example, there is an inspectorate for the police (Her Majesty's Inspectorate of Constabulary, HMIC), Her Majesty's Inspectorate of Probation (HMIP), and Her Majesty's Inspectorate of Prisons (HMIP).

Home Office The government department responsible for the criminal justice system and law and order policies.

Home secretary The minister in charge of policy at the Home Office.

House of Lords One of the two houses of Parliament, a non-elected body which scrutinizes legislation proposed by the House of Commons.

Incarceration The imprisonment of sentenced prisoners and persons awaiting trail.

Indeterminate sentence A sentence that does not have a fixed period (for instance, a life sentence). This is in contrast to a determinate sentence, which is for a fixed length of time.

Indictable offences Crimes that are tried in the Crown court.

Individualism An assumption that social life is best understood with reference to the individual social actor and that society is the sum of individual actions.

Intermittent custody A prison sentence which is spread over a longer period to ensure a prisoner can work in the week and go to prison at weekends.

Judge In the crown Court she/he summarizes the court proceedings and gives direction regarding the necessary points of law.

Jury For criminal trials held at the Crown court 12 adults are selected to decide whether the accused is guilty or not on the basis of the evidence they hear.

Just deserts According to this sentencing principle the punishment should fit the crime.

Labelling theory The theory that crime is the result of a social reaction and without this, crime does not exist. In other words, a criminal is produced by the complex activities of the criminal justice agencies and the criminal justice system.

Left realism A holistic explanation of crime that considers the complex causes of crime and solutions to offending behaviour. Left realists created the *square of crime.*

Magistrate This person is responsible for sentencing in the magistrates' courts.
Magistrates' court The lower court (the Crown court is the higher one) in which criminal cases are heard.
Modernity A belief in science and rationality, and that human beings can control their own environment.
Moral panic A reaction to a crime that is blown out of proportion to its actual seriousness.

New criminology A theoretical approach popular in the 1970s which aimed to bring together Marxism and *labelling theory.*
New Public Management (NPM) A method of public sector reform where there is an emphasis on economy, effectiveness and efficiency. Sometimes known as managerialism.
Notifiable offences The offences recorded by the police. They include most indictable offences and triable either way offences, as well as a small number of summary offences.

Offence An action that is prohibited by the criminal law.

Paedophilia Sexual attraction to children, and hence the sexually motivated abuse of children.
Parliament Both the elected House of Commons and the non-elected House of Lords. All legislation is debated and scrutinized by Parliament and must have parliamentary approval before it becomes law. The House of Commons is the most powerful body and can override a decision by the House of Lords.
Parole The early release of prisoners from custody (prison).
Parole board Takes decisions about whether, and when, to release prisoners.
Patriarchy Originally, male dominance within families. Radical feminists have adopted this idea to explain male dominance in social relations.
Plea A defendant makes a plea to indicate whether or not he or she admits to being guilty of committing the offence he or she is accused of.
Positivism This word may used in two main ways. First, it describes those theories that explain criminal behaviour as something caused or influenced by biological, psychological or environmental factors. Second, it refers to the belief that human society can be examined in the same way that natural scientists (such as physicists and chemists) study natural phenomena.
Postmodernity and the postmodern A position that challenges modernity and the principles of rationality and scientific reason. The emphasis is on discourse, diversity and fragmentation.
Pre-sentence reports These are written by the probation service for adult offenders to describe their background in an attempt to put their behaviour in context and to influence sentencing decisions.
Presumption of innocence The assumption that the prosecution must prove beyond reasonable doubt the guilt of a defendant, and that guilt should not be assumed until this has been achieved.
Probation Those activities undertaken by probation officers and the National Probation Service.

Race The use of physical markers such as skin colour to classify people into groups (such as White and Black). Note that there is no scientific evidence to support the view that biological differences result in social differences.
Racism Discrimination based on perceived differences, where social groups are arranged in a hierarchy, including dominant and subordinate groups. Racism may be manifest by an individual or it may be institutionalized.
Radical criminology This perspective is inspired by Marxism and highlights the economic and class dimensions of crime. It takes the stance that the ruling class use the law and the criminal justice system to oppress the working classes.
Rational choice theory The theory that human beings commit crime when the opportunity arises and if there is nothing to prevent them from doing so.
Recidivist A repeat and persistent offender.
Rehabilitation The aim is to reform offenders and return them to normality.
Remand The custody in which an alleged offender may be held before a trial takes place.
Reparation An offender is required to make amends to the victim and to repair the damage he or she has done.

Restorative justice An attempt to repair the damage caused by offenders by bringing them into contact with their victims.

Retribution The belief that criminals deserve to be punished because what they have done is wrong.

Right realism The theory that the criminal is a rational actor who chooses to commit a offence. The certainty of punishment may deter future offenders.

Routine activities theory The thesis that for a crime to be committed there must be an offender, a suitable target (person or property) and the absence of a capable guardian to prevent the crime from happening.

Sentence(s) The punishments imposed by the courts on those found guilty of criminal offences. They include fines and custodial or non-custodial (community-based) sentences.

Situational crime prevention The argument that crime can be prevented by making people or property more crime resistant. For example, car alarms can prevent theft of and from motor vehicles.

Social exclusion A concept used to describe those people who are not able to participate in the social activities enjoyed by most people. Invariably it is used to describe the poorest members of society.

Square of crime Invented by the *left realists*, this explanation of crime looks at the relationship between the offender, victim, state and wider society to understand not only the action but the reaction to crime.

State The more or less permanent legal and organizational framework through which society is managed and controlled, and which defines the competencies and powers of its agents (such as judges and civil servants).

Statute Law as set out in Parliament.

Stipendiary magistrate See *district judge*.

Strain theory The theory that offenders experience strain when the legitimate or legal means of satisfying their perceived needs are not available.

Subculture Criminal behaviour is an adaptation of groups, especially young people, to their material social circumstances.

Summary offence One of the three categories of criminal offences, the other two being indictable and triable either way offences. Summary offences are heard in the magistrates' court only.

Summons A written notice issued to a defendant requiring him or her to appear in court at a specified time to respond to a criminal charge.

Surveillance The systematic observation and control of people, products or places, for example using closed-circuit television (CCTV).

Suspect A person who is believed to have committed a criminal offence. He or she remains a suspect until guilt is proved beyond reasonable doubt.

Techniques of neutralization The methods offenders use to justify their criminal behaviour to themselves and other people.

Triable either way (T-E-W) The third of three categories of criminal offence. Such offences may be tried either in the Crown court or at a magistrates' court.

Underclass The poorest and most deprived social group in society, often alleged to be involved in criminal activity.

Utilitarianism The thesis that a policy, such as the criminal law and criminal justice policy, should promote the 'greatest happiness of the greatest number'.

Victim This has two general meanings. First, it describes a person who has been affected by crime and offending behaviour. Second, in England and Wales the state takes on the status of a victim when it processes offenders through the criminal justice system.

Victimology The study of victims of crime.

Victimization The processes associated with the creation of a victim.

Warrant An order of court. It may give the police the power to arrest someone, for example.

White-collar crime Crimes committed by professional people while they are at work.

Witness A person who has seen a crime committed or has information about an offence.

Youth court This court is part of the magistrates' court system but is designated for dealing with young offenders under the age of 18.

Youth Justice Board This agency has overall responsibility for youth justice policy and practice.

Youth offending team A team of criminal justice professionals established to deal specifically with young people.

References

Acheson, Sir Donald (1998) *Independent Inquiry into Inequalities in Health*. London: HMSO.

Ackroyd, S and Hughes, J. (1992) *Data Collection in Context* (2nd edn), London: Longman.

Adler, F. (1975) *Sisters in Crime: The rise of the new female criminal*. New York: McGraw Hill.

Alcock, P., Erskine, A. and May, M. (eds) (2003) *The Student's Companion to Social Policy* (2nd edn), Oxford: Blackwell.

Allahar, A. (1993) 'When black first became worth less', *International Journal of Comparative Sociology* 34(1–2): 39–55.

Anthias, F. (1990) 'Race and class revisited – conceptualising race and racisms', *Sociological Review* 38(1): 19–42.

Anti-Social Behaviour Unit (2004) *Together: Tackling anti-social behaviour pack*. London: HMSO.

Archard, P. (1979) 'Vagrancy: a literature review', in T. D. Cook (ed.), *Vagrancy: Some new perspectives*. London: Academic Press.

Armstrong, G. (1993) 'Like that Desmond Morris?', in D. Hobbs and T. May (eds), *Interpreting the Field: Accounts of ethnography*. Oxford: Clarendon Press.

Armstrong, G. (1998) *Football Hooligans: Knowing the score*. Oxford: Berg.

Ashworth, A. (1994) 'Sentencing', in M. Maguire, R. Morgan and R. Reiner (eds), *The Oxford Handbook of Criminology*. Oxford: Oxford University Press.

Ashworth, A. (2003) *The Criminal Process* (3rd edn). Oxford: Oxford University Press.

Association of Chief Police Officers (ACPO) (2004) *Community Cohesion Policing: Practice and advice*. London: National Centre for Policing Excellence, Centrex.

Atkinson, J. M. (1968) *Discovering Suicide: Studies in the organisation of sudden death*. London: Macmetc.

Audit Commission (1999) *Safety in Numbers: Promoting community safety*. London: Audit Commission.

Audit Commission (2004) *Youth Justice 2004: A review of the reformed youth justice system*. Wetherby: Audit Commission Publications.

Auld Report (2001) *Review into the Workings of the Criminal Courts in England and Wales*. London: Home Office.

Balchin, P. and Rhodes, M. (2002) *Housing Policy: An introduction* (4th edn). London: Sage.

Baldwin, J. and Kinsey, R. (1982) *Police Powers and Politics*. London: Quartet.

Bannister, J. and Scott, S. (2000) 'Assessing the cost-effectiveness of measures to deal with anti-social behaviour', Housing and Social Policy Research Group Discussion Paper 1. Glasgow: University of Glasgow.

Banton, M. (1964) *The Policeman in the Community*. London: Tavistock.

Banton, M. (1967) *Police–Community Relations*. London: Collins.

Barnes, B. (1977) *Interests and the Growth in Knowledge*. London: Routledge & Kegan Paul.

Bartol, C. A. and Bartol, A. M. (2005) *Criminal Behaviour: A Psychological Approach*. New Jersey: Pearson Education.

Barton, A. (1999), 'Breaking the crime/drug cycle: the birth of a new approach?', *Howard Journal*, 38(2): 144–57.

Barton, A. and Quinn, C. (2002), 'Risk management of groups or respect for the individual? Issues for information sharing and confidentiality in drug treatment and testing orders', *Drugs, Education, Prevention and Policy*, 9(1).

Bateman, M. (2001), 'Conflict in court?', *Nursing Times*, 97(44): 34–5.

Batty, D. (2004) 'Home Office launches "anti-social behaviour academy"', *Guardian*, 3 March.

Bauman, Z. (1991) *Modernity and Ambivalence*. Oxford: Polity.

Bauman, Z. (2000) *Liquid Modernity*. Cambridge: Polity.

Bean, P. (2002) *Drugs and Crime*. Devon: Willan.

Bean, P. (2004) *Drugs and Crime* (2nd edn). Devon: Willan.

Beccaria, C. (1963) *On Crimes and Punishment* (trans. H. Paolucci). Indianapolis: Bobbs-Merrill Educational.

Beck, U. (1992) *The Risk Society*, London: Sage.

Becker, H. (1963) *Outsiders: Studies in the sociology of deviance*. New York: Free Press.

Beirne, P. and J.W. Messerschmidt (2005) *Criminology* (4th edn). Los Angeles, Calif.: Roxbury.

Bell, C. (1969) 'A note on participant observation', *Sociology* 3: 417–18.

Bennett, T. and Holloway, K. (2005) *Understanding Drugs, Alcohol and Crime*. Maidenhead: OUP.

Beresford, P. (1979) 'The public presentation of vagrants', in T.D. Cook (ed.), *Vagrancy: Some new perspectives*. London: Academic Press.

Berkowitz, L. (1962) *Agression: A Social-Psychological Analysis*. New York: McGraw-Hill.

Berry, B. and Matthews, R. (1989) 'Electronic monitoring and house arrest: making the right connections', in R. Matthews (ed.), *Privatising Criminal Justice*. London: Sage.

Beveridge, W. (1942) *Social Insurance and Allied Services*, Cm. 604. London: HMSO.

Bevin, K. E. (2006) *Is Hip Hop Music Encouraging Gun Related Crime Among Inner City Teenagers?* Unpublished dissertation, Division of Criminology, Nottingham Trent University.

Bichard, R. (2004) *The Bichard Inquiry Report*, House of Commons HC 653. London: HMSO.

Bittner, E. (1967a) 'Police discretion in emergency apprehension of mentally ill persons', *Social Problems* 14: 257–92.

Bittner, E. (1967b) 'The police on skid row: a study of peacekeeping', *American Sociological Review* 32(5): 699–715.

Bittner, E. (1974) 'Florence Nightingale in pursuit of Willie Sutton: a theory of the police', in H. Jacobs (ed.), *Potential for Reform of Criminal Justice*. Beverley Hills, Calif.: Sage.

Black, M. and Smith, R. G. (2003) *Electronic Monitoring in the Criminal Justice System*. Series: Trends and Issues in Crime and Criminal Justice 254. Canberra: Australian Institute of Criminology.

Bottomley, K and Coleman, C. (1981) *Understanding Crime Rates: Police and public roles in the production of official statistics*. London: Gower.

Bottomley, K. and Pease, K. (1993) *Crime and Punishment: Interpreting the data*. Milton Keynes: Open University Press.

Bowling, B. (1998) *Violent Racism*. Oxford: Oxford University Press.

Bowling, B. and Foster, J. (2002) 'Policing and the police', in M. Maguire, R. Reiner and R. Morgan (eds), *The Oxford Handbook of Criminology* (3rd edn). Oxford: Clarendon Press.

Bowling, B. and Phillips, C. (2002) *Racism, Crime and Justice*. Harlow: Longman.

Box, S. (1983) *Power, Crime and Mystification*. London: Tavistock.

Box, S. (1987) *Recession, Crime and Punishment*. London: Macmillan.

Boyne, R. (2001) 'Post-panopticism', *Economy and Society* 29(2): 285–307.

Braithwaite, J. (1984) *Corporate Crime in the Pharmaceutical Industry*. London: Routledge.

Bright, M. (2002) 'Surgical tag plans for sex offenders', *Observer*, 17 November.

Brogden, M and Nijhar, P. (2000) *Crime, Abuse and the Elderly*. Cullompton: Willan.

Brown, J. and Heidensohn, F. (2000) *Gender and Policing*. London: Macmillan.

Brown, S. (1998) *Understanding Youth and Crime*. Buckingham: Open University Press.

Brownlee, I. (1998) *Community Punishment: A critical introduction*. Harlow: Longman.

Brownmiller, S. (1975) *Against Our Will*. Harmondsworth: Penguin.

Bryman, A. (2001) *Social Research Methods*. Oxford: Oxford University Press.

Bullock, K. and Tilley, N. (2002) *Shootings, Gangs and Violent Incidents in Manchester: Developing a crime reduction strategy*. Home Office Research Series Paper 13. London: Home Office.

Bulmer, M. (1984) *Social Research Methods*, London: Macmillan.

Burman, M. J., Batchelor, S. A. and Brown, J. A. (2001) 'Researching girls and violence: facing the dilemmas of fieldwork', *British Journal of Criminology* 41: 443–59.

Burney, E. (2002) 'Talking tough, acting coy: what happened to the anti-social behaviour order?', *Howard Journal* 41(5): 469–84.

Byrne, C. and Trew, K. (2005) 'Crime orientation, social relations and improvement in crime: patterns emerging from offenders' accounts', *Howard Journal* 44(2): 185–205.

Cabinet Office (2001) *National Strategy for Neighbourhood Renewal*. London: Cabinet Office.

Caddle, D. and Crisp, D. (1997) *Imprisoned Women and Mothers*. Home Office Research Study 162. London: Home Office.

Cain, M. (1973) *Society and the Policeman's Role*. London: Routledge.

Cain, M. (1990) 'Towards transgression: new directions in feminist criminology', *International Journal of the Sociology of Law* 18(1): 1–18.

Carlen, P. (1983) *Women's Imprisonment: A study in social control*. London: Routledge.

Carlen, P. (1988) *Women, Crime and Poverty*. Buckingham: Open University Press.

Carlen, P. (1989) 'Crime inequality and sentencing', in P. Carlen and D. Cook (eds), *Paying for Crime*. Milton Keynes: Open University Press.

Carlen, P. (ed.) (2002a) *Women and Punishment*. Cullompton: Willan.

Carlen P. (2002b) 'Women's imprisonment: models of reform and change', *Probation Journal* 49(2).

Carlen, P. (2002c) 'Critical criminology? In praise of an oxymoron and its enemies', in D. Carrington and R. Hogg (eds), *Critical Criminology: Issues, debates and challenges*. Cullompton: Willan.

Carlen, P. and Worrall, A. (2005) *Analysing Women's Imprisonment*. Cullompton: Willan.

Carnwath, T. and Smith, I. (2002) *Heroin Century*. London: Routledge.

Carter, P. (2003) *Managing Offenders, Reducing Crime: A new approach*. London: HMSO.

Cavadino, M. and Dignan, J. (2002) *The Penal System: An introduction* (3rd edn). London: Sage.

Chambliss, W. (1969) 'The law of vagrancy', in W. Chambliss (ed.), *Crime and the Legal Process*. New York: McGraw-Hill.

Chambliss, W. (1975) 'Towards a political economy of crime', *Theory and Society* 2: 149–70.

Chesney-Lind, M. and Pasko, L. (2004) *The Female Offender: Girls, women, and crime* (2nd edn). Thousand Oaks, Calif.: Sage.

Chibnall, S. (1977) *Law-and-Order News: An analysis of crime reporting in the British Press*. London: Tavistock.

Choongh, S. (1997) *Policing as Social Discipline*. Oxford: Oxford University Press.

Christie, N. (1977) 'Conflicts as property', *British Journal of Criminology* 17(1): 1–15.

Christie, N. (1993) *Crime Control as Industry*. London: Routledge.

Cicourel, A. V. (1976) *The Social Organisation of Juvenile Justice*. London: Heinemann.

Clarke, J. and Newman, J. (1997) *The Managerial State: Power, politics and ideology in the remaking of social welfare*. London. Sage.

Clarke, R. (1980) 'Situational crime prevention: theory and practice', *British Journal of Criminology* 20: 132–45.

Clarke, R. V. and Felson, M. (2004) *Routine Activity and Rational Choice*. USA: Transaction.

Cloward, R. and Ohlin, L. E. (1960) *Delinquency and Opportunity: A theory of delinquent gangs*. New York: Free Press

Clyde, C. (2004) *Education Policy in Britain*. Basingstoke: Palgrave Macmillan.

Cochrane, A. (2003) 'The governance of local welfare', in P. Alcock, A. Erskine and M. May (eds), *The Student's Companion to Social Policy* (2nd edn). Oxford: Blackwell.

Cohen, A. (1955) *Delinquent Boys: The culture of the gang*. New York: Free Press.

Cohen, P. (1979) 'Policing the working class city', in B. Fine, R. Kinsey, J. Lea, S. Piccioto and J. Young (eds), *Capitalism and the Rule of Law*. London: Hutchinson.

Cohen, S. (1973) *Folk Devils and Moral Panics: The creation of the mods and rockers*. London: Paladin.

Cohen, S. (1980) *Folk Devils and Moral Panics* (new edition). Oxford: Martin Robertson.

Cohen, S. (1985) *Visions of Social Control*. Cambridge: Polity.

Cohen, S. (2000) *States of Denial*. Cambridge: Polity.

Coleman, C. (1981) *In the Production of Official Statistics*. London: Gower.

Coleman, C. and Moynihan, J. (1996) *Understanding Crime Data: Haunted by the dark figure*. Milton Keynes: Open University Press.

Coleman, R. (2004) *Reclaiming the Streets: Surveillance, social control and the city*. Cullompton: Willan.

Collier, R. (1998). *Masculinities, Crime and Criminology: Men, heterosexuality and the criminal(ised) other*. London: Sage.

Collison, M. (1996) 'In search of the high life: drugs, crime, masculinities and consumption', *British Journal of Criminology* 36(3): 428–44.

Connell, R. W. (1987) *Gender and Power: Society, the person, and sexual politics.* Stanford, Calif.: Stanford University Press.

Connell, R. W. (1995) *Masculinities.* Berkeley, Calif.: University of California Press.

Connell, R. W. (2000) *The Men and the Boys.* Sydney: Allen & Unwin.

Connell, R. W. (2002) *Gender.* Cambridge, UK: Polity.

Connell, R.W. and Messerschmidt, J. (2005) 'Hegemonic masculinity: rethinking the concept', *Gender and Society* 19(6): 829–59.

Cook, D. (2006) *Criminal and Social Justice.* London: Sage.

Crawford, A. (1997) *The Local Governance of Crime.* Oxford: Oxford University Press.

Crawford, A. (2003) 'The pattern of policing in the UK: policing beyond the police', in T. Newburn (ed.), *Handbook of Policing.* Cullompton: Willan.

Crawford, A., Lister, S., Blackburn, S. and Burnett, J. (2005) *Plural Policing: The mixed economy of visible patrols in England and Wales.* Bristol: Policy Press.

Croall, H. (1998) *Crime and Society in Britain.* Harlow: Addison Wesley Longman.

Crompton, R. (1993) *Class and Stratification: An introduction to current debates.* Cambridge: Polity.

Crompton, R. (1996) 'The fragmentation of class analysis', *British Journal of Sociology* 47(1): 56–65.

Crow, I. (2001) *The Treatment and Rehabilitation of Offenders.* London: Sage.

Crowther, C. (2000a) *Policing Urban Poverty.* Basingstoke: Macmillan.

Crowther, C. (2000b) 'Crime, social exclusion and policing in the twenty-first century', *Crime Prevention and Community Safety* 2(1): 37–49.

Crowther, C. (2002) 'The politics and economics of disciplining an inclusive and exclusive society', pp. 199–224 in R. Sykes, C. Bochel and N. Ellison (eds), *Social Policy Review 14*, Bristol: Policy Press.

Crowther, C. (2004) 'Over-policing and under-policing social exclusion', in R. Hopkins Burke (ed.), *'Hard Cop/Soft Cop': Dilemmas and debates in contemporary policing.* Cullompton: Willan.

Crowther, C. and Formby, E. (2004) *An Evaluation of the Costs of Responding to and Preventing Anti-Social Behaviour in Westershire.* Research Centre in Community Justice and Centre for Social Inclusion: Sheffield Hallam University.

Daly, K. (1987/9) 'Criminal justice ideologies and practices in different voices: some feminist questions about justice', *International Journal of the Sociology of Law* 17: 1–18.

Daly, K. (1998) 'Gender, crime and criminology', in M. Tonry (ed.), *The Handbook of Crime and Punishment.* New York: Oxford University Press.

Daly, K. and Maher, L. (eds) (1998) *Criminology at the Crossroads: Feminist readings in crime and justice.* New York: Oxford University Press.

Dapp, R. (2002) 'Facts about the Lambeth cannabis pilot scheme', *Urban 75*, September.

Darwin, C. (1968) *On the Origin of the Species.* Harmondsworth: Penguin.

David, M. (1998) 'Education, education and education', in H. Jones and S. MacGregor (eds), *Social Issues and Party Politics.* London: Routledge.

Davies, D. (2004) 'Prisons without bars?', *The Times*, 20 July.

Davies, H., Nutley, S. and Smith, P. (eds) (2000) *What Works? Evidence-based policy and practice in public services*, Bristol: Policy Press.

Davies, J. (1990) *Youth and the Condition of Britain: Images of adolescent conflict.* London: Athlone Press.

Davies, M., Croall, H. and Tyrer, J. (2005) *Criminal Justice: An introduction to the criminal justice system in England and Wales.* Harlow: Pearson Longman.

De Gobineau, A. and Collins, A. (1853/1983) *The Inequality of Human Races* (2nd edn reprint). Torrance, Calif.: Noontide Press.

Dean, M. (1999) *Governmentality: Power and rule in modern society.* London: Sage.

Dean, H. (2006) *Social Policy.* Cambridge: Polity.

Demuth, C. (1978) *'Sus': A report on the Vagrancy Act 1824.* London: Runnymede Trust.

Department of Health (DoH) (2000) *The NHS Plan: A plan for investment, a plan for reform.* London: DoH.

DoH (2003) *Tackling Health Inequalities: A programme for action.* London: DoH.

DoH and Home Office (2005) *National Service Guidelines for Developing Sexual Assault Referral Centres.* London: DoH.

Department of Social Security (DSS) (1993) *Households Below Average Income 1979–1990/1.* London: HMSO.

DSS (2001) *Households Below Average Income.* London: HMSO.

Devine, F., Savage, M., Scott, J. and Crompton, R. (2004) *Rethinking Class: Culture, identities and lifestyle*. Basingstoke: Palgrave.

Dingwall, G. (2005) *Alcohol and Crime*. Cullompton: Willan.

Dixon, M., Reed, H., Rogers, B. and Stone, L. (2006) *Crime Share: The unequal impact of crime*. London: IPPR.

Dodd, T., Nicholas, S., Povey, D. and Walker, A. (2004) *Crime in England and Wales 2003/04*, Home Office Statistical Bulletin 10/04. London: Home Office.

Dodgson, K., Goodwin, P., Howard, P., Llewellyn-Thomas, S., Mortimer, E., Russell, N. and Weiner, M. (2001) *Electronic Monitoring of Released Prisoners: An evaluation of the home detention curfew scheme*, Home Office Research Study 222. London: Home Office.

Dodgson, K. and Mortimer, K. (2000) *Home Office Detention Curfew: The first year of operation*, Research Findings 110. London: Home Office.

Dollard, J., Doob, L.W., Miller, N. E., Mowrer, O. H. and Sears, R. R. (1939) *Frustration and Aggression*. New Haven, Conn.: Yale University Press.

Dominey, J. (2003) 'Community justice files', *British Journal of Community Justice* 2(2): 81–2.

Douglas, J. (1967) *The Social Meanings of Suicide*. Princeton, N.J.: Princeton University Press.

Downes, D. (1966) *The Delinquent Solution: A Study in Subcultural Theory*. London: Routledge and Kegan Paul.

Downes, D. and Rock, P. (1998) *Understanding Deviance: A guide to the sociology of crime and rule breaking* (3rd edn). Oxford: Oxford University Press.

Durkheim, E. (1970) *Suicide* (trans. S.A. Solovay and J.H. Mueller, ed. G. E. G. Catlin). New York: Free Press.

Durkheim, E. (1984) *The Division of Labour in Society* (trans. W. D. Halls). Basingstoke: Macmillan.

Dworkin, A. (1981) *Pornography: Men possessing women*. New York: Perigee Books.

Eaton, M. (1983/6) *Justice for Women?* London: Open University Press.

Eaton, M. (1985) *Women After Prison*. Buckingham: Open University Press.

Elgin, P. (1987) 'The meaning and use of official statistics in the explanation of deviance', in R. J. Anderson, J. Hughes and W. Sharrock (eds), *Classic Disputes in Sociology*. London: Unwin Hyman.

Elias, N. (1978) *The Civilising Process, Vol.1: The History of Manners*. Oxford: Blackwell.

Elias, N. (1982) *The Civilising Process, Vol. 2: State Formation and Civilisation*. Oxford: Blackwell.

Emsley, C. (2002) 'The history of crime and crime control institutions', in M. Maguire, R. Morgan and R. Reiner (eds), *The Oxford Handbook of Criminology* (3rd edn). Oxford University Press.

Ericson, R. and Haggerty, K. (1997) *Policing the Risk Society*, Oxford: Oxford University Press.

Eves, K. (2004) *Juveniles in Custody 2003–4*. London: HMIP/Youth Justice Board.

Eysenck, H. J. (1964) *Crime and Personality*. Boston: Houghton Mifflin.

Eysench, H. J. (1977) *Crime and Personality* (3rd edn). London: Routledge and Kegan Paul.

Falk, C. (2004) 'Are DTTOs working? Issues of policy, implementation and practice', *Probation Journal* 51(4): 398–406.

Farrell, G. and Pease, K. (1993) 'Once bitten, twice bitten: repeat victimisation and its implications for crime prevention', *Crime Prevention Unit*, Paper No. 46. London: HMSO.

Farrell, G. and Pease, K. (eds) (2001) *Repeat Victimisation*. Monsey, NY: Criminal Justice.

Farrell, G. and Pease, K. (2003) *Repeat Victimisation*. New York: Criminal Justice Press.

Farrington, D. P. (1994) 'Human development and criminal careers', in M. Maguire, R. Morgan and R. Reiner (eds), *The Oxford Handbook of Criminology*. London: Oxford: Oxford University Press.

Farrington, D. P., Coid, J. W., Harnett, L., Joliffe, D., Sorteriou, N., Turner, R. and West, D. J. (2006) *Criminal Careers Up To Age 50 and Life Success Up To 48*, Home Office Research Study No. 299. London: Home Office.

Farrington, D. P. and Morris, A. (1983) 'Sex, sentencing and reconviction', *British Journal of Criminology* 23.

Farris, R. E. L. (1967) *The Chicago School, 1920-1932*. Chicago: University of Chicago Press.

Fawcett Society (2004) *Commission on Women and the Criminal Justice System and Women's Offending Reduction Programme*. London: Fawcett Society.

Feeley, M. and Simon, J. (1994) 'Actuarial justice: the emerging new criminal law', pp. 173–201 in D. Nelken (ed.), *The Futures of Criminology*. London: Sage.

Field, J. (2005) *Social Capital and Lifelong Learning*. Bristol: Policy Press.

Finney, A. (2004) *Alcohol and Sexual Violence: Key findings from the research*. Findings 215. London: Home Office.

Fionda, J. (2000) 'New managerialism, credibility and the sanitisation of criminal justice', pp. 109–27 in P. Green and A. Rutherford (eds), *Criminal Policy in Transition*. Oxford: Hart.

Flynn, N. (1998) *Introduction to Prisons and Imprisonment*. London: Waterside Press.

Foster, J. (1993) *Housing, Community and Crime: Impact of Priority Estates Project (PEP)*. London: Home Office.

Foster, J. (2003) 'Police cultures', in T. Newburn (ed.), *The Handbook of Policing*. Cullompton: Willan.

Foucault, M. (1977) *Discipline and Punish*. Harmondsworth: Penguin.

Fox, R. (2001) 'Someone to watch over us: back to the panopticon', *Criminal Justice* 1(3): 251–76.

Fraser, D. (1984) *The Evolution of the British Welfare State* (2nd edn). Basingstoke: Macmillan.

Freud, S. (1961) *The Complete Works of Sigmund Freud* (Vol. 16). London: Hogarth.

Fussey, P. (2005) *Installing CCTV: A study of the networks of surveillance policy*. Unpublished PhD thesis: Brunel University.

Fyfe, N. and Bannister, J. (1996) 'City Watching: Closed Circuit Television in Public Spaces', *Area* 28(1): 37-46.

Galton, F. (1907) *Inquiries into Human Faculty and Development* (2nd edn). London: Dent and Dutton (Everyman).

Gandy, O. (1993) *The Panoptic Sort: A political economy of personal information*. Boulder: Westview Press.

Gans, H. (1968) 'The participant observer as human being: observation on the personal aspects of fieldwork', in H. S. Becker (ed.), *Institutions and the Person: Papers presented to Everett C. Hughes*. Chicago: Aldine.

Garland, D. (1985) *Punishment and Welfare: A history of penal strategies*. Aldershot: Ashgate.

Garland, D. (1997) 'Of crime and criminals: the development of criminology in Britain', in M. Maguire, R. Morgan and R. Reiner (eds), *The Oxford Handbook of Criminology*. Oxford: Oxford University Press.

Garland, D. (2001) *The Culture of Control: Crime and social order in contemporary society*. Oxford: Oxford University Press.

Gattrell, V. (1990) 'Crime, authority and the policeman state', in F. M. L. Thompson (ed.), *Cambridge Social History of Britain, 1750-1950, Vol. 3: Social Agencies and Institutions*. Cambridge: Cambridge University Press.

Gelles, R. J. and Cornell, R. (1985) *Intimate Violence in Families*. Newbury Park, Calif.: Sage.

Gelsthorpe, L. (2002) 'Feminism and criminology', in M. Maguire, R. Morgan and R. Reiner (eds), *The Oxford Handbook of Criminology* (3rd edn). Oxford: Oxford University Press.

Gelsthorpe, L. and Heddermann, C. (1997) *Understanding the Sentencing of Women*, Home Office Research Study 170. London: Home Office.

Gelsthorpe, L. and Morris, A. (1990) *Feminist Perspectives in Criminology*. Milton Keynes: Open University Press.

Gelsthorpe, L. and Padfield, N. (eds) (2003) *Exercising Discretion: Decision making in the criminal justice system and beyond*. Cullompton: Willan.

Genders, E. and Player, E. (1989) *Race Relations in Prison*. Oxford: Oxford University Press.

Gendreau, P., Goggin, C., Cullen, F. and Andrews, D. A. (2000) 'The effects of community sanctions and incarceration on recidivism', *Forum on Correctional Research* 12 (May): 10–13.

Giddens, A. (1999) *The Third Way*. Cambridge: Polity.

Gilbert, N. (ed.) (1993) *Researching Social Life*. London: Sage.

Gilroy, P. (1987) *There Ain't No Black in the Union Jack*. London: Routledge.

Gilroy, P. and Sim, J. (1987) 'Law, order and the state of the left', pp. 71–106 in P. Scraton (ed.), *Law, Order and the Authoritarian State: Readings in critical criminology*. Milton Keynes: Open University Press:

Glover, D. (1985) *The Sociology of the Mass Media*. Ormskirk: Causeway.

Goode, E. and Ben-Yehuda, N. (1994) *Moral Panics*. Oxford: Blackwell.

Goodey, J. (2004) *Victims and Victimology: Research, policy and practice*. London: Longman.

Gottfredson, M. R. and Hirschi, T. (1990) *A General Theory of Crime*. Stanford, Calif.: Stanford University Press.

Grace, S. (1995) *Policing Domestic Violence in the 1990s*. Home Office Research Study No. 139. London: HMSO.

Grace, S., Lloyd, C. and Smith, L. J. F. (1992) *Rape: From recording to conviction*. Home Office Research and Planning Unit Paper 71. London: Home Office.

Gramsci, A. (1971) *Selections from the Prison Notebooks*. London: Lawrence and Wishart.

Gross, R. (1992) *Psychology: The science of mind and behaviour*. London: Hodder and Stoughton.

Haggerty, K. and Ericson, R. (2000) 'The surveillant assemblage', *British Journal of Sociology* 51(4): 605–22.

Hales, G. (2005) *Gun Crime in Brent*. Commissioned by the London Borough of Brent Crime & Disorder Reduction Partnership. University of Portsmouth ICJS (March).

Hall, S., Critcher, C., Jefferson, T., Clarke, J. and Roberts, B. (1978) *Policing the Crisis: Mugging, the state and law and order*. Basingstoke: Macmillan.

Hall, S. and Jefferson, T. (1976) *Resistance Through Rituals: Youth subcultures in postwar Britain*. London: Hutchinson.

Halliday Report (2001) *Making Punishments Work: Review of the sentencing framework for England and Wales*. London: Home Office.

Halsbury (2005) *Halsbury's Statutes of England and Wales* (4th edn). London: Butterworth.

Ham, C. (2004) *Health Policy in Britain: The politics and organisation of the NHS* (5th edn). Basingstoke: Macmillan.

Hannah-Moffatt, K. H. (2002) 'Creating choices, reflecting on the choices', in P. Carlen (ed.), *Women and Punishment*. Cullompton: Willan.

Hargreaves, D.H. (1967) *Social Relations in a Secondary School*. London: Routledge and Kegan Paul.

Harker, J. (2006) *Delivering on Child Poverty: What would it take?* Report for the Department for Work and Pensions. London: HMSO.

Harris, J. and Grace, S. (1999) *A Question of Evidence: Investigating and prosecuting rape in the 1990s*, Home Office Research Study 196. London: Home Office.

Harrison, J., Simpson, M., Harrison, O. and Martin, E. (2005) *Study Skills for Criminology*. London: Sage.

Hawtin, M. and Kettle, J. (2000) 'Housing and social exclusion', in J. Percy-Smith (ed.), *Policy Responses to Social Exclusion: Towards inclusion*. Milton Keynes: Open University Press.

Hayward, K. H. (2004) *City Limits: Crime, consumer culture and the urban experience*. London: Cavendish/ Glasshouse Press.

Hebenton, B. and Thomas, T. (1996) 'Sexual offenders in the community: reflections on problems of law, community and risk management in the USA, England and Wales', *International Journal of the Sociology of Law* 24: 427–43.

Heddermann, C. (2004) 'Are more women being sentenced to custody?', in G. McIvor (ed.), *Women Who Offend*. London: Jessica Kingsley.

Hedderman, C. and Gelsthorpe, L. (1997) *Understanding the Sentencing of Women*. Home Office Research Study 170. London: Home Office.

Hedderman, C. and Hough, M. (1994) *Does the Criminal Justice System Treat Men and Women Differently?* Home Office Research Findings No. 10. London: HMSO.

Heidensohn, F. (1968) 'The deviance of women: a critique and an enquiry', *British Journal of Criminology* 19(2): 160–76.

Heidensohn, F. (1989) *Crime and Society*. Basingstoke: Macmillan.

Heidensohn, F. (2002) 'Gender and crime', in M. Maguire, R. Morgan and R. Reiner (eds), *The Oxford Handbook of Criminology* (3rd edn). Oxford: Oxford University Press.

Heidensohn, F. (2003) 'Gender and policing', in T. Newburn (ed.), *The Handbook of Policing*. Cullompton: Willan.

Heidensohn, F. with Silvestri, M. (1996) *Women and Crime* (2nd edn). Basingstoke: Macmillan.

Her Majesty's (HM) Crown Prosecution Service Inspectorate (HMCPSI) and HM Inspectorate of Constabulary (HMIC) (2002a) *A Report on the Joint Inspection into the Investigation and Prosecution of Cases Involving Allegations of Rape*. London: HMCPSI and HMIC.

HMCPSI and HMIC (2002b) *Action Plan to Implement the Joint Recommendations into the Investigation and Prosecution of Cases Involving Allegations of Rape*. London: HMCPSI and HMIC.

HM Government (1994) *Tackling Drugs Together: A consultation document strategy for England 1995–1998*. London: HMSO.

HM Government (1997) *Excellence in Schools*, white paper. London: HMSO.

HM Government (1998a) *Tackling Drugs to Build A Better Britain: The government's ten year strategy for tackling drugs misuse*, Cmd 3945. London: HMSO.

HM Government (1998b) *Modernizing Mental Health Services: Safe, sound and supportive*, white paper. London: HMSO.

HM Inspectorate of Constabulary (HMIC) *Neighbourhood Watch: HMIC Thematic Report*. London: HMIC.

HMIC (2001) *Thematic Review*. London: HMSO.

HM Inspectorate of Prisons (HMIP) (1997) *Thematic Review of Women in Prison*. London: Home Office.

HMIP (1999) *Suicide is Everyone's Concern: A thematic review by HM Chief Inspector of Prisons for England and Wales*. London: HMIP.

HMIP and HM Inspectorate of Probation (2001) *Through the Prison Gate: A joint thematic review by HM Inspectorates of Prisons and Probation*. London: HMSO.

Herrnstein, R. J. and Murray C. (1994) *The Bell Curve: Intelligence and Class Structure in American Society*. New York: Free Press.

Hester, M., Kelly, L. and Radford, J. (eds) (1996) *Women, Violence and Male Power*. Buckingham: Open University Press.

Hickey, E. (1991) *Serial Killers and their Victims*. Pacific Grove, Calif.: Brooks/Cole.

Hills, J. and Stewart, K. (2005) *A More Equal Society? New Labour, poverty, inequality and exclusion*. Bristol: Policy Press.

Hirschi, T. (1969) *Causes of Delinquency*. Berkeley, Calif.: University of California Press.

Hobbes, T. (1561/1968) *Leviathan*, ed. C. B. MacPherson. Harmondsworth: Penguin.

Hobbs, D. (1988) *Doing the Business: Entrepreneurship, the working class and detectives in the East End of London*. Oxford: Oxford University Press.

Hobbs, D. (1995) *Bad Business*. Oxford: Oxford University Press.

Hobbs, D. Hadfield, P., Lister, S. and Winlow, S. (2003) *Bouncers: Violence and governance in the night-time economy*. Oxford: Oxford University Press.

Hobbs, D. and May, T. (eds) (1993) *Interpreting the Field: Accounts of ethnography*. Oxford: Oxford University Press.

Hodgins, S. (ed.) (1993) *Mental Disorder and Crime*. London: Sage.

Holdaway, S. (1983) *Inside the British Police: A force at work*. Oxford: Blackwell.

Holdaway, S. (1996) *The Racialisation of British Policing*. Basingstoke: Macmillan.

Hollin, C. R. (2002) 'Criminological psychology', in M. Maguire, R. Morgan and R. Reiner (eds), *The Oxford Handbook of Criminology* (3rd edn). Oxford: Oxford University Press.

Home Office (2003) *Statistics on Women and the CJS*. London: Home Office.

Home Office (1990) *Crime Justice and Protecting the Public*. London: Home Office.

Home Office (1991) *Safer Communities: The local delivery of crime prevention through the partnership approach (Morgan Report)*. London: Home Office.

Home Office (1992–) *Criminal Statistics*, London: Home Office Statistical Department.

Home Office (1998a) *The Crime and Disorder Act: Community safety and the reduction and prevention of crime, a conceptual framework for training and the development of a professional discipline*. London: Home Office.

Home Office (1998b) *Tackling Drugs to Build a Better Britain*, white paper. London: HMSO.

Home Office (2000) *A Guide to the Criminal Justice System in England and Wales*. London: Home Office.

Home Office (2001a) *A Review of the Victim's Charter*. London: HMSO.

Home Office (2001b) 'Understanding and responding to hate crime', domestic violence factsheet. London: Home Office.

Home Office (2003a) *National Policing Plan, 2003–2006*. London: Home Office.

Home Office (2003b) *Safety and Justice: The government's proposals on domestic violence*, Cm. 5847. London: Home Office.

Home Office (2003c) *Respect and Responsibility: Taking a stand against anti-social behaviour*, Cm. 5778. London: HMSO.

Home Office (2004a) *Building Communities, Beating Crime: A better police service for the 21st century*. London: HMSO.

Home Office (2004b) *Statistics on Women and the Criminal Justice System 2203: A Home Office publication under Section 95 of the Criminal Justice System*. London: Home Office.

Home Office (2004c) *Reducing Crime, Changing Lives: The government's plans for transforming the management of offenders*. London: Home Office.

Home Office (2005a) *The National Policing Plan 2003 to 2006*. London: Home Office.

Home Office (2005b) *One Year On – TOGETHER: Tackling anti-social behaviour*. London: Home Office.

Home Office (2005c) *Statistics on Race and the Criminal Justice System – 2004*. London: Home Office.

Home Office (2005d) *Rebuilding Lives: Supporting victims of crime*, Cm. 6705. London: Home Office.

Home Office (2005e) *National Community Safety Plan 2006–2009*. London: Home Office.

Home Office (2005f) *Population in Custody Monthly Tables*. September 2005. London: Home Office.

Home Office (2006) *Report of the Zahid Mubarek Inquiry*. London: Home Office.

Home Office (nd a) 'Anti-social behaviour' (online) www.homeoffice.gov.uk (accessed 11 November 2004).

Home Office (nd b) 'Anti-social behaviour day count' (online) www.homeoffice.gov.uk (accessed 11 November 2004).

Home Office (nd c) 'The one day count of anti-social behaviour' (online) www.homeoffice.gov.uk (accessed 11 November 2004).

Home Office (nd d) 'Anti-social behaviour day count – update of results', (online) www.homeoffice.gov.uk (accessed 11 November 2004).

Home Office, DoH, Crown Prosecution Service and ACPO (2005) *Improving Outcomes for Victims of Sexual Violence: A strategic partnership approach*. Conference report: National Conference on Sexual Violence, 16–17 November 2005.

Hood, R. (1992) *Race and Sentencing: A study in Crown court*. Oxford: Clarendon Press.

Hood, R. and Cordovil, G. (1992) *A Question of Judgement: Race and sentencing: summary of a report for the Commission of Racial Equality*, London: Commission for Racial Equality.

Hopkins Burke, R. (2001) *An Introduction to Criminological Theory*. Cullompton: Willan.

Hopkins Burke, R. (2005) *An Introduction to Criminological Theory* (2nd edn). Cullompton: Willan.

Hopkins Burke, R. and Morrill, R. (2004) 'Human rights v community rights: the case of the anti-social behaviour order', in R. Hopkins Burke (ed.), *Hard Cop, Soft Cop: Dilemmas and debates in contemporary policing*. Cullompton: Willan.

Hough, M., Jacobson, J. and Millie, A. (2003) *The Decision to Imprison: Sentencing and the prison population*. London: Prison Reform Trust.

Hough, M. and Mayhew, P. (1983) *The British Crime Survey: First report*, Home Office Research Study 16. London: Home Office.

Hough, M. and Mitchell, D. (2003) 'Drug dependent offenders and justice for all', in M. Tonry (ed.), *Confronting Crime: Crime control policy under New Labour*. Cullompton: Willan.

Howard League for Penal Reform (1997) *Lost Inside: Report of the Howard League enquiry into the use of prison custody for girls under 18*. London: Howard League.

Hughes, G. (2002) 'The shifting sands of crime prevention and community safety', pp. 1–10 in G. Hughes, E. McLaughlin and J. Muncie (eds), *Crime Prevention and Community Safety: New directions*, London: Sage.

Humphreys, C. and Stantley, N. (eds) (2006) *Domestic Violence and Child Protection*. London: Jessica Kingsley.

Hutton, W. and Giddens, A. (2000) *On the Edge: Essays on a runaway world*. London: Jonathan Cape.

Ignatief, M. (1978) *A Just Measure of Pain: The penitentiary in the Industrial Revolution, 1750–1850*. New York: Pantheon.

Jefferson, T. (1990) *The Case Against Paramilitary Policing Considered*. Milton Keynes: Open University Press.

Jefferson, T. (1996a) 'Introduction', *British Journal of Criminology* 36(3): 337–47.

Jefferson, T. (1996b) 'From "Little Fairy Boy" to the "Complete Destroyer": subjectivity and transformation in the life of Mike Tyson', in M. Mac an Ghaill (ed.), *Understanding Masculinities: Social relations and cultural arenas*. Buckingham: Open University Press.

Jefferson, T. (1997) 'Masculinities and crimes', in M. Maguire, R. Morgan and R. Reiner (eds), *The Oxford Handbook of Criminology* (2nd edn). Oxford: Oxford University Press.

Jewkes, Y. (2004) *Media and Crime*. London: Sage.

Johnston, L. (2000) *Policing Britain*. Harlow: Longman.

Joint Consultative Committee (1990) *The Operational Policing Review*. Surbiton: Joint Consultative Committee of the Three Staff Associations of England and Wales.

Jones, H. (1998) 'The people's health', in H. Jones and S. MacGregor (eds), *Social Issues and Party Politics*. London: Routledge.

Jones, T. and Newburn, T. (1998) *Private Security and Public Policing*. Oxford: Clarendon.

Jones, T., Maclean, B. and Young, J. (1986) *The Islington Crime Survey*. Aldershot: Gower.

Joseph Rowntree Foundation (JRF) (2004) *Monitoring Poverty and Social Exclusion 2004. Findings*. York: JRF.

Jupp, V., Davies, P. and Francis, P. (eds) (2000) *Doing Criminological Research*. London: Sage.

Kapardis, A. and Farrington, D. (1981) 'An experimental study of sentencing by magistrates', *Law and Human Behaviour* 5: 107–21.

Keith, M. (1993) *Race, Riots and Policing*, London: UCL Press.

Kelly, L. (2001) *Routes to Injustice: A research review on the reporting, investigation and prosecution of rape cases*. London: HMCPSI.

Kemshall, H. (2003) *Understanding Risk in Criminal Justice*. Milton Keynes: Open University Press.

Kemshall, H., Mackenzie, G., Wood, J., Bailey, R. and Yates, J. (2005) *Strengthening Multi-Agency Public Protection Arrangements (MAPPAs)*. London: Home Office.

Kershaw, C., Chivitie-Matthews, N., Thomas, C. and Aust, R. (2001) *The 2001 British Crime Survey*, Home Office Statistical Bulletin 18/01. London: Home Office.

King, R and Wincup, E. (eds) (2000) *Doing Research on Crime and Justice*. Oxford: Oxford University Press.

Kinsey, R. (1984) *Merseyside Crime and Policing Survey*. Merseyside: Merseyside County Council.

Koffman, L. (1996) *Crime Surveys and Victims of Crime*. Cardiff: University of Wales Press.

Kohlberg, L. (1976) 'Moral stages and moralization: the cognitive developmental approach to socialisation', in J. Lickona (ed.), *Moral Development Behaviour: Theory, research and social issues*. New York: Harper and Row.

Koons-Witt, B. A. (2002) 'The effect of gender on the decision to incarcerate before and after the introduction to sentencing guidelines', *Criminology* 40(2): 297–328.

Koskela, H. (2003) 'Cam Era: The contemporary urban panopticon', *Surveillance and Society* 1(3): 292–313.

Labour Party (1997*) New Labour Leading Britain into the Future: Election manifesto*. London: Labour Party.

Laidler, K. J. and Hunt, G. (2001) 'Accomplishing femininity among the girls in the gang', *British Journal of Criminology* 41: 656–78.

Lea, J. (2002) *Crime and Modernity*. London: Sage.

Lea, J. and Young, J. (1984) *What is to be Done About Law and Order?* Harmondsworth: Penguin.

Lea, J. and Young, J. (1993) *What is to be Done About Law and Order? Crisis in the nineties*. London: Pluto Press.

Lee, M. and South, N. (2003) 'Drugs policing', in T. Newburn (ed.), *The Handbook of Policing*. Cullompton: Willan.

Lees, S. and Gregory, J. (1993) *Rape and Sexual Assault: A study of attrition*. London: Islington Council Police and Crime Prevention Unit.

Levitas, R. (1998) *The Inclusive Society? Social exclusion and New Labour*. Basingstoke: Macmillan.

Levitas, R. and Guy, W. (eds) (1996) *Interpreting Official Statistics*. London: Routledge.

Liddiard, M. (1998) 'Home truths', in H. Jones and S. MacGregor (eds), *Social Issues and Party Politics*. London: Routledge.

Lieb, R. (2003) 'Joined-up worrying: the multi-agency public protection panels', in A. Matravers (ed.), *Sex Offenders in the Community*. Cullompton: Willan.

Liebling, A. (1992) *Suicides in Prison*. London: Routledge.

Lister, R. (2004) *Poverty*. Cambridge: Polity.

Loader, I. and Sparks, R. (2002), 'Contemporary landscapes of crime, order and control', in M. Maguire, R. Morgan and R. Rainer (eds), *The Oxford Handbook of Criminology* (3rd edn). Oxford: Oxford University Press.

Lombroso, C. (2006) *On Criminal Man*. Durham, NC, USA: Duke University Press.

Lombroso, C. and Ferrero, G. (1895) *The Female Offender*. London: Fisher Unwin.

Lombroso, C. and Ferrero, G. (1895/2004) *Criminal Woman, the Prostitute and the Normal Woman* (Translated With a New Introduction by N. Hahn Rafter and M. Gibson). Durham, NC, USA: Duke University Press.

Long, M. (2003) 'Leadership and performance management', in T. Newburn (ed.), *The Handbook of Policing*. Cullompton: Willan.

Lovett, J., Regan, L. and Kelly, L. (2004) *Sexual Assault Referral Centres: Developing good practice and maximising potentials*, Home Office Research Study 285. London: Home Office.

Lyon, D. (1994) *The Electronic Eye: The rise of the surveillance society*. Oxford: Polity.

Lyotard, J. F. (1984) *The Postmodern Condition*. Manchester: Manchester University Press.

Macpherson, W. (1999) *The Stephen Lawrence Inquiry*: *Report of an inquiry by Sir William Macpherson of Cluny*, Cm. 4262–1. London: HMSO.

Maguire, M. and Kemshall, H. (2004) 'Multi-agency public protection arrangements: key issues', in H. Kemshall and G. McIvor (eds), *Managing Sex Offenders Risk*. London: Jessica Kingsley.

Mair, G. (2001) 'Technology and the future of community penalties', in A. Bottoms, L. Gelsthorpe and S. Rex (eds), *Community Penalties: Change and challenges*. Cullompton: Willan.

Malpass, P. (2005) *Housing and the Welfare State: The development of housing policy in Britain*. Basingstoke: Palgrave Macmillan.

Manning, P. (1977) *Police Work*. Cambridge, Mass.: MIT Press.

Martinson, R. (1974) 'What works? Questions and answers about prison reform', *Public Interest* 35: 22–54.

Marx, K. and Engels, F. (1848) *The Communist Manifesto*. Harmondsworth: Penguin.

Mason, D. (2000) *Race and Ethnicity in Modern Britain* (2nd edn). Oxford: Oxford University Press.

Mathiesen, T. (1997) 'The viewer society: Michel Foucault's "panopticon" revisited', *Theoretical Criminology* 1(2): 215–34.

Matthews, R. (1999) *Doing Time*. Basingstoke: Palgrave Macmillan.

Matza, D. (1969) *Becoming Delinquent*. Englewood Cliffs, N.J.: Prentice Hall.

Mawby, R. (2001) *Burglary*. Cullompton: Willan.

Mawby, R. and Walklate, S. (1994) *Critical Victimology*. London: Sage.

May, T. (1991) *Probation: Policy, politics and practice*. Buckingham: Open University Press.

May, T. (1997) *Social Research: Issues, method and process*. London: Sage.

May, T., Warburton, H., Turnbull, P. and Hough, M. (2002*) Times They Are-A-Changing: Policing of cannabis.* York: JRF.

Mayhew, P. (2000) 'Researching the state of crime: local, national, and international victim surveys', in R. King and E. Wincup (eds), *Doing Research on Crime and Justice.* Oxford: Oxford University Press.

Mayhew, P. et al. (1989) *The 1988 British Crime Survey* (3rd report). London: Home Office Research and Planning Unit.

Mayhew, P. et al. (1992) *The 1992 British Crime Survey.* Research Study no. 132. London: Home Office Research and Planning Unit.

McCahill, M. (1998) 'Beyond Foucault: Towards a Contemporary Theory of Surveillance', in C. Norris, J. Moran and G. Armstrong (eds.) *Surveillance, Closed Circuit Television and Social Control.* Aldershot: Avebury.

McCahill, M. (2002) *The Surveillance Web: The rise of visual surveillance in an English city.* Cullompton: Willan.

McCahill, M. and Norris, C. (2002) 'Literature Review, Working Paper No. 2', from *Urban Eye: On the threshold to urban panopticon? Analysing employment of CCTV in European cities and assessing its social and political impacts.* European Commission Project.

McConville, M. and Shepherd, D. (1992) *Watching Police, Watching Communities.* London: Routledge.

McConville, M. and Wilson, G. (eds) (2002*) The Handbook of the Criminal Process.* Oxford: Oxford University Press.

McDermott, K. (1990) 'We have no problem: the experience of race relations in prison', *New Community* 16(2): 312–28.

McGrath, J. (2004) *Loving Big Brother: Performance, privacy and surveillance space.* London: Routledge.

McLagan, G. (2003) *Bent Coppers.* London: Weidenfeld and Nicholson.

McLaughlin, E. and Muncie, J. (eds.) (2006) *The Sage Dictionary of Criminology* (2nd edn). London: Sage.

McLaughlin, E. and Murji, K. (2001) 'Lost connections and new directions: neo-liberalism, new public management and the "modernization" of the British police', pp. 104–22 in K. Stenson and R. A. Sullivan (eds), *Crime, Risk and Justice: The politics of crime control in liberal democracies,* Cullompton: Willan.

McLaughlin, E. et al. (2001) 'The permanent revolution: New Labour, public management and the modernization of criminal justice', *Criminal Justice* 1(3): 301–18.

Melossi, D. and Pavarini, M. (1980*) The Prison and the Factory: Origins of the penitentiary system* (trans. G. Cousin). London: Macmillan.

Merton, R. K. (1938) 'Social structure and anomie', *American Sociological Review* 3: 672–82.

Messerschmidt, J. W. (1993) *Masculinities and Crime: Critique and reconceptualization of theory.* Lanham, Md.: Rowman & Littlefield.

Messerschmidt, J. W. (1997) *Crime as Structured Action: Gender, race, class, and crime in the making.* Thousand Oaks, Calif.: Sage.

Messerschmidt, J. W. (2000) *Nine Lives: Adolescent masculinities, the body, and violence.* Boulder, Colo.: Westview.

Messerschmidt, J. W. (2004) *Flesh and Blood: Adolescent gender diversity and violence.* Lanham, Md.: Rowman & Littlefield.

Metropolitan Police Authority (2002) *The Lambeth Cannabis Warning Pilot Scheme,* Report 17, 26 September. London: Metropolitan Police Authority.

Metropolitan Police Authority (2004) *Gun Crime Scrutiny: Final report.* London: Metropolitan Police Authority.

Metropolitan Police Service (2000) *Clearing the Decks.* London: Metropolitan Police Service.

Miller, N. E. (1941) 'The frustration–aggression hypothesis', *Psychological Review* 48: 337–42.

Miller, W. (1958) 'Lower class culture as a generating milieu of gang delinquency', *Journal of Social Issues* 14: 5–19.

Mirrlees-Black, C. (1999) *Domestic Violence: Findings from a new British Crime Survey self completion questionnaire,* HORS 191. London: Home Office.

Mirrlees-Black, C. et al. (1998) *The 1998 British Crime Survey.* London: Home Office.

Mitchell, J. (1971) *Woman's Estate.* Harmondsworth: Penguin.

Moran, G. and Simpkin, M (2000) 'Social exclusion and health', in J. Percy-Smith (ed.), *Policy Responses to Social Exclusion: Towards inclusion.* Milton Keynes: Open University Press.

Morgan Report (1991) *Safer Communities: The delivery of crime prevention through the partnership approach.* London: Home Office.

Morris, T. (1957) *The Criminal Area: A study in social ecology.* London: Routledge.

Muncie, J. (1999) *Youth and Crime: A critical introduction.* London: Sage.

Muncie, J. (2001) 'The construction and deconstruction of crime', in J. Muncie and J. E. McLaughlin (eds), *The Problem of Crime* (2nd edn). London: Sage.

Muncie, J. and McLaughlin, J. E. (eds) (2001) *The Problem of Crime* (2nd edn). London: Sage.

Muncie, J. et al. (1996) *Criminological Perspectives.* London: Sage.

Murie, A. (1998) 'Linking housing changes to crime', in C. Jones-Finer and M. Nellis (eds), *Crime and Social Exclusion.* Oxford: Blackwell.

Murray, C. (1997) *Does Prison Work?* London: Institute for Economic Affairs.

Murray, C. (2000) 'The British underclass', *Sunday Times,* 13 February.

Myhill, A. and Allen, J. (2002a) *Rape and Sexual Assault of Women: Findings from the British Crime Survey,* Findings 159. London: Home Office.

Myhill, A. and Allen, J. (2002b) *Rape and Sexual Assault of Women: The extent and nature of the problem,* Home Office Research Study 237. London: Home Office.

Myrdal, G. (1964) *The Challenge to Affluence.* Chicago: Victor Gollancz.

Nagel, I. (1981) 'Sex differences in the processing of criminal defendants', in L. Gelsthorpe and A. Morris (eds), *Women and Crime.* Cambridge: Cambridge Institute of Criminology.

National Association for the Care and Resettlement of Offenders (NACRO) (2001) *Women Who Challenge: Women offenders and mental health issues.* London: NACRO.

National Offender Management Scheme (NOMS) (2005) *Prison Population and Accommodation Briefing for 9th December 2005.* London: NOMS Estate Planning and Development Unit.

National Probation Service (2004), *DTTOs/DRRS Advice and Information About Changes and Future Arrangements* (online) <www.probation.homeoffice.gov.uk/files/pdf/pc55.pdf> (accessed 12 March 2005).

Nellis, M. (1991) 'The electronic monitoring of offenders in England and Wales: recent developments and future prospects', *British Journal of Criminology* 31(2): 165–85.

Nellis, M. (2002) 'Electronic monitoring and family life', *Criminal Justice Matters* 50, Winter.

Nellis, M. (2003) 'Electronic monitoring and the future of the probation service', in W. Chiu and M. Nellis (eds.), *Moving Probation Forward: Evidence, arguments and practice.* Harlow: Longmans.

Nellis, M. (2004a) 'The electronic monitoring of offenders: images and arguments presented in the English media', paper presented at Elmo-Tech 10th Anniversary Conference, 20–23 October 2004, Nerola, Italy.

Nellis, M. (2004b) ' "I know where you live!": electronic monitoring and penal policy in England and Wales 1999–2003', *British Journal of Community Justice* 2(3): 33–59.

Nellis, M. (2005) 'Out of this world: the advent of the satellite tracking of offenders in England and Wales', *Howard Journal* 44(2): 125–50.

Newburn, T. (2002) 'Community safety and policing: some implications of the Crime and Disorder Act 1998', pp. 102–22 in G. Hughes, E. McLaughlin and J. Muncie (eds), *Crime Prevention and Community Safety,* London: Open University Press/Sage.

Newman, O. (1973) *Defensible Space.* London: Architectural Press.

Neyroud, P. (2003) 'Policing and ethics', in T. Newburn (ed.), *Handbook of Policing.* Cullompton: Willan.

Neyroud, P. and Beckley, A. (2001) *Policing, Ethics and Human Rights.* Cullompton: Willan.

Nicholas, S., Povey, D., Walker, A. and Kershaw, C. (2005) *Crime in England and Wales 2004/05: Home Office Statistics Bulletin.* London: Home Office.

Norris, C. and Armstrong, G. (1999) *The Maximum Surveillance Society.* Oxford: Berg.

O'Neill, M. (1997) *Prostitution and Feminism: Towards a politics of feeling.* Cambridge: Polity.

Office for National Statistics (ONS) (2001) *The National Statistics Socio-economic Classification Analytic Classes (NS-SEC).* London: ONS.

Office for Standards in Education (Ofsted) (1998) *New Start Partnership Project for 14–16 Year Olds in Schools 1997–1999.* London: Ofsted.

Ofsted (2004) *Girls in Prison: The education and training of under 18s serving detention and training orders.* London: Ofsted and HMIP.

O'Keeffe, C. (2003) *Moving Mountains.* Sheffield: Sheffield Hallam University Press.

Omaji, P. (2003) *Responding to Youth Crime.* Australia: Federation Press.

Packer, H. (1968) *The Limits of the Criminal Sanction.* Stanford, Calif.: Stanford University Press.

Padel, U. and Stevenson, P. (1988) *Insiders: Women's experience of prison.* London: Virago.

Painter, K. and Farrington, D. (1998) 'Marital violence in Great Britain and its relationship to marital and non-marital rape', *International Review of Victimology* 5(3/4): 257–76.

Pakulski, J. and Waters, M. (1996) *The Death of Class.* London: Sage.

Parisi, N. (1982) 'Are females treated differently? A review of the theories and evidence on sentencing and parole decisions', in R. Smith and K. Talmadge (eds), *Judge, Lawyer, Victim, Thief: Women, gender roles and criminal justice*. New York: North Eastern University Press.

Parker, H. (2004), 'The new drugs intervention industry: what outcomes can drugs/criminal justice treatment programmes realistically deliver?', *Probation Journal* 51(4): 379–86.

Parks, R. E., Burgess, E. W. and McKenzie, R. D. (eds) (1925) *The City*. Chicago: University of Chicago Press.

Payley, M. and Clayden, H. (2005) 'The role of the Sex Offence Liaison Officers (S.O.L.O.s)', in Home Office, DoH, Crown Prosecution Service and ACPO, *Improving Outcomes for Victims of Sexual Violence: A strategic partnership approach*. Conference report: National Conference on Sexual Violence, 16–17 November 2005.

Pearson, G. (1983) *Hooligan: A history of respectable fears*. Basingstoke: Macmillan.

Pearson, R. (1976/1981) 'Women defendants in the magistrates' courts', *British Journal of Law and Society* 3: 265–73.

Pease, K. (1997) 'Crime prevention', in M. Maguire, R. Morgan and R. Reiner (eds), *The Oxford Handbook of Criminology*. Oxford: Oxford University Press.

Pease, K. (2002) 'Crime reduction', in M. Maguire, R. Morgan and R. Reiner (eds), *The Oxford Handbook of Criminology*. Oxford: Oxford University Press.

Penhale, B. (2005) 'Global developments in elder abuse', in A. Wahidin and M. Cain (eds), *Ageing, Crime and Society*. Cullompton: Willan.

Pitts, J. (1998) 'Crime and citizenship', in A. Marlow and J. Pitts (eds), *Planning Safer Communities*. Lyme Regis: Russell House.

Pitts, J. (2003) 'Youth justice in England and Wales', in R. Matthews and J. Young (eds), *The New Politics of Punishment*. Cullompton: Willan.

Pollak, O. (1950) *The Criminality of Women*. New York: Barnes.

Poster, M. (1990) *The Mode of Information*. London: Sage.

Povey, D. (ed.) (2004) *Crime in England and Wales 2002/03: Supplementary Volume I: Homicide and Gun Crime*. London: Home Office.

Pratt, J. (2002) *Punishment and Civilisation: Penal tolerance and intolerance in modern society*. London: Sage.

Pratt, J. (ed.) (2005) *The New Punitiveness: Trends, theories, perspectives*. Cullompton: Willan.

Prison Reform Trust (2000) *Justice For Women: the Need for Reform* (Wedderburn Report). London: Prison Reform Trust.

Pryce, K. (1979) *Endless Pressure*. Harmondsworth: Penguin.

PSS Consultancy Group (2002) *Evaluation of Lambeth's Pilot of Warnings for Possession of Cannabis*. London: PSS Consultancy Group.

Quinney, R. (1977) *Class, State and Crime*. New York: David McKay.

Radford, J., Friedberg, M. and Harne, L. (eds) (2000) *Women, Violence and Strategies for Action: Feminist research, policy and practice*. Buckingham: Open University Press.

Rahman, M., Palmer, G. and Kenway, P. (2001) *Monitoring Poverty and Social Exclusion 2001*. York: JRF.

Rahman, M, Palmer, G., Kenway, P. and Howarth, C. (2000) *Monitoring Poverty and Social Exclusion 2000*. York: JRF.

Ramsbotham, D. (2003) *Prisongate*. London: Free Press.

Rawlings, P. (2001) *Policing: A short history*. Cullompton: Willan

Raynor, P. (2002), 'Community penalties: probation, punishment, and 'what works'', in M. Maguire, R. Morgan and R. Rainer (eds), *The Oxford Handbook of Criminology* (3rd edn). Oxford: Oxford University Press.

Reed Committee (2002) *Review of Health and Social Services for Mentally Disordered Offenders and Others Requiring Similar Services*. London: HMSO.

Reeve, A. (1998) 'The Panopticism of Shopping: CCTV and Leisure Consumption', in C. Norris, J. Moran and G. Armstrong (eds.) *Surveillance, Closed Circuit Television and Social Control*. Aldershot: Avebury.

Refuge (2004) *The Effects of Domestic Violence on Health*. London: Refuge.

Refuge (2005) *Refuge Assessment and Intervention for Pre-school Children Exposed to Domestic Violence*. London: Refuge.

Reiner, R. (1978) *The Blue Coated Worker*. Cambridge: Cambridge University Press.

Reiner, R. (1991) *Chief Constables*. Oxford: Oxford University Press.

Reiner, R. (2000) *The Politics of the Police* (3rd edn). Oxford: Oxford University Press.

Reiner, R. (2002) 'Media made criminality: the representation of crime in the mass media', in M. Maguire, R. Reiner and R. Morgan (eds), *The Oxford Handbook of Criminology* (3rd edn). Oxford: Clarendon Press.

Reiner, R. (2003) 'Policing and the media', in T. Newburn (ed.), *Handbook of Policing*. Cullompton: Willan.

Rock, P. (2002) 'Sociological theories of crime', in M. Maguire, R. Morgan and R. Reiner (eds), *The Oxford Handbook of Criminology*. Oxford: Oxford University Press.

Rose, L. (1988) *Rogues and Vagabonds: The vagrant underworld in Britain 1815–1985*. Oxford: Clarendon Press.

Rose, N. and Miller, P. (1992) 'Political power beyond the state: problematics of government', *British Journal of Sociology* 43(2): 172–205.

Rose, T. (1994) *Black Noise: Black music and Black culture in contemporary America*. Middle Town, Conn.: Wesleyan University Press.

Rowe, M. (2004) *Policing, Race and Racism*. Cullompton: Willan.

Rumgay, J. (2001), 'Accountability in the delivery of community penalties: to whom, for what and why?' in A. Bottoms, L. Gelsthorpe and S. Rex (eds), *Community Penalties: Change and challenges*. Cullompton: Willan.

Rusche, G. and Kirchheimer, O. (2003) *Punishment and Social Structure* (intro. by D. Melossi). New Brunswick, N.J.: Transaction.

Sanders, A. and Young, R. (2003) 'Police powers', in T. Newburn (ed.), *Handbook of Policing*. Cullompton: Willan.

Sanders, B. (2005) *Youth Crime and Youth Culture in the Inner City*. London: Routledge.

Sapsford, R. and Jupp, V. (eds) (1996) *Data Collection and Analysis*. London: Sage.

Scarman, Lord (1981) *The Brixton Disorders 10–12 April: Report of an inquiry by the Rt. Honourable Lord Scarman*, Cm 8427. London: HMSO.

Scrambler, G. and Scrambler, A. (1997) *Rethinking Prostitution: Purchasing sex in the 1990s*. London: Routledge.

Self, H. (2003) *Prostitution, Women and the Misuse of the Law: The fallen daughters of Eve*. London: Frank Cass.

Sellin, T. (1938) *Culture Conflict and Crime*. New York: Social Science Research Council.

Senior, P., Crowther-Dowey, C. and Long, M. (2007) *Understanding Modernisation*. Buckingham: Open University Press.

Shaw, C. R. and McKay, H. D. (1969) *Juvenile Delinquency and Urban Areas: A study of rates of delinquency in relation to differential characteristics of local communities in American cities*. Chicago: University of Chicago Press.

Shearing, C. D. and Stenning, P. C. (1981) 'Modern private security: its growth and implications', *Crime and Justice* 3: 193–245.

Silverman, D. (1993) *Interpreting Qualitative Data*. London: Sage

Silvestri, M. (2003) *Women in Charge: Policing, gender and leadership*. Cullompton: Willan.

Singh, G. (2000) 'The concept and context of institutional racism', in A. Marlow and B. Loveday (eds), *After Macpherson: Policing After the Stephen Lawrence Inquiry*. Lyme Regis: Russell House.

Singleton, N., Meltzer, H., Gatwood, R., Coid, J. and Deasy, D. (1998) *Psychiatric Morbidity Among Prisoners in England and Wales*. London: ONS.

Smart, C. (1977) *Women, Crime and Criminology*. London: Routledge & Kegan Paul.

Smart, C. (1990) 'Feminist approaches to criminology, or postmodern woman meets atavistic man', in A. Morris and L. Gelsthorpe (eds), *Feminist Perspectives in Criminology*. Milton Keynes: Open University Press.

Smart, U. (2006) *Criminal Justice*. London: Sage.

Smith, C. and Allen, J. (2004) *Violent Crime in England and Wales*, Home Office Online Report 18/04. London: Home Office.

Smith, D. J. and Gray, J. (1983) *Police and People in London* (Vol. 4). London: PSI.

Smith, L. (1988) 'Images of women – decision making in courts', in A. Morris and C. Wilkinson (eds), *Women and the Penal System*. Cambridge: Cambridge Institute of Criminology.

Smith, R. (2003) *Youth Justice: Ideas, policy and practice*. Cullompton: Willan.

Social Exclusion Unit (SEU) (1998) *Truancy and Social Exclusion*. London: HMSO.

SEU (2000) *Report of Policy Action Team 8: Anti-social behaviour*. London: Cabinet Office.

Solomos, J. (2003) *Race and Racism in Britain* (3rd edn). Basingstoke: Palgrave.

Southgate, P. and Ekblom, P. (1986) *Police Public Encounters*, Home Office Research Study No. 90. London: HMSO.

Spalek, B. (ed.) (2002) *Islam, Crime and Justice*. Cullompton: Willan.

Spalek, B. (2006) *Crime Victims: Theory, policy and practice*. Basingstoke: Palgrave.

Squires, P. and Stephen, D. (2005) *Rougher Justice: Anti-social behaviour and young people*. Cullompton: Willan.

Stacey, T. (1989) 'Tracking tagging: the British contribution', in K. Russell and R. Lilly (eds), *The Electronic Monitoring of Offenders*. Leicester: Leicester Polytechnic School of Law Monographs.

Stanko, B., O'Bierne, M. and Zafutto, G. (2002) *Taking Stock: What do we know about interpersonal violence*. ESRC Violent Research Programme. London: HMSO.

Stanko, E. (1985) *Intimate Intrusion*. London: Routledge and Kegan Paul.

Stanko, E. (1990) *Everyday Violence*. London: Pandora.

Stanko, E. (2001) 'The day to count: reflections on a methodology to raise awareness about the impact of domestic violence in the UK', *Criminal Justice* 1(2): 215–26.

Staples, W. (2000) *Everyday Surveillance*. Oxford: Rowman and Littlefield.

Stedman-Jones, G. (1971) *Outcast London*. London: Penguin.

Steffensmeier, D. (1980) 'Assessing the impact of the women's movement on sex-based differences in the handling of adult defendants', *Crime and Delinquency*.

Stenson, K. (2000) 'Crime control, social policy and liberalism', pp. 229–44 in G. Lewis, S. Gerwitz and J. Clarke (eds), *Rethinking Social Policy*. London: Sage.

Stenson, K. and Edwards, A. (2001) 'Crime control and liberal government: the "third way" and the return to the local', pp. 117–44 in K. Stenson and R.A. Sullivan (eds), *Crime, Risk and Justice: The politics of crime control in liberal democracies*, Cullompton: Willan.

Stone, N. (2002) *A Companion Guide to Mentally Disordered Offenders* (2nd edn). Crayford: Shaw.

Strauss, L. (1936) *The Political Philosophy of Hobbes: Its basis and genesis*. Oxford: Clarendon Press.

Sugg, D., Moore, L. and Howard, P. (2001) *Electronic Monitoring and Offending Behaviour: Reconviction results for the second year of trials of curfew orders*, Home Office Research Findings 141. London: Home Office.

Sutherland, E. H. (1938) *White Collar Crime: The uncut version*. New Haven, Conn.: Yale University Press.

Sutherland, E. H. (1947) *Principles of Criminology* (3rd edn). Philadelphia: J. B. Lipincott.

Taylor, I., Walton, P. and Young, J. (1973) *The New Criminology: For a social theory of deviance*. London: Routledge and Kegan Paul.

Tchaikovsky, C. (1997) *100 Women*. London: Women In Prison.

Temkin, J. (1999) 'Reporting in rape: a qualitative study', *Howard Journal* 38(1): 17–41.

Thomas, T. (2005*) Sex Crime: Sex offending and society*. Cullompton: Willan.

Thompson, A. (2000) 'An injection of hope?', *Community Care*.

Tombs, S. and Whyte, D. (2005) *Safety Crime*. Cullompton: Willan.

Townsend, P. (1979) *Poverty in the UK*. Harmondsworth: Penguin.

Townsend, P. (1990) 'Underclass and overclass: the widening gulf between the social classes in Britain in the 1980s', in G. Payne and M. Cross (eds), *Sociology in Action*. Basingstoke: Macmillan.

Townsend, P. and Davidson, N. (eds) (1992) *Inequality in Health: The Black Report*. London: Penguin.

Transform Drug Policy Foundation (TDPF) (2004) *After the War on Drugs: Options for control*. Bristol: TDPF.

Turk, A. (1969) *Criminality and the Social Order*. Chicago: Rand McNally.

Turnbull, P., McSweeney, T., Webster, R., Edmund, M. and Hough, M. (2000) *Home Office Research Study 212: Drug treatment and testing orders – final evaluation report* (online) < www.homeoffice.gov.uk/rds/pdfs/ hors212.pdf> (accessed 1 February 2005).

Turner, R. (2004) 'The impact of drug treatment and testing orders in West Yorkshire: six-month outcomes', *Probation Journal* 51(2): 116–32.

Underdown, A. (2001) 'Making "what works" work: challenges in the delivery of community penalties', in A. Bottoms, L. Gelsthorpe and S. Rex (eds), *Community Penalties: Change and challenges*. Cullompton: Willan.

Unell, I. (2002) 'Controlling drug use: where is the justice?' in D. Ward, J. Scott and M. Lacey (eds), *Probation: Working for justice*. Oxford: Oxford University Press.

Vanstone, M. (2004) *Supervising Offenders in the Community: A history of probation theory and practice*. Aldershot: Ashgate.

Von Hentig, H. (1948) *The Criminal and His Victim*. New Haven, Conn.: Yale University Press.

Waddington, P. A. J. (1999) *Policing Citizens*. London: UCL Press.

Waddington, P. A. J. (2003) 'Keeping stop and search in proportion', *Police*, November, pp. 17–18.

Wahidin, A. and Cain, M. (eds) (2005) *Ageing, Crime and Society*. Cullompton: Willan.

Walby, S. and Allen, J. (2004) *Domestic Violence, Sexual Assault and Stalking: Findings from the British Crime Survey*, Home Office Research Study 276. London: Home Office.

Walker, A. (1991) 'Poverty and the underclass', in M. Haralambos (ed.), *Developments in Sociology, Volume 7*. Ormskirk: Causeway Press.

Walklate, S. (2004) *Gender, Crime and Criminal Justice* (2nd edn). Cullompton: Willan.

Walkowitz, J. R. (1980) *Prostitution and Victorian Society: Women, class and the state*. Cambridge: Cambridge University Press.

Walter, I., Sugg, D. and Moore, L. (2001) *A Year on the Tag: Interviews with criminal justice practitioners and electronic monitoring staff about curfew orders*, Home Office Research Study 140. London: Home Office.

Walters, R. (2003) *Deviant Knowledge: Criminology, politics and policy*. Cullompton: Willan.

Walton, F. (2000) 'Education and training', in J. Percy-Smith (ed.), *Policy Responses to Social Exclusion: Towards inclusion*. Milton Keynes: Open University Press.

Weber, M. (1968) *Economy and Society* (ed. G. Roth and C. Wittich). New York: Bedminster Press.

Webster, C. (2004) 'The evolving diffusion, regulation and governance of closed circuit television in the UK', *Surveillance and Society* 2(2/3): 230–50.

Weeks, J. (1981) *Sex, Politics and Society: The regulation of sexuality since 1800*. London: Longman.

Weeks, J. and Porter, K. (eds) (1998) *Between the Acts: Lives of homosexual men 1885–1967* (2nd edn). London: Rivers Oram Press.

Weinberger, J., Pickstone, C. and Harrison, P. (eds) (2005) *Learning from Sure Start: Working with young children and their families*. Maidenhead: Open University Press.

West, D. and Farrington, D. P. (1977) *The Delinquent Way of Life: The third report of the Cambridge Study in Delinquent Behaviour*. London: Heinemann.

Westergaard, J. (1992) 'About and beyond the underclass: some notes on influences of climate on sociology today – BSA Address 1992', *Sociology* 26(4): 575–85.

White-Sansom, L. (2004) 'Stalking the stalker: a review of policing strategies', in R. Hopkins Burke (ed.), *Hard Cop, Soft Cop: Dilemmas and debates in contemporary policing*. Cullompton: Willan.

Whitehead, C. M. E., Stockdale, J. E. and Razzu, G. (2003) *The Economic and Social Costs of Anti-Social Behaviour: A review*. London: London School of Economics (LSE).

Whitfield, D. (1997) *Tackling the Tag*. Winchester: Waterside Press.

Whitfield, D. (2001) *The Magic Bracelet: Technology and offender supervision*. Winchester: Waterside Press.

Whyte, W. F. (1983) *Street Corner Society: The social structure of an Italian slum* (4th edn). Chicago: University of Chicago Press.

Wiles, P. (1999) 'The contribution of research to policy', Speech given at the Centre for Criminal Justice Studies (ISTD), AGM, November.

Williams, K. S. (2001) *Textbook on Criminology* (4th edn). Oxford: Oxford University Press.

Wilson, H. (1980) 'Parental supervision: a neglected aspect of delinquency', *British Journal of Criminology* 20: 315–27

Wilson, J. Q. (1983) *Thinking About Crime*. New York: Basic Books.

Wilson, J. Q. and Herrnstein, R. J. (1985) *Crime and Human Nature*. New York: Simon and Schuster.

Winlow, S. (2001) *Badfellas*. Oxford: Berg.

Wollstonecraft, M. and Mill, J. S. (1929*) The Rights of Women, The Subjection of Women* (ed. G. Catin). London: Longman.

Women's National Commission (1985) *Violence Against Women*. London: Cabinet Office.

Wootton, B. (1959) *Social Science and Social Pathology*. London: George Allen and Unwin (reprinted by Greenwood Press).

Worrall, A. (1989) *Offending Women: Female lawbreakers and the criminal justice system*. London: Routledge.

Worrall, A. (1997) *Punishment in the Community*. London: Longman.

Worrall, A. (2004) *Punishment in the Community: The future of the criminal justice system*. Cullompton: Willan.

Wright, A. (2002) *Policing: An introduction*. Cullompton: Willan.

Wright, C. (2005) *School Exclusion and the Transition into Adulthood in African-Caribbean Communities*. York: JRF.

Yar, M. (2003) 'Panoptic power and the pathologisation of vision: critical reflections on the Foucauldian thesis', *Surveillance and Society* 1(3): 254–71.

Yates, J. (2005) 'Rape action plan stocktake and the need for victim-focused policing', in Home Office, DoH, Crown Prosecution Service and ACPO (2005*) Improving Outcomes for Victims of Sexual Violence: A strategic partnership approach*, Conference Report: National Conference on Sexual Violence, 16–17 November 2005.

Young, J. (1981) 'Thinking seriously about crime: some models of criminology', in M. Fitzgerald, G. McLennan and J. Pawson (eds), *Crime and Society*. London: Routledge and Kegan Paul.

Young, J. (1992) 'Ten points of realism' in J. Young and R. Matthews (eds), *Rethinking Criminology: The realist debate*. London: Sage.

Young, J. (1999) *The Exclusive Society: Social exclusion, crime and difference in late modernity,* London: Sage.

Zedner, L. (2002) 'Victims', in M. Maguire, R. Morgan and R. Reiner (eds), *The Oxford Handbook of Criminology* (3rd edn), Oxford: Oxford University Press.

Subject index

Index of proper names

Index of legislation